OXFORD LABOUR LAW

General Editors

ALAN BOGG,
A. C. L. DAVIES,
KEITH EWING,
MARK FREEDLAND

Putting Human Rights to Work

Labour Law, the ECHR, and the Employment Relation

OXFORD LABOUR LAW

General Editors: Alan Bogg, Professor of Labour Law at University of Bristol Law School; A. C. L. Davies, Dean of the Oxford Law Faculty; Keith Ewing, Professor of Public Law at King's College London; and Mark Freedland, Emeritus Research Fellow in Law at St John's College and Emeritus Professor of Employment Law in the University of Oxford.

This series has come to represent a significant contribution to the literature of British, European, and international labour law. The series recognizes the arrival not only of a renewed interest in labour law generally, but also the need for fresh approaches to the study of labour law following a period of momentous change in the UK and Europe. The series is concerned with all aspects of labour law, including traditional subjects of study such as collective labour law and individual employment law. It also includes works that concentrate on the growing role of human rights and the combating of discrimination in employment, and others that examine the law and economics of the labour market and the impact of social security law and national and supranational employment policies upon patterns of employment and the employment contract. Two of the contributing authors to the series, Lucy Vickers and Diamond Ashiagbor, have received awards from the Society of Legal Scholars in respect of their books.

Also Available in the Series

Strike Ballots, Democracy, and Law
BREEN CREIGHTON, CATRINA DENVIR, RICHARD JOHNSTONE, SHAE MCCRYSTAL, ALICE ORCHISTON

Living Wage
Regulatory Solutions to Informal and Precarious Work in Global Supply Chains
SHELLEY MARSHALL

Bullying and Behavioural Conflict at Work
The Duality of Individual Rights
LIZZIE BARMES

The Concept of the Employer
JEREMIAS PRASSL

The Labour Constitution
The Enduring Idea of Labour Law
RUTH DUKES

The Legal Construction of Personal Work Relations
MARK FREEDLAND FBA AND NICOLA KOUNTOURIS

A Right to Care?
Unpaid Work in European Employment Law
NICOLE BUSBY

Regulating Flexible Work
DEIRDRE MCCANN

Welfare to Work
Conditional Rights in Social Policy
AMIR PAZ-FUCHS

EU Intervention in Domestic Labour Law
PHIL SYRPIS

Towards a Flexible Labour Market
Labour Legislation and Regulation since the 1990s
PAUL DAVIES AND MARK FREEDLAND

The European Employment Strategy
Labour Market Regulation and New Governance
DIAMOND ASHIAGBOR

The Law of the Labour Market
Industrialization, Employment, and Legal Evolution
SIMON DEAKIN AND FRANK WILKINSON

The Personal Employment Contract
MARK FREEDLAND

International and European Protection of the Right to Strike
A Comparative Study of Standards Set by the International Labour Organization, the Council of Europe and the European Union
TONIA NOVITZ

Freedom of Speech and Employment
LUCY VICKERS

Women and the Law
SANDRA FREDMAN

Just Wages for Women
AILEEN MCCOLGAN

Putting Human Rights to Work

Labour Law, the ECHR, and the Employment Relation

PHILIPPA COLLINS

OXFORD
UNIVERSITY PRESS

OXFORD
UNIVERSITY PRESS

Great Clarendon Street, Oxford, OX2 6DP,
United Kingdom

Oxford University Press is a department of the University of Oxford.
It furthers the University's objective of excellence in research, scholarship,
and education by publishing worldwide. Oxford is a registered trade mark of
Oxford University Press in the UK and in certain other countries

First Edition published in 2022

Impression: 1

Published in the United States of America by Oxford University Press
198 Madison Avenue, New York, NY 10016, United States of America

British Library Cataloguing in Publication Data

Data available

Library of Congress Control Number: 2021941269

ISBN 978–0–19–289459–5

DOI: 10.1093/oso/9780192894595.001.0001

Printed and bound in Great Britain by
Clays Ltd, Elcograf S.p.A.

For my parents, Alison and Steve

Editors' Preface

The past couple of decades have witnessed what might be termed a 'rights turn' in labour law. Responding to a sense that the subject is in crisis, some scholars have sought to identify a theoretical justification for labour law in the protection of the fundamental rights of working people. This project is not without controversy, sparking fears that a rights-based labour law might prove too individualistic, thereby undermining the subject's traditional emphasis on collective strength and solidarity. But, for others, it remains the most promising way of providing the discipline with a powerful philosophical underpinning.

The 'rights turn' is not, however, confined to legal theory. There is also a strongly pragmatic strand in which scholars, practitioners and activists have sought to invoke rights arguments both in political debate and in courts as a way of bolstering working people's claims. This instrumental use of rights arguments can be seen in many different fora: from the ILO's efforts to promote sustainable development and to combat the worst deregulatory excesses of globalisation, to strategic litigation before regional courts, such as the European Court of Human Rights, to day-to-day employment disputes in front of national courts and tribunals.

In this important contribution, Philippa Collins offers a rigorous and detailed analysis of whether English employment law can be said to protect working people's fundamental rights. She explains and justifies the decision to analyse the subject from a rights perspective, before evaluating the various practical manifestations of this approach. She considers the impact of the Human Rights Act 1998 on labour law and identifies significant limitations in the way in which the law purports to protect rights, from difficulties around the personal scope of labour law and questions of employment status, to weaknesses in the statute law of unfair dismissal. Collins is sceptical about the potential for the common law to step in where statute has failed or to provide an alternative route for the protection of rights. Having made good her critique, she uses the concluding chapter to develop a detailed proposal for reform by presenting a draft Bill of Rights for Workers. Collins argues that this would fulfil the UK's positive obligations under the European Convention on Human Rights and secure proper protection for fundamental rights at work.

This book represents doctrinal analysis at its very best: unflinching in its critique but constructive and ambitious in its reform agenda. It deserves to be widely read by policy-makers as well as scholars and practitioners, and we are delighted to be able to include it in the series.

ALB, ACLD, KDE, MRF
27 July 2021

Acknowledgements

A cliché no doubt, but there are too many thanks that I owe to fit them into a few short paragraphs. A number of institutions have supported this project: the Oxford Law Faculty, the UKRI Arts and Humanities Research Council and University of Bristol Law School in the form of funding; Oxford University Press and Sage Publishing through granting permission to reference previously published work, and Oxford University Press and Newgen Knowledge Works in the preparation of the manuscript. I would like to express my gratitude to all of them.

Along the journey to this point, I have been welcomed into supportive academic communities at Oxford, Exeter and most recently Bristol. The Oxford Labour Law Discussion Group, the Human Rights and Democracy Forum and the Centre for Science, Culture and the Law at the University of Exeter, the Society of Legal Scholars, the Industrial Law Society and the Centre for Law at Work at the University of Bristol have provided numerous opportunities for conversation, advice and feedback as the project progressed. At key moments, conversations with Andrew Dickinson, Séverine Saintier and Stephen Skinner encouraged me and steered me in the right direction and I am immensely grateful to them.

Looking back, it was fortunate that I chose to research and teach in Labour Law as one could not wish to join a warmer or more generous group of scholars. So many people have influenced the shape and progress of this project, and I am grateful to all of them. As examiners of the doctoral thesis, David Cabrelli, Jeremias Adams-Prassl, Keith Ewing and Mark Freedland offered the perfect mix of encouragement, guidance and questioning and thereby progressed my thinking enormously. Along with Anne Davies and Alan Bogg, Keith and Mark are also editors of this series, of which I am very privileged to be a part and I thank them all for supporting the publication of this monograph and the entire project so enthusiastically. In the final stages of writing, I benefited greatly from receiving comments and suggestions from an array of friends and colleagues and any outstanding errors are of course mine - thank you to Joe Atkinson, Anne Davies, Mark Freedland, Dimitri Kagiaros, Colm O'Cinneide, Tonia Novitz and Hugh Collins.

Without Hugh, I would never have started (let alone finished) this book and the doctoral thesis that underpinned it. Hugh's advice has been essential over the course of the project and to my navigation of the early stages of an academic career. His generosity in sharing his expertise is unparalleled and I will always be grateful to him for making my first years of research far more enjoyable and laughter-filled than I could have imagined.

Finally, to my family and friends who have been alongside me throughout the twists and turns of the journey, thank you. A complete list is impossible but special thanks are owed to Beth, Jane, Rosie, Caroline, Tom, Tommy and Jennifer, David and Katie, Dimitri, Alice, Matt and Tash, Katie and Luke and the Dentons. Every day I am grateful for the love and support of my family, Alison, Steve, Eleanor and Lydia, and my husband, Josh.

Philippa Collins
October 2021

Table of Contents

Abbreviations xv
Table of Cases xvii
Table of Legislation xxi

Introduction 1
I. An Overview of the Book 5
II. The European Convention on Human Rights and the Employer's Pervasive Prerogative 7
A. An Analysis in Accordance with the European Convention on Human Rights 7
B. The Qualified Rights within the Convention 9
C. The Employer's Authority to Dismiss, Discipline, and Manage 11
III. Notes on Terminology 13
IV. The Horizontal Effect of Human Rights at Work 15

PART I: THE ROLE OF HUMAN RIGHTS IN LABOUR (LAW)

1. Why Must We Protect the Human Rights of Workers? 21
I. The Centrality of the State in Human Rights Discourse 23
II. The Institutional Status of Employers 24
III. The Fundamental Rights of Workers Under Threat 25
IV. Not All Employers? 'Good' Employers and the Risk to Rights 29
V. The Inherent Tension Between Employment and Fundamental Rights 31
Conclusion 32

2. The Role of Human Rights in Labour Law 34
I. The Promise of a Turn Towards Human Rights in Labour Law 35
II. A Theory of Human Rights as the Foundation of Labour Law 37
A. Human Rights as a Floor, Not a Ceiling 38
B. The Shape of Labour Law on a Fundamental Rights Theory 40
C. Individualism and Collectivism in a Rights-based Theory 42
D. Two Potential Responses to the Critiques 44
III. Human Rights as One of Labour Law's Objectives 46
IV. Putting Human Rights to Work: The Distinctive Features of Labour Law 50
A. Towards a 'Human Rights Culture' in Labour Law 50

B. The Irrelevance of (Some) Doctrines of International Human Rights Law 51
C. Fit for Purpose? Human Rights *at Work* 54
Conclusion 57

3. Labour Law, the European Convention on Human Rights, and the States' Positive Obligations 58
I. *Human* Rights: The Protective Scope of the Convention 60
II. The Qualified Rights: From Interference to Necessity 62
A. The Examination of the Interference 63
B. The Justification Process 65
III. The Convention in the Context of Work 69
A. Waiver and Exit from Employment: Mitigating an Infringement? 70
B. The Interpretation and Enforcement of a Contract of Employment 72
IV. An Effective Remedy 75
Conclusion 77

PART II: UNDER PRESSURE: THE CURRENT FRAMEWORK OF LABOUR RIGHTS

4. The Existing Patchwork of Rights Protection 81
I. Mapping the Human Rights Dimensions of Labour Law's Instruments 82
A. Equality Act 2010 83
B. Trade Union and Labour Relations (Consolidation) Act 1992 85
C. The Public Interest Disclosure Act 1998 88
II. The Horizontal Effect of Convention Rights in Labour Law 89
III. The Cracks Begin to Show: The Divergence Between Domestic Duties and Convention Case Law 93
A. *Mba v Merton LBC*: Indirect Discrimination, Article 9, and Group Disadvantage 94
B. The Limits of Discrimination Law: Contentious and Political Beliefs 97
Conclusion 100

5. The Relational Scope of Labour Rights: Employees Only? 101
I. The Personal Scope of Convention Rights 103
II. The Contractual Core of Employment Status 104
A. The Existence of a Contract: The First Barrier to Enforcement 105
B. Barred by Illegality: Movement in the Right Direction? 108
III. The Categorization of the Workforce 110
A. The Trilateral Model of Rights Allocation 111
B. The 'Contract of Service': An Exclusionary Device 113
IV. Statutory Restrictions on Employment Rights 116
A. The Qualifying Period and *Redfearn v United Kingdom* 116
B. Exclusion Through Sectoral Occupation and Diplomatic Immunity 119
V. Reclassification Compelled by Human Rights Arguments 120

A. *Vining v London Borough of Wandsworth* and the Inclusion of Parks Police 120
B. *Gilham v Ministry of Justice*: Justice for Judges 122
C. An Unpredictable Artform: The Limits of Human Rights Argumentation 124
Conclusion 126

6. Human Rights and the Law of Unfair Dismissal 128
I. The Framework of the Law of Unfair Dismissal 129
II. The Standard of Review 133
A. Divergent Standards: Proportionality and the Range of Reasonable Responses 133
B. An Attempt at Reconciliation: The *X v Y* Framework for Fairness 136
III. The Tribunals' Blindspot: An Absence of Human Rights Considerations 138
IV. The Cursory Consideration of Human Rights Issues 140
V. The Remedies for an Unfair Dismissal 143
A. Non-pecuniary Loss and Injury to Feelings 144
B. The Upper Limit on a Claimant's Award 145
C. An Unbalanced Approach to the Adjustment of Awards 146
Conclusion 148

PART III: THE FUTURE OF HUMAN RIGHTS AT WORK

7. Human Rights and the Common Law of the Contract of Employment 151
I. Contractual Interpretation and Human Rights 152
II. A New Function for the Mutual Trust and Confidence Term? 156
A. Procedural Justice and the Implied Obligation 158
B. Acting 'Without Reasonable and Proper Cause' 159
C. A Lack of Respect and Concern for the Employee 161
D. The Divergence between the Implied Obligation and Human Rights Protection 163
E. Human Rights as a Mandatory Influence on the Implied Obligation? 165
III. A New Implied Obligation to Respect an Employee's Human Rights 166
A. A 'Necessary Incident' of a Contract of Employment? 168
B. A 'Sound Development' of the Common Law? 169
Conclusion 171

8. The Merits of Contractual Human Rights Protection 173
I. The Limitations of the Mutual Trust and Confidence Term 175
II. Contractual Waivers of Convention Rights and the Implied Terms 177
A. Displacing the Implied Obligation of Mutual Trust and Confidence 179
B. Would a New Human Rights Term be Derogable? 180

III. The Common Law's Relationship to the Employer's Managerial Prerogative 182
Conclusion 189

9. A Bill of Rights for Workers 190
I. The Need for Legislative Action 191
II. A Duty to Respect the Human Rights of Workers 193
A. The Requirement of Legality in the Context of Work 195
B. The Definition of an Employer's Legitimate Aims 196
C. The Proportionality of an Employer's Policy or Decision 198
III. The Parties: Defining the Duty Bearer and the Rights Holder 199
A. Who Is 'an Employer'? 199
B. Who Can Bring a Claim? 203
IV. Implementing Effective Protection for Human Rights at Work 205
A. A Pre-emptive Duty to Consider Fundamental Rights 206
B. Tackling Avoidance by Contract 208
C. An Effective Remedy for an Interference 209
V. A Tailored Connection to the ECHR 210
A. A Distinctive and Dynamic Approach to the Court's Case Law 210
B. The Interpretation and Incompatibility of Labour Law and the Common Law 212
VI. What Role for Fundamental Social Rights? 214
Conclusion 216

Bibliography 219
Index 229

Abbreviations

ACAS	Advisory, Conciliation and Arbitration Service
CAC	Central Arbitration Committee
CFREU	Charter of Fundamental Rights of the European Union
CJEU	Court of Justice of the European Union
CLJ	Cambridge Law Journal
EA 2010	Equality Act 2010
EAT	Employment Appeal Tribunal
ECHR	European Convention on Human Rights
ECSR	European Committee of Social Rights
ECtHR	European Court of Human Rights
EHRLR	European Human Rights Law Review
ERA 1996	Employment Rights Act 1996
ESC	European Social Charter
ET	Employment Tribunal
EU	European Union
HRA 1998	Human Rights Act 1998
ILJ	Industrial Law Journal
ILO	International Labour Organization
IOMTAC	Implied Obligation of Mutual Trust and Confidence
JCHR	Joint Committee on Human Rights
LQR	Law Quarterly Review
MLR	Modern Law Review
OJLS	Oxford Journal of Legal Studies
PIDA 1998	Public Interest Disclosure Act 1998
RORR	Range of Reasonable Responses
SIA 1978	State Immunity Act 1978
TULR(C)A 1992	Trade Union and Labour Relations (Consolidation) Act 1992
UDHR	Universal Declaration of Human Rights

Table of Cases

Addis v Gramophone Company Ltd [1909] AC 488 175–76
Amnesty International v Ahmed [2009] ICR 1450 .... 30–31, 163, 164n.66, 173n.1
Atkinson v Community Gateway Association [2015] ICR 1 .... 3n.11, 141n.77
Austin v A1M Retro Classics Limited [2020] ET 2500934/2020 137–38
Autoclenz Ltd v Belcher [2011] UKSC 41, [2011] 4 All ER 745 .... 112, 113n.86
Avsar v Wilson James Ltd [2020] EWHC 3412 (QB) 2n.5, 160
Bates van Winkelhof v Clyde & Co LLP [2014] UKSC 32, [2014] 1 WLR 2047 .... 113n.76
Bank Mellat v HM Treasury [2013] UKSC 38, [2014] AC 700 198
Benkharbouche v Secretary of State for Foreign and Commonwealth Affairs [2017] UKSC 62, [2017] 3 WLR 957 .... 7n.25, 119
Braine & others v The National Gallery (2019) ET 2201625/2018 115–16
British Leyland UK Ltd v Swift [1981] IRLR 91 .... 131, 134n.45
Buckland v Bournemouth University Higher Education Corporation [2010] EWCA Civ 121, [2010] 4 All ER 186 .... 161, 162–63
City and County of Swansea v Gayle [2013] IRLR 768 .... 3n.10, 185–86
Crossley v Faithful & Gould Holdings Ltd [2004] EWCA Civ 293, [2004] ICR 1615 170–71
Dunnachie v Kingston upon Hull City Council [2004] UKHL 36, [2005] 1 AC 226 .... 144–45, 147
Eastwood v Magnox Electric Plc [2004] UKHL 35, [2005] 1 AC 503 176–77
Edwards v Chesterfield Royal Hospital NHS Foundation Trust, Botham v Ministry of Defence [2011] UKSC 58, [2012] 2 AC 22 176–77
Eweida v British Airways Plc [2010] EWCA Civ 80, [2010] ICR 890 .... 2n.6, 95n.84
Forstater v CGD Europe, Centre for Global Development and Masood Ahmed [2019] ET 2200909/2019 98–99
Game Retail Limited v Laws (2014) UKEAT/0188/14/DA 141–42
Gibbins v British Council (2017) ET 2200088/2017 .... 2n.4, 139–40, 154–56, 184
Gilham v Ministry of Justice [2019] UKSC 44, [2020] IRLR 52 .... 2n.7, 10n.36, 120, 122–23, 126
GM Packaging (UK) Ltd v Haslem (2014) UKEAT/0259/13/LA 138–39
Gogay v Hertfordshire County Council [2000] IRLR 703 .... 158–59, 179n.35
Grainger Plc v Nicholson [2010] 2 All ER 253 97–99
Grant v South-West Trains Ltd [1998] IRLR 188 164
Gray v Mulberry Company (Design) Ltd [2019] EWCA Civ 1720, [2020] IRLR 29 96–97
Haddon v Van Der Bergh Foods Ltd [1999] ICR 1150 135–36
Higgs v Farmor's School [2020] ET 1401264/2019 (unreported) 99
Horkulak v Cantor Fitzgerald International [2003] EWHC 1918 (QB), [2004] ICR 697 162–63
Hounga v Allen and another [2014] UKSC 47, [2014] 1 WLR 2889 .... 109, 181n.44
Iceland Frozen Foods Ltd v Jones [1983] ICR 17 .... 131, 134–35
James v Greenwich London Borough Council [2008] EWCA Civ 35, [2008] ICR 545 .... 105–6, 107
Jivraj v Hashwani [2011] UKSC 40, [2011] 1 WLR 1872 .... 113n.77

Johnson v Unisys Ltd [2001] UKHL 13, [2003] 1 AC 518 . . . . 166, 170, 172, 176–77, 179–80
Ladele v Islington LBC [2009] EWCA Civ 1357, [2010] 1 WLR 955 . . . . 2n.6
Lee v Showmen's Guild of Great Britain [1952] 2 QB 329 181
Mackereth v Department of Work and Pensions [2019] ET 1304602/2018 98–99
Malik v Bank of Credit and Commerce International S.A. [1998] AC 20 . . . . 157, 167, 170–71
Mba v Merton London Borough Council [2013] EWCA Civ 1562, [2014] 1 WLR 1501 . . . . 2n.6, 28n.33, 94–97
McGowan v Scottish Water [2005] IRLR 167 . . . . 141n.77
Ministry of Justice v O'Brien [2013] UKSC 6, [2013] 1 WLR 522 123
Ministry of Justice v Sarfraz [2011] IRLR 562 . . . . 164n.66, 188
National Union of Professional Foster Carers v Certification Officer [2021] EWCA Civ 548 124
Norton Tool Co Ltd v Tewson [1973] 1 WLR 45 144–45
O'Kelly and Others v Trusthouse Forte Plc [1984] QB 90 . . . . 2n.5, 114–15
Okedina v Chikale [2019] EWCA Civ 1393, [2019] ICR 1635 . . . . 109, 110
Pay v Lancashire Probation Service [2004] ICR 187 . . . . 3n.9, 54n.106, 64n.33, 141n.76
Pharmacists' Defence Association Union v Boots Management Services Ltd and another [2017] EWCA Civ 66, [2017] IRLR 355 . . . . 165n.71, 211n.69
Pimlico Plumbers Ltd v Smith [2018] UKSC 29, [2018] ICR 1511 . . . . 113n.76
Plant v API Microelectronics Ltd (2017) ET 3401454/2016 139–40
Polkey v AE Dayton Services Ltd [1987] 3 WLR 1153, [1988] AC 344 147
Preece v J D Wetherspoons [2011] ET 2104806/10 142–43
Puthenveettil v Alexander, George & The Secretary of State for Business, Energy and Industrial Strategy [2020] ET 2361118/2013 . . . . 124, 126n.154
R. (on the application of the Independent Workers Union of Great Britain) v Central Arbitration Committee & Roofoods Limited t/a Deliveroo [2018] EWHC 3342 (Admin), [2019] IRLR 249 125
R. (on the application of the Independent Workers' Union of Great Britain) v Central Arbitration Committee & University of London [2019] EWHC 728 (Admin), [2019] IRLR 530 124–25
R. (on the application of the Independent Workers' Union of Great Britain) v The Secretary of State for Work and Pensions & The Secretary of State for Business, Energy and Industrial Strategy [2020] EWHC 3050 (Admin) 124
Reda v Flag Ltd [2002] UKPC 38, [2002] IRLR 747 179–80
Redbridge London Borough Council v Dhinsa and another [2014] EWCA Civ 178, [2014] ICR 834 119–20
Redfearn v Serco Ltd [2006] EWCA Civ 659, [2006] ICR 1367 . . . . . 2n.4, 30–31, 61n.21, 117
Reed and Bull Information Systems v Stedman [1999] IRLR 299 162–63
Reilly v Sandwell Metropolitan Borough Council [2018] UKSC 16, [2018] IRLR 558 140
Scally v Southern Health and Social Services Board [1992] 1 AC 294, [1991] 3 WLR 778 . . . . 166n.75, 167n.81, 170n.102
Serco Ltd v National Union of Rail, Maritime & Transport Workers [2011] EWCA Civ 226, [2011] ICR 848 91–93
Sharpe v The Bishop of Worcester and another [2015] EWCA Civ 399, [2015] ICR 1241 106
Smith v Carillion (JM) Ltd [2015] EWCA Civ 209, [2015] IRLR 467 . . . . . . 2n.5, 21–23, 107
Smith v Trafford Housing Trust [2012] EWHC 3221 (Ch), [2013] IRLR 86 . . . . . 1–3, 30–31, 151–52, 153–54, 173n.1
Steer v Stormsure Ltd [2021] IRLR 172 . . . . 10n.36, 146
Stevens v University of Birmingham [2015] EWHC 2300 (QB), [2015] IRLR 899 159

Transco Plc v O'brien [2002] EWCA Civ 379, [2002] ICR 721 159–60
Trayhorn v Secretary of State for Justice [2018] IRLR 502 96–97
TSB Bank Plc v Harris [2000] IRLR 157 159
Turner v East Midlands Trains Ltd [2012] EWCA Civ 1470, [2013] ICR 525 . . . . 53–54, 137–38
Uber BV and others v Aslam and others [2021] UKSC 5, [2021] IRLR 407 . . . . 112, 120
Vining and others v London Borough of Wandsworth [2017] EWCA Civ 1092, [2017] IRLR 1140 . . . . 119–22, 126
Wells and another v Cathay Investments 2 Ltd [2019] EWHC 2996 (QB), [2020] IRLR 281 . . . . 156n.22, 186n.66, 188
Williams v Leeds United Football Club [2015] EWHC 376 (QB), [2015] IRLR 383 . . . . 3n.11, 156n.22, 185–87, 198n.20
X v Y [2004] EWCA Civ 662, [2004] ICR 1634 . . . . 3n.9, 54n.106, 133, 136–38

COURT OF JUSTICE OF THE EUROPEAN UNION

C–81/12 *Asociatia ACCEPT v Consiliul National pentru Combaterea Discriminarii* [2013] 3 CMLR 26 . . . . 205n.44
C–54/07 *Centrum voor Gelijkheid van Kansen en voor Racismebestrijding v Firma Feryn* [2008] 3 CMLR 22 . . . . 205n.44
C–157/15 *Samira Achbita and Centrum voor gelijkheid van kansen en voor racismebestrijding v G4S Secure Solutions NV* [2017] 3 CMLR 21 . . . . 28n.32

EUROPEAN COURT OF HUMAN RIGHTS

Antović and Mirković v Montenegro Application no 70838/13 (ECtHR, 28 November 2017) 64, 184–86
Associated Society of Locomotive Engineers & Firemen (ASLEF) v United Kingdom (2007) 45 EHRR 34 . . . . 43n.40, 86n.33
Bărbulescu v Romania Application no 61496/08 (ECtHR, 5 September 2017) 63n.28, 72–73, 156, 184–85, 187
Boyraz v Turkey (2015) 60 EHRR 30 . . . . 10n.34, 84
Demir v Turkey (2009) 48 EHRR 54 . . . . 42n.33, 43n.41, 86n.30, 121–22
Denisov v Ukraine Application no 76639/11 (ECtHR, 25 September 2018) 41n.28, 41n.30, 66n.48, 129n.5, 175–76
DH and others v Czech Republic (2008) 47 EHRR 3 . . . . 70–71, 85n.23, 177–78
Enerji Yapı-Yol Sen v Turkey Application no 68959/01 (ECtHR, 21 April 2009) 42n.33, 43n.41, 86n.30
Eweida and others v United Kingdom (2013) 57 EHRR 8 . . . . 9n.32, 28n.32, 71n.73, 71, 76–77, 95–96, 145
Fuentes Bobo v Spain (2001) 31 EHRR 50 . . . . 67, 133–34, 145
Guja v Moldova (2011) 53 EHRR 16 . . . . 88n.48, 122
Halford v United Kingdom (1997) 24 EHRR 523 . . . . 72n.82
Heinisch v Germany (2014) 58 EHRR 31 . . . . 67n.49, 88n.48
Herbai v Hungary (2020) 70 EHRR 35 . . . . 59n.6, 63–64, 68–69, 156n.24, 183–84
Köpke v Germany (2011) 53 EHRR SE26 56
Kyriakides v Cyprus Application no 39058/05 (ECtHR, 16 October 2008) 75n.101
Markin v Russia (2013) 56 EHRR 8 . . . . 71n.73, 83n.10, 177–78
Martínez v Spain (2015) 60 EHRR 3 . . . . 60n.11, 69n.62, 72n.78, 108n.45, 178n.23
Mustafa and Tarzibachi v Sweden (2011) 52 EHRR 24 75
National Union of Rail, Maritime and Transport Workers v United Kingdom (2015) 60 EHRR 10 . . . . 44n.44

Niemietz v Germany (1993) 16 EHRR 97 187
Ognevenko v Russia Application no 44873/09 (ECtHR, 20 November 2018) 63n.27
Pay v United Kingdom (2009) 48 EHRR SE2 .... 64, 68n.61, 139n.66, 186n.67
Pişkin v Turkey Application no 33399/18 (ECtHR, 15 December 2020) 67–68, 129n.6, 175–76
Pla v Andorra (2006) 42 EHRR 25 .... 73–75, 152n.5, 168–69
Rantsev v Cyprus and Russia (2010) 51 EHRR 1 .... 9n.31
Redfearn v United Kingdom (2013) 57 EHRR 2 .... 59n.5, 61–62, 63, 67, 97n.96, 98n.103, 102, 116–18, 168–69
Sadik v Greece (1997) 24 EHRR 323 65
Sánchez v Spain (2012) 54 EHRR 24 .... 53–54, 68n.61, 72n.79, 139n.67
Siliadin v France (2006) 43 EHRR 16 .... 9n.31, 83n.5
Sindicatul Păstorul cel Bun v Romania (2014) 58 EHRR 10 .... 71n.73, 71n.74, 85–86, 103–4, 115, 125
Smith and Grady v United Kingdom (Just Satisfaction) (2001) 31 EHRR 24 .... 66n.44, 76–77, 145, 147
Sørensen and Rasmussen v Denmark (2008) 46 EHRR 29 .... 71n.74, 178
Taliadorou and Stylianou v Cyprus Application nos 39627/05 and 39631/05 (ECtHR, 16 October 2008) 77, 144n.89
Thlimmenos v Greece (2001) 31 EHRR 15 84–85
Vogt v Germany (1996) 21 EHRR 205 .... 72n.78, 97n.96, 98n.103, 133
Wilson and others v United Kingdom (2002) 35 EHRR 20 ..... 12–13, 51n.88, 59n.5, 86–87
Young, James and Webster v United Kingdom (1981) 3 EHRR 20 .... 12, 43n.37, 53n.99, 87n.40

Table of Legislation

UK

Agency Workers Regulations 2010 ... 107
Data Protection Act 2018 ...... 81–82, 90
The Employment Relations Act 1999 (Blacklists) Regulations 2010 ... 204–5
Employment Rights Act 1996 .... 105, 111–13, 118, 119–20, 123, 128, 129–32
  Section 86 .... 175n.5
  Section 94 .... 113n.80, 115n.95, 129–30
  Section 98(1) 130, 197
  Section 98(2) 130, 197
  Section 98(4) 131, 136–38
  Section 103A 131n.19, 188
  Section 108 116–18
  Section 119 .... 132n.30
  Section 123 .... 132n.32, 144n.92, 147n.110, 209n.64
  Section 200 120–21
  Section 230 .... 104n.15, 105n.16, 111n.63, 122n.134
Employment Rights (Increase of Limits) Order 2021 .... 132n.33, 145n.101
Enterprise and Regulatory Reform Act 2013 118
Equality Act 2006 204
Equality Act 2010 .... 5, 81–82, 83–85, 94–99, 105, 161, 164, 169–70, 193–94, 204, 206, 207–8, 212–13
  Section 10 97–99
  Section 13 84
  Section 19 .... 84–85, 94, 96–97, 196n.13
  Section 83 .... 105n.17, 111n.61
  Section 119 .... 209n.64
  Section 135 .... 209n.60
  Section 142 208
  Section 144 208
European Union (Withdrawal) Act 2018 .... 7n.24
Health and Safety at Work etc. Act 1974 .... 81–83, 200–1
Human Rights Act 1998 ...... 5, 8, 16–17, 45, 50–51, 52, 92, 93, 116, 151–52, 157, 158, 165, 183, 190–91, 192–93, 205, 216–17
  Section 2 ..... 211n.67, 211–12, 216–17
  Section 3 .... 82, 91, 95–96, 107, 120, 121–22, 123, 127, 128, 136–37, 213
  Section 4 .... 119, 210
  Section 6 ..... 151–52, 165, 181–82, 193
  Section 7 .... 122, 193
Immigration, Asylum and Nationality Act 2006 109
Modern Slavery Act 2015 .... 41n.26, 81–82
National Minimum Wage Act 1998 .... 111n.64, 152n.8
Public Interest Disclosure Act 1998 ...... 81–82, 88–89, 212–13
State Immunity Act 1978 119
Trade Disputes Act 1906 48
Trade Union Act 1871 48
Trade Union and Labour Relations (Consolidation) Act 1992 .... 5, 81–82, 85–88, 91–92, 93–94, 105, 111–12, 120–22, 124, 161, 169–70, 193–94, 212–13
  Section 1 .... 86n.32, 111n.66, 124
  Section 137 87
  Section 146 .... 87, 111n.67, 160
  Section 152 87
  Section 219 .... 86n.36, 91n.66
  Section 296 .... 105n.19
  Schedule A1 .... 86n.34, 124
Working Time Regulations 1998 ... 111n.64

INTERNATIONAL AND EUROPEAN UNION

Council Directive 97/80/EC of 15 December 1997 on the burden of proof in cases of discrimination based on sex [1998] OJ L14/6....... 209n.60

Council Directive 2000/43/EC of 29 June 2000 implementing the principle of equal treatment between persons irrespective of racial or ethnic origin [2000] OJ L180/2 . . . . 83n.14
Council Directive 2000/78/EC of 27 November 2000 establishing a general framework for equal treatment in employment and occupation [2000] OJ L303/16 . . . 83n.15
Directive 2006/54/EC of the European Parliament and of the Council of 5 July 2006 on the implementation of the principle of equal opportunities and equal treatment of men and women in matters of employment and occupation [2006] OJ L204/23 . . . . 83n.13
European Convention on Human Rights 5, 7–9, 37–38, 40–42, 52–53, 82, 101, 128–29, 193, 210–14, 215–16
Article 1 60
Article 4 . . . . 10, 35–36, 82–83
Article 6 . . . 10–11, 70, 119, 146, 158, 159
Article 8 . . . . 9–11, 28, 41–42, 58, 65–66, 67–68, 72–73, 77, 82–83, 90, 120–21, 128–29, 130–31, 137–38, 139–40, 155–56, 164, 184–86, 188, 207
Article 9 . . . . 9–11, 58, 65–66, 71, 94–97, 137, 155–56
Article 10 . . . . 9–11, 58, 61, 63–64, 65–66, 75, 88–89, 94, 97–99, 106, 122, 130–31, 133–34, 137, 139–40, 141–43, 155–56, 183–84
Article 11 . . . . 9–11, 42, 43–44, 58, 61–62, 65–66, 85–88, 92, 93–94, 103–4, 116, 117–18, 120–22, 124, 130–31, 201, 213
Article 13 . . . . 75–76, 143–44, 145
Article 14 . . . . 9–10, 60, 73–74, 83–85, 120–21, 122, 123, 143–44, 146, 159–60, 164, 207
Article 41 76–77
European Social Charter 7–9, 40–41, 43–44, 45, 214–16
International Covenant on Economic, Social and Cultural Rights 7–8, 214–15
Regulation (EU) 2016/679 of the European Parliament and of the Council of 27 April 2016 on the protection of natural persons with regard to the processing of personal data and on the free movement of such data, and repealing Directive 95/46/EC [2016] OJ L119/1 . . . . 83n.7
The Charter of Fundamental Rights of the European Union [2016] OJ C202/389 . . . . 7, 43–46, 55, 119, 214–15
Universal Declaration of Human Rights 7–8, 37–38, 44–45

Introduction

'<Gay church "marriages" set to get the go-ahead.>[1] *An equality too far*'

On his personal Facebook page, Mr Smith described himself as a 'full on charismatic Christian'. He used his Facebook page to discuss football and motorsports, as well as to keep in touch with his Christian community and other friends and colleagues. In February 2011, he posted a link to a BBC article reporting that the then Equalities Minister had expressed a view that civil partnerships should be permitted to take place in religious settings, such as churches. Mr Smith thought that the development would interest members of the Christian community abroad and he posted the comment quoted at the beginning of the chapter. Amongst the 200 or so people that Mr Smith was connected to on Facebook were some of his colleagues from the Trafford Housing Trust, where he was a manager. One of these colleagues responded to Mr Smith's post, asking him whether he disapproved of the report's contents and to explain his viewpoint further. Mr Smith responded as follows:

> I don't understand why people who have no faith and don't believe in Christ would want to get hitched in church the bible is quite specific that marriage is for men and women if the state wants to offer civil marriage to same sex then that is up to the state; but the state shouldn't impose [its] rules on places of faith and conscience.

For these two online comments, Mr Smith faced disciplinary action by his employer, the Housing Trust. He sought to explain that he had intended his comments to be thought-provoking. Mr Smith admitted that he had made an error by making those comments in circumstances where the reader would also be able to link him to his employer, as his position was listed elsewhere on his page. During the investigation, his colleagues described Mr Smith's comments as 'silly' and 'out of order' but one employee—the same colleague who had asked Mr Smith to elaborate on his

[1] Mr Smith's post included a link to a BBC article regarding the possible introduction of gay marriages in churches.

Putting Human Rights to Work. Philippa Collins, Oxford University Press. © Philippa Collins 2022.
DOI: 10.1093/oso/9780192894595.003.0001

views—categorized the exchange as an instance of 'blatant homophobia'.[2] This evidence was relied on to hold that Mr Smith was guilty of causing offence and upset to his colleagues, of creating a risk to the Trust's reputation and of impermissibly promoting his religious views contrary to the employer's Code of Conduct. The outcome of that process was Mr Smith's permanent demotion and a 40 per cent reduction in his salary.

Many would find this decision by his employer, a Housing Trust, deeply concerning. A permanent demotion for a mild-mannered exchange on social media appears entirely out of proportion. A written warning to be more careful in his interactions online would surely have sufficed. In addition, the circumstances of the penalty against Mr Smith invoke a concern for several of his fundamental rights. The employer's disciplinary process violated Mr Smith's right to privacy because the Trust accessed, read, and relied upon materials shared by Mr Smith in a personal capacity on a forum that he used outside of working time. Mr Smith's right to freedom of expression extended to the views that he expressed on Facebook, even though they may be disagreeable or offensive to some. The sanction meted out by the employer infringed upon that fundamental right, as well as no doubt discouraging other employees in the workplace from exercising their right to express their opinions in future. In addition, Mr Smith's perception of the possibility of gay marriages in churches was reflective of his own Christian faith, a fundamental element of his identity. The employer, despite the importance of these rights that Mr Smith was entitled to exercise, decided that a final written warning for gross misconduct, a permanent demotion, and a pay cut was the most appropriate response in the circumstances.

Mr Smith convinced the High Court that his employer's action had been in breach of the terms of his contract of employment.[3] Mr Smith's success is an anomaly in a mass of cases where individuals seek to challenge an employer's interference with their human rights. Workers have been dismissed for expressing their political views[4] or associating with a trade union in order to protect their interests.[5] They have suffered detriment as a result of expressing or seeking to adhere to their faith,[6] 'blowing the whistle' on potentially unlawful conduct within their employer's organization,[7] or expressing their personal views on social media.[8]

[2] *Smith v Trafford Housing Trust* [2012] EWHC 3221 (Ch), [2013] IRLR 86, [37].

[3] ibid.

[4] *Redfearn v Serco Ltd* [2006] EWCA Civ 659, [2006] ICR 1367; *Gibbins v British Council* (2017) ET 2200088/2017.

[5] *O'Kelly and Others v Trusthouse Forte Plc* [1984] QB 90; *Avsar v Wilson James Ltd* [2020] EWHC 3412 (QB); *Smith v Carillion (JM) Ltd* [2015] EWCA Civ 209, [2015] IRLR 467.

[6] *Eweida v British Airways Plc* [2010] EWCA Civ 80, [2010] ICR 890; *Ladele v Islington LBC* [2009] EWCA Civ 1357, [2010] 1 WLR 955; *Mba v Merton London Borough Council* [2013] EWCA Civ 1562, [2014] 1 WLR 1501.

[7] *Gilham v Ministry of Justice* [2019] UKSC 44, [2020] IRLR 52; *Royal Mail Ltd v Jhuti* [2019] UKSC 55, [2020] 3 All ER 257.

[8] *Smith v British Waterways Board (t/a Scottish Canals)* (2015) UKEATS/0004/15, [2015] All ER (D) 126.

Employees' right to respect for their private life have been infringed upon through invasive investigations and dismissals justified by reference to reasons that relate to a person's intimate and personal life.[9] A worker's privacy can be further threatened by extensive monitoring of their movements, both within and beyond the workplace,[10] and employers probing their personal correspondence and communication through email, social media, and private messages.[11] Individuals who have been subjected to these kinds of infringements have fought hard to receive recognition of the wrongs that they have suffered at the hands of their employer.[12]

In rare cases, such as Mr Smith's, the worker's challenge is successful. Mr Smith's victory, however, was pyrrhic: he was awarded only £98 in damages,[13] a paltry sum in the light of the lasting financial consequences for Mr Smith of the Trust's decision to demote him. The court acknowledged that the primary purpose of Mr Smith's case was to restore his reputation after being wrongfully accused of gross misconduct. Nevertheless, he was not reinstated in his former position[14] and, as noted by the judge in the case, the award ordered 'leaves the uncomfortable feeling that justice has not been done to him in the circumstances.'[15] Certainly, the trivial sum awarded did little to remedy the serious infringement upon Mr Smith's human rights committed by his employer. Examining Mr Smith's case exposes a myriad of urgent questions. Why was the law's response to his claim so meagre? Why did the employer perceive Mr Smith's demotion as an appropriate response to his expression of his personal views outside of work? What could be done to ensure that individuals like Mr Smith enjoy effective protection for their rights in the workplace?

This book addresses many of these questions. The overarching theme is whether labour law's response to an infringement upon a worker's human rights by an employer is adequate. In the absence of a general obligation on employers to respect the fundamental rights of their workers, individuals often turn to the structures of employment and labour law to seek vindication. Is labour law, as it is currently framed and applied, capable of providing effective protection for our fundamental rights when they are contravened by employers? To be clear from the outset,

[9] *X v Y* [2004] EWCA Civ 662, [2004] ICR 1634; *Pay v Lancashire Probation Service* [2004] ICR 187; *Percy v Church of Scotland Board of National Mission* [2005] UKHL 73, [2006] 2 AC 28; *Lawrence v Secretary of State for Justice* (2017) ET 3401016/2016.

[10] *City and County of Swansea v Gayle* [2013] IRLR 768; *McGowan v Scottish Water* [2005] IRLR 167.

[11] *Atkinson v Community Gateway Association* [2015] ICR 1; *Williams v Leeds United Football Club* [2015] EWHC 376 (QB), [2015] IRLR 383; *Kianchehr v Tesco Stores Limited* (2020) ET 1404529/2019.

[12] Whilst these cases are drawn from the UK, they are mirrored in cases from other jurisdictions that have been litigated in the European Court of Human Rights (ECtHR). See, for example, *Vogt v Germany* (1996) 21 EHRR 205; *Sánchez v Spain* (2012) 54 EHRR 24; *Martínez v Spain* (2015) 60 EHRR 3; *Bărbulescu v Romania* Application no 61496/08 (ECtHR, 5 September 2017); *Herbai v Hungary* (2020) 70 EHRR 35.

[13] For the decision regarding remedies, see *Smith v Trafford Housing Trust* [2012] EWHC 3320 (Ch), [2012] All ER (D) 273.

[14] ibid [14]–[15].

[15] *Smith v Trafford Housing Trust* (n 2) [106].

although there are some areas which may lead us to be optimistic in the debate regarding human rights at work, I will argue that the answer to this question is 'no'.

The examination offered explores the point of intersection between a group of fundamental rights, the protection of which is acknowledged internationally to be a matter of urgent priority and moral necessity, and a context which is crucial to the survival and flourishing of the majority of people. Human rights possess a special normative weight in debates, both political and legal. They are enjoyed equally by all people, whether or not they are protected by the laws of a particular country at a particular time.[16] The precise values or justifications that underpin these rights are contested,[17] but the ability to exercise one's human rights freely contributes to a person's sense of dignity, their freedom, and their autonomy amongst many other values. A decent life of work makes a significant contribution to those same ends: as Bob Hepple noted, 'Work is, for most people, the way in which they can best express their dignity and autonomy as human beings and contribute to society.'[18] It provides opportunities for self-realization, membership of a community, and a sense of self-worth.[19] The value and importance of work in modern society and in the lives of individuals who seek to perform it is incontrovertible.

Perhaps because 'employment is *the* enabling opportunity',[20] relationships between workers and their employers are complex. Self-fulfilment and a range of advantages may flow from the provision of work, but the employment relationship is also characterized by adverse traits, such as subordination, inequality, and one party's dependence upon the other. These features generate an inherent tension between the free exercise of human rights by members of the workforce and the existence of a relationship of employment.[21] The context of work is too central to our lives to allow it to be untouched by a concern for the human rights of workers. Effective legal guarantees must be in place to ensure that workers do not suffer unjustified infringements upon their most fundamental rights. By protecting their *human* rights, we recognize and confirm the dignity of workers as individuals and push against the commodification of labour.[22] The overarching objective of this work is at once timeless and timely: we shall see how the human rights of workers

[16] See Pablo Gilabert, 'Labor Human Rights and Human Dignity' (2015) 42 Philosophy & Social Criticism 171, 176.

[17] See Rowan Cruft, S Matthew Liao, and Massimo Renzo (eds), *Philosophical Foundations of Human Rights* (Oxford University Press 2015) Part I.

[18] Bob Hepple, 'European Rules on Dismissal Law?' (1997) 18 Comparative Labour Law Journal 204, 204.

[19] Hugh Collins, 'Is There a Human Right to Work?' in Virginia Mantouvalou (ed), *The Right to Work: Legal and Philosophical Perspectives* (Hart Publishing 2015) 35.

[20] Tarunabh Khaitan, *A Theory of Discrimination Law* (Oxford University Press 2015) 210.

[21] Hugh Collins, 'Is the Contract of Employment Illiberal?' in Hugh Collins, Gillian Lester, and Virginia Mantouvalou (eds), *Philosophical Foundations of Labour Law* (Oxford University Press 2018) 62–63.

[22] Hugh Collins, 'Justice at Work' (2020) 1 Revista Forumul Judecatorilor 59, 67.

remain under threat despite decades of discourse regarding the urgency of their proper protection.

I. An Overview of the Book

Before commencing the detailed explanation of the scope and approach of the work, I will sketch its main components and key arguments. The chapters are divided into three parts. Part I investigates the relationship between work, labour law, and human rights. Chapter 1 recounts the essential characteristics of modern employment relationships and demonstrates that the relationship of employment generates a risk to the worker's human rights, both within the workplace and beyond it. Perhaps in implicit response, I will argue in Chapter 2, one aim of the discipline of labour law has always been to protect the fundamental rights of workers from violation by their employer. Human rights law has also responded to the risk to rights posed by private actors and Chapter 3 will discuss how the European Convention on Human Rights (ECHR or the Convention) has been interpreted to counter this threat. An account of the doctrine of positive obligations, which have been developed by the European Court of Human Rights (ECtHR or the Court) and applied to labour disputes over many years, will be offered. These chapters form the normative foundation of the rest of the work, as well as providing a set of standards, derived from the case law of the ECtHR, against which domestic laws and practice can be assessed.

The focus of Part II is upon the mechanisms through which workers may already attempt to enforce their fundamental rights in England and Wales. Throughout, I have sought to reflect the law as it stood on 1 May 2021. In the UK, the Human Rights Act 1998 (HRA 1998) gives domestic effect to the ECHR rights, particularly by imposing an obligation upon all public authorities, including courts and tribunals, to act compatibly with those rights.[23] The Act also requires that existing legislation be interpreted in a manner that is compatible with the Convention rights as far as it is possible to do so. Chapter 4 expands upon the various ways in which the HRA 1998 impacts upon labour law, or has the potential to do so, particularly in the light of the statutory foundations of many key employment rights. The chapter highlights the extent to which employment and labour laws already impose duties upon employers in relation to specific human rights, such as freedom of association or expression. I will also begin to describe the discrepancies between the Convention's principles and the safeguards provided by statutes such as the Equality Act 2010 and the Trade Union and Labour Relations (Consolidation) Act 1992.

[23] HRA 1998, section 6.

Despite the strong interpretive obligation of the HRA 1998, and the moral urgency of the rights-protective ambitions of labour law, the second part of this book exposes a range of difficulties and limitations upon the capacity of existing employment rights to protect the human rights of workers. The relational scope of employment rights is a significant barrier to anyone who seeks to vindicate their human rights through these mechanisms. Important rights are restricted in their availability to the legal category of 'employee'/'worker' or even by the number of years of service that the individual has completed. Halting and occasional progress has been made in opening up some rights to a wider group of beneficiaries, but Chapter 5 shows that the universal entitlement to human rights remains a challenge that employment law has yet to confront fully. Chapter 6 turns to the right not to be unfairly dismissed. Human rights arguments have been a notable presence in the case law and discussion of the law of unfair dismissal in its recent history. Chapter 6 will demonstrate that the law of unfair dismissal has not yet fulfilled its potential as a source of effective protection for the human rights of workers. Unfair dismissal cases are regularly decided without any reference to the individual's Convention rights at all or after only the most fleeting review of the justification for an infringement.

The third and final part of the book turns to alternative methods which could be relied upon to guarantee the exercise and enforcement of human rights at work. Once we have concluded that the statutory possibilities are flawed for a variety of reasons, a prominent alternative is the common law and the wrongs that flow from the terms and obligations of the contract of employment. The current and future direction of the common law regarding human rights is discussed in Chapter 7 where I observe that pockets of protection can be seen alongside serious divergences from human rights standards. This chapter anticipates a judicial reluctance to engage in a swift refashioning of the common law implied terms in order to provide full protection for an individual's Convention rights. Chapter 8 goes on to assess the desirability of protecting human rights, as mandatory and universal rights, through the common law and through contractual means in particular. Interestingly, many of the deficiencies in the application of the statutory rights are mirrored in their common law counterparts, in addition to concerns about the contractual foundation of this alternative in the presence of a significant imbalance of bargaining power between the parties.

To conclude Part III and indeed the entire book, an ambitious Bill of Rights for Workers will be proposed and detailed in Chapter 9. This novel legislative solution is tailored to the specific context of the workplace and consciously breaks away from many of the existing patterns and problems of labour law exposed in the prior chapters. The elements suggested draw upon the successes of labour law, equality law, and human rights law to craft an effective mechanism of human rights protection for workers against infringements by their employers. The proposal would fulfil the UK's positive obligations under the Convention and answer the pressing need, underscored in the early chapters, for human rights to be respected and protected in working relationships.

II. The European Convention on Human Rights and the Employer's Pervasive Prerogative

The outline in section I indicates some of the limitations on the scope of this book which will be explored further in this section. First, I will explain the choice to focus upon the ECHR, as a classic example of a document containing civil and political human rights, rather than a document more inclusive of social and economic fundamental rights. More specifically, the detailed analyses offered in Chapter 3 onwards focus upon the qualified rights contained in the ECHR. In section II.C, I outline the aspects of domestic employment law that are central to Parts II and III of the work. The regulation of employer's power to dismiss a worker, as the ultimate sanction that reinforces the individual's subordination to the employer's authority, is key to the doctrinal analysis. The assessment offered here does, however, extend to how workers are protected from other forms of detriment and restrictions which constitute infringements upon their fundamental rights.

A. An Analysis in Accordance with the European Convention on Human Rights

Until recently, any scholar from the UK seeking to discuss only the ECHR would have to defend themselves from the charge that the focus of their research was unduly narrow. This charge has less force with the departure of the UK from the EU. The Charter of Fundamental Rights of the European Union contains an array of rights and principles that are highly relevant to the world of work and its potential is only beginning to be realized in decisions at EU and domestic level. Although the link between the Charter and UK law has been expressly severed because of Brexit,[24] the Charter has already formed part of important victories for working people in the UK courts[25] and it will be mentioned when relevant throughout the text.

The UK's exit from the EU explains the relative absence of the Charter, but what of other human rights documents that have (or should have) influence in the UK? Many such documents have more direct relevance to the world of work than the Convention. The European Social Charter—the Council of Europe treaty and the

[24] See European Union (Withdrawal) Act 2018, section 5(4).

[25] Most notably *Benkharbouche v Secretary of State for Foreign and Commonwealth Affairs* [2017] UKSC 62, [2017] 3 WLR 957.

counterpart of the ECHR—contains a variety of fundamental social rights that are directly applicable to the workplace: the right to just conditions of work and the right to a fair remuneration, for example.[26] The Conventions and Recommendations of the International Labour Organization (ILO), particularly the core conventions highlighted by the ILO Declaration on Fundamental Principles and Rights at Work,[27] contain crucial guidance regarding the proper safeguarding of rights in the workplace. From the range of United Nations documents, one might highlight the Universal Declaration on Human Rights, the International Covenant on Economic, Social and Cultural Rights, and the Guiding Principles on Business and Human Rights as relevant to the shape and substance of any regime of labour laws. Undoubtedly, a study of UK labour law in accordance with the demands and principles of each would be an important exercise.

Nevertheless, the scope of this work is confined to an examination of the European Convention, the UK's obligations under it, and the case law of the ECtHR. In contrast to some of the other documents listed, these rights are justiciable and enforceable before national courts and tribunals under the HRA 1998. The Act also includes important tools, particularly the obligation to interpret statutes compatibly with the Convention rights where it is possible to do so, that have already demonstrated their potential to reshape how employment rights are applied. As will be seen, however, significant deficiencies remain when one examines the extent to which these fundamental rights of members of the workforce are protected in domestic law.

The focus upon the ECHR is in no way intended to reinforce the 'deeply rooted prejudice' against economic, social, and cultural rights that has been present in modern discourse regarding human rights.[28] This prejudice has been undermined on many occasions and on a variety of grounds[29] and I do not subscribe to it. Rather, in Chapter 2, I express serious concerns about the narrow scope that would follow from a theory of labour law grounded within a so-called 'first generation' rights document such as the Convention. Such an enterprise would risk the erosion of any claims on behalf of labour that are unconnected to the limited list of civil and political human rights. The boundaries and concerns of labour law would be substantially contracted without reference to fundamental social rights such as those contained in the European Social Charter. The discussion of the Bill of Rights in Chapter 9 takes into account these concerns. I consider how fundamental social rights could be incorporated into the legislative scheme, reflecting the ECtHR's

[26] European Social Charter, Article 2 and Article 4, respectively.

[27] ILO Declaration on Fundamental Principles and Rights at Work, adopted by the International Labour Conference, 86th Session, Geneva, June 1998, [2].

[28] Filip Dorssemont, 'The European Convention on Human Rights as a Fountain of Labour Rights' in Janice R Bellace and Beryl ter Haar (eds), *Research Handbook on Labour, Business and Human Rights Law* (Edward Elgar Publishing 2019) 314.

[29] See Sandra Fredman, *Comparative Human Rights Law* (Oxford University Press 2018) chapter 3.

own 'integrated approach' which draws on fundamental social rights in its interpretation of the Convention.[30]

B. The Qualified Rights within the Convention

From the full list of Convention rights, the focus of this work is narrowed further. The main assessment of the labour law of England and Wales will be conducted in accordance with the qualified rights of the ECHR: Article 8 (the right to respect for private life), Article 9 (freedom of thought, conscience, and belief), Article 10 (freedom of expression), and Article 11 (freedom of assembly and association). Reasons of limited space aside, this subset of Convention rights was selected for two reasons: one descriptive and one normative. Firstly, the qualified rights have differences in phrasing, but they are nevertheless applied and developed in a fairly consistent manner by the Court. Secondly, although some of the most egregious human rights violations in the context of work are examined under other Convention rights,[31] the qualified rights are regularly invoked in disputes between workers and employers. These rights appear particularly vulnerable to interference and restriction in the context of work.

From a descriptive perspective, the way that the qualified rights are applied and, for the purposes of this work, the obligations that they impose upon member states are comparable. The qualified rights under Articles 8–11 require the application of a two-pronged analysis: the question of whether an interference with a right has occurred followed by the assessment of whether the interference was justified. The case law on the qualified rights has generally developed consistently and the Court draws on principles expressed in the case law regarding one qualified right in decisions relating to another.[32] There are unique positive obligations imposed on member states under each right.[33] Notwithstanding these specific obligations, Chapter 3 will demonstrate that a common set of obligations can be drawn from the Strasbourg case law with respect to how member states should protect the qualified rights in the context of employment relations.

Another right—the prohibition on discrimination contained in Article 14—will also be mentioned occasionally throughout the chapters. Article 14 is a 'parasitic'

[30] See Virginia Mantouvalou, 'Labour Rights in the European Convention on Human Rights: An Intellectual Justification for an Integrated Approach to Interpretation' (2013) 13 Human Rights Law Review 529.

[31] Examples of egregious treatment of people at work can be found in Article 4 cases such as *Siliadin v France* (2006) 43 EHRR 16; *Rantsev v Cyprus and Russia* (2010) 51 EHRR 1; *C.N. and V. v France* Application no 67724/09 (ECtHR, 11 October 2012).

[32] In the employment context, a recent, notable example of this approach of this 'cross-fertilization' is *Eweida and others v United Kingdom* (2013) 57 EHRR 8, [83].

[33] See Alastair Mowbray, *The Development of Positive Obligations under the European Convention on Human Rights by the European Court of Human Rights* (Hart Publishing 2004) chapters 6 and 7.

right: it relies upon the circumstances of the case falling 'within the ambit' of another Convention right in order to permit an individual to argue that they have been discriminated against in the way that their rights have been secured by a member state.[34] Article 14 will be breached if a difference in treatment between persons in comparable circumstances is not met with an 'objective and reasonable justification'.[35] This standard of justification, which has been 'read in' to the Article by the ECtHR, also entails that the difference in treatment is shown to pursue a legitimate aim. In addition to a discussion of how the right not to be discriminated against has been guaranteed in working relations in the UK, we will see instances where Article 14 has been crucial in challenging distinctions drawn between groups of workers within the domestic system of employment rights.[36]

The rights contained in Article 4 and Article 6 are beyond the scope of this study. Although both are relevant to the relationship between employers and individuals, the nature of the rights themselves and the obligations that they entail are quite different to the qualified rights. Article 4, the prohibition of slavery, servitude, and forced labour, is an absolute right which admits of no qualification. As observed by Vladislava Stoyanova,[37] states are under an obligation to criminalize any act that maintains a person in slavery, servitude, or forced labour. There is also an obligation to investigate allegations that an individual has been a victim of these forms of abuse and to develop effective regulatory frameworks that protect individuals from a violation of their Article 4 right. The positive obligations that are imposed upon states under Article 4 are distinct compared to those that we will discuss with relation to the qualified rights throughout this work. Article 4 has been analysed in detail in other work,[38] but it will not be a significant focus herein.

Similarly, the right to a fair trial, contained in Article 6, has a distinct nature when contrasted with the qualified rights. In fact, it is used as a paradigm example of a 'vertical' human right which is applicable between citizen and state and incurs substantial duties only upon the state to provide the structures and means of providing a fair trial.[39] That is not to say that Article 6 has lacked impact on labour disputes. Sébastian Van Drooghenbroeck observes both the 'conventionalisation' of labour law litigation and the 'labourisation' of fair trial standards.[40] Through

[34] See *Boyraz v Turkey* (2015) 60 EHRR 30, [40].

[35] ibid [50].

[36] See, for example, *Gilham v Ministry of Justice* (n 7); *Steer v Stormsure Ltd* [2021] IRLR 172.

[37] See Vladislava Stoyanova, *Human Trafficking and Slavery Reconsidered: Conceptual Limits and States' Positive Obligations in European Law* (Cambridge University Press 2017) chapter 8.

[38] See ibid; Virginia Mantouvalou, 'The Prohibition of Slavery, Servitude and Forced and Compulsory Labour under Article 4 ECHR' in Filip Dorssemont, Klaus Lörcher, and Isabelle Schömann (eds), *The European Convention on Human Rights and the Employment Relation* (Hart Publishing 2013).

[39] Ian Leigh and Roger Masterman, *Making Rights Real: The Human Rights Act in its First Decade* (Hart Publishing 2008) 241.

[40] Sébastien Van Drooghenbroek, 'Labour Law Litigation and Fair Trial under Article 6' in Filip Dorssemont, Klaus Lörcher, and Isabelle Schömann (eds), *The European Convention on Human Rights and the Employment Relation* (Hart Publishing 2013).

these trends, the Court has expanded its jurisdiction under Article 6 to encompass a wider variety of labour litigation, whilst also appreciating the specificities of litigation in the labour context. Article 6 has been invoked to guarantee a right to access a court for embassy and diplomatic employees, a right to a fair trial for a candidate who was refused a teaching post without sufficient reasons from the employer or adequate review by the national court, and a right to a fair trial within a reasonable time for an employee who suffered sex discrimination.[41] Occasionally, I will discuss procedural issues associated with disciplinary decisions made by employers, such as the need to conduct adequate investigations in a manner that minimizes the interference with the fundamental rights of employees. Although these expectations are connected to the same value of procedural justice that underpins Article 6, I will tend to rely upon cases related to Articles 8–11 which also include similar requirements.

The second reason that justifies focusing particularly upon the qualified ECHR rights is that they appear to be particularly under threat within relationships of employment. Workers repeatedly have cause to argue that their employer's actions or decisions amount to an interference with the right to respect for one's private life, to freedom of belief, opinion, and expression and to freedom of association. As Chapter 1 will show, the dynamics of the employment relationship—subordination, dependence, and an imbalance of bargaining power—generate a risk to the individual's ability to exercise their human rights freely. The particular forms of authority that employers hold over their workforce can be used in numerous ways to restrict and infringe upon the human rights of the workers. From the apparently innocuous ability to determine a dress code for the workplace through to the power to discipline and dismiss individuals, each prerogative generates a threat to the rights contained in Articles 8–11 of the Convention.

C. The Employer's Authority to Dismiss, Discipline, and Manage

The origin of this work was a comprehensive analysis of the law of unfair dismissal and the extent to which it provides an effective route for workers to vindicate their human rights.[42] To a degree, an examination of how the law restrains the employer's power to dismiss workers remains central to the analysis presented here. It is the apex of the employer's disciplinary powers, the ultimate sanction. A dismissal from employment has a huge impact upon the individual, depriving them of the wide

[41] See *Cudak v Lithuania* (2010) 51 EHRR 15; *Lombardi Vallauri v Italy* Application no 39128/05 (ECtHR, 20 October 2009); *Boyraz v Turkey* (n 34), respectively.

[42] My key findings were shared in Philippa Collins, 'The Inadequate Protection of Human Rights in Unfair Dismissal Law' (2018) 47 ILJ 504.

range of opportunities and benefits, financial and non-tangible, that are provided by a job. In his seminal work on *Justice in Dismissal*, Hugh Collins observed that:

> Although the harm caused to the employee by dismissal will depend heavily on how quickly and in what capacity he or she regains employment elsewhere, there can be little doubt that in many instances the disciplinary power of an employer is equivalent or greater in its effects to that exercised by the criminal courts.[43]

In *Young, James and Webster v UK*, the ECtHR observed that 'a threat of dismissal involving a loss of livelihood is a most serious form of compulsion'.[44] This quotation recognizes the power of the *threat* to dismiss: such a threat provides a potent incentive for individuals to comply with their employer's demands, however unreasonable the worker may believe them to be. Employers exercising the power to terminate the employment relationship in a manner that interferes with human rights is the central focus that runs through this book.

An emphasis only on dismissal would neglect the many other ways in which an employer can interfere with the fundamental rights of their staff. Analysis of the legal protection against these infringements will be entwined with the consideration of the termination of employment. Mr Smith's case, recounted earlier, demonstrates that lesser disciplinary sanctions, such as suspensions from work and the power to demote particular individuals, undoubtedly have serious implications for the employee and their willingness to exercise their rights freely. Both the reason for a disciplinary measure *and* how it is investigated or carried out could infringe upon the human rights of the individual. An employer's investigations may breach the right to respect for one's private life, whilst the reason for the dismissal may relate to how the employee has chosen to live their private life, for example.[45] An analysis of only the manner of a disciplinary measure or the reason for it would therefore be incomplete.

Beyond disciplinary scenarios, the employer's determining influence on the organization of work, how it should be performed and their interpretation and enforcement of the employee's responsibilities to the employing organization are also crucial to whether an individual is able to exercise their rights both within and beyond the workplace. Several chapters investigate the deliberate or unintentional manipulation of the individual's entitlement to important employment rights and their ability to exercise their human rights. Prior cases, most notably *Wilson and others v UK*,[46] have demonstrated how the employer can use their superior

[43] Hugh Collins, *Justice in Dismissal: The Law of Termination of Employment* (Oxford University Press 1992) 2.

[44] (1981) 3 EHRR 20, [55].

[45] Prominent examples of these two scenarios are *Bărbulescu v Romania* (n 12); *Martínez v Spain* (n 12).

[46] (2002) 35 EHRR 20.

financial resources to induce employees to give up particular aspects of their fundamental rights. We must even consider whether the employer might demand that employees waive their human rights in the context of the relationship between those two parties, objectionable though that prospect is. In these ways, this book goes beyond the regulation of the power to dismiss and considers the myriad of other ways that employers can restrict or interfere with the Convention rights of their workers.

III. Notes on Terminology

Here, I use 'labour law' and 'employment law' fairly interchangeably in referring to the discipline as a whole. Occasionally, the former may denote a reference to the regulation of collective aspects of the discipline where the latter points towards the regulation of the relationship between a single worker and their employer, although the respective spheres are intimately connected.[47] Similarly, I refer to the Convention rights as 'human rights' or 'fundamental rights'. Where I discuss rights outside this category, I use the language of 'fundamental social rights' or 'fundamental labour rights' in order to denote this shift beyond the ECHR rights. Finally, my tendency is to refer to the employing organization in the singular. In reality, labour law literature teaches us that the functions and powers of the employer may be divided and subdivided across a variety of entities without affecting the reality of working life for the individual.[48] Attributing responsibility for workers across multilateral arrangements is a challenge for the UK system of employment rights and I will discuss its impact upon the enforcement of Convention rights in Chapter 5.

A more difficult issue is how to refer to the individual or individuals who argue that their fundamental rights have been breached by an employer. The category of people that I am interested in is deliberately broad. The rights are *human* rights and the entitlement to them is universal. However, the context that I examine is that of work, which serves to limit my focus. In line with the exposition here and in Chapter 1, my view is that all people who are placed at increased risk of a human rights infringement by reason of their provision of work for another *should* receive protection for those rights. I refer to the people so entitled as 'workers' or 'individuals' wherever possible. I am conscious that this characterization goes well beyond the relational scope traditionally associated with labour law norms, but it is

[47] For a recent examination of the meaning of the two terms, see Volume 43 of the *Dalhousie Law Journal*, a special issue which reflects upon Langille's earlier piece, Brian Langille, 'Labour Law is a Subset of Employment Law' (1981) 31 University of Toronto Law Journal 200.

[48] See David Weil, *The Fissured Workplace: Why Work Became So Bad for So Many and What Can Be Done to Improve It* (Harvard University Press 2014).

necessary in order to achieve effective protection of human rights wherever they are placed under threat in the context of work.

The characteristics of subordination, dependence, and inequality of bargaining power which generate a potential threat to human rights, however, do not apply to every situation where labour or services are provided. Excluded from the scope of this work are genuinely independent contractors who can negotiate on an equal basis with another business or organization for the provision of labour and for the safeguards that they may need. Those who retain independence from other businesses or individuals may well be entitled to forms of human rights protection, but this would be a separate matter regarding the influence of human rights norms upon commercial or contract law. In applying this boundary, we must be alive to any attempts by a dominant party who *might be* an employer on the approach taken here to create a sense of entrepreneurship artificially within the working life of an individual. Such artifices must be scrutinized in order to expose the reality of the relationship. If the relationship functions as one of employment and suffers from the same aforementioned characteristics, then the individual must be safeguarded against the consequent risk to their human rights.

There is a dissonance between the sense in which I refer to 'workers' as described earlier and the categorization of an individual as a worker by law. Filip Dorssemont touched upon this issue when he observed that:

> Some of these [fundamental] rights are concerned with human beings offering their labour on the labour market. The question whether they actually have concluded a contract of employment is immaterial. Furthermore, the mere fact whether an employment relation has been based upon a valid employment contract is not decisive, nor whether people are seeking to conclude such a valid employment contract.[49]

'Employee' or 'worker' is a descriptive label which connotes the law's classification of their contract for work and indicates that an individual enjoys a particular set of employment rights. When discussing a specific right, I adopt the relevant descriptive label, so in Chapters 6, 7, and 8 the term 'employee' appears as that is the group entitled to the statutory and common law safeguards against dismissal. This terminology should not be taken as an endorsement of the narrow relational scope of these particular rights, however. Chapter 5 is dedicated to charting and analysing the generally restrictive scope of these terms when viewed through the lens of human rights. The narrow scope of key rights is a significant difficulty for those seeking to enforce human rights through the means already provided by labour law.

[49] Dorssemont (n 28) 315.

IV. The Horizontal Effect of Human Rights at Work

Although most of the chapters of this book focus on the effective implementation of the Convention rights, there are several recurring themes that intersect with this question. The first is the divide between the disciplines of public law and private law. More specifically, the project can be situated within a wider debate regarding the proper relationship between human rights norms and the rules of private law disciplines. In my view, intimately connected to this question is the consideration of the shape and meaning of human rights when they are applied in the context of an employment relationship. Even if human rights are given the fullest legal protection possible in the private sphere, the rights must be interpreted in a manner that is suitable for that context for their effect to be felt in practice.

An assumption underlying the entire project is that it is beneficial for workers to be able to exercise and enforce their fundamental rights in their employment relationship. Although this assumption, I believe, is now uncontroversial,[50] it amounts to a clear challenge to the distinction that has been drawn for many decades between 'private law' and 'public law' disciplines.[51] Human rights norms are seen as part of public law, which regulates the relationship between a citizen and the state. Private law disciplines, such as tort law and contract law, are generally applicable and regulate all relationships between persons without distinction between public and private actors. This conceptual distinction has led to two types of arguments: first, that extending human rights to the private sphere may weaken their normative force and diminish their symbolic value;[52] second, that such an extension would unduly limit the autonomy of private parties.[53] On the latter point, this book adopts the opposite view within the context of labour relations: *without* the application of human rights in this particular sphere, the autonomy of workers will never be realized fully.

[50] See, for example, Collins, *Justice in Dismissal: The Law of Termination of Employment* (n 43) 183; Lord Wedderburn, *Labour Law and Freedom: Further Essays in Labour Law* (Lawrence & Wishart 1995) 350; Keith Ewing, 'Rights at the Workplace: An Agenda for Labour Law' in Aileen McColgan (ed), *The Future of Labour Law* (Cassell 1996) 9–10; James A Gross, *A Shameful Business: The Case for Human Rights in the American Workplace* (Cornell University Press 2010) 7; Hazel Oliver, 'Employment Law' in David Hoffman (ed), *The Impact of the UK Human Rights Act on Private Law* (Cambridge University Press 2011) 344; Manfred Weiss, 'Re-Inventing Labour Law?' in Brian Langille and Guy Davidov (eds), *The Idea of Labour Law* (Oxford University Press 2011) 50; Elizabeth Anderson, *Private Government: How Employers Rules our Lives (and Why We Don't Talk about It)* (Princeton University Press 2017) 68.

[51] For sceptical accounts of the current use of the public–private divide, see Dan Priel, 'The Political Origins of English Private Law' (2013) 40 Journal of Law and Society 481; Karl Klare, 'The Public/Private Distinction in Labour Law' (1981) 130 University of Pennsylvania Law Review 1358.

[52] See Clapham's account of this objection: Andrew Clapham, *Human Rights Obligations of Non-State Actors* (Oxford University Press 2006) 25–26.

[53] See, for example, Lillian BeVier and John Harrison, 'The State Action Principle and its Critics' (2010) 96 Virginia Law Review 1767; Jan Smits, 'Private Law and Fundamental Rights: A Sceptical View' in Tom Barkhuysen and Siewert Lindenberg (eds), *Constitutionalisation of Private Law* (Martinus Nijhoff Publishers 2006) 19–21.

Another way of answering these concerns would be to question the place of labour law itself on the public–private divide. Perhaps labour law, despite its usual classification as an area of private law due to its connection to the law of contract, is itself a hybrid discipline which draws readily upon norms and values from both sides of the divide.[54] Many pieces have relied upon the analogy between employment relations and the relation between citizen and state to explain labour law's imposition of duties would usually be associated with public law,[55] as well as observing that employment law and public law at times pursue similar aims such as the prevention of abuse of power.[56] Chapters 1 and 2 align well with this direction of argument, in highlighting the characteristics of the employment relationship that distinguish employers from other private actors and justify the imposition of rights-based duties upon employers. Further, I put forward the observation that the protection of the human rights of workers has always been a part of the objectives of labour law.

At a lesser level of abstraction, much has also been said about *how* human rights should come to influence the private sphere. Which form, or indeed forms, of 'horizontal effect' between private parties (as opposed to 'vertical effect' between citizen and state) should human rights be permitted or required to entail?[57] The debate has its own nuances in each jurisdiction.[58] Some observers argued that the UK's HRA 1998 gave the Convention rights full horizontal effect.[59] A private party, on this model, would be able to bring a suit against another private party for a violation of their Convention rights. If no suitable private law mechanism existed, a new cause of action would have to be created in order to enable the rights to be enforced between the parties. It seems that full, direct horizontal effect has been ruled out by the courts: new causes of action have not been created,[60] although the distinction between the evolution of existing legal rights and the creation of new ones has

[54] Mark Freedland, 'Employment Law' in John Bell, Sophie Boyron, and Simon Whittaker (eds), *Principles of French Law* (2nd edn, Oxford University Press 2008) 483–88. See further Paul Davies and Mark Freedland, 'The Impact of Public Law on Labour Law, 1972–1997' (1997) 26 ILJ 311; ACL Davies, 'Labour Law as Public Law' in Alan Bogg and others (eds), *The Autonomy of Labour Law* (Hart Publishing 2015).

[55] See, for example, Oliver (n 50) 344; Anderson (n 50) chapter 2; Khaitan (n 20) 204.

[56] See John Laws, 'Public Law and Employment Law: Abuse of Power' [1997] Public Law 455; Dawn Oliver, *Common Values and the Public-private Divide* (Cambridge University Press 2010) 129–48.

[57] Alison Young has provided a useful 'map' of the different possible forms of horizontal effect: Alison Young, 'Mapping Horizontal Effect' in David Hoffman (ed), *The Impact of the UK Human Rights Act on Private Law* (Cambridge University Press 2011).

[58] See the chapters within Dawn Oliver and Jörg Fedtke (eds), *Human Rights and the Private Sphere: A Comparative Study* (Routledge-Cavendish 2007).

[59] Sir William Wade, 'Horizons of Horizontality' (2000) 116 LQR 217; Jonathan Morgan, 'Questioning the True Effect of the Human Rights Act' (2002) 22 Legal Studies 259.

[60] As argued by Gavin Phillipson, 'Privacy: The Development of Breach of Confidence—the clearest case of Horizontal Effect?' in David Hoffman (ed), *The Impact of the UK Human Rights Act on Private Law* (Cambridge University Press 2011); Leigh and Masterman (n 39) chapter 9; for a contrasting viewpoint, see Jonathan Morgan, 'Privacy, Confidence and Horizontal Effect: "Hello" Trouble' (2003) 62 CLJ 444.

been proved to be slim.[61] *Indirect* horizontal effect, whereby human rights influence the development of existing private law rules,[62] has been embraced. Human rights have reshaped common law doctrines of private law, as well as having an impact upon how statutes and statutory instruments are interpreted. Employment law doctrines can thus be checked against the standards set under the Convention and various modes of indirect horizontal effect deployed to correct deficiencies where it is possible to do so.

A second set of questions, linked again to the application of human rights in the private sphere, must also be discussed in order to offer the optimal standard of human rights protection in the context of work. Hugh Collins observes that human rights, which have been developed primarily in the light of the relationship between citizen and state, should not be transplanted straightforwardly into other contexts.[63] In our case, the relationship between employer and worker has different characteristics and dynamics which must be considered if human rights are to be protected effectively. For example, the state's interest in public safety may necessitate that an individual's rights are infringed upon by the issuing of criminal sanctions in response to unlawful behaviour. Employers, in general, do not have the same degree of interest in public safety so would not have a justification for taking disciplinary action in response to the same behaviour, particularly where the worker's actions occurred outside of work and had little connection to the relationship between worker and employer.[64] The problems that arise from the uncritical transplantation of rights from the public sphere into that of employment will emerge occasionally throughout this work. In employment cases, the rights are often conceptualized narrowly and in a manner that does not acknowledge the full challenge posed by the worker's fundamental rights to the employer's entrenched managerial authority.

To guarantee the highest standard of protection for workers, the meaning of human rights must be tailored to the employment context. The principles developed by the ECtHR in relation to the protection of rights in an employment relationship have thus far been sensitive to the unique dynamics between the two

61 Mattias Kumm, 'Who is Afraid of the Total Constitution? Constitutional Rights as Principles and the Constitutionalization of Private Law' (2006) 7 German Law Journal 341, 352; Olha Cherednychenko, 'Subordinating Contract Law to Fundamental Rights: Towards a Major Breakthrough or towards Walking in Circles?' in Stefan Grundmann (ed), *Constitutional Values and European Contract Law* (Kluwer Law International 2008) 57; Hugh Collins, 'The Challenges Presented by Fundamental Rights to Private Law' in Kit Barker, Karen Fairweather, and Ross Grantham (eds), *Private Law in the 21st Century* (Hart Publishing 2017) 227.

62 A consistent advocate of indirect horizontal effect under the HRA has been Gavin Phillipson, 'The Human Rights Act, 'Horizontal Effect' and the Common Law: A Bang or a Whimper?' (1999) 62 MLR 824; Phillipson, 'Privacy' (n 60).

63 Hugh Collins, 'On the Incompatibility of Human Rights Discourse and Private Law' in Hans W Micklitz (ed), *Constitutionalization of European Private Law* (Oxford University Press 2014) 46–48.

64 Virginia Mantouvalou, 'Human Rights and Unfair Dismissal: Private Acts in Public Spaces' (2008) 71 MLR 912, 931 onwards.

parties. In the domestic context, as will be discussed in Chapter 2, some features of international human rights law must be disregarded in order to ensure an appropriate standard of scrutiny is applied to an employer's infringement upon a worker's ECHR rights. Understanding the protection of human rights as an organic concern of labour law encourages us to think further about the shape of the rights themselves, in addition to the question of how they are best enforced. Whilst the focus of this work is mostly upon the latter question, only when *both* issues are tackled will workers enjoy full protection of their human rights.

PART I

THE ROLE OF HUMAN RIGHTS IN LABOUR (LAW)

1
Why Must We Protect the Human Rights of Workers?

David Smith was unable to find work in his chosen sector for some eighteen years. After a twenty-year career in the construction industry, suddenly he found was no longer being hired. Mr Smith was an active member of the trade union, UCATT. He had been a shop steward on some sites, as well as acting as a health and safety representative. In 1997, he worked for six months on a project for John Mowlem & Co. Unbeknownst to Mr Smith, John Mowlem was one of the many companies who used the services of The Consulting Association. The Consulting Association operated a secret database containing files on several thousand construction workers, those who were perceived as 'troublemakers'.[1] Most workers on the database had been active union members, shop stewards, or health and safety representatives. Much of the information held on the database was alleged by its subjects to be false. The workers were seen as a disruptive influence and, as a result, they were refused employment and excluded from the industry.

In 2009, the database was discovered. John Mowlem & Co had contributed information to the file held on Mr Smith. The existence of Mr Smith's file on the database was the reason he had been pushed out of the construction industry for eighteen years. Along with Mr Smith, some 3,000 workers had been affected by the Consultation Association's blacklisting activities. Excluded from his chosen profession for half of his career, Mr Smith brought claims against the companies responsible for his blacklisting before an Employment Tribunal (ET).[2] His case was unsuccessful, and he was left with no recompense.

What insights can we learn from Mr Smith's case? Mr Smith's situation shows the vulnerability of employees in their relationship with their employer. Even though Mr Smith had only worked for John Mowlem for six months, the information provided by the company deprived him of his livelihood for eighteen years. The impact of his one-time employer's decision upon the course of the rest of Mr Smith's life is shocking. Mr Smith was also unaware of the threat to his profession. He was therefore unable to challenge the decision made by the companies to refuse him

[1] For a fuller account of the investigation, impact, and legal consequences of The Consulting Association's activities, see Keith Ewing, *Ruined Lives: Blacklisting in the UK Construction Industry* (Institute of Employment Rights 2009).

[2] *Smith v Carillion (JM) Ltd* [2015] EWCA Civ 209, [2015] IRLR 467.

Putting Human Rights to Work. Philippa Collins, Oxford University Press. © Philippa Collins 2022.
DOI: 10.1093/oso/9780192894595.003.0002

employment for unlawful reasons. This sense of powerlessness is common to many employees when in dispute with their employer.[3] Although they might have the ability to appeal internally against a decision to dismiss them,[4] they cannot force the employer to change its decision.

The example of The Consulting Association also shows how employers, as a group, hold the ability to change decisively the fortunes of large numbers of workers. The Consulting Association's clients included many large construction companies, such as Balfour Beatty and Kier. Through the companies' communally exercised power to hire and fire workers, they prevented any number of workers from earning a living. The livelihoods of all workers are dependent upon the whim of employing companies.

The final twist of the knife for Mr Smith was that employment law was unable to protect him against the wrongdoing of his past employer. His case shows that the law may fail completely to protect our most basic rights from violation by our employers. Mr Smith suffered several serious violations of his human rights. The Consulting Association's blacklist interfered with his right to work in his chosen profession, resulted in reputational harm and damaging consequences for his personal life, as well as constituting a serious infringement upon his data privacy rights. All of these unlawful activities were pursued for the sole purpose of excluding from the construction industry workers who were considered undesirable. Most were classified as such because of their trade union affiliation and activities.[5] The actions of the employers amounted to an egregious breach of Mr Smith's freedom to associate with whomever he chose and his right to join a trade union for the protection of his professional interests. It is difficult to imagine a more serious infringement upon Mr Smith's human rights that could be perpetrated by an employer. Yet employment law provided no remedy for the severe damage that he suffered.

Mr Smith's case impresses upon us the need to restrain employers through a duty to respect the human rights of their workers, a stance that is the foundation of this work. This position runs contrary to the state-centred view which is present in the current discourse regarding the appropriate duty bearers of the human rights of individuals and will be outlined in the first section of this chapter. The remaining sections provide a response to this view in the form of an analysis of the institutional status of employers in our society and the respective powers and duties of the parties to an employment relationship which give rise to a risk to the human rights of workers. The chapter culminates with the argument that the relationship

[3] For an excellent contemporary account of the experience of claimants in the ET system, see Nicole Busby and Morag McDermont, 'Fighting with the Wind: Claimants' Experiences and Perceptions of the Employment Tribunal' (2020) 49 ILJ 159.

[4] See Advisory, Conciliation and Arbitration Service, *Code of Practice on Disciplinary and Grievance Procedures* (2015), [26]–[29].

[5] Department for Business, Innovation and Skills, *The Blacklisting of Trade Unionists: Consultation on Revised Draft Regulations* (July 2009) [1.11].

between an employer and a worker is inconsistent with the free enjoyment and exercise of the worker's human rights. As observed by Henry Shue, 'to enjoy something only at the discretion of someone else, especially someone powerful enough to deprive you of it at will, is precisely not to enjoy a right to it'.[6] I argue that an employer is just such a powerful person and that the law must intervene to ensure that workers are granted effective protection for their human rights to rectify this situation.

I. The Centrality of the State in Human Rights Discourse

The founding premise of this book is that employers are, or should be, under a duty to respect the human rights of their workforce. Although many scholars of labour law and human rights agree with this proposition,[7] this position faces an objection that must be addressed or overcome. On a state-centred view of human rights, duties are only imposed on governmental decision-makers. For example, international treaties bind state signatories and individuals can argue that the state has interfered with their human rights. This view is founded upon the assumptions that the state alone guarantees fundamental rights *and* that it poses the most significant threat to those rights.[8] It follows from this view that private citizens and non-state actors are not bound by human rights or public law norms more generally.[9] Private individuals are entitled to a realm of private freedom, in which they pursue their preferences without being required to consider the rights of others or the interests of society.[10]

Eleni Frantziou, in her work on the horizontality of fundamental rights, warns that one must not underestimate the strength of the state-centred view of human rights.[11] Taking heed of Frantziou's caution, I turn to examine the impact of this view on my claim that employers should be subject to a duty to respect their workers' human rights. An employment relationship is almost always classified as a private relationship. At its centre, we often find a contract of employment. The specialized body of law that applies to the employment relationship is layered on to this foundation or develops from a core of contract law. The parties to the contract, notwithstanding Otto Kahn-Freund's reminder that the contract acts as a 'conceptual screen' for subordination and unequal power between employer and worker,[12]

[6] Henry Shue, *Basic Rights: Subsistence, Affluence, and U.S. Foreign Policy* (40th Anniversary edn, Princeton University Press 2020) 78.

[7] See n 50 in the Introduction.

[8] Eleni Frantziou, *The Horizontal Effect of Fundamental Rights in the European Union: A Constitutional Analysis* (Oxford University Press 2019) 18.

[9] See Jan Smits, 'Private Law and Fundamental Rights: A Sceptical View' in Tom Barkhuysen and Siewert Lindenberg (eds), *Constitutionalisation of Private Law* (Martinus Nijhoff Publishers 2006) 19.

[10] ibid.

[11] Frantziou (n 8) 17.

[12] Mark Freedland and Paul Davies, *Kahn-Freund's Labour and the Law* (3rd edn, Stevens 1983) 15.

are seen as private actors. The contract formed is an exercise of their freedom to contract, to choose with whom they work, what work to do and upon which terms. On a state-centred view of human rights, the employer is a private party and therefore unrestrained by a duty to respect the human rights of others.

There are two responses to this position which will be developed throughout this chapter. The first reply is that employers are not equivalent to other private actors. As we can see in the example of Mr Smith, between them, employers distribute opportunities crucial to a fulfilling and dignified life. This status as a community of gatekeepers justifies the imposition of a requirement that opportunities should not be distributed based on irrelevant or unjust criteria such as an individual's trade union membership, political beliefs, or private activities outside of work. The second response is that the employment relationship is not equivalent to a contractual relationship between two private individuals. Entering an employment relationship puts the individual's human rights at an unavoidable risk due to the imbalance of power, the dependency of one party upon the other, and the subordination to an organizational hierarchy that it entails. Once the relationship of employment is seen through this lens, it becomes unthinkable to treat employers like any other private actor and to permit them free rein to restrict the rights of their workers. As observed by Clyde Summers, '[c]onstitutional values cannot be fully realized in the face of unrestrained private power'.[13]

II. The Institutional Status of Employers

When an employer refuses an individual a job, the act is somehow different in quality from a person choosing their friends or buying a car. Employers have a 'quasi-public' role in modern life,[14] by reason of what John Gardner described as their 'special privileged position in the distributive mechanics of society'.[15] Holding the power to select amongst a mass of applicants, the employer's decision fundamentally affects the life chances of the individual who is hired and the individual who is not. Then, one single incident of choice is multiplied exponentially across companies and sectors. Together, employers control the fate of workers in a manner not seen in a typical private relationship. As argued by Frances Raday:

> In employing a workforce, employers are carrying out a function which is so central to the determination of socio-economic opportunity and human dignity that

[13] Clyde W Summers, 'The Privatization of Personal Freedoms and Enrichment of Democracy: Some Lessons From Labor Law' (1986) 1986 University of Illinois Law Review 689, 693.

[14] Frances Raday, 'Constitutionalization of Labour Law' in Roger Blanpain and Manfred Weiss (eds), *The Changing Face of Labour Law and Industrial Relations* (Nomos 1993) 106.

[15] John Gardner, 'Liberals and Unlawful Discrimination' (1989) 9 OJLS 1, 11.

> they are bound to a standard of behaviour which is not imposed on all private actors.[16]

To appreciate the role of employers as 'gatekeepers of opportunities' fully,[17] we must delve further into the value of work for individuals. The significances of a job for an individual are manifold, as summarized by the Council of Europe's Committee on Economic, Social and Cultural Rights:

> The right to work is essential for realizing other human rights and forms an inseparable and inherent part of human dignity. Every individual has the right to be able to work, allowing him/her to live in dignity. The right to work contributes at the same time to the survival of the individual and to that of his/her family, and insofar as work is freely chosen or accepted, to his/her development and recognition within the community.[18]

Most individuals rely on their wage to fulfil their basic needs and it enables a minimum standard of living. Beyond that, a job provides an opportunity to work as a part of a group, to form connections with others and to be a productive member of a wider community. Work is often a means by which an individual finds self-respect and earns status within society. Having a job matters for our sense of 'self-fulfilment'[19] as well as the fulfilment of our essential needs.

Their communal control over access to '*the* enabling opportunity'[20] distinguishes employers from other private actors in society. The degree of control held by employers over the fate of others must not be left unchecked. This feature has been deployed to justify the imposition of duties not to discriminate on the grounds of protected characteristics.[21] Going further and imposing a duty to respect the human rights of workers would ensure that individuals are not routinely excluded because of the way they choose to exercise their rights.

III. The Fundamental Rights of Workers Under Threat

The earlier exposition of the value and importance of work to individuals also uncovers an important dynamic of the relationship between workers and their employers: dependence. Jean Thomas, in discussing which actors should be bound by

[16] Raday (n 14) 106.
[17] Tarunabh Khaitan, *A Theory of Discrimination Law* (Oxford University Press 2015) 209.
[18] Committee on Economic, Social and Cultural Rights, *The Right to Work* (Economic and Social Council, General Comment No. 18, adopted on 24 November 2005) [1].
[19] Hugh Collins, 'Is There a Human Right to Work?' in Virginia Mantouvalou (ed), *The Right to Work: Legal and Philosophical Perspectives* (Hart Publishing 2015) 32.
[20] Khaitan (n 17) 210.
[21] ibid; Gardner (n 15) 11.

public law rights (including fundamental rights), considers the relational context of dependence to be of great significance.[22] In the arena of labour law, Guy Davidov observes that workers are dependent on their employer in an economic sense, as well as for the fulfilment of their social and psychological needs.[23] He highlights this dependency as one of the key vulnerabilities that are present within an employment relationship which labour law is invoked to address.[24] It is easy to see how the sense of dependence on an employer for the fulfilment of this variety of needs translates into a risk to that person's human rights.[25] A person is more likely to accept and work under conditions in which those rights are restricted or interfered with if they depend upon their work for the employer for this range of tangible and non-tangible needs.

Dependence is not the only feature of employment relations that contributes to the risk of human rights infringements. Mentioned above was the employer's capacity to choose amongst many willing workers. This oversupply enables the employer to offer terms that they consider acceptable on a 'take it or leave it' basis to the candidate and to keep searching for a worker willing to accept its terms. The employer's superior resources generate an inequality of bargaining power between the parties. Counteracting this disparity was described influentially by Otto Kahn-Freund as 'the main object of labour law'.[26] Whilst the inequality of bargaining power is most evident at the commencement of the relationship, it continues throughout its lifetime through the employer's capacity to vary the terms and conditions of work unilaterally. The worker's only chance to resist the employer's desire to change the conditions of their daily life is through collective action, challenging the legality of the variation or by exit from the relationship.

The unilateral determination of terms and conditions feeds into the employer's bureaucratic control of the workplace. The worker is subordinated to the norms of the business, placed within an organizational hierarchy. The institution of employment and the contract of employment, as it is formed and understood in our society, grant the employer practical authority over its staff.[27] The employer possesses the 'power of an autonomous legislature'[28] in determining the minutiae of how employees should behave at work. An individual's responsibilities, tasks, standard of performance, hours, rest breaks, dress code, and many other details are provided

[22] Jean Thomas, *Public Rights, Private Relations* (Oxford University Press 2015) chapter 9.

[23] Guy Davidov, *A Purposive Approach to Labour Law* (Oxford University Press 2016) 43–48.

[24] ibid 48.

[25] See Virginia Mantouvalou, 'Human Rights and Unfair Dismissal: Private Acts in Public Spaces' (2008) 71 MLR 912, 925–26.

[26] Freedland and Davies, *Kahn-Freund's Labour and the Law* (n 12) 18.

[27] Hugh Collins, 'Is the Contract of Employment Illiberal?' in Hugh Collins, Gillian Lester, and Virginia Mantouvalou (eds), *Philosophical Foundations of Labour Law* (Oxford University Press 2018) 55.

[28] Raday (n 14) 106.

for in the employer's 'miniature legal system'.[29] The individual is subordinated to the employer's jurisdiction during their working life. The threat to the worker's human rights is thereby compounded, in the context of a relationship upon which that person depends heavily for financial and personal value.

The one act that poses the most significant single risk to the individual worker, their prospects, and their human rights is that of dismissal. The employer's power to dismiss is the apex of disciplinary capacity: it reinforces both the employer's disciplinary processes and their authority over the day-to-day running of the enterprise. A dismissal has drastic long- and short-term consequences for the individual worker. As Hugh Collins argues:

> Although the harm caused to the employee by dismissal will depend heavily on how quickly and in what capacity he or she regains employment elsewhere, there can be little doubt that in many instances the disciplinary power of an employer is equivalent or greater in its effects to that exercised by the criminal courts.[30]

If anyone fails to comply with the company Code of Conduct, the ultimate sanction is dismissal although the impact of lesser sanctions, such as demotion, suspension, pay-based sanctions, warnings, and reassignment, should not be underestimated. As examples throughout the course of these chapters will demonstrate, employers deploy their disciplinary powers in a manner that interferes with the fundamental rights of workers with regularity.

The end of the employment relationship is not the only event that places the exercise of fundamental rights in jeopardy. At the opposite end of the chronology, by signing the contract of employment, an individual may sign away their right to conditions that are sensitive to the exercise of their human rights. These measures might be generally hostile to the worker's ability to make valuable choices, such as long working hours with limited rest periods or time to develop relationships with others, or contain more specific, restrictive terms. Examples of the latter might include a term that requires invasive pre-employment testing or extensive screening of the individual's online activities that breaches the individual's right to privacy. In addition, the terms of the contract can be used to disincentivize the exercise of rights. For example, by including a term permitting deduction from wages for part- or non-performance of duties, the employer can lawfully refuse to pay employees who exercise their right to strike. Severe pay deductions are an effective method of discouraging employees from engaging in strike action.

[29] Hugh Collins, 'Market Power, Bureaucratic Power and the Contract of Employment' (1986) 15 ILJ 1, 4.

[30] Hugh Collins, *Justice in Dismissal: The Law of Termination of Employment* (Oxford University Press 1992) 2.

The legislative power of employers to write the rule book of the enterprise is commonly exercised, perhaps unintentionally, in a manner that limits or infringes upon the fundamental rights of its workforce. Even the most apparently routine tasks of an employer—setting the dress and appearance code—have the capacity to interfere with an individual's human rights. Article 8 could be invoked where an individual does not wish to adhere to a requirement that they dress in clothing conventional to their biological sex.[31] A rule that states that individuals should maintain a 'professional' or 'neutral' appearance, which may include a requirement to refrain from wearing head-coverings, amounts to a severe curtailment of the ability of religious individuals to manifest their religious faith whilst retaining their position.[32] Similarly, inflexible shift patterns or working hours can interfere with an employee's religious observances.[33]

With the rise of technology in the workplace, the threat to an employee's privacy is significant. IT policies subject employees to constant monitoring to ensure consistent productivity. Employers can access and read the private communications of individual employees where they suspect that the employee has breached a prohibition on private use of the employer's equipment and resources.[34] These examples demonstrate how an employer's bureaucratic powers can be exercised in a way that interferes with the exercise of fundamental rights during working time.

More worryingly, employers may extend the subordination of their workforce beyond working time.[35] Any activities outside of work that could have a negative impact upon the employer's business or reputation can place the employee at risk of being in breach of an employer's rule book. A Code of Conduct typically prohibits bringing the employer into disrepute. This wide prohibition can be relied upon to discipline workers for a range of conduct, some of which amount of an exercise of the worker's human rights. Under this general rule, conduct protected by the Convention's qualified rights is treated as legitimate grounds for disciplinary action and dismissal. 'Social media dismissals' are increasingly common.[36] Complaints made about colleagues and superiors, criticism of the employer's products online, and content that the employer deems to be offensive are considered

[31] *Kara v United Kingdom* (1999) 27 EHRR CD272.

[32] The major cases on this issue are *Eweida and others v United Kingdom* (2013) 57 EHRR 8; C-157/15 *Samira Achbita and Centrum voor gelijkheid van kansen en voor racismebestrijding v G4S Secure Solutions NV* [2017] 3 CMLR 21.

[33] *Ahmad v United Kingdom* (1982) 4 EHRR 126; *Mba v Merton London Borough Council* [2013] EWCA Civ 1562, [2014] 1 WLR 1501.

[34] *Bărbulescu v Romania* Application no 61496/08 (ECtHR, 5 September 2017).

[35] See Mantouvalou (n 25); Astrid Sanders, 'The Law of Unfair Dismissal and Behaviour Outside Work' (2014) 34 Legal Studies 328.

[36] See Virginia Mantouvalou, '"I Lost My Job over a Facebook Post: Was that Fair?" Discipline and Dismissal for Social Media Activity' (2019) 35 International Journal of Comparative Labour Law and Industrial Relations 101; David Mangan, 'Social Media in the Workplace' in David Mangan and Lorna E Gillies (eds), *The Legal Challenges of Social Media* (Elgar Publishing 2017).

grounds for dismissal,[37] despite the right to respect for one's private life and correspondence and to freedom of expression. The individual's other fundamental rights can be invoked where their online exchanges express their religious or philosophical beliefs.[38] All of these examples demonstrate the risk to human rights generated by vesting a unilateral, rule-setting capacity in employers which extends beyond the bounds of working time and space.

An employer might also consider an individual's political activities to be a legitimate ground for dismissal,[39] particularly where the political party in question is controversial and the employer considers a perceived association between itself and the party through the employee's activities to be undesirable. Another form of expression damaging to the employer is whistleblowing, where an employee discloses information that they believe to be in the public interest but, as it damages the employer's business interests, they are dismissed as a result.[40] Drug and health screening also impact upon the way that an employee may spend their time outside work, with the threat of dismissal apparent even where drug use has no impact upon their performance at work.[41] Similarly, personal information such as HIV status has led to detrimental treatment by employers.[42] Even more intrusive are employers' actions that have regard to an individual's intimate and sexual preferences and choices, whether that be engaging in an affair or involvement in the BDSM community.[43]

These examples show that employers possess the capacity to interfere with the human rights of their workers in a myriad of ways. In the pursuit of their own goals, employers make decisions that do infringe upon those rights. The significant risk of interference with human rights within the employment relationship justifies placing of constraints upon employers. They should be under a duty to act in a manner that complies with the human rights of their workforce. The law must ensure that the employer does not exercise their control and authority in a manner that infringes the human rights of individuals.

IV. Not All Employers? 'Good' Employers and the Risk to Rights

An easy response to the account given in section III would be that these are examples of 'bad employers'. Not all employers are villains. Several counterarguments

[37] *British Waterway Board v Smith* (2015) UKEATS/0004/15/SM; *Game Retail Limited v Laws* (2014) UKEAT/0188/14/DA; *Crisp v Apple Retail UK Ltd* [2011] ET 1500258/11.

[38] *Smith v Trafford Housing Trust* [2012] EWHC 3221 (Ch), [2013] IRLR 86; *Gibbins v British Council* (2017) ET 2200088/2017.

[39] *Redfearn v Serco Ltd* [2006] EWCA Civ 659, [2006] ICR 1367; *Vogt v Germany* (1996) 21 EHRR 205.

[40] See *Heinisch v Germany* (2014) 58 EHRR 31.

[41] *Kuehne & Nagel Ltd v Cosgrove* (2013) UKEAT/0165/13/DM.

[42] *IB v Greece* Application no 552/10 (ECtHR, 3 October 2013).

[43] See respectively *Percy v Church of Scotland Board of National Mission* [2005] UKHL 73, [2006] 2 AC 28; *Pay v Lancashire Probation Service* [2004] ICR 187.

can be made here. First, any risk to human rights should be minimized and protected against, even if there is only a serious risk of infringement within a small percentage of companies and organizations. In addition, an individual's awareness that their employer *could* censure them for how they choose to exercise their fundamental rights is wrong in itself. The majority of workers are likely to have altered their behaviour or choices in order to please or appease their employer. Alan Bogg and Cynthia Estlund observe that this adjustment to conform with the employer's wishes and requirements is itself an unfreedom:

> Even if there is no actual interference in choices, *the vulnerability to interference* is a form of unfreedom, for it forces one to anticipate and accommodate oneself to the other's desires, backed as they are by the power to interfere.[44]

From this insight, one learns that it may not matter if the employer actually exercises their powers over a particular worker by, for example, embarking upon a disciplinary process. The individual has already lost one aspect of their freedom by living 'in the shadow of managerial prerogative':[45] the ability to make autonomous choices free of outside influence. They assess and reassess their preferences and goals in light of their employer's likely inclinations. The employer's dominant sway over the individual's choices 'creates a kind of *potential* for detriment, or threat, to well-being'.[46] This influence should be countered by constraining the employer's permissible range of conduct.

Secondly, a survey of the cases indicates that the initial claim is not true. Even 'good employers' who are trying to do their best for the workforce and their customers make decisions that infringe the human rights of individuals. We can highlight three situations where this might occur. The first might be labelled the 'customer protective' decision. An example of this category is *Redfearn v Serco*.[47] Anxieties regarding the safety of Serco's vulnerable passenger groups were cited to justify dismissing Mr Redfearn after he was elected as a local councillor representing the British National Party, a far-right, anti-immigration group. Secondly, we might think of 'workforce protective' decisions such as in *Smith v Trafford Housing Trust*.[48] Mr Smith was subject to disciplinary proceedings following an exchange on Facebook about gay marriage. The employer noted that Mr Smith's comments had upset his colleagues: protecting other members

[44] Alan Bogg and Cynthia Estlund, 'Freedom of Association and the Right to Contest' in Alan Bogg and Tonia Novitz (eds), *Voices at Work: Continuity and Change in the Common Law World* (Oxford University Press 2014) 151 emphasis added.

[45] Collins, *Justice in Dismissal: The Law of Termination of Employment* (n 30) title of chapter 6.

[46] Thomas (n 22) 195.

[47] *Redfearn v Serco* (n 39) [8].

[48] *Smith v Trafford Housing Trust* (n 38).

of staff from distress was one part of the employer's justification for his demotion.[49] The third instance is less common, but it is the 'worker protective' decision such as in *Amnesty International v Ahmed*.[50] Miss Ahmed worked for Amnesty International and was of Sudanese descent. Her application for a new role, the remit of which would include research and visiting the Sudan, was refused. Whilst the primary reason for Amnesty International's decision was a concern regarding the perceived vested interests of staff members, the employer also observed that staff who visit countries from which they appear to originate are at a greater risk of ill-treatment or violence than an 'outsider'.[51] In part, the organization's rules were in place to protect its own staff against infringements upon their rights by others.

In these cases, the employer was seeking to protect their customers or service users, the other members of the workforce, or even the individual themselves. Even benevolent aims can be pursued in a manner that infringes a person's human rights. Understanding that all kinds of employers pose a danger to the human rights of their workers offers a strong justification for the imposition on employers of a duty to respect the human rights of their workers.

V. The Inherent Tension Between Employment and Fundamental Rights

The culmination of these observations is that there is an inherent conflict between the free enjoyment of human rights and an employment relationship. Hugh Collins argues that characteristics of the employment relationship intrinsically conflict with the exercise of fundamental rights by workers. He contends that:

> the relation of subordination is inherently opposed to the enjoyment of civil liberties [because] civil liberties must be exercisable as of right, whereas in the context of employment the enjoyment of civil liberties is normally dependent on permission from the employer or is subject to the employer's legitimate aims and purposes.[52]

For example, whether an individual enjoys privacy in communicating with their family whilst at work depends upon the terms of the employer's policies. Exercising the right to manifest one's faith or attend worship during the week relies upon the

[49] ibid [38].
[50] [2009] ICR 1450.
[51] ibid [8].
[52] Collins, 'Is the Contract of Employment Illiberal?' (n 27) 58.

employer's dress code or express permission to be absent during working hours. Rather than the employee making decisions in accordance with their priorities and preferences, they must seek the employer's consent to the manner in which they wish to exercise their rights. It is perhaps this inherent collision between the free exercise of rights and the employment relationship that has turned employment law's attention towards the protection of human rights over the course of its development. Chapter 2 will explore this argument further.

Conclusion

It would be utterly unacceptable to allow this clash between fundamental rights and employment to persist unregulated. The law must impose constraints on the employer's capacity to deny workers the right to exercise their human rights. It should be unlawful for an employer to act in contravention of their workers' human rights. Although employers may be notionally private actors, the employment relationship is rare in incurring a structural risk to the workers' fundamental rights. This threat to the rights of individuals justifies strong duties of respect for those rights. As will be demonstrated in Chapters 3 and 4, both the European Convention on Human Rights and many domestic legal frameworks have recognized this risk, either explicitly or implicitly. These systems have responded by imposing duties, either directly or as a consequence of the state's obligations, upon employers which require them to respect the fundamental rights of the workforce to a greater or lesser degree.

The role of businesses as employers discussed here is one element of a wider picture. Business enterprises impact upon human rights in many other ways, both directly and indirectly. The 'authoritative focal point' of the global recognition of that impact and progress to eliminate it is the UN Guiding Principles on Business and Human Rights.[53] Now in their tenth year, the Guiding Principles rest on three pillars: the state's duty to protect human rights, the duty of enterprises to respect human rights, and the need for human rights to be supported by an appropriate remedy. One of the foundational principles is that '[b]usiness enterprises should respect human rights. This means that they should avoid infringing on the human rights of others and should address adverse human rights impacts with which they are involved.'[54] A duty on businesses to respect the human rights of their workforce (broadly defined) would contribute to the fulfilment of this principle, as well

[53] Report of the Special Representative of the Secretary-General on the issue of human rights and transnational corporations and other business enterprises, *Guiding Principles on Business and Human Rights: Implementing the United Nations 'Protect, Respect and Remedy' Framework* (A/HRC/17/31, United Nations, 2 March 2011) [5].

[54] ibid Annex, [11].

as making progress towards both the 'respect' and 'remedy' pillars of the Guiding Principles. Whilst the remaining chapters are framed in terms of the European Convention obligations, many of the critiques and recommendations would equally be relevant to the question of the UK's implementation of the Guiding Principles.[55]

[55] For the current version of the UK National Action Plan, see The Secretary of State for Foreign and Commonwealth Affairs, *Good Business: Implementing the UN Guiding Principles on Business and Human Rights* (CM 9255, May 2016).

2
The Role of Human Rights in Labour Law

Employers hold significant power over their workforce, sufficient to justify the imposition upon them of a duty to respect the human rights of individual workers. Yet there is an additional way that we might frame the argument that employers should be required to respect their workers' fundamental rights. We could argue that these duties are required because safeguarding the human rights of workers is an important aim of employment law. Only in recent years have scholars rephrased long-established goals of employment law in the language of human rights. On this view, the protection of workers' basic rights against infringement by their employer has always been, and must continue to be, an essential part of employment and labour law. Such protection necessitates imposing corresponding duties upon employers.

A view of labour law that includes a strong human rights dimension has several normative strengths and practical benefits, which will be explored in section I. There are two ways in which we might conceptualize the relationship between human rights and labour law. I will sketch an emerging version in section II, which sees human rights as the foundation of labour law. Although this view has merits, this chapter will note several concerns about its consequences. Instead, I would adopt a pluralist approach which is discussed in section III. On this view, the protection of workers' human rights is one purpose of employment law amongst several, specific concerns that are important to the development of the discipline.

Seeing labour law as a distinctive discipline with its own unique combination of aims and values, as recommended in section III, also has the benefit of maintaining a sense of autonomy for labour law and a clear boundary between labour law and its neighbouring disciplines. In turn, the existence of a disciplinary boundary—porous though it is—encourages a 'translation process' to occur as human rights ideas move from the public/international sphere to the distinctive setting of work relationships. Human rights principles have predominantly developed on the international stage, regulating states in their actions and choices in relation to their citizens. When human rights concepts are applied in disputes between workers and their employers, those concepts must be adapted to ensure that workers receive the most effective protection in their daily lives. This translation process is the focus of section IV.

Putting Human Rights to Work. Philippa Collins, Oxford University Press. © Philippa Collins 2022.
DOI: 10.1093/oso/9780192894595.003.0003

I. The Promise of a Turn Towards Human Rights in Labour Law

The inclusion of an express discourse around the human rights of workers in labour law has one very apparent benefit: the increased likelihood that those rights will be adequately protected. The significant risk to fundamental rights was highlighted in Chapter 1 and argued to be inherent in a relationship between employer and worker, broadly defined. Once expressly recognized, we can consider which mechanisms might minimize that risk effectively, change the behaviour of employers, and provide appropriate remedies to individuals who have suffered this specific type of wrong. Such an enterprise depends on the context, jurisdiction, and constitutional and working arrangements in which the analysis arises. Parts II and III of this work are an attempt to provide such an analysis in the context of England and Wales.

Several qualities that are attributed to human rights are powerful within a labour law context. In an area of law that is often locked in a political stalemate, human rights have the potential to transcend party politics. As Joe Atkinson summarized, the consensus amongst philosophers in this area is that human rights 'are individual entitlements, whose normative force does not depend on legal or political recognition, that are distinct from other norms in some important way, and which all people hold equally'.[1] Human rights have a special moral status and normative force within any argument. The effect of rights on debates and particular decisions was described influentially by Dworkin as 'rights as trumps'.[2] The language of human rights enables us to draw upon their strong moral force and their capacity to transcend other interests or concerns, such as productivity, competitiveness, or efficiency, in discussions regarding the future of labour law. Ensuring the proper protection of human rights is an urgent issue in most jurisdictions and 'gives rise to global in addition to merely local concern',[3] an essential feature in a global labour market.[4]

Human rights are universal and inalienable.[5] Everyone has human rights. One cannot simply sign away the right to those rights, and any restriction upon them

[1] Joe Atkinson, 'Human Rights as Foundations for Labour Law' in Hugh Collins, Gillian Lester, and Virginia Mantouvalou (eds), *Philosophical Foundations of Labour Law* (Oxford University Press 2018) 125.

[2] Ronald Dworkin, *Taking Rights Seriously* (Harvard University Press 1977) introduction and chapter 12.

[3] Pablo Gilabert, 'Labor Human Rights and Human Dignity' (2015) 42 Philosophy & Social Criticism 171, 176.

[4] The increased focus on human rights at work has been thought to coincide with the globalization of markets: see Janice R Bellace and Beryl ter Haar, 'Perspectives on Labour and Human Rights' in Janice R Bellace and Beryl ter Haar (eds), *Research Handbook on Labour, Business and Human Rights Law* (Edward Elgar Publishing 2019) 3.

[5] See the preamble to the UDHR (10 December 1948) UNGA Res. 217 A (III).

will be carefully examined.[6] Some human rights are unqualified, such as the prohibition of forced labour contained in Article 4 European Convention on Human Rights (ECHR), but many rights that are relevant to the world of work are qualified rights. Any restriction or infringement upon those rights must be justified in accordance with the text and principles of the relevant human rights document. The adjudicating authority, such as a court or tribunal, must assess whether an interference is justified, following a structured framework: the infringing measure must be shown to be lawful, a legitimate aim should be identified, and finally, the necessity and proportionality of the measure to its aim must be assessed. If an individual's human rights have been violated, they must receive an effective remedy from the court or tribunal. The practical enjoyment and enforcement of one's rights in a particular jurisdiction relies on measures being taken by the relevant authorities. To this end, supervisory bodies place obligations on those actors to take positive steps, to establish appropriate legal frameworks or systems of protection, and to ensure that individuals are protected from a range of threats to their human rights, including where the origin of that threat is a non-state actor. The nature and extent of these obligations within the ECHR system will be investigated in detail in Chapter 3.

A human rights lens provides an opportunity to re-examine long-established balances that have been struck within employment and labour law.[7] The features of human rights law described here have been developed and tested over many years, for example, through the decisions of the European Court of Human Rights (the ECtHR or the Court) and national bodies that apply human rights norms. To this extent, they are an external set of principles and norms that can be used in making a critical analysis of the doctrines, rules, and mechanisms of employment and labour law.[8] Hugh Collins and Virginia Mantouvalou's observation encapsulates this process of critical review:

> a human rights perspective offers … a presumption that the personal scope of employment law and associated statutory rights should be universal. In so far as rights under the contract of employment or statutory regulation are perceived to be founded on fundamental rights, any exclusions from those rights would receive strict scrutiny and require justification.[9]

[6] Hugh Collins and Virginia Mantouvalou, 'Human Rights and the Contract of Employment' in Mark Freedland (ed), *The Contract of Employment* (Oxford University Press 2016) 200.

[7] This point is made more generally by Oliver Gerstenberg, 'Private Law and the New European Constitutional Settlement' (2004) 10 European Law Journal 766, 767.

[8] Hugh Collins, 'On the Incompatibility of Human Rights Discourse and Private Law' in Hans W Micklitz (ed), *Constitutionalization of European Private Law* (Oxford University Press 2014) 41.

[9] Collins and Mantouvalou (n 6) 199.

The independently developed principles of human rights thereby provide a fresh perspective upon the established patterns of labour law. They prompt scholars and policymakers to seek to justify discrepancies where they arise. Where a deficiency in protection cannot be justified, their normative status as human rights provides impetus to amend the inconsistency as a matter of moral urgency.

II. A Theory of Human Rights as the Foundation of Labour Law

The next question is, then, how to conceive of the relationship between human rights and labour law. Theories of labour law have been the subject of increased debate in recent years,[10] prompted in part by dramatic empirical changes in the world of work and a crisis of confidence in the founding concepts of the discipline.[11] Human rights principles have indeed formed part of the challenge to the established patterns of labour law, as can be seen throughout this work, but could human rights be part of the theoretical solution? If so, how? Regarding the interaction between human rights and labour law, the optimal theory would combine the benefits just outlined with a reasonable degree of descriptive fit to the current shape of labour law regimes. The theory would also avoid any foreseeable negative consequences for the future of labour law when viewed from an instrumentalist or strategic perspective. In this section, I will investigate the possibility of an exclusive foundation for labour law based solely upon human rights before considering a more pluralistic alternative.

We might see fundamental or human rights as the very foundations of labour law. Labour law would thus draw upon the 'pre-emptive force' and 'special weight' of fundamental rights, meaning labour law's 'foundations would be much more secure'.[12] Thus far, only preliminary steps have been taken to conceptualize the whole system of labour law as an elaboration of workers' fundamental rights.[13] Such a perspective might start from a particular political theory or, if taking a more 'positivist' approach,[14] adopt the list of human rights that can be found in an international

[10] See Guy Davidov and Brian Langille (eds), *Boundaries and Frontiers of Labour Law: Goals and Means in the Regulation of Work* (Hart Publishing 2006); Guy Davidov and Brian Langille (eds), *The Idea of Labour Law* (Oxford University Press 2011); Hugh Collins, Gillian Lester, and Virginia Mantouvalou (eds), *Philosophical Foundations of Labour Law* (Oxford University Press 2018).

[11] Brian Langille, 'Labour Law's Theory of Justice' in Guy Davidov and Brian Langille (eds), *The Idea of Labour Law* (Oxford University Press 2011) 101.

[12] Hugh Collins, 'Theories of Rights as Justifications for Labour Law' in Brian Langille and Guy Davidov (eds), *The Idea of Labour Law* (Oxford University Press 2011) 139.

[13] Initial outlines of this kind of theory of labour law can be found in Atkinson (n 1); Collins, 'Theories of Rights as Justifications for Labour Law' (n 12); Hugh Collins, 'Justice at Work' (2020) 1 Revista Forumul Judecatorilor 59.

[14] See the different approaches to these questions outlined in Virginia Mantouvalou, 'Are Labour Rights Human Rights?' (2012) 2 European Labour Law Journal 151.

human rights instrument such as the ECHR or UN Universal Declaration of Human Rights (UDHR). How could such a theory be constructed? Are they likely to be successful when measured against the criteria suggested earlier?

This section highlights the most likely areas of difficulty for a 'labour law as human rights' theory, along with possible responses that a theorist could make. It charts a concern that human rights, as they appear in the current discourse, reflect a basic set of guarantees for a decent life, placing in jeopardy labour's claims to equality, distributive justice, or fairness. Founding a theory upon the ECHR would also risk a serious contraction of labour law's breadth as well as possibly reconstituting its priorities with individualist concerns taking the fore and collective rights being pushed aside. Underpinning these different strands of critique is a concern regarding the possible or likely consequences we would see if a 'labour law as human rights' theory became dominant. The loss of priority and urgency for any claim or interest that cannot be expressing in terms of a human right is a serious challenge. As observed by Colin Fenwick and Tonia Novitz:

> understanding the protection of workers' interests as human rights is likely to broaden their appeal at a time of marginalisation of trade unions as antiquated and outdated organisations. *What may be problematic... is that one may implicitly denigrate the status of workers' claims where it is more difficult to phrase them in terms of human rights.*[15]

A. Human Rights as a Floor, Not a Ceiling

Samuel Moyn argues that 'Before the age of human rights came, dreams of equality were taken quite seriously, both nationally and globally. In the age of human rights, the pertinence of fairness beyond sufficiency has been forgotten.'[16] If a system of rights focuses on sufficiency, it examines the position of the least well-off, asking how far they are away from having nothing and whether they surpass the 'bottom line' of goods and services necessary to live a minimally decent life. Huge disparities in wealth, power, and access to goods and services in a society is not a worry on this view, providing everyone is guaranteed enough to survive. These disparities, however, would be a significant concern for a proponent of equality. Hierarchies amongst society should be tackled and a limit placed on the extent of inequality within a society. On Moyn's interpretation, the age of human rights has sought to

[15] Tonia Novitz and Colin Fenwick, 'The Application of Human Rights Discourse to Labour Relations: Translation of Theory into Practice' in Tonia Novitz and Colin Fenwick (eds), *Human Rights at Work: Perspectives on Law and Regulation* (Hart Publishing 2010) 24 emphasis added.

[16] Samuel Moyn, *Not Enough: Human Rights in an Unequal World* (Harvard University Press 2018) 3.

guarantee sufficiency whilst permitting inequality between the rich and poor to persist and grow.[17]

What is the relevance of this bold statement regarding the priorities of the age of human rights to our discussion of a 'labour law as human rights' view? Labour law has long been associated with a concern for distributive justice, rebalancing the scales of power and wealth between capital and labour. Stripping the foundations of labour law to a concern only for the protection of human rights could lead us to focus on the very basics, achieving sufficiency for everyone, and to lose sight of aspirations of equality between groups. The most obvious instance of this consequence is the regulation of wages. Human rights give an individual the capacity to challenge pay disparities on the basis of specified grounds, such as one's sex, race, or religion. The fulfilment of human rights obligations could be considered to require a minimum wage such that the individual is able to meet their basic needs,[18] a concern for sufficiency only. Campaigns to redistribute wealth, in the form of increased wages for workers, may not find a strong foundation in a human rights view. They could be perceived as attacking the human rights of capital, of the employing organization, particularly the right to enjoy one's property and possessions or the freedom to contract.[19] In this sense, human rights assist us in achieving a floor of sufficiency for all, but not in striving for equality and distributive justice in the relationship between workers and employers.

There is a second sense in which human rights protections represent a floor rather than a ceiling, which poses a difficulty for a 'labour law as human rights' theory. The prohibitions contained and the duties incurred through human rights documents, which prevent the worse treatment of individuals by more powerful parties, can be considered minimal when compared with the detailed regulation laid down by most labour laws. Jill Murray observes that human rights often provide a 'weak signal' to law and policymakers when devising detailed regulation in the sphere of work, taking as an example the question of how women's participation in the workforce should be supported and the reconciliation of home and work life enabled.[20] Similarly, a right to respect for one's private life may guarantee some time away from work, but would leave open many questions regarding the precise manner in which working time should be regulated.[21] Elizabeth Anderson notes

[17] ibid 5–6.

[18] See *MSS v Belgium and Greece* (2011) 53 EHRR 2.

[19] This line of argument was most stark in the *Lochner* era in the US, *Lochner v New York* 198 US 45 (1905), and the CJEU has been accused of using the CFREU's article on the freedom to conduct a business in a 'deregulatory thrust' against workers' rights: Stephen Weatherill, 'Use and Abuse of the EU's Charter of Fundamental Rights: On the Improper Veneration of "Freedom of Contract"' (2014) 10 European Review of Contract Law 167, 179 on C-426/11 *Alemo-Herron v Parkwood Leisure Ltd* [2014] 1 CMLR 21.

[20] Jill Murray, 'Taking Social Rights Seriously: Is There a Case for Institutional Reform of the ILO?' in Tonia Novitz and Colin Fenwick (eds), *Human Rights at Work: Perspectives on Law and Regulation* (Hart Publishing 2010) 369.

[21] See McCann's commentary on the importance of working time practices for workers' participation in community and social activities, reconciliation with caring responsibilities, and the exercise of other

that '[t]here are limits ... to how far a bill of rights can go in protecting workers from abuse ... they can at best offer a minimal floor'.[22] Human rights are *necessary* but not *sufficient* in the pursuit of a workplace where the fair and decent treatment of workers is guaranteed.

A proponent of a 'labour law as human rights' view would have to defend the theory from the objection that the theory only prescribes a floor of protection. Workers are empowered to exercise their human rights without interference and, through work, are able to obtain the goods and services that are required to live a minimally dignified life. The theory does not assist legislators in making complex regulatory choices and balancing different values and consequences. Advocating for improved terms and conditions, equality, and distributive justice in the workplace would be more challenging. Indeed, we must acknowledge the risk that, in re-organizing employment law around a human rights theory, we would lose the 'directness and specificity' of labour rights that are well-established in domestic legal systems.[23] Deirdre McCann notes that existing regulatory mechanisms may offer more 'sophisticated mechanisms' than those that would be available under a human rights-based view.[24] This risk remains even when we take into account the set of positive obligations that the ECtHR has developed and imposed upon member states, discussed further in Chapter 3.

B. The Shape of Labour Law on a Fundamental Rights Theory

McCann's observation leads us to a broader point regarding the mismatch between the content of labour law in most jurisdictions and the extent of the recognized human rights of workers. As noted, the prohibitions could be perceived as minimal, but their range is also limited. The ECHR, particularly as it was originally drafted, maps onto a narrow group of rights and interests when compared to the labour law regimes in most European jurisdictions. Keith Ewing noted in 1998 that the ECHR's interest in labour law matters was largely incidental: '[u]nlike the Council of Europe's Social Charter—which deals with recognisable issues such as pay, working time, occupational health and safety, collective bargaining and the right to strike—the ECHR is silent on questions relating directly to the province of labour law'.[25] Although the ECHR has been interpreted in a manner that increases

human rights such as freedom to manifest one's religion: Deirdre McCann, 'Decent Working Hours as a Human Right: Intersections in the Regulation of Working Time' in Tonia Novitz and Colin Fenwick (eds), *Human Rights at Work: Perspectives on Law and Regulation* (Hart Publishing 2010) 519–20, 522.

[22] Elizabeth Anderson, *Private Government: How Employers Rules our Lives (and Why We Don't Talk about It)* (Princeton University Press 2017) 69.

[23] McCann (n 21) 527.

[24] ibid.

[25] Keith Ewing, 'The Human Rights Act and Labour Law' (1998) 27 ILJ 275, 278.

its capacity to ground a range of important labour rights, the derivative manner in which some of those rights are protected may remain a source of concern.

If we traced the Convention's application to labour disputes, labour law would undoubtedly be concerned with prohibiting forced labour, compulsory labour, slavery, or servitude.[26] The right against forced labour would require employment law to protect against unpaid work or work to which the individual has not consented. In addition, health and safety regulation would be necessary to provide protection for the right to life of the workforce,[27] as well as their physical and psychological integrity which is protected by Article 8 ECHR. From the right to respect for private and family life, we might derive protection from excessive working hours that leave little space for activities outside work, an entitlement to leave in order to care for family members, and limitations upon the surveillance of workers. An emphasis on freedom of association and non-discrimination would be maintained, although more emphasis might be placed on the right to freedom of expression and the right to privacy within the workplace. The right to a fair trial in Article 6 would guarantee procedural rights if the individual is at risk of being deprived of a civil right, such as the right to the continuation of an employment relationship,[28] as a result of the dispute in question.

There is one significant problem with this ECHR-inspired account. It appears to be an incomplete picture of modern employment law. We might consider the right not to be dismissed unfairly which is a cornerstone of many systems of labour rights but cannot be easily grounded within a civil liberties foundation of labour law. Only in very recent years has it been possible to derive a right against unjustified dismissal from the case law on Article 8 ECHR.[29] Even then, Article 8 will only be engaged where the dismissal has 'serious negative effects on the individual's private life',[30] a significant limitation on the scope of the right itself.[31] Whilst such negative consequences might be relevant to a domestic tribunal's determination of an unfair dismissal case, the right not to be unjustifiably dismissed is not usually limited to such cases. Even on a wide interpretation of Article 8, we do not see a general right not to be subject to an unjust dismissal as it appears in many systems of labour law.[32]

[26] ECHR, Article 4, recently reflected in the Modern Slavery Act 2015.

[27] See Emily A Spieler, 'Risks and Rights: The Case for Occupational Safety and Health as a Core Worker Right' in James A Gross (ed), *Workers' Rights as Human Rights* (Cornell University Press 2003) 94 on the relationship to the right to life. See also *Brincat and Others v Malta* Application no 60908/11 (ECtHR, 24 July 2014).

[28] See *Denisov v Ukraine* Application no 76639/11 (ECtHR, 25 September 2018) [46].

[29] Hugh Collins, 'An Emerging Human Right to Protection against Unjustified Dismissal' (2021) 50 ILJ 36.

[30] *Denisov v Ukraine* (n 28) [107].

[31] Collins, 'An Emerging Human Right to Protection against Unjustified Dismissal' (n 29) 61.

[32] See Samuel Estreicher and Jeffrey M Hirsch, 'Comparative Wrongful Dismissal Law: Reassessing American Exceptionalism' (2014) 92 North Carolina Law Review 343, 445–48.

One might argue that, although a significant development in the jurisprudence of Article 8, this secondary form of protection does not accord well with the status of the right not to be dismissed unfairly as a core and fundamental right of workers upon most views of labour law. Similar questions may be asked about the derivative status of several collective rights. The right to bargain collectively with an employer and the right to take industrial action to protect the interests of a trade union and its members have been 'read into' the right to freedom of association under Article 11.[33] These decisions represent major victories for the labour movement. Nonetheless, given that these rights are so crucial upon most views of labour law, their status as derived from a 'higher' right may give rise to an expressive concern. Even if the evolving interpretation of the right to freedom of association has led to the incorporation of these collective rights within the realm of human rights, a 'labour law as human rights' view might be considered to reinforce a hierarchy in which the narrow right as it was originally drafted is given prominence over the broader conception favoured by labour law scholars.

C. Individualism and Collectivism in a Rights-based Theory

The perception of a hierarchy between the individual's right to freedom of association and the protection of the capacity of unions to organize and protect their members' interests is one aspect of the longstanding scepticism of human rights arguments within labour law. It has been argued that by focusing upon the individual's rights, the claims of the collective are injured.[34] David Kennedy argues that a focus upon individuals as rights holders changes our perspective: 'the human rights movement intensifies the sense of entitlement in individuals and groups at great cost to their ability to participate in collective political life and to their understanding of own lives as part of a more diverse community'.[35] A major function of labour law has always been conceived to be the enhancement of the collective voice of workers, deployed to secure a better deal for workers. Jay Youngdahl argues that 'Elevating human rights to the dominant position within labor ideology will eviscerate support for the common concerns of all workers that is the keystone of labor solidarity'.[36]

[33] *Demir v Turkey* (2009) 48 EHRR 54, [154]; *Enerji Yapı-Yol Sen v Turkey* Application no 68959/01 (ECtHR, 21 April 2009) [24].

[34] This point has been argued persuasively in Jay Youngdahl, 'Solidarity First: Labor Rights are Not the Same as Human Rights' (2009) 18 New Labour Forum 31 and is also noted by Collins as a likely consequence of a Rawlsian approach to a rights-based account of labour law: Collins, 'Theories of Rights as Justifications for Labour Law' (n 12) 150–51.

[35] David Kennedy, 'International Human Rights Movement: Part of the Problem?' (2002) 15 Harvard Human Rights Journal 101, 112–13.

[36] Youngdahl (n 34) 32.

In the earlier years of the debate, in the UK particularly, there was a sense of caution and concern regarding the role of human rights in labour disputes. The rights given initial prominence under Article 11 of the ECHR had focused upon the individual's rights. Lord Wedderburn observed in 1987 that the judges of the ECtHR were not willing to imbue Article 11 with positive rights to organize and to bargain through a union. Instead, the ECtHR judges implied a 'negative' right not to associate for individual non-unionists leading to a finding that closed shops were a disproportionate interference with that implied right.[37] Ten years on, upon the enactment of the Human Rights Act (HRA) 1998, Keith Ewing surveyed the Convention case law again, observing that 'the contribution of article 11 to date has been disappointing, failing to deliver any meaningful protection for trade union activities, while being used as an instrument for undermining trade union security'.[38] The shape of the rights themselves, with their focus on the individual rather than the collective, and the turn towards courts who had been 'deaf' to the calls of labour in the past, caused consternation for both authors.

Although scepticism regarding the role of courts and Convention rights resurfaces when unions or workers suffer key defeats in litigation,[39] there has been a rebalancing of the Article 11 jurisprudence. Whilst the rights of individuals emerged first, some years later they were followed by rights centred upon trade unions, their autonomy, and their mandate to protect the interests of their members. The rights of unions to control their own affairs[40] and to represent their members' interests through bargaining and strike[41] have been upheld in recent ECtHR cases. In doing so, the Court drew upon international documents that protect and detail fundamental social rights such as the Council of Europe's European Social Charter (ESC), the EU Charter of Fundamental Rights, and International Labour Organization (ILO) Conventions.[42] ACL Davies observes that, in these cases, 'the ECtHR has seized the opportunity to locate article 11 in a collectivist framework. It has accepted the importance of trade union autonomy and has refused to give priority to the rights of individuals'.[43] From a descriptive perspective, although there are instances where one might think the courts could do *more* to support the trade

[37] Lord Wedderburn, 'Freedom of Association or Right to Organise?' (1987) 18 Industrial Relations Journal 244, 248, commenting upon the Railwaymen's Case: *Young, James and Webster v United Kingdom* (1981) 3 EHRR 20.

[38] Ewing (n 25) 279.

[39] For a sceptical review of the approach at domestic and European level, see Keith Ewing and John Hendy QC, 'The Trade Union Act 2016 and the Failure of Human Rights' (2016) 45 ILJ 391, 412–20.

[40] *Associated Society of Locomotive Engineers & Firemen (ASLEF) v United Kingdom* (2007) 45 EHRR 34.

[41] See *Demir v Turkey* (n 33) [154]; *Enerji Yapı-Yol Sen v Turkey* (n 33) [24].

[42] See, for example, *Demir v Turkey* (n 33) [147]–[150].

[43] ACL Davies, 'Workers' Human Rights in English Law' in Tonia Novitz and Colin Fenwick (eds), *Human Rights at Work: Perspectives on Law and Regulation* (Hart Publishing 2010) 183.

union movement,[44] we can see that human rights discourse can have an important role in upholding the rights of collective organizations and their members.

This descriptive view feeds into a more general response to the concerns regarding the fate of collective agendas under theory of labour law influenced by human rights. As Alan Bogg comments, 'a successful legal regime' combines both individual and collective rights within its strategy, where workers and unions reap the benefits of mutually supportive individual *and* group rights to freedom of association.[45] A union enjoying a strongly protected right to strike would be almost useless, for example, if individual union members were not safeguarded from detriment or discipline on the grounds that they joined such a strike. To prevent discriminatory dismissals of union members is also to protect the union's position in the workplace and to remove a strong deterrent that employers could otherwise use to limit union power. Effective collective organizing, from the formation and recognition of a union through to collective bargaining and industrial action, relies upon an interconnected web of individual *and* collective rights. A concern regarding the impact of human rights on labour collectives should not therefore be taken to rule out a 'labour law as human rights' theory.

D. Two Potential Responses to the Critiques

A 'labour law as human rights' theory is faced with several challenges: a foundation grounded in potentially minimal prohibitions against infringements upon a worker's human rights, a narrowed focus when compared to existing labour law regimes, and a consequential concern about priorities or agendas that cannot be phrased in fundamental rights terms. There are two ways that a theorist might seek to address these points. Either we might adopt a framework that encompasses a wider group of human rights, or we could admit some plurality: alongside fundamental rights, there are other elements that are necessary within a theory of labour law. A plural perspective is detailed in section III.

There are several choices, from a positivist's perspective, if we were to take the former option. The EU Charter of Fundamental Rights contains civil liberties and a number of social or 'solidarity' rights[46] which provide a basis for a greater proportion of employment law's scope. Article 30 protects against unjustified dismissal; Article 31 provides a right to fair and just working conditions, including limits upon working time, and collective bargaining and rights to consultation of the workforce are included.[47] A similarly extensive list of rights applicable to

[44] See *National Union of Rail, Maritime and Transport Workers v United Kingdom* (2015) 60 EHRR 10; Alan Bogg and Keith Ewing, 'The Implications of the RMT Case' (2014) 43 ILJ 221.

[45] Alan Bogg, '"Individualism" and "Collectivism" in Collective Labour Law' (2017) 46 ILJ 72, 101.

[46] The Charter of Fundamental Rights of the European Union [2016] OJ C202/389, Chapter IV.

[47] CFREU, Articles 30, 31, 28, 27.

employment are included in the ESC, the companion to the ECHR. The UN UDHR contains rights that could provide a foundation for various labour standards. In her work examining the ILO perspective on human rights at work, Jill Murray references a 'confluence of broadly defined social rights and the ILO's own concept of decent work'[48] which would incorporate a range of key principles drawn from a variety of ILO documents.

A theory of employment law grounded upon a larger category of fundamental rights is likely to be more persuasive to labour scholars. It recognizes the importance of labour rights in their own right, rather than as derivatives of classic civil and political rights, and accounts for the breadth of labour laws found in most countries more successfully and accurately. However, it is not without its own difficulties. This theoretical move risks the theorist becoming embroiled in the debate regarding what may properly be considered a 'human right', an issue that is contested in relation to important rights of workers,[49] and potentially being faulted for furthering the proliferation of rights and thereby damaging the power of existing rights claims.[50]

A theorist would also have to confront the possibility that, in drawing upon a more inclusive group of rights, they may sacrifice the normative or legal force of their argument. The UK is a good example of a jurisdiction where the perceived divide between civil and social human rights is reflected in their legal status and justiciability. The ECHR rights are justiciable against public authorities as a result of the HRA 1998 under section 6, as well as influencing the interpretation of other legislative instruments via section 3. In contrast, the European Committee of Social Rights (ECSR) monitors and reports upon the UK's implementation of the ESC. The ECSR's criticism is often not acted upon by the UK government. Colm O'Cinneide has argued that the social dimension of 'rights talk' is completely absent in the UK and its record on social rights contains numerous 'serious failings'.[51] As observed by Judy Fudge, 'justiciable and legally enforceable rights are regarded as the most powerful'[52] and therefore would provide the strongest foundations for labour law.

Particularly in countries where the divide between civil liberties and socio-economic rights remains prominent, adopting a broader foundation across both sides of the distinction may sacrifice the universal appeal in practice and in politics that

[48] Murray (n 20) 381.

[49] See, for example, Atkinson (n 1) 130 for an investigation of the status of labour rights on a Razian view; James Griffin, *On Human Rights* (Oxford University Press 2008) 207 for a rejection of a human right to work. For typography of approaches to this question in the labour law context, see Mantouvalou (n 14).

[50] See Philip Alston, 'Conjuring up New Human Rights: A Proposal for Quality Control' (1984) 78 American Journal of International Law 614; Dominique Clément, 'Human Rights or Social Justice? The Problem of Rights Inflation' (2018) 22 International Journal of Human Rights 155.

[51] Colm O'Cinneide, 'The European Social Charter and the UK: Why It Matters' (2018) 29 Kings Law Journal 275, 275–76.

[52] Judy Fudge, *Constitutionalizing Labour Rights in Europe* (Oxford University Press 2011) 244.

a theorist would seek. Whilst the 'first generation' human rights have become a global, moral *lingua franca*,[53] the position of social and economic rights is still contested. The prospect of legally binding social rights—particularly the right not to be unjustifiably dismissed and the right to collective bargaining and action—caused such consternation that the UK government sought an 'opt-out' from the EU Charter of Fundamental Rights.[54] It was also a target during the process of the UK's withdrawal from the EU. The Charter has been expressly and deliberately excluded from retained law post-Brexit, indicating the level of hostility towards the document that remains.[55] The sudden 'death of the Charter' in the UK indicates that a theory of labour founded on a broader base of civil and social fundamental rights may not enjoy support from all quarters.

An alternative response to the difficulties of a 'labour law as human rights' would be to draw on the essential prohibitions contained in human rights instruments *and* complementary features or aspirations that form part of the theory of labour law. Pablo Gilabert creates a conceptual distinction between basic and maximal labour rights: 'Whereas the former focus on workers' access to a decent life, the latter go further by tracking workers' access to a flourishing life.'[56] His theory of labour law would thus combine protection for basic labour rights, including human rights, with more aspirational rights which enable our 'full human development at work'.[57] Virginia Mantouvalou, in discussing whether some labour rights are human rights, distinguishes between human rights and other labour standards 'that involve the detailed regulation of the employment relation' and 'focus on the particular challenges that workers in a specific sector face, making the general human rights principles more subtle and precise'.[58] Admitting that not all aspects of employment law can be grounded upon human rights and that some of its usual provisions are instead 'labour standards' may allow a human rights-based theory to maintain both the strong normative claims of human rights and the comprehensive regulation that has developed in response to the unique relational dynamics between employers and workers.

III. Human Rights as One of Labour Law's Objectives

An alternative perspective on the relationship between human rights and labour law is that the protection of workers' human rights has always been *one of* labour

53 Moyn (n 16) ix.

54 Catherine Barnard, 'So Long, Farewell, Auf Wiedersehen, Adieu: Brexit and the Charter of Fundamental Rights' (2019) 82 MLR 319, 352.

55 ibid 365.

56 Pablo Gilabert, 'Dignity at Work' in Hugh Collins, Gillian Lester, and Virginia Mantouvalou (eds), *Philosophical Foundations of Labour Law* (Oxford University Press 2018) 80.

57 ibid.

58 Mantouvalou (n 14) 169–70.

law's central objectives. Two of the authors mentioned earlier, for example, have developed theories in which human rights are an important component, but ultimately part of a wider perspective or objective. Gilabert's is a dignitarian account of the subject.[59] A suite of basic (and fundamental) and maximal labour rights is necessary in order to ensure that every person's dignity is respected and that their pursuit of a decent and flourishing life is supported.[60] In contrast, Mantouvalou highlights how human rights analysis and accountability can be important in tackling structural injustices that lead to individuals being placed in positions where they are vulnerable to exploitation.[61] A pluralist view of the goals of labour law is able to capture all the benefits set out in section I, whilst avoiding the criticisms that can be made of a more exclusive 'labour law as human rights' theory. A pluralist account of labour law includes the protection of human rights at work as a key component alongside other abstract values and more concrete aims and agendas.

Labour law has been considered to pursue a variety of goals, such as the redistribution of power from capital to labour,[62] concerns regarding social justice,[63] and tackling the particular vulnerabilities of workers, such as subordination and dependency upon their employer.[64] Higher order values such as equality,[65] freedom,[66] autonomy,[67] and dignity[68] ground theories of labour law. Conceiving the whole of labour law as a singular elaboration of human rights risks neglecting these objectives and ideals which have been said to underpin the discipline of labour law. What is crucial when positioning the protection of human rights within a broader theoretical framework is not to eclipse this array of important, specific, and unique values and objectives that employment law has pursued and achieved for many years.

Equally as important is to acknowledge the longstanding role of the protection of the fundamental rights of workers as an aspect of labour law's functions.

[59] Gilabert, 'Dignity at Work' (n 56); Gilabert, 'Labor Human Rights and Human Dignity' (n 3).

[60] Gilabert, 'Dignity at Work' (n 56).

[61] Virginia Mantouvalou, 'Structural Injustice and the Human Rights of Workers' (2020) 73 Current Legal Problems 1.

[62] Mark Freedland and Paul Davies, *Kahn-Freund's Labour and the Law* (3rd edn, Stevens 1983) 18.

[63] See Ruth Dukes, 'Constitutionalizing Employment Relations: Sinzheimer, Kahn-Freund, and the Role of Labor Law' (2008) 35 Journal of Law and Society 341, 345. More recently, social justice as an ideal for labour law was strongly defended by Supiot:Emilios Christodoulidis and Ruth Dukes, 'Dialogue & Debate: Labour, Constitution and A Sense of Measure: A Debate with Alain Supiot' (2010) 19 Social & Legal Studies 217, 221.

[64] Guy Davidov, *A Purposive Approach to Labour Law* (Oxford University Press 2016) chapter 3, part I.

[65] Judy Fudge, 'Labour As a "Fictive Commodity": Radically Reconceptualizing Labour Law' in Guy Davidov and Brian Langille (eds), *The Idea of Labour Law* (Oxford University Press 2011).

[66] Langille (n 11) 112 and Alan Bogg and Cynthia Estlund, 'Freedom of Association and the Right to Contest' in Alan Bogg and Tonia Novitz (eds), *Voices at Work: Continuity and Change in the Common Law World* (Oxford University Press 2014) 151–59.

[67] As in Spector's theory of 'equal autonomy': Horacio Spector, 'Philosophical Foundations of Labor Law' (2006) 33 Florida State University Law Review 1119.

[68] David C Yamada, 'Human Dignity and American Employment Law' (2009) 43 University of Richmond Law Review 523; Gilabert, 'Dignity at Work' (n 56).

Although the terminology of 'fundamental' or 'human' rights was a comparatively late arrival, both the past and the present of labour law invoke a concern to safeguard a range of important rights that vest in individual workers. As thoughtfully observed by Janice Bellace and Beryl ter Haar, '[o]ver the past century, the terminology may have changed, from labour standards to labour rights to human rights, but the values are timeless'.[69] A more precise mapping of the current regime of employment and labour rights and their relationship to the ECHR rights will be offered in Chapter 4, so here I will focus more on the evolution of labour law to this point.

Very early legislation of the workplace, notably the Factory Acts, limited the number of hours that children could work in factories and introduced some basic safety requirements. These early safeguards were later supplemented with a common law duty upon the employer to provide a safe working environment for their employees.[70] Similarly, a concern for continuation of the unions' ability to act on the behalf of their members led to the Trade Union Act 1871 which protected the unions from liability under common law doctrines such as restraint of trade. The Trade Disputes Act 1906 similarly protected unions from liability for inducing breach of contract and interference with a business. This mode of providing unions with immunity against existing wrongs remains a part of modern employment law.[71] These early rules prevented onerous child labour, protected the workers' right to life by improving conditions in the workplace, and provided the basics of a right to engage in collective action. All three themes can be seen in the modern human rights documents and principles.

The common law also provides protection for the worker's freedom from coerced labour and their liberty to exit the relationship. Tort law would intervene to protect an individual from wrongs such as battery, false imprisonment, or intentional infliction of psychiatric injury.[72] Contract law, as it applies to contracts of employment, ensures that employees receive a wage in return for their work[73] and the entitlement to terminate the contract by giving notice protects the individual from forced labour. If an employee is found to breach their contract, the courts will not use their remedial powers to force an employee to continue working for an employer against their wishes,[74] a position which 'bears witness to the ... presence of the anti-slavery norm'.[75] Other areas of the common law, based implicitly or directly

[69] Bellace and Haar (n 4) 14.

[70] *Wilsons & Clyde Coal Company Ltd v English* [1938] AC 57.

[71] Trade Union and Labour Relations (Consolidation) Act 1992, section 219.

[72] See Pam Stewart, 'Tortious Remedies for Deliberate Wrongdoing to Victims of Human Trafficking and Slavery in Australia' (2011) 34 University of New South Wales Law Journal 898.

[73] See *Bryant v Flight* (1839) 5 M & W 114.

[74] See *De Francesco v Barnum* (1890) 45 Ch D 430, 438 (Fry LJ).

[75] Todd D Rakoff, 'Enforcement of Employment Contracts and the Anti-Slavery Norm' in Dan Friedmann and Daphne Barak-Erez (eds), *Human Rights in Private Law* (Hart Publishing 2003) 291.

upon norms of public policy, similarly provide protection to human rights such as the freedom to choose one's occupation or the right to non-discrimination.[76]

Hugh Collins and Virginia Mantouvalou have observed that the common law's accomplishments regarding the protection of human rights will always be complex in nature, due to the subordination and imbalance of power inherent in the employment relationship that the common law preserves.[77] Nevertheless a theme of protecting workers from forced labour, as well as other fundamental rights, is certainly discernible. These common law principles and statutory standards grant piecemeal protection to the human rights of workers, a theme which will be picked up in Chapter 4 through an examination of the major pieces of recent legislation. At this point, it is sufficient to draw upon Collins and Mantouvalou's observation:

> In retrospect, it is possible to see that the enactment of various statutory employment rights in the 1970s, such as the right not to be unfairly dismissed and the laws against sex and race discrimination, were inspired, at least in part, by a human rights perspective on the tasks for labour law ... the individual was provided with a mandatory right as the basis for a legal claim for compensation against an employer.[78]

It is opportune to note a final consequence of the acknowledgement that employment law has a history of protecting the human rights of workers. If human rights are considered an organic concern of employment law, then the importance of the theoretical divide between private law disciplines (which would usually be considered to include employment or labour law)[79] and public law and human rights norms diminishes. The resistance that might otherwise be encountered by a project that is seen to fundamentally challenge that divide is therefore unnecessary. It is important to realize the extent to which employment law and public law face similar concerns,[80] which explains the propensity of labour law to 'borrow' public law concepts and use them in the regulation of working relationships.[81] As will be detailed in the final part of this chapter, any transference of concepts between these disciplines must be sensitive to the differences in their surrounding social and legal context.

[76] See, for example, the doctrine of unlawful restraint of trade and cases such as *Nagle v Fielden* [1966] 2 QB 633, discussed further in Chapter 8, section II.

[77] Collins and Mantouvalou (n 6) 193–94.

[78] ibid 195.

[79] For a critical reflection on this classification, see Mark Freedland, 'Employment Law' in John Bell, Sophie Boyron, and Simon Whittaker (eds), *Principles of French Law* (2nd edn, Oxford University Press 2008).

[80] See John Laws, 'Public Law and Employment Law: Abuse of Power' [1997] Public Law 455.

[81] ACL Davies, 'Labour Law as Public Law' in Alan Bogg, Cathryn Costello, ACL Davies, and Jeremias Prassl (eds), *The Autonomy of Labour Law* (Hart Publishing 2015); Paul Davies and Mark Freedland, 'The Impact of Public Law on Labour Law, 1972–1997' (1997) 26 ILJ 311.

IV. Putting Human Rights to Work: The Distinctive Features of Labour Law

Having engaged with such an impressive plurality of ideas and ideals as those presented here, a singular foundation for labour law based upon the protection of human rights is troubling. One consequence of a 'labour law as human rights' approach that has not yet been explored is the possibility that the conception of those human rights, having been primarily developed in the relationship between citizen and state, would be uncritically transplanted into labour relations.[82] Maintaining the boundaries of labour law as an autonomous discipline allows us to fit the protection of human rights within a wide variety of aims, but also to investigate how the context of work affects their meaning and the mechanisms by which they should be protected. This re-conceptualization ensures that workers receive a high standard of protection, whilst recognizing that new factors and features must be taken into account.

In the final section of this chapter, I discuss what the effective protection of human rights at work requires. The ideal response from the legislature and the courts, as key actors that must ensure fundamental rights are respected and must embody a culture of human rights, will be outlined. Aware of the risks of straightforward transplantation of ideas from an international human rights context to the domestic regulation of working relationships, I will consider whether doctrines such as the 'margin of appreciation' which are applied by the ECtHR have any role to play in the latter setting. Finally, I will discuss adjustments and specificities that a court or regulator must take into account in order to ensure that the scope and shape of human rights are tailored to the context of work.

A. Towards a 'Human Rights Culture' in Labour Law

ACL Davies calls for a 'human rights culture' in labour law.[83] A human rights culture describes 'an ideal situation in which key actors in the legal system regard compliance with human rights norms as an important goal which takes priority over other considerations and which should be pursued with vigour'.[84] In the courts, it 'would be evidenced by careful consideration to determine whether rights were relevant to any decision, a generous interpretation of what those rights required … and, in appropriate cases, rigorous scrutiny of any interference with rights using the proportionality test'.[85] The government, within its sphere, would

[82] Hugh Collins, 'Utility and Rights in Common Law Reasoning: Rebalancing Private Law Through Constitutionalization' (2007) 30 Dalhousie Law Journal 1, 21.
[83] Davies, 'Workers' Human Rights in English Law' (n 43) 183.
[84] ibid 183.
[85] ibid 183.

actively promote the enjoyment of human rights through legislative review and engagement with international human rights bodies, and it must avoid actions that infringe human rights.[86] Davies does swiftly note, however, that 'there is, as yet, little evidence of the emergence of a human rights culture in the United Kingdom since the enactment of the Human Rights Act 1998'.[87]

Davies' vision for a human rights culture depicts the ideal response from key actors to the claim that the protection of human rights is an important function of labour law. Looking more particularly at the role of the courts, in areas where human rights influences can already be seen in the applicable doctrines and provisions, the responsibility of the court is to ensure that the standards and rules set out in the legislation are purposively applied to grant the most effective protection to the claimant's human rights as possible.[88] In some cases, however, employment law may not reflect the need to protect the human rights of workers. As we have shown that human rights *should* be reflected within labour law, the aim of the court must be to rectify the deficiency. The provisions of the HRA 1998 confer a wide competency, even an obligation, upon the courts to engage in judicial development of the law.[89] In a blossoming culture of human rights, the courts would engage with this obligation to correct inadequacies in the domestic system of employment law wherever possible.[90]

B. The Irrelevance of (Some) Doctrines of International Human Rights Law

A further consequence of human rights being legitimately part of employment law's aims is that human rights ideas should continue to be 'translated' into a form that is suitable for the workplace and relationships of employment. Protection of human rights should not be perceived as a 'top-down' imposition, which is straightforwardly transplanted onto the existing regime of employment law. This subsection tackles the elements of international human rights law which should be disregarded in this translation process, whereas the final subsection of the chapter

86 ibid 184.

87 ibid 184. Whilst the culture around human rights in labour law has improved since Davies was writing in 2010, the thrust of the chapters that follow would support this claim.

88 One instance where the courts failed to perform this function was *Associated Newspapers Ltd v Wilson, Associated British Ports v Palmer* [1995] 2 AC 454, [1995] 2 WLR 354. The House of Lords read the statutory protection for trade union members in a narrow fashion so as to exclude the use of collective bargaining. The court's interpretation of the statute led to a successful complaint in Strasbourg: *Wilson and others v United Kingdom* (2002) 35 EHRR 20.

89 See Murray Hunt, 'The "Horizontal Effect" of the Human Rights Act' [1998] Public Law 423, 440; *X v Y* [2004] EWCA Civ 662, [2004] ICR 1634, [58].

90 As will be discussed further in Chapter 4, there are some limits on the capacity of the courts to seek outcomes compatible with the Convention, and where these limits would be exceeded the court must make a declaration of incompatibility under HRA 1998, section 4.

recounts key characteristics that must be actively considered when bringing human rights into the workplace.

The first point is specific to the process of drawing on Convention rights in domestic employment law. Human rights were conceived in relation to the state and its functions and Convention rights have been developed by a court with an international supervisory remit. These features have led to the development of two doctrines that are used regularly by the ECtHR in examining employment-related cases but should play no role in a domestic tribunal's scrutiny of an employer's actions. The doctrines are the 'margin of appreciation' and the positive obligations placed on Council of Europe states. Their application entails a more lenient approach to the process of justifying an infringement. Both are only relevant where the defendant in the case is a member state which is entitled to a degree of deference.

The 'margin of appreciation' is a recognition of the principle of subsidiarity[91] and that the member states could protect and fulfil Convention rights via several routes, balancing rights in different ways. The margin is used 'to balance the sovereignty of the Contracting States with the need to secure protection of the rights embodied in the Convention.'[92] The Court has stated that '[b]y reason of their direct and continuous contact with the vital forces of their countries ... it is for the national authorities to make the initial assessment of the reality of the pressing social need implied by the notion of "necessity" in this context.'[93] It is applied, for example, where a state has a piece of legislation which is intended in part to protect a particular right but the legislature had to reach a compromise between the enforcement of the right and other important societal interests[94] or where the ECtHR is reviewing a national court's decision that an infringement upon an individual's Convention right was necessary in order to pursue a legitimate aim.[95] As the 'margin of appreciation' is a feature of an *international* system of judicial supervision, it has no role in the deliberations of national courts.[96] This has been recognized by the judiciary: '[i]n applying the Convention rights which have been reproduced as part of domestic law by the Human Rights Act 1998, the concept of the margin of appreciation has, as such, no application.'[97]

A similar analysis can be applied to the ECtHR's doctrine of positive obligations or positive duties. The Court has long held that the states' obligations under several of the Convention's articles extend beyond the 'primarily negative undertaking[s]'[98]

[91] George Letsas, 'Two Concepts of the Margin of Appreciation' (2006) 26 OJLS 705, 721.

[92] ibid 720.

[93] *Handyside v United Kingdom* (1979) 1 EHRR 737, [48].

[94] *Redfearn v United Kingdom* (2013) 57 EHRR 2, [48].

[95] *Sánchez v Spain* (2012) 54 EHRR 24, [54].

[96] David Pannick, 'Principles of Interpretation of Convention Rights under the Human Rights Act and the Discretionary Area of Judgment' [1998] Public Law 545, 548; Keir Starmer, *European Human Rights Law: the Human Rights Act 1998 and the European Convention on Human Rights* (Legal Action Group 1999) 190.

[97] *R. (SB) v Governors of Denbigh High School* [2006] UKHL 15, [2007] 1 AC 100, [63] (Lord Hoffman).

[98] *Martínez v Spain* (2015) 60 EHRR 3, [114].

contained in the ECHR text. The Court has imposed a duty on member states to ensure that the national framework provides effective protection for human rights. Importantly, the member states are under an obligation to protect individuals from interferences with their ECHR rights by other private parties.[99] This principle extends the Court's purview to reviewing private law legislation that offers this protection between private individuals and to examining the reasoning and outcomes reached by national courts in determining private law disputes.[100]

An important factor that appears in the workplace cases and influences whether the Court considers the positive obligation to be fulfilled in a particular case is whether a 'fair balance' has been struck between the fundamental right and any countervailing interests.[101] This standard of scrutiny varies and can be applied fairly loosely by the ECtHR in assessing whether, for example, a national court has struck that fair balance in the circumstances of a particular case.[102] In *Sánchez v Spain*, the Strasbourg Court examined whether a national court's decision regarding the lawfulness of a dismissal had failed to fulfil the state's positive obligations under Article 10. The ECtHR held that the state would only have failed to strike a fair balance if the dismissal was 'manifestly disproportionate or excessive' such that intervention by the courts was required.[103] Although the result was strongly questioned by a dissenting opinion, the majority of the Court held that the domestic court's consideration of the case had satisfied the state's positive obligation. This reasoning was influenced by the operation of the margin of appreciation and has been cited by Laurens Lavrysen as an example of the Court granting greater deference to the national authority because it had attempted to conduct its own proportionality analysis.[104]

As with the margin of appreciation mentioned earlier, the less searching scrutiny that positive obligations cases can entail should not be taken into account by the domestic courts. Tribunals must give due regard to the human rights of the individual and thoroughly examine the justification and necessity of any infringements in the case before them, as will be seen in Chapter 3. The 'fair balance' style of analysis applied by the ECtHR to give deference to the national authorities and courts who have direct contact with the evidence and the social context of the dispute should not be drawn upon by national courts in setting the standards of review at a domestic level. Excerpts from *Sánchez*, for example, were relied upon

[99] *Young, James and Webster v UK* (n 37) [49].

[100] See, for example, *Redfearn v UK* (n 94) and *Eweida and others v United Kingdom* (2013) 57 EHRR 8 respectively. For further detail, see Chapter 3.

[101] *Abdulaziz, Cabales and Balkandali v United Kingdom* (1985) 7 EHRR 471, [67].

[102] For a comparison of the Court's standard of scrutiny under negative obligations and positive obligations, see Laurens Lavrysen, *Human Rights in a Positive State: Rethinking the Relationship between Positive and Negative Obligations under the European Convention on Human Rights* (Intersentia 2017) 233–35.

[103] *Sánchez v Spain* (n 95) [77].

[104] Lavrysen (n 102) 181–82.

by the English Court of Appeal in *Turner v East Midlands Trains Ltd* to bolster the court's view that domestic law already offered sufficient protection to certain aspects of an individual's human rights at work.[105] I would argue that such an interpretation of the relationship between ECtHR decisions and domestic law is ill-conceived. The 'leeway' granted by the Strasbourg Court to national authorities under the doctrine of positive obligations must not be taken as a reason to maintain less rigorous standards of review at the domestic level.

C. Fit for Purpose? Human Rights *at Work*

Just as ideals such as justice or freedom can be expounded in a manner that is more or less sensitive to the peculiarities of the working relationship, so can human rights concepts. It has been demonstrated that transferring the meaning and scope of human rights that have been developed in international and domestic cases against the state can lead to severe deficiencies in the standard of protection offered to individuals.[106] As Collins argues, '[e]xisting declarations of the rights of citizens can be drawn upon by analogy, but the context of the workplace requires a more refined and differentiated discourse to protect employees against the arbitrary use of managerial power'.[107]

We might consider first the factual differences between the powers and capacities of the state as opposed to the employer. Although the similarities between the state and the employer are sufficient that they attract interest from employment and human rights commentators alike,[108] there are important differences.[109] Whilst a state can lawfully remove the liberty of those within its jurisdiction whereas an employer cannot, the state cannot act in certain ways which are available to employers. It cannot straightforwardly offer financial inducements to its citizens to give up fundamental rights that they enjoy. The state cannot 'downgrade' a citizen's status to express disapproval of their actions, in the way that an employer can demote an employee. A democratic state cannot unilaterally determine the rules of the relationship and thereby restrict the exercise of fundamental rights in a major sphere of an individual's life. An employer's powers are more immediate and intrusive

105 [2012] EWCA Civ 1470, [2013] ICR 525.

106 See, for example, the conception of privacy adopted in *X v Y* (n 89); *Pay v Lancashire Probation Service* [2004] ICR 187; Virginia Mantouvalou's arguments that it was inappropriate for application to the employment relationship: Virginia Mantouvalou, 'Human Rights and Unfair Dismissal: Private Acts in Public Spaces' (2008) 71 MLR 912, 922 onwards.

107 Hugh Collins, 'The Productive Disintegration of Labour Law' (1997) 26 ILJ 295, 306.

108 See, for example, Hazel Oliver, 'Employment Law' in David Hoffman (ed), *The Impact of the UK Human Rights Act on Private Law* (Cambridge University Press 2011) 344; Dawn Oliver, *Common Values and the Public-private Divide* (Cambridge University Press 2010) chapter 6.

109 The limitations of the analogy between governing and employing relations has been highlighted by Frances Raday: Frances Raday, 'Constitutionalization of Labour Law' in Roger Blanpain and Manfred Weiss (eds), *The Changing Face of Labour Law and Industrial Relations* (Nomos 1993) 106.

than those possessed by a state. In the 'panoptic design' of the workplace,[110] a manager can watch an employee throughout the day, noting how often and for how long they interact with others, or they can closely surveil their activity through IT systems or productivity monitoring. These distinctive ways in which the employer can exercise their prerogative must be considered in applying human rights standards to the workplace if we are to provide effective protection to workers.

These differences between employers and the state as holders of power point to the first major feature of the employment relationship to which a conception of human rights must respond. A state cannot enter into an agreement with an individual that they should not exercise their fundamental rights for a certain period of time or in certain ways. The contractual foundation of the working relationship means that such an action is entirely possible. Restrictions on fundamental rights are regularly included in contracts of employment and employees could, in theory at least, waive their rights altogether under the terms of the contract. The principles and mechanisms that protect human rights in the employment sphere must be conscious of this key difference and respond appropriately.[111] How the ECtHR has approached the contractual diminution of human rights will be examined in Chapter 3, section III.

The second difficulty in translating human rights from international human rights law into employment disputes is that, in the latter setting, both sides have rights. Inserting the mode of analysis used to check whether a state has disproportionately infringed the rights of an individual in its pursuit of the communal interest straight into an examination of an employment dispute creates a risk that the employer's rights will be overlooked. The state is not a rights holder and it should only act in the general interest of society when it restricts the rights of individuals. In contrast, the employer has a variety of contractual and statutory rights that are protected by private law.[112] The right to property and the right to protect one's reputation can be called to the employer's aid in a variety of situations when justifying an infringement with an individual's fundamental right. In some human rights frameworks, such as the EU Charter of Fundamental Rights, an employer could also rely on their freedom to conduct a business.[113] The move from the vertical scenario, where only one party holds rights, to the horizontal setting must be sensitive to the need to reconcile two sets of rights.[114]

[110] Guy Mundlak, 'Human Rights and the Employment Relationship: A Look Through the Prism of Juridification' in Daniel Friedmann and Daphne Barak-Erez (eds), *Human Rights in Private Law* (Hart Publishing 2002) 323.

[111] See Collins and Mantouvalou (n 6) 200–02.

[112] Whether a corporation can have 'human rights' could be questioned on theoretical grounds: see Anat Scolnicov, 'Lifelike and Lifeless in Law: Do Corporations Have Human Rights?' (2013) University of Cambridge Legal Studies Research Paper Series, Paper No 13/2013 <http://ssrn.com/abstract=2268537> accessed 16 November 2020.

[113] CFREU, Article 16.

[114] See Collins, 'On the Incompatibility of Human Rights Discourse and Private Law' (n 8) 50.

An observer of labour law, particularly one that is sceptical of an employer's motives, cannot leave the point there. There is another risk in human rights analyses making the jump from public to private. The risk is the opposite one: that employers will be given *too much* leeway in the protection of their fundamental rights in a manner that is deeply detrimental to the standard of protection available to individual workers. We must be careful to distinguish between two types of claims. The first type of claim is that an employer's rights are genuinely under threat or have been infringed, for example, where an employee makes public accusations to harm the reputation of the employer without evidence or justification. Another example of this type of case is *Köpke v Germany*,[115] in which the employer introduced video surveillance to gather proof that an employee had committed theft of company property. In these kinds of situations, the employer has a legitimate reason to interfere with an employee's rights, providing the infringement goes no further than was necessary in order to protect the employer's property and so forth.

In some situations, however, the claim to property rights or reputation management may be decoded as an appeal to run a business in the most profitable way. Through this route, considerations of 'economic efficiency' re-enter the discussion and threaten to limit the effectiveness of any duty on employers. This must be strongly resisted. As argued firmly by Manfred Weiss, '[f]undamental values expressed by fundamental rights cannot be pushed aside by business interests or economic considerations'.[116] This view is shared by other commentators[117] and is supported by the analyses of John Rawls that 'justice requires that liberty may only be limited for the sake of liberty and *not for the sake of other social and economic advantages*'.[118] In applying human rights standards in labour law, we must be alert to the risk that the rights of workers might be compromised on account of considerations of economic or managerial efficiency. A commercial agenda is not of sufficient importance to justify an infringement on fundamental rights, even if the arguments are delivered through the medium of the right to enjoyment of property or the right to protect the reputation of an enterprise. The ECtHR could be criticized in failing to be attentive to this risk in some cases, depending heavily on the

[115] (2011) 53 EHRR SE26.

[116] Manfred Weiss, 'Re-Inventing Labour Law?' in Brian Langille and Guy Davidov (eds), *The Idea of Labour Law* (Oxford University Press 2011) 50.

[117] Mantouvalou, 'Are Labour Rights Human Rights?' (n 14) 171; Spector (n 67) 1146; Judy Fudge, 'The New Discourse of Labor Rights: From Social to Fundamental Rights' (2007) 29 Comparative Labour Law and Policy Journal 29, 39; Sandra Fredman, 'Equality Law: Labour Law or an Autonomous Field?' in Alan Bogg, Cathryn Costello, ACL Davies, and Jeremias Prassl (eds), *The Autonomy of Labour Law* (Hart Publishing 2015) 273.

[118] HLA Hart, 'Rawls on Liberty and Its Priority' (1973) 40 University of Chicago Law Review 534, 534 emphasis added.

necessity and proportionality assessments rather than analysing the legitimate aim relied on by the member state closely.[119]

Conclusion

The protection of workers' human rights is an important objective of labour law and there are many benefits to the integration of a human rights perspective within the analysis and theorization of labour law. In addition, although we must be cautious in conceptualizing labour law founded upon human rights alone, effective protection for human rights undoubtedly contributes to the achievement of a number of the broader values and aims of the discipline. In this chapter, it has been made clear, however, that the ideas and concepts used within the human rights discourse must not be transplanted uncritically into employment disputes. The peculiarities of the employment relationship mean that the concepts and approach towards the application of human rights standards must be adjusted to take into account its contractual and horizontal nature. In Chapter 3, the manner in which the European Convention has evolved to counteract the threat to human rights posed by non-state actors will be investigated and the expectations held by the ECtHR of a national labour law system, iterated through its doctrine of positive obligations, will be explored.

[119] See further Chapter 3, section II; Filip Dorssemont, 'The European Convention on Human Rights as a Fountain of Labour Rights' in Janice R Bellace and Beryl ter Haar (eds), *Research Handbook on Labour, Business and Human Rights Law* (Edward Elgar Publishing 2019) 331.

3

Labour Law, the European Convention on Human Rights, and the States' Positive Obligations

In order to assess whether the domestic system of protection of rights at work is adequate, we must understand the standards established under the European Convention on Human Rights (ECHR or the Convention) by the European Court of Human Rights (ECtHR or the Court). The aim of this chapter is to consider in detail the case law of the ECtHR and to translate it into a framework for analysis which may be applied to any national system of labour law. The focus here, and throughout the remaining chapters, is upon the qualified rights contained in Articles 8–11.[1] I highlight three obligations upon member states that are relevant to the design and application of labour laws:

(a) the obligation to extend any domestic right that enforces a fundamental right to all people, unless a restriction is justified under the Convention;
(b) the obligation to examine an interference with a Convention right seriously and to assess whether it is justified in a manner that aligns with the ECtHR's own case law; and
(c) the obligation to offer an effective remedy where a Convention right has been violated.

In order to derive a framework that can be applied to the rights of all workers across the private and public sectors, this chapters focuses on the positive obligations of member states. When an individual works for the state, they may bring a complaint before the ECtHR against that state as their employer.[2] Where an individual's complaint relates to their treatment by a non-state actor, such as a private employer, the ECtHR applies the doctrine of positive obligations. Positive obligations were developed by the Court to render the Convention rights practical and effective,[3] moving

[1] Some aspects of the framework set out here may be applicable to other Convention rights that are relevant to workplace disputes such as Article 4 (the prohibition on forced labour), Article 6 (the right to a fair trial) and Article 14 (prohibition of discrimination in the enjoyment of the Convention rights).

[2] See, for example, *Vogt v Germany* (1996) 21 EHRR 205; *Guja v Moldova* (2011) 53 EHRR 16.

[3] Dean Spielmann, 'The European Convention on Human Rights: The European Court of Human Rights' in Dawn Oliver and Jörg Fedtke (eds), *Human Rights and the Private Sphere: A Comparative Study* (Routledge-Cavendish 2007) 428.

Putting Human Rights to Work. Philippa Collins, Oxford University Press. © Philippa Collins 2022.
DOI: 10.1093/oso/9780192894595.003.0004

beyond the negative prohibitions on member states interfering with those rights. The Council of Europe member states are under an obligation to protect individuals from infringements on their rights by all parties, including private actors, and to establish a legal framework that effectively guarantees those rights and provides appropriate review and remedies where they are infringed upon. Laurens Lavrysen terms these obligations 'horizontal positive obligations', as they are focused on the state regulation of a private law relationship such as employment.[4] These obligations are essential to ensuring that individuals at work enjoy full and effective protection of their human rights in their relationship with an influential actor in their life: their employer.

While it is the member state that is bound by the obligation to take positive steps to protect human rights, where the duty to discharge the obligation falls in a particular situation depends upon the context of the dispute and the legal structures in place in the relevant jurisdiction. In some situations, an amendment to a statutory provision may be necessary to comply with the state's positive obligations.[5] The doctrine of positive obligations has also been applied to review decisions of national courts where the complainant alleges that the outcome infringes upon their Convention rights.[6] In these cases, an adjustment in the practice of national courts may be required in order to fulfil the state's obligations in the future. In relation to the qualified rights discussed herein, the 'fair balance' test is central to the Court's decision regarding whether the state's positive obligation has been fulfilled in a particular case.[7] Failure to strike a 'fair balance ... between the competing interests of the individual and of the community as a whole' will result in a finding that the state has failed to discharge its positive obligations to protect the complainant's Convention rights adequately.[8]

Three key positive obligations can be derived from the Court's case law. They are relevant to how labour rights should be designed, as well as how national courts should examine cases where fundamental rights have been invoked. Section

[4] Laurens Lavrysen, *Human Rights in a Positive State: Rethinking the Relationship between Positive and Negative Obligations under the European Convention on Human Rights* (Intersentia 2017) 89.

[5] See, for example, *Redfearn v United Kingdom* (2013) 57 EHRR 2; *Wilson and others v United Kingdom* (2002) 35 EHRR 20; which were followed by legislative amendments in the Enterprise and Regulatory Reform Act 2013, section 13 and the Employment Relations Act 2004, section 29, respectively.

[6] For a recent example, see *Herbai v Hungary* (2020) 70 EHRR 35.

[7] Janneke Gerards, *General Principles of the European Convention on Human Rights* (Cambridge University Press 2019) 110–11. The Court may also have regard to 'the diversity of situations obtaining in Contracting States and the choices which must be made in terms of priorities and resources' as well as seeking to ensure that the obligation imposed upon a state is not disproportionate: see *Ilaşcu v Moldova and Russia* (2005) 40 EHRR 46, [332].

[8] See *Sánchez v Spain* (2012) 54 EHRR 24, [62]. For the invocation of the concept of a 'fair balance' within the positive obligation cases relating to the workplace, see, for example, *Köpke v Germany* (2011) 53 EHRR SE26, [51]; *Redfearn v UK* (n 5) [47]; *Eweida and others v United Kingdom* (2013) 57 EHRR 8, [94] and [109]; *Bărbulescu v Romania* Application no 61496/08 (ECtHR, 5 September 2017) [141]; *Herbai v Hungary* (n 6) [51].

I recounts the obligation to extend rights widely, to ensure that all individuals have access to the opportunity to raise a human rights issue before a tribunal and to receive a ruling that balances their rights against the arguments raised by their employer. The breadth of this entitlement can be seen in the range of vocations, employment, and occupational statuses of the individuals who have litigated in Strasbourg. In sections II and III, the state's obligation to provide a forum in which the rights and interests are balanced against each other in accordance with the ECtHR's principles of necessity and proportionality will be explored. The ways in which the consideration of human rights is shaped by the context of the employment relationship, such as its contractual nature, are also noted here. The final obligation, discussed in section IV, is to offer an effective remedy to an individual who has been held to have suffered an infringement of their Convention rights. Although this obligation is less developed and precise than the other obligations discussed, it is nevertheless an important element of the framework for the protection of fundamental rights in the employment context.

I. *Human* Rights: The Protective Scope of the Convention

Everyone is entitled to the rights contained in the European Convention. According to Article 1 of the ECHR, '[t]he High Contracting Parties shall secure to *everyone* within their jurisdiction the rights and freedoms defined in Section I of this Convention'.[9] This guarantee is mirrored in the other articles, which commence 'Everyone has the right to ...' or 'No one shall be ...'. The fact that everyone enjoys the Convention's protection equally and without distinction is reinforced by Article 14's prohibition on discrimination between persons in the enjoyment of ECHR rights and freedoms.[10] The Convention's broad scope of application gives rise to the first positive obligation upon member states: to offer safeguards and adjudicative consideration to the human rights of all individuals within their jurisdiction.

The core of this obligation is ensuring that, where national labour rights provide an opportunity to challenge a human rights infringement, those rights and their remedies must be widely available. The Court has demonstrated this inclusivity by hearing employment-centred complaints raised by a diverse range of applicants. It shows no regard for the employment status of the individual, nor the legal form of the relationship between the individual and the actor who interferes with their rights. The ECtHR has examined a complex joint hiring process of a state school's teacher of religion which required the recommendation of a third party (the Church),[11] the dismissal from office of a judge,[12] and the dismissal of

[9] ECHR, Article 1 emphasis added.
[10] ibid, Article 14.
[11] *Martínez v Spain* (2015) 60 EHRR 3.
[12] *Kudeshkina v Russia* (2011) 52 EHRR 37.

a whistleblowing civil servant,[13] as well as the complaints of a bus driver,[14] a domestic worker,[15] a member of the military,[16] and a cabaret hostess.[17] An applicant is entitled to exercise and vindicate their Convention rights before Strasbourg irrespective of their migration status,[18] whether their work was lawful under the state's immigration rules, and even if their activities were criminal in nature. The ECtHR, for example, has considered the infringement of the fundamental rights of an individual who had committed fraud in applying for a job with a fake passport.[19] These cases show that 'the only condition for being entitled to human rights is the status of being human'[20]—contractual details, the rules of national regulatory systems, migration status, and illegality are irrelevant to the ECtHR.

In Chapter 2, it was observed that one of the purposes of employment and labour law systems is to offer protection for the human rights of workers against infringement by their employer. Where a domestic labour right provides safeguards to a human right, the positive obligation to protect *everyone* from violations of their Convention rights obliges national legislators and adjudicators to ensure that the labour right is widely available and that its scope is interpreted in a manner that coheres with the inclusivity of human rights protection. The force of this positive obligation was shown clearly in *Redfearn v United Kingdom*. Mr Redfearn was dismissed by his employer, a private company providing transport services, after being elected to the local council as a representative of the right-wing British National Party (BNP). Although Mr Redfearn sought to challenge his dismissal in the Employment Tribunal (ET), he was prevented from using the most appropriate mechanism—unfair dismissal law—by the operation of the qualifying period of continuous employment.[21] At the relevant time, the qualifying period was one year in length, but Mr Redfearn had been employed some seven months. He was therefore left without a credible domestic cause of action and went on to present a complaint under Articles 10 and 11 before the ECtHR.[22] Mr Redfearn's arguments focused on the UK's failure to comply with its positive obligations, particularly the obligation 'to enact legislation which would have afforded him protection from the termination of his employment by Serco on the ground of his involvement with the BNP'.[23]

13 *Guja v Moldova* (n 2).
14 *Redfearn v UK* (n 5).
15 *Siliadin v France* (2006) 43 EHRR 16.
16 *Markin v Russia* (2013) 56 EHRR 8.
17 *Rantsev v Cyprus and Russia* (2010) 51 EHRR 1.
18 *Siliadin v France* (n 15).
19 See *Paulet v United Kingdom* (2015) 61 EHRR 39.
20 Hugh Collins and Virginia Mantouvalou, 'Human Rights and the Contract of Employment' in Mark Freedland (ed), *The Contract of Employment* (Oxford University Press 2016) 198.
21 See *Redfearn v Serco Ltd* [2006] EWCA Civ 659, [2006] ICR 1367, [9]–[13].
22 Mr Redfearn's complaint also included Articles 13 (the right to an effective remedy) and 14 (non-discrimination) but the ECtHR found that its consideration of his Article 11 complaint adequately addressed the matter: see *Redfearn v UK* (n 5) [62] and [66].
23 ibid [33].

The UK's positive obligation to provide safeguards that were generally available, and not contingent upon a period of service, were at the heart of the case. Having found that the dismissal infringed upon Mr Redfearn's Article 11 rights, the Court considered whether the UK had taken 'reasonable and appropriate measures' to protect his rights, in light of the detriment caused to Mr Redfearn by the qualifying period.[24] The UK put forward a justification for the existence of the qualifying period, namely, to allow employers time to assess the suitability of employees free of a concern regarding potential interference by the ETs. Nonetheless, the ECtHR held that the UK legislation was 'deficient': the UK was under an obligation to protect *all* employees from dismissal on political grounds, including those with a short period of service.

In its decision in *Redfearn*, the Court stated that 'what is decisive in such cases is that the domestic courts or tribunals be allowed to pronounce on whether, in the circumstances of a particular case, the interests of the employer should prevail over the art.11 rights asserted by the employee'.[25] The decision is an excellent demonstration of the operation of the positive obligation to ensure that any individual is able to raise a human rights complaint within their national system and that the domestic courts have the opportunity to engage in a balancing of the competing interests at stake in the particular case. *Redfearn* emphasizes that any restriction on the ability of an individual to have their case heard will be subject to detailed consideration of its necessity in light of legitimate aim relied upon by the member state.

II. The Qualified Rights: From Interference to Necessity

The second positive obligation that can be identified from the Strasbourg case law primarily falls on the national courts and tribunals that hear and decide upon cases. There is an obligation to consider the individual's arguments regarding the infringement of a Convention right seriously and, where a qualified right is engaged upon the facts, to examine whether the infringement was justified in the circumstances of that case. This assessment may be framed in accordance with the national constitution, for example, but national courts must 'take due account of the standards for review developed in the Court's case law'.[26] It is important for national courts to give regard to the proper scope of the Convention rights, as indicated by the ECtHR's jurisprudence, as well as consider a range of factors that have emerged from the Court's case law regarding the necessity of any restriction upon

[24] ibid [52].
[25] ibid [56].
[26] Janneke Gerards, 'Procedural Review by the ECtHR: A Typology' in Janneke Gerards and Eva Brems (eds), *Procedural Review in European Fundamental Rights Cases* (Cambridge University Press 2017) 138.

that right. Further, the surrounding legal framework must allow for that consideration.[27] Here, I will divide the discussion into the two prongs of analysis that are familiar in cases that involved qualified rights: interference and justification.

A. The Examination of the Interference

The first requirement is that the tribunal must have the opportunity to engage with the substance of the interference, and actually do so. The national tribunal, in cases related to employment disputes, must consider the human rights dimensions of both the process leading to a dismissal or disciplinary action, for example, where the investigation of misconduct infringes on the individual's right to privacy,[28] and the reason underlying the employer's decision itself. *Redfearn* is an example of the latter category of case and the inability of the UK courts to engage with the infringement upon Mr Redfearn's freedom of association was key to the finding that the UK had failed to fulfil its positive obligations in that situation.

Similarly, in *Herbai v Hungary*, the Court was critical that a dispute between a senior employee and his employing bank had been determined 'purely by contractual considerations' in the national tribunals.[29] The applicant had been dismissed after contributing to a website that shared good practice and information about human resources management. Mr Herbai had raised freedom of expression arguments in the domestic litigation, but the national courts focused wholly on the contractual issues between the parties. Consequently, the ECtHR considered that Mr Herbai's rights-based arguments were rendered ineffective and not given due consideration at the national level.[30] Therefore, the ECtHR concluded, the member state had failed to secure Mr Herbai's right to freedom of expression in the course of the litigation and had failed in its positive obligations under the Convention.

Where we see a deficiency in a member state's compliance with this obligation, one common cause is divergence in the perception of the scope of the relevant right. The judiciary of a particular member state may have a more conservative view on the applicability of a Convention right, leading to the conclusion that it is not engaged on the facts and does not need to be considered. In *Herbai v Hungary*, for example, the Constitutional Court relied upon its own prior practice in settling the scope of freedom of expression, asking whether the opinions expressed by the complainant had 'public characteristics' or were linked to matters of public

[27] See *Ognevenko v Russia* Application no 44873/09 (ECtHR, 20 November 2018) [82]; *Redfearn v UK* (n 5) [56].

[28] See *Bărbulescu v Romania* (n 8) [122] on the express requirement that an employee who has been monitored must have access to a remedy before a judicial body able to decide whether the surveillance was lawful.

[29] *Herbai v Hungary* (n 6) [50].

[30] ibid [50].

interest.[31] This approach led to the conclusion that the articles published were professional in nature, rather than related to issues of public interest, and that those circumstances disclosed no connection to a fundamental right. The ECtHR disagreed with the national Constitutional Court, holding that 'workplace-related free speech does not only protect comments that demonstrably contribute to a debate on a public matter'.[32] Thus, the Strasbourg Court found that the national courts *had* been under an obligation to engage with Mr Herbai's right to freedom of expression which it had failed to fulfil.

Evidence of other discrepancies between local and European interpretations of a right can be found elsewhere. In *Pay v United Kingdom*, in relation to whether one's right to private life could be engaged by performances in a public space, the UK tribunal's view of Article 8 was narrower than the one adopted by the ECtHR.[33] In *Antović and Mirković v Montenegro*, the ECtHR disagreed with the national courts' view that the taking and storage of video recordings of University lecturers in amphitheatres did not invoke a right to privacy.[34] These cases demonstrate that it is essential that the national courts take into account the proper scope of the relevant right, as defined by ECtHR jurisprudence. The consequence of a divergence of views at this stage is often that the individual's Convention right receives no substantial examination by the national courts and particularly on the point of whether the infringement was justified. A finding that the state had breached its obligation to provide that right with effective protection is in turn rendered more likely.

Because of the centrality of this aspect of the state's positive obligation to provide effective enforcement of human rights at the domestic level, it might be expected that the Strasbourg Court demand that national adjudicators should introduce human rights issues of their own motion. Such a stipulation from the ECtHR could have a significant effect upon the utilization of rights in daily legal practice. Elsewhere, the requirement that courts introduce considerations not argued before them is one element of the EU's regulation of unfair consumer terms. This element of the regime was initiated by the European Court of Justice and justified on the basis that it would ensure the effectiveness of EU consumer protection.[35] Such a requirement could have a particular impact in employment disputes, where the individual may not have the benefit of legal expertise in preparing their case[36]

[31] ibid [19].

[32] ibid [43].

[33] Contrast *Pay v United Kingdom* (2009) 48 EHRR SE2, 24–25 with *Pay v Lancashire Probation Service* [2004] ICR 187, [36]–[37].

[34] Contrast the national court's reasoning found at [14] and [16] with that of the ECtHR at [44] in *Antović and Mirković v Montenegro* Application no 70838/13 (ECtHR, 28 November 2017).

[35] See Joined cases C-430/93 and C-431/93 *van Schijndel and van Veen v Stichting Pensioenfonds voor Fysiotherapeuten* [1995] ECR I-4705; Joined cases C-240/98 to C-244/98 *Océano Grupo Editorial SA v Roció Murciano* [2000] ECR I-4941.

[36] In 2018/2019, 21 per cent of claimants before the ETs in England and Wales had no legal representation recorded: see Ministry of Justice, *Tribunal Statistics Quarterly: April to June 2019* (12 September 2019).

and therefore may not realize the potential of the human rights arguments in their favour.

Despite the potential efficacy of this option, an obligation upon national courts to introduce Convention rights of their own motion into cases has not been embraced by the ECtHR. In *Sadik v Greece*, one issue before the Court was whether the complainant had exhausted their domestic remedies before launching their suit in Strasbourg. The majority of the Court held that the complainant should have raised the human rights arguments that he later submitted before the ECtHR before the national courts.[37] This remained the case '[e]ven if the Greek courts were able, or even obliged, to examine the case of their own motion under the Convention'.[38] We can see that, despite the clear positive obligation upon domestic tribunals to consider an individual's argument that their human right has been infringed upon, the Convention has not been interpreted to demand that adjudicators raise rights-based issues of their own motion to ensure effective protection of those rights.

B. The Justification Process

The second element of this positive obligation is to scrutinize, in line with the Convention text and jurisprudence, whether an interference with the fundamental right was justified. In disputes in the employment context where the relevant rights are often the qualified rights in Articles 8–11, this stage is particularly important. Once the Court establishes that a dismissal invokes an infringement of an ECHR right, the member state must satisfy the Court of three main elements of justification:

1. That the interference was 'prescribed by law'. In most cases, the interference is in accordance with the terms of the domestic labour code, although it may be authorized by a consistent line of authority from the courts regarding the particular type of conduct.[39]
2. That the interference pursued a 'legitimate aim' as listed by the Convention. In employment cases that arise in the private sector, often the 'protection of the rights and freedoms of others' will be relied upon. This may include the protection of the rights of the business' customers or the employer's own interest in running their business including engaging in monitoring of their workforce or their public reputation.[40]

37 *Sadik v Greece* (1997) 24 EHRR 323, [33].
38 ibid.
39 *Köpke v Germany* (n 8) [44].
40 See respectively Ms Ladele's case and Ms Eweida's case in *Eweida v UK* (n 8); *Bărbulescu v Romania* (n 8) [127]; *Heinisch v Germany* (2014) 58 EHRR 31, [49].

3. That the interference was 'necessary in a democratic society'. This final stage will be elaborated on later.

In employment cases, the member state may be involved as the employer—in which case the standard of scrutiny is more searching[41]—or the adjudicator of the dispute, in the case of private sector litigation where the doctrine of positive obligations is invoked. In the latter case, the national courts are not expected to frame the justification process in precisely the same terms as used under the ECHR. Nevertheless, a domestic tribunal that strays too far from the considerations that the ECtHR would deem to be relevant in a justification analysis may find itself to be at the centre of a finding of a violation of the Convention. A 'fair balance' between the rights of the individual and the countervailing interests of others would not have been struck, leading to the conclusion that the member state has failed to fulfil its positive obligation towards the complainant.

What questions should a domestic court ask in order to ensure that the infringement was 'necessary' in Convention terms? Here, the ECtHR's considerations are far from consistent across the case law, but a set of relevant factors can nevertheless be discerned. The infringing measure should answer a 'pressing social need' identified in that member state[42] and the reasons presented to the court must be 'relevant and sufficient' to justify an infringement upon a fundamental right.[43] Further, a sense of proportionality is embedded into the Court's analysis: a serious infringement upon the individual's right must be met with a very weighty justification and sufficient supporting evidence.[44]

In examining whether the dismissal was proportionate, the ECtHR has repeatedly expressed the view that dismissal is a serious or severe sanction.[45] The Court takes into account, in its assessment, the consequences of the dismissal for the individual complainant. These consequences might include the difficulty of finding another job, whether by reason of a specialist vocation[46] or because of the claimant's particular circumstances,[47] in addition to the impact on an individual's private life and reputation that may be concurrent with a dismissal.[48] In cases of freedom of

[41] See Lavrysen's discussion of the use of qualifying terms in the positive obligations case law in Lavrysen (n 4) 158 onwards.

[42] See *Vogt v Germany* (n 2) [52]; *Fuentes Bobo v Spain* (2001) 31 EHRR 50, [44].

[43] *Fuentes Bobo v Spain* (n 42) [44].

[44] *Smith and Grady v United Kingdom* (2000) 29 EHRR 493, [94].

[45] See, for example, *Fuentes Bobo v Spain* (n 42) [49]; *Eweida v UK* (n 8) [109]; *Herbai v Hungary* (n 6) [49].

[46] *Vogt v Germany* (n 2) [60]; *Schüth v Germany* (2011) 52 EHRR 32, [73]; *Martínez v Spain* (n 11) [113].

[47] *Smith and Grady v United Kingdom* (n 44) [92]; *Schüth v Germany* (n 46) [73].

[48] ibid [67]; *Martínez v Spain* (n 11) [145]. If the consequences of a dismissal for an individual's private life are sufficiently serious, such consequences may be sufficient to engage Article 8 ECHR without more: see *Denisov v Ukraine* Application no 76639/11 (ECtHR, 25 September 2018) [107]–[109], discussed further in Chapter 2, section II(B).

expression, the chilling effect of the dismissal on the exercise of rights by others in the workplace is considered by the ECtHR and reinforces the seriousness of the interference with the Convention right.[49] These consequences of the dismissal should be taken into account and weighed against the countervailing legitimate aim put forward by the employer.

Finally, the Court may assess whether the cited aim could have been achieved by less restrictive means. References to the 'less restrictive means' question appear to be growing in prominence in the ECtHR's decisions, although 'such references are not systematic in any line of case law to date'.[50] When considering whether a national tribunal has reached a fair balance between the rights and interests at stake in the case, the existence of a clear alternative to dismissal may be taken into account by the Strasbourg Court. We see this factor considered in *Fuentes Bobo v Spain* and *Redfearn v UK*,[51] for example. The presence of the 'less restrictive means' question in the Court's reasoning arguably translates to an expectation that national adjudications should consider a comparable question: could the employer have selected an alternative route which would have had a lesser impact on the individual's human rights?[52] This consideration can be particularly important in an employment law case, where dismissal is the most serious sanction available and the employer has an array of other disciplinary measures that are less drastic that they might have employed.

We can see that the ECtHR requires a national court to engage in a substantive review of the decision to dismiss. What was the employer seeking to achieve? Was the measure necessary and proportionate to that objective? In addition to the issue of *why* an individual was dismissed, scrutiny of *how* the decision to dismiss was reached may be necessary. Tribunals must seek evidence from the employer that satisfies them that the dismissal pursued a legitimate aim, for example. Particularly in cases of alleged misconduct, an employer must conduct an investigation in order to establish the grounds for a dismissal.[53] In *Pişkin v Turkey*, the ECtHR stated a general principle that 'the Court must examine whether the decision-making process leading to measures of interference was fair and such as to afford due respect to the interests safeguarded to the individual by Article 8'.[54] In this case, the complainant had been dismissed pursuant to emergency legislation regarding those with connections to terrorist organizations. No evidence was

[49] *Heinisch v Germany* (n 40) [91].

[50] Eva Brems and Laurens Lavrysen, '"Don't Use a Sledgehammer to Crack a Nut": Less Restrictive Means in the Case Law of the European Court of Human Rights' (2015) 15 HRLR 139, 166.

[51] *Fuentes Bobo v Spain* (n 42) [49]; *Redfearn v UK* (n 5) [45].

[52] See Hugh Collins and Virginia Mantouvalou, 'Redfearn v UK: Political Association and Dismissal' (2013) 76 MLR 909, 919–21; Philippa Collins, 'Square Peg vs a Round Hole? The Necessity of a Bill of Rights for Workers' (2020) 11 European Labour Law Journal 199, 206–07.

[53] See *Özpınar v Turkey* Application no 20999/04 (ECtHR, 19 October 2010); *Vogt v Germany* (n 2) [60].

[54] *Pişkin v Turkey* Application no 33399/18 (ECtHR, 15 December 2020) [214].

presented to the ECtHR or, it seemed, to the domestic courts regarding why Mr Pişkin had been assessed as falling into this category.[55] The Court concluded that the national judicial review of his dismissal was 'inadequate' and the applicant's Article 8 rights had been breached.[56] The need for a dismissal to be supported by evidence, obtained through appropriate investigations, and to follow from a fair process of decision-making[57] are articulated most clearly in cases regarding the state as an employer. Elsewhere, however, the ECtHR has also imposed a positive obligation upon member states to ensure that Article 8 rights are adequately safeguarded where employers engage in surveillance or monitoring of their staff.[58]

Although the aforementioned factors demonstrate that the ECtHR is sensitive to the peculiarities of the employment context, there remains one area where the Court's approach is variable and has resulted in some criticism of its practice.[59] The question of whether a legitimate aim applies to a particular case could be an opportunity for the Court to scrutinize and test the objective that the employer considers so imperative that it could outweigh the fundamental right of their employee. Instead, the Court can be quick to accept the existence of a pressing social need which could justify the complainant's dismissal. This problem seems to arise where the employer seeks to justify the dismissal on grounds of self-protection, instances where labour law scholars would be most sceptical of the legitimate aim.[60] Examples of the legitimate aims cited but inadequately analysed by the Court include a risk of damage to the employer's business interests and a risk to the employer's own reputation or the reputation of a senior member of staff.[61] On some occasions, the state has not been expected to provide evidence that the risk to the employer was substantial or genuine. This lax approach creates a possibility that the individual's right will be restricted on grounds that have not been seriously investigated by the Court and it relies heavily on the necessity and proportionality assessment to perform the bulk of the analytical work.

It may be that this trend of straightforward acceptance of an employer's reliance on a risk to their own rights and interests is shifting, however. In several cases regarding dismissals from employment in a religious organization, the Court directed national courts to consider the reality of the threat to the Church's religious autonomy in the circumstances. Did the continued employment of the individual pose a 'probable and substantial' threat to the organization's autonomy

[55] ibid [183] and [226].

[56] ibid [228]–[229].

[57] For a discussion of the role of procedural review in the ECtHR's case law more generally, see Gerards, 'Procedural Review by the ECtHR: A Typology' (n 26).

[58] See *López Ribalda v Spain* (2020) 71 EHRR 7, [114].

[59] See, for example, ACL Davies, 'Judicial Self-restraint in Labour Law' (2009) 38 ILJ 278, 299–300.

[60] See Chapter 2, section IV(C).

[61] See, for example, *Pay v UK* (n 33) 25 and *Sánchez v Spain* (n 8) [64]–[68].

in the selection of its personnel?[62] Moving in a similar direction of probing the employer's claim to a legitimate purpose is *Herbai v Hungary*.[63] The employer claimed that Mr Herbai's online publications could adversely affect its business interests, but the national appeal court sought no evidence to substantiate the claim. The ECtHR criticized the court and the employer for the failure to prove this claim,[64] and ultimately held that Mr Herbai's right to freedom of expression had been breached. These more recent cases show an emerging willingness to scrutinize the strength of an employer's justification and to ensure that there is evidence of the existence of a real threat to the employer's interests. This engagement goes some way to counteract the breadth of interests that have been accepted as legitimate under the wide banner of 'the protection of the rights and freedoms of others'.

III. The Convention in the Context of Work

In order to understand the role of positive obligations in the labour law context, we must consider the relationship between contracts, their terms, and the exercise of fundamental rights. In most jurisdictions, the core of an employment relationship is a contract. The existence and terms of the contract could be used to negate or shape the exercise of rights by the individual who has signed the arrangement. How much weight does the ECtHR give to that signature? Olivier de Schutter observes that the Court has 'generally adopted the view that, while the consent of the individual may be *necessary* to justify certain restrictions on his rights, such a consent, as expressed in contractual clauses, should never be considered, as such, a *sufficient* justification'.[65] Further, incidents of the contract or the work itself, such as duties of loyalty or adherence to specified behavioural standards, are examined carefully where they restrict or impact upon the individual's exercise of their Convention rights. The ECtHR has even gone as far as requiring national courts to interpret private law documents compatibly with the Convention, an obligation which could have significant impact upon labour relations if applied widely. These broader issues will be investigated after a brief discussion of the ECtHR's approach to waiving one's Convention rights in the employment setting.

[62] *Martínez v Spain* (n 11) [132]. We see similar issues arise in other cases involving religious employment such as: *Travaš v Croatia* Application no 75581/13 (ECtHR, 4 October 2016) [102]; *Schüth v Germany* (n 46) [60].
[63] *Herbai v Hungary* (n 6).
[64] ibid [48].
[65] Olivier de Schutter, 'Human Rights in Employment Relationships: Contracts as Power' in Filip Dorssemont, Klaus Lörcher, and Isabelle Schömann (eds), *The European Convention on Human Rights and the Employment Relation* (Hart Publishing 2013) 138.

A. Waiver and Exit from Employment: Mitigating an Infringement?

We must investigate two arguments that could shape an employee's capacity to rely upon their Convention rights in an employment context dramatically. If either argument were to be successful, it would relieve national tribunals of their obligation to examine a potential infringement upon an individual's Convention right. The first argument is that the employee has waived their Convention right by signing a contract which contains terms that conflict with or contradict that right. An alternative argument could be that there is no infringement upon the relevant right because the individual could easily exercise their rights if they resign from their job and find an alternative role more compatible with their choices. The ECtHR has now rejected the second argument in the context of work and claims regarding waivers of rights are thoroughly investigated, as explained below. It therefore seems that the positive obligations outlined earlier will take effect in most cases.

The issue of waiving a Convention right appears with most regularity within the context of Article 6, more specifically the question of whether a criminal defendant has waived their right to claim an aspect of their fair trial rights.[66] In disputes regarding the employment context, the argument is raised rarely and often unsuccessfully.[67] Understandably, the Court has created a high threshold before it will agree that a right has been waived. In *DH and others v Czech Republic*,[68] the applicants challenged the authorities' method of testing the learning needs of school children, which resulted in a disproportionate number of Roma children being placed in an alternative stream of education. These children were provided with a reduced curriculum and there was little chance that they would join the mainstream system in the future. One of the government's arguments was that the Roma parents had consented to their child's placement in a special school. The Court reiterated its principles:

> In view of the fact that a difference in treatment has been established in the instant case, it follows that any such consent would signify ... a waiver of the right not to be discriminated against. However, under the Court's case law, the waiver of a right guaranteed by the Convention—in so far as such a waiver is permissible—must be *established in an unequivocal manner*, and be given *in full knowledge of the facts*, that is to say on the *basis of informed consent* and *without constraint*.[69]

[66] See, for example, *Jones v United Kingdom* (2003) 37 EHRR CD269; *Pfeifer v Austria* (1992) 14 EHRR 692, [37]–[38].

[67] For example, in two employment cases, *Smith and Grady v United Kingdom* (n 44) and *Martínez v Spain* (n 11), the government might have argued that the applicants had waived aspects of their fundamental rights by signing a contract of employment. Waiver arguments were absent in both.

[68] (2008) 47 EHRR 3.

[69] ibid [202] emphasis added.

The Court expressed concern that informed consent had not been given by signing 'a pre-completed form that contained no information on the available alternatives', with incomplete information provided by the authorities and a lack of awareness of the consequences of their signature for their children's future.[70] On these grounds, the Court refused to accept that a waiver had taken place.

In the employment context, this reasoning would indicate that the employer would have to engage in an extensive explanation of the effects of and alternatives to signing a document before the Court would consider a waiver to be effective. Such an explanation may make the 'without constraint' criterion difficult to satisfy, particularly if the only other option open to the individual is refusing the position and possibly becoming unemployed as a result. Gillian Morris has argued that any threat of dismissal or other detriment because of a worker's refusal to waive a right would amount to constraint and a resultant waiver of a Convention right should not be considered effective.[71] If employees can be said to have 'no real choice' regarding whether or not to sign a contract,[72] the principles under the Convention would dismiss any waiver included in a contract between employer and employee. The brevity of the Court's consideration of waivers in employment cases supports this conclusion.[73]

A member state or, in a local dispute, an employer might seek to rely on the individual's voluntary acceptance of the position and the existence of alternative employment which they could resign in favour of to negate an infringement. Although this argument has not been accepted under the other qualified rights,[74] it was relied upon successfully several times in relation to the right to manifest one's religious beliefs under Article 9.[75] In *Eweida and others v UK*,[76] the ECtHR reversed its position. Relying on the treatment of the same point under Articles 8, 10, and 11, the Court held that 'the better approach' would be to consider the possibility of resignation amongst other factors in the final balancing stage.[77] Thus, this second route by which it could be argued that a Convention right should not be examined in a dispute was closed.

[70] ibid [203].

[71] Gillian Morris, 'Fundamental Rights: Exclusion by Agreement?' (2001) 30 ILJ 49, 54.

[72] Hazel Oliver, 'Email and Internet Monitoring in the Workplace: Information Privacy and Contracting-out' (2002) 31 ILJ 321, 333.

[73] See *Sindicatul Păstorul cel Bun v Romania* (2014) 58 EHRR 10, [146]; *Eweida v UK* (n 8) in *Ladele* at [106]; *McFarlane* at [109]; *Schüth v Germany* (n 46) [71]; and *Markin v Russia* (n 16) [150].

[74] *Smith and Grady v United Kingdom* (n 44) [70]–[71]; *Sørensen and Rasmussen v Denmark* (2008) 46 EHRR 29, [60]–[62].

[75] See, for example, *Ahmad v United Kingdom* (1982) 4 EHRR 126; *Konttinen v Finland* Application no 24949/94 (EComHR, 3 December 1996); *Stedman v United Kingdom* (1997) 23 EHRR CD 168.

[76] *Eweida v UK* (n 8).

[77] ibid [83].

B. The Interpretation and Enforcement of a Contract of Employment

The approach iterated in *Eweida* has also been followed in relation to other contractual terms and rules of the organization that restrict or influence the individual's exercise of their Convention rights. For example, work in particular organizations may result in the imposition of limits upon the employee's freedom of expression or right to respect for their private life. Duties of confidentiality or loyalty to a set of values and principles—such as those of a particular religious organization—can circumscribe the employee's range of action and will be considered as one part of the necessity assessment.[78] Occasionally, the Court could be criticized for erring too far in the employer's favour in this aspect of their reasoning.[79] Nevertheless, the careful examination of restrictions or influences upon an individual's ability to exercise their Convention rights derived from the contractual arrangement or institutional status of their employment is a well-established element of the balancing process. The Court's own approach is a strong indicator of the direction that practice in national courts and tribunals should take and the ECtHR has criticized national courts' reasoning where this feature has been absent.[80]

A case of note regarding the interaction between employers' rules and the Convention rights is *Bărbulescu v Romania*.[81] After earlier cases relating to communications monitoring by employers, there was a possibility that the organization's rulebook could operate to remove any 'reasonable expectations of privacy' within the workplace.[82] The employee would then face an uphill battle in demonstrating that Article 8 ECHR was infringed upon by the employer's monitoring practices. Fortunately, the ECtHR clarified its position. Mr Bărbulescu was a sales engineer who had been dismissed after the employer had monitored his communications during working time and found that he was using his computer for personal use. This use was contrary to the employer's regulations and a recent notice that was circulated around the office prohibiting personal use of computers. The government argued that Mr Bărbulescu had no reasonable expectation of privacy under Article 8, as he had failed to tell the employer that some of his messages were personal during the internal proceedings and he had been informed of the company policies and of the ongoing monitoring.[83]

The ECtHR held that an individual's reasonable expectation of privacy 'is a significant though *not necessarily conclusive* factor'[84] and ultimately found that

[78] See, for example, *Vogt v Germany* (n 2) [59]; *Martínez v Spain* (n 11) [119] and [131].

[79] See, for example, the Dissenting Opinion in *Sánchez v Spain* (n 8).

[80] See, for example, *Herbai v Hungary* (n 6) [50]; *Schüth v Germany* (n 46) [66]–[69].

[81] *Bărbulescu v Romania* (n 8).

[82] See the commentary upon *Halford v United Kingdom* (1997) 24 EHRR 523 by Morris (n 71) and Oliver (n 72).

[83] *Bărbulescu v Romania* (n 8) [65].

[84] ibid [73] emphasis added.

Mr Bărbulescu's right to private life was engaged upon the facts. Of interest for the purposes of this chapter is the ECtHR's statement that:

> [i]t is open to question whether—and if so, to what extent—the employer's restrictive regulations left the applicant with a reasonable expectation of privacy. Be that as it may, *an employer's instructions cannot reduce private social life in the workplace to zero*. Respect for private life and for the privacy of correspondence continues to exist, even if these may be restricted in so far as necessary.[85]

The statement provides further support to the claim made earlier that national courts must scrutinize an infringement upon a Convention right, even in face of an express contrary instruction by the employer in the case. *Bărbulescu* demonstrates that the interest of the ECtHR in a Convention infringement will not be affected by the argument that it was provided for in a contract of employment and legitimate by the standards of domestic law. Any restriction upon a right must be examined and demonstrated to be necessary in the pursuit of a legitimate aim.

More than simply taking into account contractual factors in the consideration of cases, the Court has gone further in requiring national courts (in rare cases) to interpret and enforce private law instruments in a manner that is compatible with the Convention. These decisions indicate that the positive obligations upon the member states stretch well into the private sphere. The challenge in *Pla and Puncernau v Andorra*[86] regarded the Andorran High Court's interpretation of a will written by an ancestor of the complainants. The court had to consider whether the phrase 'son or grandson of a lawful and canonical marriage' in the ancestor's will excluded an adopted grandson. The Andorran court held that only biological grandchildren could inherit under the will. The decision was challenged on behalf of an adopted grandson before the ECtHR. The majority of the Court found in his favour. The decision was found to be within the scope of Article 8, meaning that Article 14 could be applied to the facts on the grounds that the Andorran court's decision discriminated against adopted children.[87]

The majority of the ECtHR was critical of the Andorran court's interpretation, arguing that there was no express exclusion of adopted children in the will and therefore the national court's decision on interpretation amounted to a 'judicial deprivation of an adopted child's inheritance rights' that could not be justified under Article 14.[88] The majority stated that national courts should endeavour to make a will effective 'without overlooking the importance of interpreting the testamentary

85 ibid [81] emphasis added.
86 (2006) 42 EHRR 25.
87 ibid [55].
88 ibid [60] and [61].

disposition in the manner that most closely corresponds to domestic law and to the Convention as interpreted in the Court's case-law'.[89] This statement may appear innocuous but it has latent significance for the interpretation of legal instruments created by private parties, including the contract of employment.

The majority decision imposes an obligation upon national courts to interpret private law instruments compatibly with the Convention.[90] The case is controversial for at least two reasons. Firstly, *Pla* was a clear example of the growing 'horizontal effect' of the ECHR, as opposed to its vertical effect between individual and state that the text indicates.[91] Richard Kay observes that, following the majority decision in *Pla and Puncernau*, 'the prospects for European supervision of national law appear endless'.[92] Cherednychenko expressed concern that 'the Court clearly demonstrated its readiness to extend its control not only to the law of succession, but also the field of general contract law'.[93] The capacity of private individuals to make decisions without regard to the human rights of other individuals, and have any private law instruments that reflect those decisions enforced by a national court, appear to be placed in jeopardy by the Court in *Pla*.[94] In the case of employment relationships characterized as they are by subordination, dependence, and an imbalance of power, however, preserving the power of an employer to restrict a worker's human rights via contract is not a concern.

The second reason that the decision in *Pla* is controversial is the ambiguity regarding whether it was a case of *direct* horizontal effect or *indirect* horizontal effect. The latter is reflected in the case law on positive obligations: the obligation to respect human rights is placed on the national authorities which has an effect on the regulation of private relations.[95] The former denotes a situation where Convention rights are directly applicable in a dispute between private parties, the ultimate consequence of which would be that private actors are under a duty to respect the fundamental rights of others. Judge Garlicki, in his dissenting judgment in *Pla*, indicated that he perceived the majority's decision as going beyond indirect horizontal effect and thereby limiting the capacity of the testatrix, a private actor, to exercise her freedom to dispose of her property by reference to the Convention rights of another individual.[96] Although from the perspective of a labour lawyer more searching scrutiny of employers' decisions would be welcome, imposing obligations directly onto private actors would be novel for the Strasbourg Court.

[89] ibid [62].

[90] Spielmann (n 3) 437.

[91] See further Malu Beijer, *The Limits of Fundamental Rights Protection by the EU* (Intersentia 2017) chapter 4. The various forms of horizontal effect will also be discussed in Chapter 4, section II.

[92] Richard S Kay, 'The European Convention on Human Rights and the Control of Private Law' (2005) 5 EHRLR 466, 478.

[93] Olha Cherednychenko, 'Towards the Control of Private Acts by the European Court of Human Rights?' (2006) 13 Maastricht Journal of European & Comparative Law 195, 207.

[94] ibid.

[95] See Spielmann (n 3) 436.

[96] *Pla v Andorra* (n 86) [O-II4].

Scholars have observed that, in practice, the distinction between strong indirect horizontal effect and direct horizontal effect can be paper-thin.[97] The majority in *Pla* was at pains to emphasize that 'Only the interpretation of the testamentary disposition falls to be considered.'[98] In the subsequent case of *Mustafa and Tarzibachi v Sweden*,[99] an Article 10 complaint regarding the landlord's termination of a lease, the ECtHR emphasized that it was the national court's ruling that the lease should be terminated was at issue.[100] Even if the *Pla* and *Mustafa* cases stay on the orthodox side of the boundary between direct and indirect horizontal effect, they demonstrate that the Court's scrutiny of the practice and decisions of national courts can push Convention rights into the heart of private disputes. Not only is the national tribunal's reasoning and overall balancing open to question by the ECtHR but the interpretation of a private law document and the consequences of the court's enforcement of its terms may also be examined for compliance with the Convention. Given that the basis of most employment relationships is a contract of some kind, these decisions could hold great significance for future complaints regarding a worker's treatment by their employer.

IV. An Effective Remedy

If an infringement upon a Convention right is found not to be justified, the final positive obligation on member states is to offer a remedy to the individual. An element of the broader requirement that states should 'set up a system for [the right's] effective protection and implementation in cases of unlawful interference falling within its scope',[101] there is a clear requirement to offer an adequate remedy. This obligation may be expressed and examined as one component of the broader issue of whether a particular Convention right has been properly protected by the national authorities.[102] It is also reflected expressly in Article 13: 'Everyone whose rights and freedoms as set forth in this Convention are violated shall have an effective remedy before a national authority.'[103] Precisely what constitutes an effective package of remedies is more difficult to grasp from the Court's case law.

[97] Mattias Kumm, 'Who is Afraid of the Total Constitution? Constitutional Rights as Principles and the Constitutionalization of Private Law' (2006) 7 German Law Journal 341, 352; Hugh Collins, 'The Challenges Presented by Fundamental Rights to Private Law' in Kit Barker, Karen Fairweather, and Ross Grantham (eds), *Private Law in the 21st Century* (Hart Publishing 2017) 230; Olha Cherednychenko, 'Subordinating Contract Law to Fundamental Rights: Towards a Major Breakthrough or towards Walking in Circles?' in Stefan Grundmann (ed), *Constitutional Values and European Contract Law* (Kluwer Law International 2008) 57.

[98] *Pla v Andorra* (n 86) [57].

[99] (2011) 52 EHRR 24.

[100] ibid [34] and [36].

[101] *Kyriakides v Cyprus* Application no 39058/05 (ECtHR, 16 October 2008), [53]–[54].

[102] See, for example, *Taliadorou and Stylianou v Cyprus* Application nos 39627/05 & 39631/05 (ECtHR, 16 October 2008) [49] onwards.

[103] ECHR, Article 13.

Despite the existence of a dedicated Convention right regarding remedies, the case law on Article 13 provides limited guidance regarding precisely how national tribunals should respond to successful claimants. The Court has repeatedly expressed the importance of the principle of subsidiarity under Article 13. The ECtHR's role on remedies is seen as subsidiary to that of national authorities, resulting in a wide margin of appreciation where those authorities have taken up responsibility to offer domestic remedies.[104] The margin of appreciation is applied to the aggregate of remedies available to the individual at domestic level for the harm suffered.[105] In addition, where a breach of another article has been established, the Court may not examine the Article 13 complaint at all.[106] This practice limits the number of cases in which Article 13 is successfully invoked. The result of these principles is that Article 13 does not provide extensive detail on which precise financial remedies, for example, should be available to a victim of a rights violation.

One might turn instead to Article 41 ECHR and the Court's own capacity to 'afford just satisfaction to the injured party' if it has found a Convention violation and considers it necessary to do so. The Court's practice in offering remedial measures to the complainant could indicate what is expected of national tribunals in exercising their remedial powers.[107] The first difficulty here is that the ECtHR relies on a broad, 'equitable assessment' in offering just satisfaction to the complainant, which has made it 'difficult to extract clear criteria from the case-law' to guide remedial choices at a national level.[108] Nonetheless, we can detect some principles from the Court's practice in exercising its jurisdiction under Article 41 to give awards to complainants. The main concern of the ECtHR is to return the complainant to the position they would have been in if the interference they suffered had not occurred,[109] comparable to the tortious measure of damages in English remedial principles. A punitive motive may influence the Court's 'equitable assessment',[110] with particularly serious infringements recognized by higher awards in favour of the complainant.

In employment cases, the individual may receive a sum for pecuniary damages reflecting past and future loss of earnings[111] and an important element of most awards is compensating for non-pecuniary damage. This component ranges from €2,000 for Ms Eweida's anxiety, frustration, and distress caused by British Airways'

[104] *Scordino v Italy (No.1)* (2007) 45 EHRR 7, [188]–[189].

[105] *Klass v Germany* (1978) 2 EHRR 214, [71]–[72].

[106] See, for example, *Young, James and Webster v United Kingdom* (1981) 3 EHRR 20, [67]; *Redfearn v UK* (n 5) [61]–[63]; *Pişkin v Turkey* (n 54) [233].

[107] For a critical perspective on this question more generally, see Jason N E Varuhas, 'Damages: Private Law and the HRA—Never the Twain Shall Meet?' in David Hoffman (ed), *The Impact of the UK Human Rights Act on Private Law* (Cambridge University Press 2011).

[108] Luzius Wildhaber, 'Article 41 of the European Convention on Human Rights: Just Satisfaction under the European Convention on Human Rights' (2003) 3 Baltic Yearbook of International Law 1 6.

[109] *Smith and Grady v United Kingdom (Just Satisfaction)* (2001) 31 EHRR 24, [18].

[110] Wildhaber (n 108) 6, 12, 17.

[111] *Smith and Grady v UK (Just Satisfaction)* (n 109) [25].

uniform code[112] to £19,000 each for Ms Smith and Mr Grady in light of the 'profoundly destabilising events' of having one's private life investigated as well as the continuing emotional and psychological impact of those events.[113] Particularly in Article 8 cases, the consequences of some dismissals for an individual's private life, reputation, and 'psychological integrity' leads the Court to be particularly concerned that they receive 'moral damages' or damages that recognize the distress and pain that the events caused.

In *Taliadorou and Stylianou v Cyprus*,[114] for example, a group of police officers were dismissed after an investigation into allegations that they tortured suspects to acquire information. The decision was annulled on the basis that it had breached a number of fair trial principles and the officers applied for compensation for the unlawful administrative act. Although a lower court awarded a sum for moral damage, this decision was overturned by the Supreme Court with very little explanation of the reasoning behind their decision. The complainants alleged that the denial of these damages in such circumstances constituted an infringement of their Article 8 rights. The ECtHR examined the infringement as an element of the state's positive obligations to put in place a system that offered full and effective protection to individuals who have suffered a violation of their human rights.[115] The lack of a remedy for the moral damage suffered by the complainants combined with the limited explanation by the national court to justify that deprivation led to a finding that Article 8 had been breached.[116] The decision emphasizes the importance of granting non-pecuniary damages in cases where the dismissal had consequences for the individual's private life. The state's failure to do so prompted a finding that it had not complied with the positive obligation to offer an effective system of rights protection.

Conclusion

Absent the expansion of the ECtHR's purview into the private sphere, through the mechanism of positive obligations, the protection of an individual's human rights would be fundamentally incomplete. As observed by Filip Dorssemont:

> The Court has progressively recognized the relevance of Convention rights *at* or rather, *despite* the workplace. It has refused to consider that the workplace as a

[112] *Eweida v UK* (n 8) [114].
[113] *Smith and Grady v UK (Just Satisfaction)* (n 109) [13].
[114] *Taliadorou and Stylianou v Cyprus* (n 102).
[115] ibid [55].
[116] ibid [58].

realm of subordination could ever be a place where the exercise of human rights could evaporate or be suspended.[117]

Chapter 1 argued that the powers and privileges vested in employers and maintained through the operation of labour law pose a significant threat to the practical enjoyment of one's human rights. This risk is cemented by the imbalance in power, the dynamic of dependence and the characteristic subordination of the employment relationship. The employment context has been a site where a range of positive obligations have been developed and applied by the ECtHR, which have been set out here.

In this chapter, a framework of standards has been devised against which national systems of labour rights should be measured. Are they providing effective protection for the Convention rights of individuals at work? Some obligations are structural and fall upon the legislature in designing the system of rights, ensuring that rights are applied broadly and that violations can be scrutinized and remedied effectively with the framework of law. Once the overarching scheme is devised, 'judicial authorities have an important task of their own to make sure individual decisions and judgments are in conformity with the Convention standards as defined by the Court'.[118] As observed in Chapter 2, human rights principles serve as an external check on the compromises and long-held traditions of labour law and prompt us to question whether the shape of key rights and duties can be justified in light of their challenge.

Even a cursory examination of many systems of labour rights would show how these positive obligations hold significant potential to disrupt long-established principles, compromises, and doctrines regarding the regulation of working relationships. Does the system of labour and employment rights in England and Wales offer an adequate framework through which individuals can enforce their human rights when they are infringed by their employer? Has the inherent risk posed to human rights by the existence of an employment relationship been sufficiently offset by the regulation in place? These are the questions considered in Part II.

[117] Filip Dorssemont, 'The European Convention on Human Rights as a Fountain of Labour Rights' in Janice R Bellace and Beryl ter Haar (eds), *Research Handbook on Labour, Business and Human Rights Law* (Edward Elgar Publishing 2019) 327.

[118] Gerards, 'Procedural Review by the ECtHR: A Typology' (n 26) 140.

PART II

UNDER PRESSURE: THE CURRENT FRAMEWORK OF LABOUR RIGHTS

4
The Existing Patchwork of Rights Protection

Whilst dismissal law is the primary focus of this text, it is not the only means by which the UK fulfils the positive obligations outlined in Chapter 3. Several other employment rights play an important role in protecting specific aspects of the qualified rights against infringement by an employer. The common law of the contract of employment, for example, protects a worker against forced and unwaged labour whilst tort law, through the employer's duty of care and the torts against the person, protects their physical and mental health.[1] This chapter focuses on the statutes that impose responsibilities upon employers that match closely an obligation not to interfere with a particular Convention right. It will be shown how these statutes operate to constrain employers by several (partial) duties to respect the Convention rights of their workers.

Some of the measures are not often described in terms of their rights-protective function and their origins may not have been a desire to protect the fundamental rights of workers. For example, a need for protection for whistleblowers against detriment and dismissal by their employer, later introduced in the Public Interest Disclosure Act 1998, was exposed by inquiries into a series of major incidents, from financial scandals to health and safety disasters.[2] Recalling that the human rights of workers are at the centre of a number of important labour statutes reinforces the fallacy of the claim that employers are private actors like any other, free from any duty to respect the fundamental rights of others. This chapter also picks up the theme developed in Chapter 2, where it was argued that the protection of the fundamental rights of workers has long been a function of employment and labour rights.

In the first section, the human rights elements of three legislative instruments are analysed. Several pieces of legislation, such as the Modern Slavery Act 2015, the Health and Safety at Work etc Act 1974, and the Data Protection Act 2018, play important roles in the protection of human rights at work. For reasons of space, my focus in section I will be on the Equality Act 2010 (EA 2010), the Trade Union and Labour Relations (Consolidation) Act 1992 (TULR(C)A 1992), and the Public Interest Disclosure Act 1998 (PIDA 1998) as examples of labour law legislation with the clear rights dimensions. Between them, they provide important

[1] For further discussion of the common law's role in protecting fundamental rights, see Chapter 2, section III and Chapters 7 and 8.

[2] See Lucy Vickers, *Freedom of Speech and Employment* (Oxford University Press 2002) 2–10.

Putting Human Rights to Work. Philippa Collins, Oxford University Press. © Philippa Collins 2022.
DOI: 10.1093/oso/9780192894595.003.0005

safeguards for aspects of the qualified rights and contribute to the UK's compliance with its positive obligations under the Convention.

In section II, the methods by which existing mechanisms of protection can be adapted so that they are more closely aligned to human rights principles will be considered. In an area of law that is dominated by statutory provisions, the duty of compatible statutory interpretation set out in section 3 of the Human Rights Act 1998 (HRA 1998) is crucial to this process. The *ad hoc* evolution of labour law through this route is a recurring theme throughout this work: it provides instant relief for the claimant but ultimately leaves the wider problem of systematic compliance with the UK's obligations under the European Convention on Human Rights (ECHR or the Convention) unsolved. The final section will demonstrate that, despite this combination of statutory provisions and compliant interpretation, deficiencies in the standard of protection for human rights remain. I will draw on examples from discrimination law, where indirect but imperfect protection is offered to other human rights such as the freedom of belief and manifestation of that belief contained in Article 9 ECHR. Where these disparities exist, we begin to see the necessity of a 'backstop' of strong human rights protection, whether that is through dismissal law or some other mechanism.

I. Mapping the Human Rights Dimensions of Labour Law's Instruments

Several statutes impose duties upon employers to respect the human rights of workers, albeit that the legislation is often specific to a particular right and the duty may not be framed in general terms, but rather as a series of prohibitions or restrictions. In some instances, employers will be amongst a group of duty bearers from the private sector that might also include landlords, education or service providers, and trade unions.[3] This section focuses only on the duties of employers under these statutes and how they correspond to ECHR rights held by individuals. The discussion serves to highlight the important role of the legislature in ensuring that the human rights are guaranteed effectively within our system of labour law.[4]

Before turning to the three legislative instruments that are the main focus of this chapter, it is interesting to step back briefly and survey the wider context of labour regulation and human rights. Some human rights relevant to the world of work, such as Article 4, which protects all individuals from slavery, servitude, and forced

[3] See, for example, the duties imposed upon trade unions, landlords, and service providers by the EA 2010.

[4] See further Alan Bogg, 'Freedom of Association: Courts and Legislatures' (2020) 36 International Journal of Comparative Labour Law and Industrial Relations 409; Grégoire Webber and Paul Yowell, 'Securing Human Rights through Legislation' in Grégoire Webber and others (eds), *Legislated Rights: Securing Human Rights through Legislation* (Cambridge University Press 2018).

or compulsory labour, necessitate criminal sanctions[5] as well as regulation via private law. The right to health and safety at work, which has properly been held to be encompassed within Article 8 of the European Convention,[6] is embodied in the Health and Safety at Work etc Act 1974. Data protection law imposes responsibilities upon employers as 'data controllers' which reflect the individual's right to the protection of their personal data,[7] one element of the wider right to respect for one's private life.[8] Equal pay legislation protects against wage discrimination between men and women,[9] whilst family leave rights and the regulation of working time enable employees to strike a balance between working obligations and the right to enjoy a private and family life.[10] We begin to see that, in modern employment law, many of the duties imposed on employers are co-extensive with or an elaboration upon an obligation to respect the human rights of employees or workers.

A. Equality Act 2010

The right to equality or non-discrimination is a human right. Within the European Convention, there is no freestanding right to equality, but discrimination in the enjoyment of the other Convention rights is prohibited unless it can be justified as proportionate.[11] Thus, another human right must be engaged by the facts before the Court will examine a possible breach of Article 14. In many of the Council of Europe member states, anti-discrimination legislation is heavily derived from EU law. Equal treatment is a well-established general principle of EU law[12] and EU directives prohibit discrimination on the grounds of sex[13] and racial or ethnic origin,[14] as well as one's religion or belief, disability, age, or sexual orientation.[15]

[5] See *Siliadin v France* (2006) 43 EHRR 16 and the Modern Slavery Act 2015, sections 1 and 2. For a comprehensive analysis of the role of criminal sanctions in the law of work, see Alan Bogg and others (eds), *Criminality at Work* (Oxford University Press 2020).

[6] See *Brincat and Others v Malta* Application no 60908/11 (ECtHR, 24 July 2014); *Vilnes v Norway* Application no 52806/09 (ECtHR, 5 December 2013).

[7] Regulation (EU) 2016/679 of the European Parliament and of the Council of 27 April 2016 on the protection of natural persons with regard to the processing of personal data and on the free movement of such data, and repealing Directive 95/46/EC [2016] OJ L119/1, Article 1(2).

[8] See *I v Finland* Application no 20511/03 (ECtHR, 17 July 2008) [47].

[9] Equal Pay Act 1970.

[10] See respectively *Markin v Russia* (2013) 56 EHRR 8; International Labour Office, *Hours of Work: From Fixed to Flexible? Report of the Committee of Experts on the Application of Conventions and Recommendations* (International Labour Office 2005) [317] and [331].

[11] ECHR, Article 14, although see also Protocol No 12 to the ECHR which contains additional protections against discrimination.

[12] C-144/04 *Mangold v Helm* [2006] 1 CMLR 43, [75]–[76].

[13] Directive 2006/54/EC of the European Parliament and of the Council of 5 July 2006 on the implementation of the principle of equal opportunities and equal treatment of men and women in matters of employment and occupation [2006] OJ L204/23.

[14] Council Directive 2000/43/EC of 29 June 2000 implementing the principle of equal treatment between persons irrespective of racial or ethnic origin [2000] OJ L180/2.

[15] See Council Directive 2000/78/EC of 27 November 2000 establishing a general framework for equal treatment in employment and occupation [2000] OJ L303/16.

The UK's EA 2010 adds marriage and civil partnership, gender reassignment, and pregnancy and maternity to its list of protected characteristics.[16] As will be discussed in section III, the confinement of the EA's protections to these enumerated characteristics and the manner in which they are defined by the courts limits the capacity of the Act to protect other fundamental rights such as a worker's freedom of association or freedom of thought. It must also be noted that the 2010 Act's list of protected characteristics is closed and limited when contrasted with the longer, open-ended list contained in Article 14 of the ECHR. The latter includes, for example, language, political or other opinion, and social origin.

Where the EA does offer a worker protection from discrimination, it does so in a manner that coheres well with the Convention. Direct discrimination, where A is treated less favourably than B because of a protected characteristic, is prohibited by section 13.[17] The Strasbourg Court has held that Article 14 can be violated in such circumstances. For example, in *Boyraz v Turkey*, the European Court of Human Rights (ECtHR or the Court) held that a dismissal from employment on the sole ground of an individual's sex engages the right to respect for one's private and family life under Article 8. The Court restated that any difference in treatment on grounds of sex between persons in a comparable situation must be met with a reasonable and objective justification.[18] In that particular case, the government was unable to convince the Court that the dismissal of Ms Boyraz from her post as a security officer pursued a legitimate aim and Article 14 was thereby violated.[19] In this regard, the EA goes beyond the standard of protection offered under the Convention as direct discrimination can only be justified in limited circumstances, whereas the Court permits national authorities to attempt to justify discrimination in all cases.

The EA also tackles indirect discrimination which occurs when B applies a facially neutral provision, criteria, or practice which puts a protected group of which A is a member at a particular disadvantage that cannot be justified.[20] Indirect discrimination has been recognized to constitute an infringement of the Convention's prohibition on discrimination. In *Thlimmenos v Greece*,[21] the applicant was refused an appointment as an accountant on the grounds that he had previously committed a felony. The felony was insubordination in the armed forces, which had been motivated by the applicant's religious beliefs as a Jehovah's Witness thereby engaging the applicant's right under Article 9. By treating a felony motivated by religious beliefs in the same way as all other felonies, the rules breached Article 14. The national authorities should have treated individuals like Mr Thlimmenos

[16] EA 2010, section 4.
[17] EA 2010, section 13.
[18] *Boyraz v Turkey* (2015) 60 EHRR 30, [50].
[19] ibid [54]–[56].
[20] EA 2010, section 19.
[21] (2001) 31 EHRR 15.

differently:[22] a facially neutral rule had a discriminatory impact on his particular religious group. In a more recent case regarding the provision of education, the ECtHR has adopted the language of indirect discrimination for the first time, holding that it constitutes a breach of Article 14.[23]

The EA, within its scope of application, protects individuals from discrimination of various kinds and in a manner that reflects the case law of the ECtHR that applies Article 14. We can see that actors who are subject to the duties contained in the EA must be considered to be duty bearers of the fundamental right not to suffer discrimination. The EA's provisions extend the duties broadly, imposing them upon employers with regard to their employees, workers under a contract personally to do work, and agency workers.[24] Equality law, as it applies to employment relations, clearly places employers under extensive and detailed duties to respect this particular fundamental right, not only in relation to their current staff but also candidates seeking employment and those who had worked for the employer previously.[25]

B. Trade Union and Labour Relations (Consolidation) Act 1992

The ECHR guarantees every individual the right to freedom of association. Article 11 includes within this freedom 'the right to form and to join trade unions for the protection of his interests'. The case law of the ECtHR shows that this human right entails several specific guarantees for individuals including protection against infringements by private employers, as well as national regulation that permits unions to form and to ensure that they can act in the interests of their members. The right to freedom of association is a qualified right, which may be restricted to protect the rights and interests of others, such as employers, amongst other legitimate aims.[26] States enjoy a margin of appreciation in establishing a regime that guarantees the Article 11 rights of individuals and unions and determining how the right to freedom of association should be reconciled with countervailing rights and the public interest.[27]

With regard to the rights of trade unions, in *Sindicatul Păstorul cel Bun v Romania*, the Court stated that 'What the Convention requires is that under national law trade unions should be enabled, in conditions not at variance with Article 11, to strive for the protection of their members' interests'.[28] The 'constituent

[22] ibid [44] and [48].
[23] *DH and others v Czech Republic* (2008) 47 EHRR 3, particularly [182]–[184].
[24] EA 2010, sections 39, 83(2), and 55 respectively.
[25] EA 2010, sections 39, 40, and 108.
[26] ECHR, Article 11(2).
[27] See *Sindicatul Păstorul cel Bun v Romania* (2014) 58 EHRR 10, [130]–[133].
[28] ibid [134].

elements of the right to organise' that have been recognized by the ECtHR include the rights to form a trade union, to seek to persuade employers to hear its views,[29] to collectively bargain, and to strike.[30] Extensive regulation is necessary in order to give shape to these elements and provide mechanisms by which they are enforced.[31] This elaboration is contained in the UK's TULR(C)A 1992. Through the Act's provisions, unions' rights under Article 11 are given effect and the individual workers' right to freedom of association are guaranteed.

Starting with the collective aspects of Article 11, TULR(C)A 1992 sets out the definition of a 'trade union' and establishes a list of trade unions held by the Certification Office,[32] reflecting the right to form a union and have it registered under national law. TULR(C)A also defines the parameters of trade union's autonomy in their own organizational affairs, another element of Article 11.[33] The process of 'recognition', by which an employer agrees to bargain with a union on particular issues, is the mechanism by which unions may persuade employers to hear the views of their members. Although voluntary agreement between a union and employer is prioritized by the provisions of TULR(C)A, there is a statutory process which *requires* an employer to recognize a union for collective bargaining if the union can satisfy the conditions and win a ballot of the workers.[34] The Act places obligations upon employers in connection with collective bargaining such as the duty to disclose information and to consult a worker representative before a redundancy occurs.[35] Finally, it regulates the union's ability to embark on industrial action to protect the interests of its members through a system of immunities from liability for economic torts which a union would otherwise incur to the employer.[36] The extensive regulation in place under the 1992 Act shows that freedom of association is the 'quintessential "legislated right". There could be no "right to form and join trade unions", no right to collective bargaining, no right to strike, without a complex statutory structure of labour law.'[37]

With regard to individual rights, the Court stated in *Wilson and Palmer v UK* that:

> it is of the essence of the right to join a trade union for the protection of their interests that employees should be free to instruct or permit the union to make representations to their employer or to take action in support of their interests on

[29] ibid [135].

[30] *Demir v Turkey* (2009) 48 EHRR 54; *Enerji Yapı-Yol Sen v Turkey* Application no 68959/01 (ECtHR, 21 April 2009) [24].

[31] Bogg (n 4).

[32] TULR(C)A 1992, sections 1 and 2.

[33] *Associated Society of Locomotive Engineers & Firemen (ASLEF) v United Kingdom* (2007) 45 EHRR 34, [38].

[34] TULR(C)A 1992, Schedule A1.

[35] TULR(C)A 1992, sections 181 and 188.

[36] TULR(C)A 1992, section 219.

[37] Bogg (n 4) 421.

> their behalf. If workers are prevented from so doing, their freedom to belong to a trade union, for the protection of their interests, becomes illusory.[38]

Workers should not be subject to disincentives or restraint by their employer with regard to their association with a union.[39] The ECtHR has found that Article 11 protects individuals from discrimination on grounds of their trade union membership, or lack thereof, in applying for positions.[40] The imposition of discipline because an individual has participated in industrial action or supported a union has been found to violate the individual's freedom of association.[41] In *Wilson and Palmer* itself, the UK was held to be in breach of its obligations under Article 11 as employers were permitted to use financial incentives to induce workers to give up rights that they held as union members, thereby undermining the strength of the union in the workplace.[42]

The Court's declarations regarding the necessary protections for individual employees are reflected in a series of prohibitions within the 1992 Act in relation to employers' behaviour prior to, during, and in the termination of employment. For example, under section 137, it is unlawful to refuse a person employment because they are, or are not, a member of a trade union.[43] This provision protects a worker's freedom to join and freedom not to join a union at the point of entry into employment. Sections 146 and 152 protect workers and employees from detriment and dismissal respectively on grounds related to their union membership and activities.[44] Employees who participate in lawful and official strike action are protected against dismissal under section 238A. In addition, and in direct response to the ECtHR's ruling in *Wilson and Palmer v UK*,[45] a worker has the right not be made an offer, the sole or main purpose of which is to induce the worker to not become a member of a union, to not take part in its activities or make use of its service, or to achieve the result that the worker's terms are no longer negotiated by collective agreement.[46] Although the provisions are undoubtedly imperfect in places,[47] the statute operates in a manner that places a duty upon employers to respect their workers' right to freedom of association under Article 11.

[38] *Wilson and others v United Kingdom* (2002) 35 EHRR 20, [46].
[39] ibid [47].
[40] See *Young, James and Webster v United Kingdom* (1981) 3 EHRR 20, [52] and [55].
[41] See *Ognevenko v Russia* Application no 44873/09 (ECtHR, 20 November 2018); *Matelly v France* Application no 10609/10 (ECtHR, 2 January 2015).
[42] *Wilson v UK* (n 38) [47]–[48].
[43] TULR(C)A 1992, section 137.
[44] TULR(C)A 1992, sections 146 and 152.
[45] *Wilson v UK* (n 38).
[46] TULR(C)A 1992, sections 145A and 145B.
[47] See Hugh Collins, Keith Ewing, and Aileen McColgan, *Labour Law* (2nd edn, Cambridge University Press 2019) 466–67; ACL Davies, 'Workers' Human Rights in English Law' in Tonia Novitz and Colin Fenwick (eds), *Human Rights at Work: Perspectives on Law and Regulation* (Hart Publishing 2010) 185–86.

TULR(C)A 1992 lays out the prohibitions, requirements, and mechanisms by which the right to freedom of association is given effect. The Act provides the foundations for the status of unions in the legal regime, grants them the capacity to be listed and recognized, as well as protection from liability if they conduct lawful industrial action to protect their members' interests. The individual worker's right to be free from restraint, disincentives, or retaliation by their employer is reflected in provisions preventing employers from discriminating against workers on grounds of their membership status or activities as a union member. It is in this regard that the employer's duty to respect the freedom of association of workers is most evident. Employers are required by the Act to refrain from interfering with an individual's Article 11 rights throughout the employment relationship, from selecting between candidates through to its power to dismiss an employee.

C. The Public Interest Disclosure Act 1998

Whistleblowing—the making of a disclosure of unlawful conduct in the public interest—has been held by the ECtHR to be one aspect of the right to freedom of expression under Article 10.[48] Dismissal from one's employment as a result of blowing the whistle is considered to be a serious infringement upon the individual's Article 10 rights and the Court is mindful of the 'chilling effect' of such a dismissal, both within the workplace and potentially beyond it.[49] The protection of the individual is circumscribed, however, by their duty of loyalty and discretion to their employer and the Court takes into account the damage suffered by the employer as a result of the individual's disclosure. These factors are weighed in the analysis of the necessity of the infringement, along with other specific considerations: whether any public disclosure was a last resort or whether alternative, effective methods of disclosure existed; whether the authenticity of the information had been verified as far as possible in the circumstances; and whether the individual was acting in good faith and regard must be had to the public interest served by the disclosure.[50]

The Public Interest Disclosure Act (PIDA) 1998 is an instance where the legislation was introduced well before the principles on whistleblowing were enunciated by the ECtHR. The parallels, however, are striking. At the centre of PIDA is the idea of a 'qualifying disclosure'. The disclosure must be made in good faith and the individual must have a reasonable belief that the information tends to show wrongdoing such as the commission or likely commission of a criminal offence

[48] See *Guja v Moldova* (2011) 53 EHRR 16, [53]; *Heinisch v Germany* (2014) 58 EHRR 31, [43]. More recently, the EU has introduced a Whistleblowing Directive which draws from the Article 10 case law: Directive (EU) 2019/1937 of the European Parliament and of the Council of 23 October 2019 on the protection of persons who report breaches of Union law [2019] OJ L305/17, preamble 31.

[49] *Heinisch v Germany* (n 48) [91].

[50] ibid [64]–[70].

or failure to comply with a legal obligation.[51] As under the Convention principles, the worker must seek to disclose the information to the employer first and can only make the disclosure more generally if they believe that they will be subject to detriment, that the employer may conceal or destroy the evidence or the worker has already disclosed the information to the employer.[52] Many other factors specified by the ECtHR are mirrored within the PIDA regime: good faith and personal gain, reasonable belief in the substantial truth of the information, the duty of confidentiality to the employer, and the seriousness of the failure. The provisions within the domestic law can be seen to perform a similar balancing between the public interest, the potential harm to the employer, the duties of the employee, and the need to protect the individual from reprisals as a result of speaking out.

What specific protections does the individual worker receive? A 'protected disclosure' is any qualifying disclosure made by a worker in accordance with the principles of the Act. Workers are protected from being subjected to detriment on the grounds that they have made a protected disclosure.[53] Where an employee can satisfy an Employment Tribunal (ET) that the principal reason for their dismissal was that they made a protected disclosure, the dismissal will be automatically unfair.[54] It is therefore significantly more straightforward for a whistleblower to succeed in an unfair dismissal claim, in addition to the removal of the two year qualifying period of continuous employment that would otherwise be required.[55] In situations of detriment or dismissal, the individual is entitled to such compensation as is considered just and equitable by the ET,[56] and the amount is not subject to the same cap as applies to other cases.[57] Given the close alignment between the provisions of PIDA and the scope of Article 10's protection for whistleblowers, it may be considered another instance where employers are under a duty to respect one dimension of a particular fundamental right of their workers.

II. The Horizontal Effect of Convention Rights in Labour Law

What does an examination of these legislative instruments tell us about the responsibilities of employers with regard to their workers' regarding human rights? Employers are already subject to legislative duties that overlap with the requirements of the Convention. This range of duties shows that labour law has been consistently concerned with protecting employees from interference with their human

[51] PIDA 1998, section 1 inserting Employment Rights Act 1996, section 43B(1).
[52] PIDA 1998, section 1 inserting ERA 1996, section 43G(1) and (2).
[53] PIDA 1998, section 2.
[54] PIDA 1998, section 5.
[55] ERA 1996, section 108(3)(ff).
[56] Respectively ERA 1996, sections 49(2) and 123.
[57] ERA 1996, section 124(1A).

rights. In this section, we will see how the provisions of these statutes can be drawn into even closer alignment with the Convention through the operation of the HRA 1998.

Whilst human rights duties and disputes traditionally exist in the vertical domain between a citizen and the state, the 'horizontal effect' of a human right refers to the extent to which it influences a private dispute. I argue that the statutes set out in section I give *de facto* direct horizontal effect to the human rights of workers, the strongest form of horizontal effect. The operation of these statutes imposes duties, albeit incomplete ones, upon employers to respect the fundamental rights of their workers (and sometimes candidates for work) which match so closely to the Convention that they can be considered examples of direct horizontal effect. Where the domestic provisions and ECHR principles diverge, the power to interpret statutes can be deployed to bridge the gap and give effect to Convention rights where possible. In areas of labour law where the common law dominates, such as in the law of wrongful dismissal and breach of contract, indirect horizontal effect could be influential in the development of the law.

In the literature, a distinction has been drawn between forms of 'direct horizontal effect' and 'indirect horizontal effect'.[58] The *direct* horizontal effect of human rights indicates that a private party is able to make a claim against another private party for an infringement of their human rights. For example, A sues B, a private sector employer, for a breach of their Article 8 right to respect for their private life. The mechanisms outlined earlier give direct horizontal effect to many aspects of the human rights of employees or workers in all but name.[59] Although we do not usually think of the statutes in these terms, they give direct horizontal effect to the rights not to suffer discrimination, to enjoy freedom of association, and to be protected from detriment as a result of blowing the whistle. Perhaps similar arguments could be made in relation to the aspects of Article 8 ECHR that are protected by health and safety legislation and the data privacy rights contained in the Data Protection Act 2018. These mechanisms show that horizontal effect can be tailored to a particular relationship and context, ensuring appropriate protection for the right itself but also weighing in the balance the other party's rights and interests.

In addition to *de facto* direct horizontal effect, there are two further modes of horizontal effect that are—or could be in the future—important to the development of labour law. The first is *indirect* horizontal effect. This effect occurs when existing common law doctrines or rights are altered to incorporate or reflect the

[58] See further Ian Leigh, 'Horizontal Rights, the Human Rights Act and Privacy: Lessons from the Commonwealth?' (1999) 48 International & Comparative Law Quarterly 57; Alison Young, 'Mapping Horizontal Effect' in David Hoffman (ed), *The Impact of the UK Human Rights Act on Private Law* (Cambridge University Press 2011).

[59] For an analysis of the blurring in practice of the boundaries between different modes of horizontal effect, see Eleni Frantziou, *The Horizontal Effect of Fundamental Rights in the European Union: A Constitutional Analysis* (Oxford University Press 2019) 47–48.

human rights of one or both of the parties. For example, A might sue B for a breach of the terms of their contract and argue that the common law of the contract of employment should be developed in a manner that reflects their Convention right. If the indirect horizontal effect of a fundamental right is fully embraced within a particular norm of private law, the result can in practice be the same as direct horizontal effect: B is put under a common law duty to respect A's Article 8 right to respect for their private life.[60] This form of horizontal effect has thus far been seen most prominently in tort law.[61] How this form of horizontal effect may influence the development of dismissal law will be investigated in Chapter 7.

A more regular feature of reasoning in labour disputes is statutory horizontality.[62] Central to statutory horizontality is a strong obligation upon the courts to interpret legislative instruments in a manner that is compatible with human rights. Section 3 of the HRA sets out just such an obligation, demanding that '[s]o far as it is possible to do so, primary legislation and subordinate legislation must be read and given effect in a way which is compatible with the Convention rights'.[63] In a case invoking statutory horizontality, A would sue B based on a pre-existing statutory right, such as the right not to be dismissed unfairly under the Employment Rights Act 1996. The question of whether that existing right has been violated would be assessed in a way that gives due regard to A's Article 8 ECHR right.[64] How this argument has played out in the law of unfair dismissal will be discussed in Chapter 6, but the interpretive obligation is a powerful tool if one is seeking a closer fit between any existing statutory duties and a Convention right.

We might draw on one example, *Serco Ltd v RMT*,[65] to demonstrate how direct statutory horizontality can have a corrective effect upon the interpretation of a statute. Domestic law protects unions and their members in the organization and in the carrying out of strikes through a system of immunities. TULR(C)A 1992 protects unions from liability for economic torts, such as inducing a breach of contract, by providing a carefully crafted immunity.[66] The immunity can only be obtained if the union fulfils a complex bundle of balloting and notification requirements. If the employer suspects that the union has failed to comply with the conditions for immunity, the employer can seek an interim injunction to prevent the strike from going ahead. In applying the statutory requirements necessary to

[60] Mattias Kumm, 'Who is Afraid of the Total Constitution? Constitutional Rights as Principles and the Constitutionalization of Private Law' (2006) 7 German Law Journal 341, 352–53.

[61] See *Campbell v MGN Ltd* [2004] UKHL 22, [2004] 2 AC 457; Gavin Phillipson, 'Privacy: The Development of Breach of Confidence—The Clearest Case of Horizontal Effect?' in David Hoffman (ed), *The Impact of the UK Human Rights Act on Private Law* (Cambridge University Press 2011).

[62] Ian Leigh and Roger Masterman, *Making Rights Real: The Human Rights Act in its First Decade* (Hart Publishing 2008) 246–47.

[63] HRA 1998, section 3(1).

[64] See, for example, *X v Y* [2004] EWCA Civ 662, [2004] ICR 1634 discussed further in Chapter 6.

[65] *Serco Ltd v National Union of Rail, Maritime & Transport Workers* [2011] EWCA Civ 226, [2011] ICR 848.

[66] TULR(C)A 1992, section 219.

receive immunity, a common law rule developed that the statute should be applied strictly against the union. In the words of Lord Denning,

> [Parliament] did not give [unions] a right to break the law or to do wrong by inducing people to break contracts. It only gave them immunity if they did. In construing this immunity … the words of the statute are not to be construed widely so as to give unlimited immunity to law-breakers. They are to be construed with due limitations so as to keep the immunity within reasonable bounds.[67]

In *Serco v RMT*,[68] this manner of interpreting union immunities was challenged. The two unions involved, RMT and ASLEF, had made several small mistakes in the balloting process and there were issues with the notification of industrial action that had been given to the employer. The lower courts had issued interim injunctions that prevented the unions from calling a strike on the basis of narrow and prescriptive interpretations of the statutory requirements. For example, on one issue, the judge held an error in sending ballots to two members who were not entitled to vote could not be disregarded because the union had not demonstrated that the accident was both 'unintentional and unavoidable'.[69] In the Court of Appeal, Lord Justice Elias adopted a different approach, bearing in mind the international recognition of the right to strike.

Commencing his judgment Lord Justice Elias noted that, whilst the common law has never conferred a right to strike, international documents recognize such a right. He observed that the right to strike has been recognized by the ECtHR as an element of Article 11 ECHR, which is given effect in the UK by the HRA 1998.[70] His Lordship considered the existence of the right to strike to be relevant to the issue of how the statutory regime should be construed and applied. Elias LJ argued that:

> if one starts from the premise that the legislation should be strictly construed against those seeking the benefit of the immunities, the effect is the same as it would be if there were a presumption that Parliament intends that the interests of the employers should hold sway unless the legislation clearly dictates otherwise. I do not think this is now a legitimate approach, if it ever was. In my judgment the legislation should simply be construed in the normal way, without presumptions one way or the other.[71]

[67] *Express Newspapers Ltd v McShane* [1979] ICR 210, 218.
[68] *Serco v RMT* (n 65).
[69] ibid [44].
[70] ibid [8].
[71] ibid [9].

In the remainder of his judgment, his Lordship's 'self-consciously neutral approach'[72] towards the interpretation of TULR(C)A led him to accept a number of the unions' arguments. For example, he held that there was no obligation on the union to improve its record-keeping[73] and *obiter* that, where specific statutory defences do not apply to a 'trifling mistake', a *de minimus* doctrine is available to the union where an immaterial or accidental mistake would otherwise invalidate a ballot.[74] The outcome of the case was that the Court of Appeal found in favour of the unions and the injunctions were discharged.

In *Serco v RMT*, the international recognition of the right to strike inclined the court to reject the restrictive common law approach to the application of statutory immunities in industrial action disputes. The Court of Appeal adopted a neutral interpretative approach which led to a rare union victory. Although the neutral approach has not been universally adopted, Elgar and Simpson note that subsequent decisions reflect Elias LJ's approach towards injunction applications.[75] It has already been noted that TULR(C)A's provisions impose a duty upon employers to respect their workers' right to freedom of association. The *RMT* decision demonstrates how the horizontal effect of human rights can provide impetus to re-examine long-established doctrines. Although the courts could go further in using the tools within the HRA 1998 to give effect to the union's right to organize industrial action,[76] the Court of Appeal's decision ensure the law is applied in a manner that aligns better with Convention rights.

III. The Cracks Begin to Show: The Divergence Between Domestic Duties and Convention Case Law

Despite the overlap that has been established between the Convention and the duties and rights available in English employment law, there are clear points of divergence. We might consider, following Keith Ewing's powerful argument, whether the system of immunities outlined earlier is an appropriate mechanism through which to safeguard a fundamental right of both unions and their members.[77] In light of more recent ECtHR case law, Ewing has also challenged the detailed regulation of unions' relations with their members and queried whether TULR(C)A goes far enough in protecting the unions' rights to organize their own affairs and choose

[72] Ruth Dukes, 'The Right to Strike under UK Law: Something More Than a Slogan?' (2011) 40 ILJ 302, 306.

[73] *Serco v RMT* (n 65) [75].

[74] ibid [86].

[75] Jane Elgar and Bob Simpson, 'The Impact of the Law on Industrial Disputes Revisited: a Perspective on Developments over the last Two Decades' (2017) 46 ILJ 6, 17.

[76] See, for example, the response to the union's section 3 HRA argument in *Metrobus Ltd v Unite the Union* [2009] EWCA Civ 829, [2010] ICR 173, [113].

[77] See Keith Ewing, 'The Right to Strike' (1986) 15 ILJ 143.

with whom to associate.[78] On the individual aspects of Article 11, the situation is perhaps better overall but limitations nevertheless exist. For example, to gain protection from detriment, the worker must convince an ET that their employer's 'sole or main purpose' for offering an inducement or the 'principal reason' for their dismissal was connected to their trade union membership or activities.[79] We could ask whether the existence of a potentially legitimate reason alongside a reason that interferes with the individual's Article 11 negates the existence or seriousness of that infringement.[80]

In this section, I will examine two deficiencies in the EA's operation when viewed from a Convention perspective. It has already been observed that the EA's primary purpose is to safeguard and elaborate upon the right to equality and non-discrimination. It also has a role to play in providing protection for other Convention rights. For example, the prevention of discrimination and harassment on the grounds of one's sex, sexual orientation, marriage or civil partnership status, or gender reassignment bolster the right to respect for one's private life in the workplace. The characteristic of religious and philosophical belief has a strong link to Articles 9 and 10: the right to freedom of thought, conscience and religion and the right to freedom of expression. There are discrepancies, however, between the principles laid down by the ECtHR and the operation of the EA.

A. *Mba v Merton LBC*: Indirect Discrimination, Article 9, and Group Disadvantage

Preventing discrimination and harassment on the grounds of an individual's religious or philosophical belief enables them to exercise their right to freedom of thought and belief. There is, however, a limitation upon the capacity of the EA to protect the individual's right under Article 9 ECHR. Protection under Article 9 generally depends upon the individual's own beliefs and there is no threshold that the belief must be shared with others.[81] In contrast, the definition of indirect discrimination—invoked to challenge policies with a discriminatory effect upon a claimant—includes a 'group disadvantage requirement'. To prove that an individual has been a victim of indirect discrimination, they must prove that the employer's apparently neutral practice 'puts, or would put, persons with whom B shares the characteristic at a particular disadvantage when compared with persons with whom B does not share it'.[82] There is thus a disconnect between the EA's provisions and the principles of the Convention.

[78] Keith Ewing, 'The Implications of the ASLEF Case' (2007) 36 ILJ 425.
[79] See respectively TULR(C)A 1992, sections 145A, 145B, and 152.
[80] Keith Ewing, 'The Implications of *Wilson and Palmer*' (2003) 32 ILJ 1, 20.
[81] See the discussion of *Eweida and others v United Kingdom* (2013) 57 EHRR 8 in this section.
[82] EA 2010, section 19(2)(b).

This discrepancy was exposed clearly in the case of *Eweida v UK*.[83] The ECtHR heard four complaints regarding the compatibility of the UK's discrimination legislation with Article 8, and in one case Article 14. The claimants had been disciplined or dismissed for reasons that related to the manifestation of their religious beliefs in their professional lives. Ms Eweida was employed by British Airways as cabin crew. She wished to wear a Christian cross at work, but she was not permitted to work whilst wearing a visible cross outside her uniform. Ms Eweida chose not to return to work until the company policy was changed and she made an indirect discrimination claim when the employer refused to pay her for the period that she did not work. Her claim was unsuccessful in the national courts because she failed to prove that she was a member of a group who shared a protected characteristic (their religion) that was disadvantaged by British Airways' policy.[84] She based her arguments solely on the impact that the airline's policy had on her, rather than establishing the existence of a broader group of Christians who would be similarly disadvantaged.

Ms Eweida directly challenged the 'group disadvantage' requirement in her arguments before the ECtHR. She argued that she had been 'denied protection under national law . . . because she was unable to adduce evidence that this was a scriptural requirement or a widely practised manifestation of belief'.[85] The ECtHR analysed what amounts to a 'manifestation of belief' entitled to protection within Article 9. Required is an act that is 'intimately linked to the religion or belief' held by the individual and the Court stated that 'there is no requirement on the applicant to establish that he or she acted in fulfilment of a duty mandated by the religion in question'.[86] Applying these principles, the Court considered that Ms Eweida's conduct was a manifestation of her religious belief attracting the protection of Article 9. By refusing to allow Ms Eweida to remain in her post whilst wearing a cross, the employer had infringed that right. The Court's finding was that the national authorities had failed to fulfil the positive obligations under Article 9 by according too much weight to the company's desire to project a corporate image within the balancing exercise.[87]

Ronan McCrea observed that, following *Eweida v UK*, the domestic approach of requiring proof of some kind of group disadvantage was exposed as 'out of line' with Strasbourg's view of Article 9, and possibly Article 14.[88] These fundamental rights do not entail that a group, however small, should be placed at a disadvantage by the employer's policy. Section 3 of the HRA, the duty of compatible interpretation, could provide a solution for this problem by reinterpreting the definition of

[83] *Eweida v UK* (n 81).
[84] See *Eweida v British Airways Plc* [2010] EWCA Civ 80, [2010] ICR 890, [8].
[85] *Eweida v UK* (n 81) [66].
[86] ibid [82].
[87] ibid [94]–[95].
[88] Ronan McCrea, 'Religion in the Workplace' (2014) 77 MLR 277, 287–88.

indirect discrimination in cases where Article 9 is relevant. The first opportunity to address the discrepancy arose, albeit as an *obiter* point, before the Court of Appeal in *Mba v Merton London Borough Council*.[89]

Ms Mba is a Christian. She worked as a care assistant at a children's home. According to her contract, she was required to work on Sundays as and when required. Ms Mba held a sincere belief that Sunday was a day of worship and made a request not to be rostered for Sunday shifts, which her employers endeavoured to comply with wherever possible. Eventually Ms Mba was required to work a Sunday shift and her refusal to do so led to disciplinary proceedings against her. Her indirect discrimination claim was unsuccessful before the courts. The employer's shift policy was held to be justified by the need to run their service, in the light of their staffing requirements and cost considerations. In *obiter* comments, the Court of Appeal addressed the dissonance between anti-discrimination law and Article 9 as applied in *Eweida v UK*.

The Lord Justices of Appeal were divided on whether the operation of indirect discrimination posed a problem under Article 9 and whether section 3 HRA could be used to address it. Lord Justice Maurice Kay was reluctant to alter the interpretation of the domestic provision, as he was not convinced that it generated a breach of Article 9. Lord Justice Elias dealt directly with the discrepancy, stating 'it is simply not possible to read down the concept of indirect discrimination to ignore the need to establish group disadvantage'.[90] Only Lord Justice Vos found that the relevant provision could be 'equally well read' to exclude a group disadvantage requirement 'on the ground that article 9 does not require any test of group disadvantage, and concentrates only on the religious freedom of the individual concerned'.[91]

The Court of Appeal has subsequently upheld Elias LJ's opinion on the possibility of 'reading down' the group disadvantage requirement under section 3. In *Gray v Mulberry*, the court held *obiter* that it is 'simply not possible to ignore (by reading it down) the threshold requirement of group disadvantage in the concept of indirect discrimination'.[92] The Employment Appeal Tribunal (EAT) in *Trayhorn v Secretary of State for Justice* also followed *Mba* in preserving the group disadvantage requirement and applied it to an indirect discrimination complaint by a prison employee. There was no evidence before the tribunal that the application of the employer's disciplinary policies put Christians at a particular disadvantage as a group. The disciplinary measures taken against Mr Trayhorn for comments made during a sermon therefore did not constitute indirect discrimination on the grounds of religion. The EAT was 'without doubt' that, after *Mba*, proof of group disadvantage remains a 'statutory threshold' for the application of section 19 EA

[89] [2013] EWCA Civ 1562, [2014] 1 WLR 1501.
[90] ibid [35].
[91] ibid [41].
[92] *Gray v Mulberry Company (Design) Ltd* [2019] EWCA Civ 1720, [2020] IRLR 29, [41].

2010.[93] The EA's provisions gave Mr Trayhorn no protection from detrimental treatment connected to the expression of his Christian faith.

The judgments in *Mba, Gray*, and *Trayhorn* show that the courts are reluctant to use section 3 to adjust the application of indirect discrimination in a manner that would provide greater protection for the individual's right to freedom of belief and to the manifestation of that belief. The decisions demonstrate that gaps and deficiencies do exist in the current patchwork of safeguards for a worker's qualified rights. Pressing a mechanism that was designed to perform one function (here, to embody the right to equality and non-discrimination) to protect fundamental rights with a very different shape and focus cannot always be expected to succeed.

B. The Limits of Discrimination Law: Contentious and Political Beliefs

A further gap in protection exists at the intersection of the EA 2010 and freedom of expression, association, or belief in controversial or political viewpoints. The Convention is applied broadly in all of these areas of Articles 9, 10, and 11. The ECtHR has reiterated many times that freedom of expression under Article 10 applies equally to inoffensive and mundane speech as to ideas that 'offend, shock or disturb'.[94] The Court has even considered hate speech to be within the scope of Article 10, although the protection of the rights and interests of others provides a strong justification for restricting or penalizing such expression.[95] Dismissal on the grounds that an individual associates with or publicly expresses alignment with political parties which might not be considered 'mainstream', such as the German Communist Party or the British National Party, is considered to be a serious infringement upon the complainant's Article 10 and/or Article 11 rights.[96] How does the scope of the safeguards contained in the EA 2010 compare with the ECtHR's approach to such questions?

One of the protected characteristics in the UK framework is philosophical belief, contained in section 10 of the EA 2010 alongside religion and religious beliefs. The definition of a philosophical belief is found in the case of *Grainger Plc v Nicholson*.[97] In summary, the philosophical belief must be genuinely held, and it must be a belief rather than an opinion. The belief must relate to a 'weighty and substantial aspect' of life and should attain a certain level of cogency, seriousness, cohesion, and importance.[98] Finally, the belief 'must be worthy of respect

93 *Trayhorn v Secretary of State for Justice* [2018] IRLR 502, [73].
94 *Vogt v Germany* (1996) 21 EHRR 205, [52].
95 See *Vejdeland v Sweden* (2014) 58 EHRR 15.
96 See *Vogt v Germany* (n 94); *Redfearn v United Kingdom* (2013) 57 EHRR 2.
97 [2010] 2 All ER 253.
98 ibid [24].

in a democratic society, not be incompatible with human dignity and not conflict with the fundamental rights of others'.[99] This fifth criteria has been criticized by Lucy Vickers as an opportunity for 'courts to make their own judgments about the content of beliefs', leading to questions regarding the courts' neutrality between different belief systems.[100] The effect of the *Grainger* criteria on contentious or offensive beliefs will be returned to later.

A major gap in protection created by the reasoning in *Grainger* is the exclusion of political party beliefs and even some political philosophies from the scope of 'philosophical belief'. In *Grainger* itself, Mr Justice Burton stated that it 'surely must be so' that support for a political party does not meet the description of a philosophical belief.[101] In 2010, an ET ruled that a belief in Marxist political philosophies should not be protected as a philosophical belief, on the grounds that the belief is not worthy of respect in a democratic society as the it invoked ideas of revolution outside the democratic process.[102] A commitment to a certain school of political thought or a particular political party can be an important part of a person's identity and the ECHR certainly protects against detrimental treatment on the grounds of one's political affiliation or philosophy.[103] Under the current interpretation of 'philosophical belief', the EA 2010 would not reliably provide protection from detriment suffered on the grounds of one's political convictions.[104] A significant limitation on the Act's capacity to protect the full range of the Articles 10 and 11 rights held by workers under the Convention is thereby exposed.

Collectively, the *Grainger* criteria also have the effect of removing beliefs that are contentious or may offend others from the scope of an accepted 'philosophical belief', leaving the belief-holder without protection under the EA 2010.[105] In *Forstater v CGD Europe*, an ET was asked to rule on whether Ms Forstater's gender critical beliefs regarding the immutability of one's sex could be classified as a 'philosophical belief'.[106] The Employment Judge found that, due to their absolutist nature, the claimant's beliefs were incompatible with the fundamental rights of others, particularly transgender people. The beliefs were not worthy of respect in a

[99] ibid.

[100] Lucy Vickers, *Religious Freedom, Religious Discrimination and the Workplace* (Hart Publishing 2016) 28.

[101] *Grainger Plc v Nicholson* (n 97) [28].

[102] *Kelly and others v Unison* (2010) ET/2203854/08, [130]–[134].

[103] See ECHR, Article 14 as well as cases such as *Vogt v Germany* (n 94), *Redfearn v UK* (n 96), and *United Communist Party of Turkey and Others v Turkey* (1998) 26 EHRR 121.

[104] Vickers, *Religious Freedom, Religious Discrimination and the Workplace* (n 100) 29–30.

[105] See also *Arya v London Borough of Waltham Forest* [2013] ET/3200396/11 (unreported) and *McClintock v Department of Constitutional Affairs* [2008] IRLR 29.

[106] *Forstater v CGD Europe, Centre for Global Development and Masood Ahmed* [2019] ET 2200909/2019.

democratic society and therefore not within the scope of the EA.[107] A different ET in *Mackereth v DWP* went one step further in stating that aspects of Dr Mackereth's faith (Christianity) also failed to satisfy the *Grainger* criteria insofar as there was a conflict between his faith and the fundamental rights of transgender people.[108] Ms Forstater has appealed to the EAT and the decision in her case has been criticized both by observers and other tribunal judges.[109]

In the subsequent case of *Higgs v Farmor's School*, in which the employee was dismissed for expressing her view that one's biological gender is immutable on Facebook, the tribunal stated that:

> Essentially, to find as the tribunals did in the cases to which we were referred would amount to a declaration that it is 'open season' on people that hold and express the beliefs in question—that they do not deserve protection. That seemed to us to be a strange and somewhat disturbing conclusion.[110]

Such a position would also be difficult from the perspective of Article 10, which protects expression that offends or shocks its audience.

One might argue that the preferable way to deal with these contentious beliefs is to admit them as 'philosophical beliefs', provided they meet the first four *Grainger* criteria. In an indirect discrimination case, the employer would then be given the opportunity to justify their policy or practice.[111] This solution is itself imperfect because if the case was one of direct discrimination, the employer is not afforded a general opportunity to justify their decision.[112] For example, if an employer decided to dismiss an individual on the grounds that they did not agree with ideas of gender fluidity, such a dismissal would amount to direct discrimination. Aside from arguing that a belief in gender fluidity was a genuine requirement of the particular occupation, the employer would have had no chance to justify their policy. Such an opportunity would be permitted under Articles 9, 10, and 14 of the Convention, demonstrating again the difficulties of using discrimination law to protect the qualified rights that are relevant to the workplace.

[107] ibid [84]–[85]. The same conclusion was reached in *Mackereth v Department of Work and Pensions* [2019] ET 1304602/2018, [202].

[108] *Mackereth v Department of Work and Pensions* (n 107) [231].

[109] See Karon Monaghan, 'The Forstater Employment Tribunal judgment: a critical appraisal in light of Miller' (*UK Labour Law Blog*, 19 February 2020) <https://uklabourlawblog.com/2020/02/19/the-forstater-employment-tribunal-judgment-a-critical-appraisal-in-light-of-miller-by-karon-monaghan/> accessed 19 November 2020; Robert Wintemute, 'Belief vs. Action in Ladele, Ngole and Forstater' (2021) 50 ILJ 104; *Higgs v Farmor's School* [2020] ET 1401264/2019 (unreported).

[110] *Higgs v Farmor's School* (n 109) [42].

[111] EA 2010, section 19(2)(d).

[112] See Hugh Collins, 'A Missing Layer of the Cake with the Controversial Icing' (*UK Labour Law Blog*, 4 March 2019) <https://uklabourlawblog.com/2019/03/04/a-missing-layer-of-the-cake-with-the-controversial-icing-hugh-collins/> accessed 19 November 2020.

Conclusion

Important elements of labour law impose duties upon employers to respect the human rights of members of their workforce. Through statutory duties and a layer of statutory horizontality, the employer is bound by an obligation not to infringe specific fundamental rights as they have been explained and developed in Strasbourg. This realization reinforces the argument that employers cannot be considered an unencumbered private actor, free from 'public law' constraints, but instead they must be respectful of the fundamental rights of their workforce to a significant degree.

The discussion of the other major rights that employees have access to also provides crucial context to the discussion of dismissal law that follows this chapter. The law of dismissal is general in nature, able to address a wide range of complaints including human rights issues that fall outside the scope of the specific provisions set out here. The remaining chapters will investigate whether dismissal law is an appropriate mechanism through which to fulfil the positive obligations placed on the UK by the ECHR, as outlined in Chapter 3. Continuing the theme developed in section III, a range of deficiencies and shortcomings will be observed in the chapters that follow relating to the structure and application of the law of dismissal. With workers still vulnerable to infringements upon their human rights, these chapters lead ultimately to the conclusion that a new approach is needed in the form of a Bill of Rights for Workers.

5

The Relational Scope of Labour Rights

Employees Only?

Human rights are universal entitlements. Chapter 3 set out member states' obligation to ensure that all persons are able to challenge actions that they believe have infringed upon those rights. Under the European Convention on Human Rights (ECHR or the Convention), this obligation extends to all individuals, no matter their immigration, employment, or contractual status. Decisions of the European Court of Human Rights (ECtHR or the Court) demonstrate that any rule which prevents an individual from enforcing their fundamental rights must be justified as a necessary pursuit of a legitimate aim.[1] We have seen that employment rights play an important role in protecting an individual's human rights against interference by their employer. Thus, those rights—encompassing discrimination law, trade union regulation, and general rights such as the right not to be dismissed unfairly—*should* be available to any person whose human rights are placed at risk by their employment relationship. After explaining how the ECtHR approaches the question of identifying an employment relationship, we investigate whether the relational scope of employment rights match these expectations.

The overarching framework and doctrines associated with questions of the 'personal scope' of labour laws are undoubtedly restrictive. Built upon an intuition that such rights should be available to those close to a 'paradigm employee' (i.e. full-time, permanent, dependent, and subordinated staff), this area of labour law is a mass of statutory restrictions and common law rules that consistently confine the availability of rights. Whilst this situation has been criticized for a range of reasons,[2] this chapter examines it through the lens of the universal protection of human rights that is offered by the Convention.

Alongside these restrictions on the class of employment relationship that are regulated by employment law, we could also consider procedural restrictions that may prevent an individual from enforcing their human rights through the Employment Tribunals (ETs). Examples may include short time limits, the

[1] *Redfearn v United Kingdom* (2013) 57 EHRR 2; discussed further in Chapter 3, section I.

[2] See, amongst many others, Hugh Collins, 'Independent Contractors and the Challenge of Vertical Disintegration to Employment Protection Laws' (1990) 10 OJLS 353; Mark Freedland, *The Personal Employment Contract* (Oxford University Press 2003) chapter 1; Jeremias Prassl and Einat Albin, 'Employees, Employers, and Beyond: Identifying the Parties to the Contract of Employment' in Mark Freedland (ed), *The Contract of Employment* (Oxford University Press 2016).

Putting Human Rights to Work. Philippa Collins, Oxford University Press. © Philippa Collins 2022.
DOI: 10.1093/oso/9780192894595.003.0006

potential return of fees to launch a claim in the ET, and the lack of access to legal aid to support litigants in vindicating their employment rights. Nevertheless, this chapter focuses on the substantive legal doctrines that restrict the scope of employment rights, affecting significant parts of the workforce and preventing them from using employment law to vindicate their human rights.

After section I sets out the ECtHR perspective on questions of personal scope, the chapter is divided into three groups of constraints upon the scope of employment rights. Section II discusses the requirement for a contract between the two parties and the other private law doctrines that affect the scope of labour rights. In section III, the approach to classifying an individual as either an 'employee' entitled to protection *versus* an 'independent contractor' will be critiqued and specific statutory exclusions, such as the qualifying period that was challenged in *Redfearn v United Kingdom*, examined in section IV. These rules impact wide swathes of the workforce, from new recruits to agency workers to atypical working arrangements, and many more. These groups are left without recourse to employment law if their employer infringes upon their human rights.

In the final section, a concerted shift in the case law is examined. Particularly occurring in the senior courts, human rights arguments have been used to reverse an existing position that a person or group is not entitled to the benefit of an employment right in several recent cases. Decisions thus far have related to members of the Parks Police Service who raised Article 11 arguments to attack a specific occupational exclusion,[3] a whistleblowing District Judge,[4] and a member of embassy staff who challenged the application of diplomatic immunity with the right to a fair trial.[5] These victories should be celebrated: they displayed a receptive judicial attitude towards human rights arguments and allowed the claimants' litigation to progress in a time where legislative change does not appear to be forthcoming.

These dramatic successes have not prompted a wider, systematic review of the relational scope of employment laws, however. Although litigation is one of the few effective tools currently available to working people, an approach driven by legal disputes has less than desirable consequences. The outcomes are very targeted: narrowly defined exemptions or reversals in a handful of cases. The rules and doctrines explored here continue to apply to the vast majority of cases. A hierarchy has thus arisen between potential claimants: many will fall at the first hurdle as a result of the maze of restrictions and exclusions, whilst the minority that can hook their case onto a human right will succeed.[6] Success or failure can be arbitrary,

[3] *Vining and others v London Borough of Wandsworth* [2017] EWCA Civ 1092, [2017] IRLR 1140.

[4] *Gilham v Ministry of Justice* [2019] UKSC 44, [2020] IRLR 52.

[5] *Benkharbouche v Secretary of State for Foreign and Commonwealth Affairs* [2017] UKSC 62, [2017] 3 WLR 957.

[6] An earlier iteration of this argument was made in Philippa Collins and Paul Fradley, 'Policing the Boundaries of Articles 8 and 11 ECHR' (2019) 48 ILJ 225.

depending on the context and argument in one's case, which generates a sense of injustice for those who are unable to take advantage of the rapid changes that are ongoing in this area. What is needed is a systematic review of the accessibility of domestic employment rights, not only in light of the positive obligation to offer universal rights and judicial review but also more generally to assess whether the current framework meets the needs of a modern workforce.

I. The Personal Scope of Convention Rights

There is only one Convention right which is occasionally seen as limited to an employment relationship by the ECtHR. Article 11 guarantees freedom of association which includes the 'right to form and to join trade unions for the protection of his interests'. Under Article 11, trade unions receive additional protection, albeit qualified, which may be the subject of a complaint before the Court. This protection consists of the rights to be legally recognized,[7] to bargain collectively,[8] and to strike.[9] In some cases therefore the ECtHR may first establish whether the members of the association can be considered workers entitled to form a trade union to protect their working interests.[10] For example, in *Sindicatul Păstorul cel Bun v Romania*,[11] the applicant union was formed to protect the interests of clergy and lay members of the Romanian Orthodox Church. The member state authorities refused to register the group as a union on the basis that it would contravene the Church's rules to do so. The union took a challenge based on Article 11 ECHR to Strasbourg.

The first question for the ECtHR was whether the collective aspects of Article 11 were applicable: Were the union members performing their duties for the Church as part of an employment relationship?[12] The Court drew two points from the materials of the International Labour Organization (ILO).[13] First, the existence of an employment relationship should be determined by a consideration of the facts, rather than how it is characterized in any agreement between the parties. Second, ILO conventions make clear that workers have the right to establish collective organizations without any distinction. The Court went on to find that the duties carried out by the union's members had many of the 'characteristic features of an

[7] *Sindicatul Păstorul cel Bun v Romania* (2014) 58 EHRR 10.
[8] *Demir v Turkey* (2009) 48 EHRR 54.
[9] *National Union of Rail, Maritime and Transport Workers v United Kingdom* (2015) 60 EHRR 10.
[10] This stage does not invariably occur, see: *Sigurdur Sigurjónsson v Iceland* (1993) 16 EHRR 462, [32]; commentary on the 'continuous' approach to Article 11 in Joe Atkinson and Hitesh Dhorajiwala, 'IWGB v RooFoods: Status, Rights and Substitution' (2019) 48 ILJ 278, 283.
[11] *Sindicatul Păstorul cel Bun v Romania* (n 7).
[12] ibid [141].
[13] ibid [142].

employment relationship'.[14] The bishop appointed the individuals and set out their rights and obligations. Under his leadership, they carried out their assigned tasks, being paid by the Church or through state funds. Employer's tax contributions were paid by the Church and the individuals were entitled to the same range of welfare and social security benefits as ordinary employees. The 'special features' of their work—the spiritual purpose of their role and the heightened duty of loyalty to which the members were subject—were not sufficient to remove the individuals from the scope of Article 11's protection. The association was therefore entitled to rights as a trade union.

What principles can be extracted from *Sindicatul Păstorul cel Bun*? Firstly, the Court aims to include individuals within the protective sphere of the Convention where possible. The Court demonstrated that commitment by taking the view that the clergymen were protected by Article 11 *unless* special features of their role took them outside the scope of the right. The Court's starting position was that the union members were within the scope of the Convention right until the member state could prove otherwise. The ECtHR examined the substance of the relationship, making broad assessment of the features of the relationship, without getting caught in technical contractual detail. Finally, the Court did not defer to the national regulatory system's classification of the priests as outside the scope of labour law. From this example, we can see that, in the rare instances where the Convention's guarantees are not a universal entitlement, the Court ensures that they apply as broadly as possible and without arbitrary or unjustified distinctions between different groups of individuals.

II. The Contractual Core of Employment Status

At the centre of all employment statuses—the contract of employment, and the additional definitions of worker—is a contract. Although the statutory requirements regarding the form of the contract are very minimal as it may be oral or implied,[15] the requirement for a contractual link between the putative employer and the individual operates to exclude some categories of worker. Their predicament will be discussed in subsection A. In addition, the contractual underpinning of the relationship introduces other doctrines into the arena of employment law's personal scope. In subsection B, the focus will be on the doctrine of illegality. This area of private law has undergone rapid evolution in recent years—thankfully in a manner that improves the probability that an individual will be able to enforce their fundamental rights through employment law. Some gaps nevertheless remain.

[14] ibid [143].
[15] ERA 1996, section 230.

A. The Existence of a Contract: The First Barrier to Enforcement

All of the major employment statuses in England and Wales include the requirement of a contract between the individual and the entity for whom they work. We see this requirement in the *contract* of employment,[16] the *contract* personally to provide work under the Equality Act 2010 (EA 2010),[17] and the 'worker' *contract* which appears in the Employment Rights Act 1996 (ERA 1996)[18] and the Trade Union and Labour Relations (Consolidation) Act 1992 (TULR(C)A 1992),[19] amongst others. The groups within the workforce that are excluded from the scope of key employment rights by the application of this requirement are disparate, ranging from priests to sub-contractors to agency workers. In some cases, the relevant legislation has been drafted to include groups in the workforce that are known to face difficulties because of this contractual requirement. Nevertheless, it remains a substantial barrier to the ability of many individuals to enforce their human rights through employment mechanisms.

The common law doctrine that might assist individuals without an express contract between themselves and their putative employer is that of contractual implication. The claimant would argue that the court should imply a contract, where one does not exist, to permit their claim to progress. Contract law requires necessity to imply a contract where one does not exist.[20] After a brief period in which the courts appeared to be willing to relax this standard to permit claimants to surpass this hurdle,[21] the Court of Appeal swiftly reasserted of the contractual orthodoxy in *James v London Borough of Greenwich*.[22] In a case regarding an unfair dismissal claim by an agency worker, Lord Justice Mummery stated that:

> In many cases agency workers will fall outside the scope of the protection of the 1996 Act because neither the workers nor the end-users were in any kind of express contractual relationship with each other and it is not necessary to imply one in order to explain the work undertaken by the worker for the end-user.[23]

Where other obligations, contractual or otherwise, explain the actions of the parties, the implication of a contract will not be necessary. The application of an unmodified contract law approach to the relationship between worker and end user

[16] ERA 1996, section 230(1).
[17] EA 2010, section 83(2)(a).
[18] ERA 1996, section 230(3)(b).
[19] TULR(C)A 1992, section 296(1)(b).
[20] See *The Aramis* [1989] 1 Lloyd's Rep 213, 224.
[21] See *Franks v Reuters Ltd* [2003] EWCA Civ 417, [2003] ICR 1166; *Dacas v Brook Street Bureau (UK) Ltd* [2004] EWCA Civ 217, [2004] ICR 1437; *Cable & Wireless plc v Muscat* [2006] EWCA Civ 220, [2006] ICR 975.
[22] *James v Greenwich London Borough Council* [2008] EWCA Civ 35, [2008] ICR 545.
[23] ibid [51].

allows a very narrow scope for the implication of a contract. The worker is thereby exposed to behaviour that would otherwise be unlawful by the end user, such as an unfair dismissal[24] or discrimination.[25]

Further groups within the workforce may be affected by the requirement for a contract, cutting across sectors and occupations. 'Office holders' who are appointed under statute or other institutional rules, such as those of a particular church, have been distinguished from employees with a contract of employment.[26] An office holder's appointment is explicable by reference to the relevant rules, and it is therefore not necessary to imply a contract between the individual and their employer. For example, in *Sharpe v Bishop of Worcester and another*,[27] Mr Sharpe was a minister in the Church of England who sought protection from detriment as a whistleblower in addition to claiming that he had been constructively dismissed. The Court of Appeal found that there was no contract in place between the claimant and defendant.[28] Lady Justice Arden considered that there was a lack of intention to create legal relations and no need to imply a contract because Mr Sharpe's role was carried out in accordance with the terms of his office which were defined by law.[29] Despite his status as a potential whistleblower who should have been entitled to protection due to the broad scope of Article 10 ECHR, Mr Sharpe was left with no route to asserting his human rights against his employer, the Church.

Elsewhere, there are significant groups of working people who are barred from employment rights for the same reason. Subcontractors are hired to provide services by a contractor, and they may be classified as an employee or self-employed in that relationship. However, they work under the direction of a principal who may hold significant control over the subcontractor's working life. There is usually no direct link between the subcontractor and the principal so, without the aid of an express provision permitting it,[30] it is difficult for the subcontractor to challenge that principal in the tribunals. Similarly, as observed by Michael Ford, the provision of work through personal service companies, which in some cases may be a condition of receiving an offer of work, allows the employer to retain the ability to coordinate, control, and discipline the worker but leaves the individual with very limited rights under employment legislation.[31] People working through personal service companies are therefore in a position of subordination that is comparable to that of employees. Nevertheless, on the issue of implication, Ford notes that 'there is

[24] ibid [51].
[25] See *Muschett v HM Prison Service* [2010] EWCA Civ 25, [2010] IRLR 451.
[26] See *Ridge v Baldwin* [1964] AC 40, 65–66.
[27] [2015] EWCA Civ 399, [2015] ICR 1241.
[28] ibid [80].
[29] ibid [44]–[47].
[30] See, for example, the extension of the protections contained in the EA 2010 to 'contract workers' and the extended definition of 'worker' in relation to whistleblowing protections: EA 2010, section 41 and ERA 1996, section 43K(1)(a) respectively.
[31] Michael Ford, 'The Fissured Worker: Personal Service Companies and Employment Rights' (2020) 49 ILJ 35.

probably little scope for finding an implied contract between the individual and the client'.[32] HMRC has estimated that more than 250,000 individuals provide work through this type of mechanism.[33] Again, without relying on provisions with extended scope, their claims would flounder for want of a contract between the individual and the employer/client.[34]

Agency workers are the most numerically significant group who provide services without a contract with the party for whom they work. Data from the Office for National Statistics states that there are 723,000 agency workers in the UK.[35] Most agency workers do not have an express contract with the business for which they provide their services, the end user. Their work is provided in accordance with the worker's contract with the agency and the agency's agreement with the end user. As we saw in *James v Greenwich LBC*, the application of a standard of necessity before a contract is implied prevents many agency workers from challenging their treatment at the hands of the end user. In *Smith v Carillion JM Ltd*,[36] Mr Smith was a construction worker who was placed on a blacklist by a company called JM, whom he had worked for via an agency. His argument that a contract should be implied was rejected by the Court of Appeal.[37] The outcome was particularly disappointing as section 3 of the Human Rights Act 1998 (HRA 1998), the duty of compatible interpretation, would have bolstered his position but came into effect a matter of months after the wrongs occurred.[38]

Due to the devastating effect on Mr Smith's life and the seriousness of the violation upon his human rights committed by JM,[39] *Smith v Carillion JM Ltd* is possibly the starkest example of how the contractual rules of implication prevent individuals from vindicating their human rights through litigation. The legal position has been softened by the introduction of provisions specific to agency workers, such as the Agency Workers Regulations 2010. Nevertheless, the general rule remains that an agency worker will not be able to enforce their human rights against the end user through key mechanisms such as unfair dismissal law or anti-discrimination law due to the lack of a contract between those two parties.

A move away from the doctrine of necessity and the focus upon a bilateral, contractual model for the allocation of employment rights would be welcome. Mark Freedland and Paul Davies have noted a 'demand for imaginative legal recognition

[32] ibid 74.
[33] HMRC, *Intermediaries Legislation (IR35): discussion document* (17 July 2015) 4.
[34] See *Croke v Hydro Aluminium Worcester Ltd* [2007] ICR 1303, [48]–[49].
[35] Office for National Statistics, *Employees in temporary and permanent agency roles by demographic and employment variables, UK* (2020).
[36] [2015] EWCA Civ 209, [2015] IRLR 467.
[37] ibid [37].
[38] ibid [43].
[39] Discussed further in Chapter 1.

of complex multipolar personal work situations'[40] and commentators have suggested a range of alternatives that might be adopted. We may consider introducing joint and several liability for entities involved in triangular employment relations,[41] adopting a functional approach to identifying who the responsible employer should be, in light of the purpose of the particular piece of regulation,[42] or abandoning the contractual element altogether in favour of 'personal work relations'.[43] Any of these options would align more closely with the ECtHR's approach to the question of entitlement.[44] The Court looks past the legal form of the relationship[45] and focuses only upon whether the worker's fundamental rights are adequately protected against a breach from any source—whether that is the supplier, the end user/client, or the government. As will be seen, the senior courts have shown willing to overlook the absence of a contract between the parties where this is required to comply with EU law or the ECHR. Progress in the right direction, although inconsistent, has therefore begun.

B. Barred by Illegality: Movement in the Right Direction?

The contractual core of an employment relationship introduces another potential hurdle to the enforcement of one's labour rights, and thereby one's human rights. Based on a concern to preserve the integrity of the legal system and its internal consistency, the illegality doctrine states that '[n]o court will lend its aid to a man who founds his cause of action on an immoral or an illegal act'.[46] The doctrine of illegality has several strands, applicable in the different situations, and divided—at least in theory—between contractual illegality and tortious illegality. Both strands of case law have relevance to employment law, as some causes of action (such as a discrimination claim) are treated as statutory torts, whilst many others rely either on the terms of the contract or on major contractual events such as its termination. In employment cases, the illegality at the heart of the case is often linked to the individual's right to work in the UK and the extent to which a lack of the correct documentation or permissions taints the contract and renders it unenforceable. It

[40] Paul Davies and Mark Freedland, 'The Complexities of the Employing Enterprise' in Guy Davidov and Brian Langille (eds), *Boundaries and Frontiers of Labour Law: Goals and Means in the Regulation of Work* (Hart Publishing 2006) 290.

[41] Guy Davidov, 'Joint Employer Status in Triangular Employment Relationships' (2004) 42 British Journal of Industrial Relations 727.

[42] Jeremias Prassl, *The Concept of the Employer* (Oxford University Press 2015) chapters 5 and 6; Simon Deakin, 'The Changing Concept of "Employer" in Labour Law' (2001) 30 ILJ 72.

[43] Mark Freedland and Nicola Kountouris, *The Legal Construction of Personal Work Relations* (Oxford University Press 2011).

[44] See also Ford (n 31) 68.

[45] See *Martínez v Spain* (2015) 60 EHRR 3 for the Court's approach to a complex appointment process divided between the state and the Church.

[46] *Holman v Johnson* (1775) 1 Cowp 341, 343 (Mansfield CJ).

is worth remembering that many of the individuals at the centre of such disputes are in an already vulnerable position because of their status as a migrant worker.[47] They are more likely to be marginalized within the workforce and less likely to enforce their employment rights[48] or seek other support from the community.

A variety of tests have been applied to assess whether a contract is void for reasons of illegality. The dominant test in contract law—the 'reliance' test[49]—was more stringent than the tortious test, which sought an inextricable link between the illegality and the claim.[50] After a period of recent activity around the doctrine of illegality, the two strands appear to be more united. A novel balancing approach to the illegality defence was first adopted in a discrimination case before the UK Supreme Court, *Hounga v Allen and another*.[51] Following the balancing approach, a judge must weigh the public policy both for and against the illegality defence applying in a particular instance in the balance and assess whether the denial of the individual's claim is proportionate to the illegality.[52] In the employment context, this balancing approach has been confirmed to apply to contractual cases of potential illegality in the recent case of *Okedina v Chikale*.[53]

Ms Chikale was a domestic worker, brought to the UK by Mrs Okedina from Malawi. Unbeknownst to Ms Chikale, her visa expired, rendering her continued employment problematic from the perspective of the Immigration, Asylum and Nationality Act 2006. When Ms Chikale was summarily dismissed, she made claims for wrongful and unfair dismissal as well as race discrimination and unlawful deduction of wages. The employer relied on illegality as a defence: their primary argument was that the statute impliedly prohibited contracts for employment where the worker did not have appropriate leave to remain in the UK. In the Court of Appeal, Lord Justice Underhill imbued his interpretation of the 2006 Act with public policy concerns regarding the protection of the rights of vulnerable foreign nationals.[54] This interpretation leant against the application of statutory illegality. Regarding common law illegality, it remained conclusive—despite the recent developments in this doctrine—that the claimant had no knowledge of or participation in the illegality.[55] The court concluded that the employers could not rely on statutory illegality or common law illegality to defeat Ms Chikale's claims.

47 Cathryn Costello, 'Migrants and Forced Labour: A Labour Law Response' in Alan Bogg and others (eds), *The Autonomy of Labour Law* (Hart Publishing 2015).

48 For a study of the enforcement of rights by migrant workers from the EU-8 counties, see Catherine Barnard and Amy Ludlow, 'Enforcement of Employment Rights by EU-8 Migrant Workers in Employment Tribunals' (2016) 45 ILJ 1.

49 See *Tinsley v Milligan* (1994) 1 AC 340.

50 See *Hall v Woolston Hall Leisure* [2001] 1 WLR 225, [42].

51 [2014] UKSC 47, [2014] 1 WLR 2889, particularly the majority judgment of Lord Wilson.

52 *Patel v Mirza* [2016] UKSC 42, [2017] AC 467, [120].

53 [2019] EWCA Civ 1393, [2019] ICR 1635.

54 ibid [48]–[50].

55 ibid [62].

The adoption of a more moderate approach towards the illegality doctrine can only be welcomed from a human rights perspective. Where the individual is using an employment law claim to enforce their human rights, this fact should be weighed directly in the balancing exercise in their favour in the same way that the senior courts have referenced the UK's obligations under international conventions towards victims of trafficking.[56] The positive obligation upon the UK to ensure that all people, no matter what their status or the context of their claim, receive protection of their fundamental rights could form an important element in public policy discussions in future cases.

Alter the facts of *Chikale* slightly, however, and there would be less cause to celebrate. By confirming the continued application of the common law's 'knowledge plus participation' test,[57] the *dicta* in *Chikale* leaves open the possibility that any claimant who is a knowing participant in the illegality will be barred from any employment claims. In the eyes of the ECtHR, fundamental rights are not just enjoyed or enforceable by the virtuous.[58] All potential applicants, whether complicit in illegal conduct or not, should be able to bring a claim to court. Any instance in which the illegality doctrine prevents the vindication of fundamental rights by an individual puts employment law out of line with the Convention.

III. The Categorization of the Workforce

Whilst everyone protected by employment rights must have a contract with their employer, not everyone in that group is entitled to the protection of dismissal law. Dismissal law, along with other key rights, safeguards only the most privileged group: employees with a contract of service. To qualify, an individual must satisfy a battery of indicators that are applied by the tribunals to their working arrangement. Developed through the common law with no statutory intervention, Mark Freedland rightly observes that the 'accumulation of case law has added weight rather than wisdom' on the topic.[59] The tests have been powerfully criticized by Hugh Collins as both insufficiently determinate and dysfunctional when applied to some working scenarios.[60] They are restrictive in their operation and deprive many people of the opportunity to challenge the treatment of their employer. This

[56] See Alan Bogg and Sarah Green, 'Rights Are Not Just for the Virtuous: What Hounga Means for the Illegality Defence in the Discrimination Torts' (2015) 44 ILJ 101, 112–13; Alan Bogg, 'Illegality, Public Policy and the Contract of Employment' in Mark Freedland (ed), *The Contract of Employment* (Oxford University Press 2016) 406.

[57] For examples of the knowledge and participation factors barring enforcement of statutory employment rights, see *Vakante v Addey & Stanhope School* [2004] EWCA Civ 1065, [2005] 1 CMLR 3; *Zarkasi v Anindita and another* [2012] ICR 788.

[58] See *Paulet v United Kingdom* (2015) 61 EHRR 39.

[59] Freedland (n 2) 20.

[60] Collins (n 2) 369.

effect has clear implications for the capacity of employment rights to vindicate an individual's human rights, if they are required to do so. This impact will be investigated below through the consideration of two decided cases, after setting out the wider context of how employment rights are allocated in England and Wales.

A. The Trilateral Model of Rights Allocation

For several decades, the outer boundary of labour laws was defined by reference to the distinction between a contract *of* service (employees) and a contract *for* services (independent contractors). The modern picture of personal scope is more complex. Two further categories—variants of the definition of 'worker'—were introduced: one within the EA 2010 and one in other pieces of legislation from the 1990s onwards. The former definition requires only that the individual agrees to provide personal service to another in a contract.[61] The latter reflected a desire to extend the entitlement to fundamental social rights to a larger proportion of the workforce.[62] Although there are small differences in the statutory phrasing, a 'worker' is a person who provides their services personally, under a contract, to someone who is not a client or customer of their business.[63]

Workers under this second definition enjoy minimum wage and working time rights,[64] as well as protection from detriment in response to any disclosure they make in the public interest (whistleblowing).[65] The 'worker' category is also central to several aspects of collective activities. Qualifying as a trade union under the TULR(C)A 1992 depends on whether the membership of the association consists 'wholly or mainly of workers'.[66] It is through this avenue that a union may seek recognition and collective bargaining rights and engage in industrial action. On the individual side, workers are entitled to the right not to be subject to detriment as a result of their membership or union activities.[67] The 'worker' category has been held to encompass a variety of workers in the gig or on-demand economy,[68] as well as plumbers, construction workers, law firm partners, and surgeons.[69] Generally,

[61] EA 2010, section 83(2)(a).

[62] Alan Bogg and Michael Ford, 'Between Statute and Contract: Who is a Worker?' (2019) 135 LQR 347, 351.

[63] ERA 1996, section 230(3)(b).

[64] See National Minimum Wage Act 1998, section 1 and The Working Time Regulations 1998.

[65] ERA 1996, section 47B.

[66] TULR(C)A 1992, section 1.

[67] TULR(C)A 1992, section 146.

[68] See, for example, *Dewhurst v Citysprint UK Ltd* (2017) ET 2202512/2016; *Uber BV and others v Aslam and others* [2021] UKSC 5, [2021] IRLR 407.

[69] See respectively *Pimlico Plumbers Ltd v Smith* [2018] UKSC 29, [2018] ICR 1511; *Redrow Homes (Yorkshire) Ltd v Wright* [2004] EWCA Civ 469, [2004] ICR 1126; *Bates van Winkelhof v Clyde & Co LLP* [2014] UKSC 32, [2014] 1 WLR 2047; *Hospital Medical Group Ltd v Westwood* [2012] EWCA Civ 1005, [2013] ICR 415.

the definition of worker has significantly increased the availability of these key social rights to individuals who would previously have been considered self-employed, and therefore outside the scope of any employment rights.

The case law on these two statutory worker concepts is mixed and at times confused. One significant step forward in the area of personal scope has been the evolution in the courts' approach to finding the true agreement between the parties. Previously, the terms of the contract had been taken as decisive in almost all cases. Personal service, for example, could be negated by the insertion of a term in the contract which permitted substitution or delegation by the individual.[70] Moving away from the established approach, the UK Supreme Court in *Autoclenz v Belcher* expressly recognized that the imbalance of bargaining power between the parties could heavily influence the terms of the contract.[71] The relative bargaining power of the parties, the court said, 'must be taken into account in deciding whether the terms of any written agreement in truth represent what was agreed and the true agreement will often have to be gleaned from all the circumstances of the case, of which the written agreement is only a part'.[72]

Building on *Autoclenz*, the UK Supreme Court in *Uber BV v Aslam and others* held that the classification exercise must be undertaken with the aims of the relevant statutes in mind.[73] For example, in construing the relational scope of working time regulation, we should aim to ensure that the result ultimately protects vulnerable workers from being exploited through excessive working hours. In addition, the courts should be aware of the dependency and subordination that characterizes employment relationships and may affect the terms of the agreement reached by the parties.[74] Any contractual terms that attempt to force a particular status upon the individual will be disregarded and, when considering whether a claimant is a 'worker' under the relevant statute, the degree of control exercised by the putative employer will be relevant.[75] As a very recent judgment that emphasizes the need for a purposive approach, it is not clear yet how far it will represent a shift in the tribunals' approach to questions of classification. In pushing towards inclusivity and with its sensitivity to the realities of the employment relationship, the *Uber* approach may complement human rights arguments well—these will be discussed further in section V.

Elsewhere, however, we see concerning trends. Senior members of the judiciary see the two statutory definitions as raising the same issues, blurring the lines between the 'worker' categories despite the differences in statutory phrasing and

[70] See for example *Express & Echo Publications Ltd v Tanton* [1999] ICR 693.
[71] *Autoclenz Ltd v Belcher* [2011] UKSC 41, [2011] 4 All ER 745, [34].
[72] ibid [35].
[73] *Uber BV and others v Aslam and others* (n 68) [70]–[71].
[74] ibid [75].
[75] ibid [87].

contextual background to the legislation.[76] This approach is particularly worrying considering the second trend: the introduction of factors often associated with the restrictive definition of a 'contract of employment' in the assessment of whether an individual is a 'worker'. Features such as subordination to direction,[77] mutuality of obligation,[78] and integration into the enterprise[79] have appeared in judgments explaining and applying the 'worker' definitions. A collapse of the boundaries between the three categories is occurring, leading to the precise problems of exclusivity that the 'worker' categories were intended to avoid. Thus, the broad, fundamental rights-inspired definitions are being impaired by the narrow factors that we see in the 'contract of employment' case law.

B. The 'Contract of Service': An Exclusionary Device

Despite these additional categories, the distinction between independent contractors and employees remains central to the personal scope of employment law's protection. To pursue an unfair dismissal claim[80] or a common law claim for wrongful dismissal,[81] the claimant must satisfy the court that they work under a contract of service/employment. It is a difficult distinction to apply, and the courts have developed a variety of factors that they will consider to reach a decision. Does the employer control the activities to be done and how they should be done?[82] Is the individual in business on their own account? Do they take a risk of profit and loss?[83] Are they integrated into the employer's business?[84] In some cases, the courts search for a contract between the parties by examining whether there is an 'irreducible minimum' of promises between the parties: an ongoing obligation upon the company to offer work and a corresponding obligation upon the worker to accept it.[85] As with the aforementioned 'worker' categories, the courts are more willing to look to the realities of the way in which the relationship is conducted, rather than how it is described in the contractual documentation, in order to apply this crucial distinction.[86]

76 *Bates van Winkelhof v Clyde & Co* (n 69) [31]-[32] and *Pimlico Plumbers v Smith* (n 69) [14]–[15].

77 *Jivraj v Hashwani* [2011] UKSC 40, [2011] 1 WLR 1872, [45]; *Bates van Winkelhof v Clyde & Co* (n 69) [39].

78 *Windle v Secretary of State for Justice* [2016] EWCA Civ 459, [2017] 3 All ER 568, [23].

79 *Bates van Winkelhof v Clyde & Co* (n 69) [39].

80 ERA 1996, section 203.

81 See, for example, Lord Steyn's observation that the implied term of mutual trust and confidence is 'an incident of all contracts of employment': *Malik v Bank of Credit and Commerce International S.A.* [1998] AC 20, 45.

82 *Ready Mixed Concrete (South East) Ltd v Minister of Pensions and National Insurance* [1968] 2 WLR 775, [1968] 2 QB 497, 515.

83 *Market Investigations Ltd v Minister of Social Security* [1969] 2 QB 173, 184.

84 *Beloff v Pressdram Ltd* [1973] FSR 33, 42.

85 *Nethermere (St Neots) Ltd v Gardiner and another* [1984] ICR 612, 624 (Stephenson LJ).

86 See *Autoclenz v Belcher* (n 71).

One problem persists: 'those who describe themselves as self-employed often manifest many of the characteristics of employees—they may in practice be dependent, have inferior bargaining power and they risk exploitation'.[87] Nevertheless, they are excluded from the protection of employment law as independent contractors. Concerningly from an ECHR perspective, this exclusion stands even where the individual has suffered a breach of their human rights at the hands of their employer. Two cases demonstrate this deficiency in domestic employment law's capacity to enforce the fundamental rights of all individuals.

The case of *O'Kelly v Trusthouse Forte*[88] discloses a serious infringement of the workers' right to freedom of association. The infringement went unnoticed and unremedied by the court. A hotel assigned work to a pool of 'regulars'—casual waiters who the company relied upon and offered work to regularly. Some of the regulars worked between thirty and forty hours a week. If a waiter failed to work an assigned shift, they would not be allocated future work—a level of disciplinary control usually associated with contracts of employment. For many of the workers, the hotel was their only source of income. The three waiters in question were members and stewards for the Hotel Catering Workers Union. Not long before their dismissal, the claimants began asserting that the regulars should receive contracts of employment, with the help of a union. They each received a letter from the hotel employer stating that their services were no longer needed. The waiters made a claim for unfair dismissal before the Industrial Tribunal, arguing that they had been dismissed for an inadmissible reason: their trade union membership and activities.

The first task for the tribunal was to classify their working arrangements. The waiters' claim was rejected at this initial stage. The court considered that the claimants did not have a contract. The 'commanding economic power' of the defendants and the advantages for the claimants of being offered work consistently led to a firm expectation of work allocation but 'it was not a contractual promise'.[89] The only possible contractual arrangement was 'a contract to offer and accept individual contracts of employment' for particular engagements.[90] In addition, the Court of Appeal agreed with the Industrial Tribunal's original finding that, if there had been a contract in place, it would not have been one of employment.[91]

Although the waiters behaved as employees whilst at work and relied on the income that their shifts provided, the tribunal considered them to be independent contractors. On the Article 11 dimension of *O'Kelly*, Mark Freedland and Nicola

[87] Catherine Barnard and Alysia Blackham, 'Discrimination and the Self-Employed: The Scope of Protection in an Interconnected Age' in Hugh Collins (ed), *European Contract Law and the Charter of Fundamental Rights* (Intersentia 2017) 198.
[88] *O'Kelly and Others v Trusthouse Forte Plc* [1984] QB 90.
[89] ibid 116 (Ackner LJ), 124 (Donaldson MR).
[90] ibid 125.
[91] ibid 117 (Ackner LJ), 122 (Fox LJ), 125 (Donaldson MR).

Kountouris observe that '[t]here seems to have been no suggestion whatsoever that the engagement of this fundamental collective right should have commanded a specially inclusive approach to the construction of the personal scope provision'.[92] I have argued that, if considered today, the ECtHR would find that the decision in *O'Kelly* amounted to a breach of the workers' Article 11 rights and a failure on behalf of the UK to fulfil its positive obligations to safeguard those rights.[93]

More recently, in *Braine & others v National Gallery*,[94] a group of educators for the Gallery sought the right to be collectively consulted about a reorganization and the right not to be dismissed unfairly, amongst other rights. Both these rights are available only to employees.[95] Whilst the unfair dismissal complaints may have raised issues relating to Article 8 ECHR,[96] the focus here will be on the right to freedom of association. Prior to the *National Gallery* case, the Court of Appeal held that the right to collective consultation 'falls squarely within the "essential elements" protected by Article 11'.[97] Therefore, stated the Court of Appeal, 'any provision of [the TULR(C)A] scheme which restricts its availability to particular classes of workers requires to be justified'.[98] *Sindicatul Păstorul cel Bun*, discussed in section I, demonstrated that the ECtHR would seek to include the workers within the scope of the right if at all possible. The Article 11 dimension of the case was raised by the claimants in argument.[99] Would the human right at stake in the case make any difference to the outcome of the case?

Examining the facts, one can see that it was a finely balanced case. In their contracts, the terms rejected any mutuality of obligations and stated that the contract was not one of employment. The educators worked variable hours but were always given notice of when they were to run a session and the Gallery was keen to avoid cancelling a scheduled session. The educators provided personal service during the sessions according to the Gallery's schedule and they were also invited to Gallery training and events along with the salaried staff. They were given extensive training and regular guidance on the performance of their duties, as well as performance evaluations by colleagues. The educators attended group meetings regularly and were presented to the public as representatives and expert staff of the Gallery. From this range of factors, there is a tenable route to the conclusion that the educators worked under a contract of employment, especially during the times where an individual was subordinated to the control of the gallery on a particular assignment.

[92] Mark Freedland and Nicola Kountouris, 'Some Reflections on the "Personal Scope" of Collective Labour Law' (2017) 46 ILJ 52, 59.

[93] Philippa Collins, 'The Inadequate Protection of Human Rights in Unfair Dismissal Law' (2018) 47 ILJ 504, 514–15.

[94] (2019) ET 2201625/2018.

[95] See TULR(C)A 1992, section 188 and ERA 1996, section 94 respectively.

[96] See the ECtHR's 'consequence-based' approach set out in *Denisov v Ukraine* Application no 76639/11 (ECtHR, 25 September 2018) and discussed in Chapter 2, section II(B).

[97] *Vining v Wandsworth* (n 3) [63].

[98] ibid [64].

[99] *Braine v The National Gallery* (n 94) [97].

In these circumstances, a concern that the educators must be able to enforce their human right to freedom of association should have guaranteed this outcome.

The ET rejected the existence of a long-term contract of employment. The tribunal held 'there was no obligation between assignments to offer or accept work and that was fatal to the Claimants' case'.[100] This finding prevented the Gallery staff from accruing the necessary period of qualifying service required for an unfair dismissal claim. Further, when assessing the educators' status during an individual assignment, the judge was persuaded by the *differences* between the educator group and the salaried staff.[101] This approach runs directly counter to the ECtHR's approach outlined earlier: looking for similarities (e.g. control, integration, personal service) between the individual and an employment relationship. Even after they had called upon Article 11 ECHR and the HRA 1998 in their arguments, as well as comparable points under EU law, the claimants faced the same fate as Mr O'Kelly and his fellow waiters. Both the *National Gallery* case and *O'Kelly* demonstrate that there are significant difficulties in using employment rights as a vehicle for the enforcement of an individual's fundamental rights.

IV. Statutory Restrictions on Employment Rights

The final category of structural restrictions on the personal scope of employment rights are statutory. Here, the focus is particularly on the limitations on the scope of unfair dismissal law as this cause of action has so far been the primary arena for litigation with a human rights angle between employer and employee. One statutory restriction, the qualifying period of continuous employment, has been the subject of a challenge in the ECtHR. The other set of limitations, targeting particular occupations, has received attention in the domestic courts recently and will be explored further later.

A. The Qualifying Period and *Redfearn v United Kingdom*

An individual wishing to make an unfair dismissal claim faces further obstacles that may prevent a tribunal from examining the substance of their complaint. Section 108 of the ERA 1996 provides that the right not to be dismissed unfairly is subject to the individual completing a period of continuous service with the employer that they intend to claim against.[102] The qualifying period is currently set at two years,[103] with a list of exemptions from the qualifying period where employees

[100] ibid [76].
[101] ibid [88].
[102] ERA 1996, section 108.
[103] ERA 1996, section 108.

are dismissed for impermissible reasons.[104] On the basis of data held by the OECD (Organisation for Economic Co-operation and Development), approximately nine million employees held their current job for less than one year in 2019.[105] Whilst there is no specific data regarding the number of employees with tenure less than two years, it is likely to be another significant group who would also be excluded from the protection of unfair dismissal. This restriction upon one's eligibility to make a claim leads to a serious inadequacy in the capacity of the law of unfair dismissal to assist individuals who wish to vindicate their human rights.

We encountered Mr Redfearn's litigation in Chapter 3 as an example of a clear statement from the ECtHR regarding the positive obligation upon member states to extend any guarantees of fundamental rights broadly.[106] In brief, Mr Redfearn was dismissed from his position as a driver by Serco after being elected as a councillor for the British National Party. To justify its decision, Serco cited several risks for the company: its concern that Mr Redfearn's presence would cause anxiety amongst passengers who were vulnerable people of primarily Asian origin or that damage would be caused to Serco's reputation, and that the situation would put the company's contract with the local City Council in jeopardy. As Mr Redfearn did not meet the one-year qualifying period of continuous service required to launch an unfair dismissal claim at the time, his only option was to attempt a race discrimination claim which was rejected by the Court of Appeal.[107]

Mr Redfearn took his case to the ECtHR alleging that the domestic system failed to protect his ECHR rights. The Court considered his complaint under Article 11 read in light of Article 10.[108] He argued that his fundamental rights must be effective from the first day of employment, and not rendered illusory by the requirement that an employee's rights can only be enforced after the completion of a period of service with the relevant employer. The UK government argued that it had fulfilled its positive obligations in this case and that the qualifying period was within its margin of appreciation because it pursued a legitimate aim: creating greater employment opportunities by encouraging recruitment.[109]

The majority of the Court found in favour of Mr Redfearn. Considering the seriousness of the sanction and its consequences, the majority held that the dismissal could strike at the substance of his Article 11 rights. The Court held that the operation of the qualifying period had deprived the applicant of the only effective means of challenging his dismissal.[110] Had the UK thereby exceeded the

[104] ERA 1996, section 108(3), (4), and (5).

[105] OECD, *Labour Market Statistics: Employment by job tenure intervals 1976–2019* (UK Data Service, 2020).

[106] See Chapter 3, section I.

[107] *Redfearn v Serco Ltd* [2006] EWCA Civ 659, [2006] ICR 1367.

[108] *Redfearn v UK* (n 1) [31].

[109] ibid [38].

[110] ibid [52].

margin of appreciation available to it in implementing the domestic system of rights protection at issue? The Court accepted that the qualifying period was a reasonable means to bolster the domestic labour market, but it was concerned that a system which could allow a dismissal purely on grounds of political affiliation carried the potential for abuse.[111] The Court found that it was incumbent on the UK to take appropriate measures to protect employees—including those with less than one year of service—from dismissal for reasons related to their political opinions.[112] As the UK had failed to take these steps, it was in breach of its positive obligation to secure adequate protection for the applicant's Article 11 rights.

The impact of *Redfearn* in the UK was the introduction of an exception to the qualifying period in the Enterprise and Regulatory Reform Act 2013. Section 13 inserted a provision into ERA 1996 stating that '[the qualifying period] does not apply if the reason (or, if more than one, the principal reason) for the dismissal is, or relates to, the employee's political opinions or affiliation'.[113] This change brings the UK into line with the letter of the Strasbourg *dicta*. As has been observed by Hugh Collins and Virginia Mantouvalou, however, the Court's reasoning in *Redfearn* 'is equally applicable to all Convention rights that create positive obligations on parties to the Convention',[114] which currently includes Article 8's right to respect for private life, Article 9 on freedom of religion, and Article 10's freedom of expression. The Court has previously transferred its reasoning between Articles 8, 9, 10, and 11[115] so it is very likely that the positive obligations as phrased in *Redfearn* under Article 11 would be similarly applicable to the other articles.

The consequence of this analysis is that the government's amendment is 'apparently inadequate to address the full challenge posed by the ECtHR to the qualifying period for unfair dismissal'.[116] Collins and Mantouvalou suggest that a broader exception would be appropriate: for cases where a Convention right has been invoked and there is an interference with that right inherent in the reason for dismissal, the qualifying period should not apply.[117] It is likely that a further challenge to the qualifying period, either domestically or before the ECtHR, is needed before any modification along these lines might be implemented.

[111] ibid [52] and [55].
[112] ibid [57].
[113] Enterprise and Regulatory Reform Act 2013, section 13.
[114] Hugh Collins and Virginia Mantouvalou, '*Redfearn v UK*: Political Association and Dismissal' (2013) 76 MLR 909, 915.
[115] See, for example, *Eweida and others v United Kingdom* (2013) 57 EHRR 8 at [83].
[116] Collins and Mantouvalou (n 114) 915.
[117] ibid 916.

B. Exclusion Through Sectoral Occupation and Diplomatic Immunity

From outside employment law, the State Immunity Act 1978 (SIA 1978) has an impact on the capacity of individuals to vindicate their rights through employment law. Section 4 of that Act sets out detailed regulation regarding the application of diplomatic immunity to a contract of employment and section 16 provides immunity from any claim relating to the employment of a person on a diplomatic mission. Two domestic workers employed by embassies in the UK challenged the application of diplomatic immunity to their employment law claims, arguing on the basis of the right to a fair trial under the Convention and the EU Charter of Fundamental Rights.

In *Benkharbouche v Embassy of the Republic of Sudan*,[118] the UK Supreme Court found that the application of immunity to contracts of employment went beyond what was expected in international law. The application of the SIA 1978 was held to be in breach of Article 6 ECHR, the right to a fair trial.[119] Whilst diplomatic immunity could in principle be consistent with the right to a fair trial, the scope of the immunity under the Act was too broad: it went beyond acts of state sovereignty and covered acts of a private nature.[120] A declaration of incompatibility was made under section 4 HRA 1998. Even further, the Supreme Court held that Article 47 of the EU Charter (the right to an effective remedy and a fair trial) had direct effect in national legal systems. Consequently, any inconsistent national provisions contained in the SIA should be disapplied where an EU-derived legal right was concerned. Thus, the discrimination and working time claims were permitted to proceed, whereas the unfair dismissal and minimum wage claims were founded solely in domestic law so could not be rescued by EU law's direct effect.[121] To date, no changes have been made in response to the Supreme Court's concerns.[122] Therefore workers in the diplomacy sector relying on domestic employment rights will still be affected by the SIA's operation.

The Employment Rights Act 1996 also excludes particular occupations from some of its elements. Numerically less significant than many of the other groups unable to claim employment rights, the targeted occupations include members of the police force and mariners.[123] The broad application of the exclusion of members of the police force was confirmed in *Redbridge LBC v Dhinsa* to include

[118] *Benkharbouche v Secretary of State for Foreign and Commonwealth Affairs* (n 5).
[119] ibid [76].
[120] ibid [66]–[67] and [69].
[121] ibid [78].
[122] See a report in 2020 that the government was still considering how to respond to the section 4 declaration in *Benkharbouche*: Ministry of Justice, *Responding to human rights judgments: Report to the Joint Committee on Human Rights on the Government's response to human rights judgments 2019–2020* (CP 347, December 2020) 38.
[123] ERA 1996, sections 199 and 200.

members of the Parks Police Service, who hold rights in relation to open spaces.[124] The issue was soon reopened in *Vining v London Borough of Wandsworth*, discussed in section V.

V. Reclassification Compelled by Human Rights Arguments

We can see that, contrary to the ECHR's universality, many groups of workers are excluded from vindicating their rights against their employer following an infringement. Statutory provisions and common law doctrines combine to narrow the scope of protection offered by employment law, and particularly the law of unfair dismissal. The Supreme Court's strongly purposive approach to the discernment of the true nature of the agreement between the parties, set out most recently in *Uber v Aslam*, may begin to soften the sharper edges of the rules on employment status. The terms of the contract are no longer determinative, or even a primary reference point, in determining these questions,[125] and the purposive approach may encourage tribunals to take an inclusive approach where the enforcement of a fundamental right is at stake.

Elsewhere, rapid progress has been made under the banner of human rights in this area. Two cases have seen dramatic reversals of the position of the claimants before the courts based on their human rights arguments: *Vining v London Borough of Wandsworth*[126] and *Gilham v Ministry of Justice*.[127] Where both litigants had previously been held to be outside the scope of the relevant provision, the senior courts applied the duty of compatible interpretation under the HRA 1998 to reach the opposite result. Whilst the claimants benefit from an exception or reversal in their case, the litigation exposed the need for systematic consideration of the strictures of employment law's personal scope and leaves the law in a somewhat tangled state. The difficulties of this *ad hoc* and litigation-driven evolution process will be discussed in the final section, where these two decisions will be contrasted with two cases where the workers were held to be outside the scope of the relevant employment rights.

A. *Vining v London Borough of Wandsworth* and the Inclusion of Parks Police

The claimants in *Vining* were two Parks Police officers and their union, UNISON. The employees were made redundant and alleged that they had been unfairly

[124] *Redbridge London Borough Council v Dhinsa and another* [2014] EWCA Civ 178, [2014] ICR 834.
[125] *Uber BV and others v Aslam and others* (n 68) [76].
[126] *Vining v Wandsworth* (n 3).
[127] *Gilham v Ministry of Justice* (n 4).

dismissed. They were barred from making a claim due to section 200 ERA 1996 which excludes members of the police force and the Court of Appeal's decision in *Dhinsa*. Their argument was that their exclusion from the scope of unfair dismissal law amounted to an infringement of their Article 8 rights either alone or combined with Article 14 ECHR. UNISON was also party to the case and sought an award for a failure to consult collective representatives during the redundancy process under TULR(C)A 1992. Employees in police service are also excluded from redundancy consultation rights[128] and here the union argued that their inability to represent their members in a consultation process was an infringement of the right to freedom of association in Article 11 ECHR. The individual employees and their union argued that the relevant provisions excluding Parks Police from the scope of protection should be interpreted compatibly with their Convention rights. The claims would therefore be allowed progress beyond the preliminary stage. The Court of Appeal found in favour of the union but rejected the individual claimants' arguments.

In addressing the individuals' Article 8 arguments, the court held that the 'mere fact of dismissal from employment' was not sufficient to engage Article 8.[129] The court acknowledged decisions from the ECtHR regarding when the consequences of a dismissal may engage the individual's private life, such as reputation damage or an effect on the individual's self-esteem and self-respect.[130] However, the Court of Appeal considered that these special factors were not present. There was no suggestion that the claimants had engaged in wrongful conduct and no stigma attached to the dismissal.[131] Difficulty finding new employment occurs to some extent after every dismissal and that was insufficient alone to engage Article 8. This finding also led to the rejection of the arguments made based on Article 14, which relied upon Article 8 being engaged. Section 200 applied to the claimants' case without alteration and the unfair dismissal claims were therefore rejected.

UNISON's arguments based on Article 11 were met with a different response. The court viewed the right to be consulted before dismissals to be an essential element of Article 11, either as an aspect of collective bargaining as recognized in *Demir v Turkey* or as an activity analogous to it.[132] Under Article 11, the state has a positive obligation to put in place a legislative scheme that strikes a fair balance between the relevant competing interests and 'any provision of that scheme which restricts its availability to particular classes of workers requires to be justified, albeit that the state is recognised to have a wide margin of appreciation'.[133] Because the government had not advanced any justifications regarding why members of the

[128] TULR(C)A 1992, section 280.
[129] *Vining v Wandsworth* (n 3) [43].
[130] ibid [47]
[131] ibid [49].
[132] ibid [63].
[133] ibid [64].

police force should be excluded from TULR(C)A's scope, the court found a breach of Article 11. Turning to the interpretive obligation in section 3 HRA, the court was unable to find a reformulation of the statutory language that drew the line between workers where the exclusion was justified and those where it was unjustified. Nevertheless, the outcome reached by the court was that, through an application of section 3 HRA, the relevant exclusionary provision does not apply to members of the Parks Police where Article 11 is engaged by the complaint. UNISON was therefore able to pursue their consultation complaint in the tribunal.

B. *Gilham v Ministry of Justice*: Justice for Judges

The case of *Gilham v Ministry of Justice* followed a similar pattern. Judge Gilham was seeking protection under the ERA against detriment after making protected disclosures—she perceived herself to be a whistleblower. Her claim was rejected by the ET on the basis that she did not possess the requisite 'worker' status: an individual who undertakes by contract to perform work personally for an entity that is not a client or customer of theirs.[134] The tribunal considered her to be an office holder, meaning that her engagement was based on a statutory appointment rather than a contract.

Before the Court of Appeal, Judge Gilham relied heavily on Article 10 ECHR, the right to freedom of expression, and the HRA 1998. Safeguards against detriment for whistleblowing workers is one aspect of Article 10, as evidenced by a line of ECtHR cases originating in *Guja v Moldova*,[135] and the Court has examined a complaint similar to Judge Gilham's in relation to a Russian judge.[136] Judge Gilham's alternative argument invoked Article 10 in combination with Article 14, which prohibits discrimination against individuals in the enjoyment of their human rights.[137] She argued that her occupation as a judge constituted a status under Article 14 and that she was disadvantaged in terms of protection as a whistleblower when compared to other, contractually engaged workers. Either of these arguments could be combined with the HRA's duty of compatible interpretation to reverse the tribunal's decision on her exclusion from whistleblowing protection.

The Article 10 ECHR argument was rejected by both the Court of Appeal and the UK Supreme Court. As the defendant was a public authority, Judge Gilham could enforce her human rights using the direct action provided for by section 7 HRA. Therefore, the courts considered that the law provided an adequate remedy for any infringement upon her human rights and there was no need to construe the ERA in a manner that extended its safeguards to Judge Gilham.[138]

[134] ERA 1996, section 230(3)(b).
[135] *Guja v Moldova* (2011) 53 EHRR 16.
[136] *Kudeshkina v Russia* (2011) 52 EHRR 37.
[137] ECHR, Article 14.
[138] *Gilham v Ministry of Justice* (n 4) [27].

The alternative argument, based on the combination of Articles 10 and 14, was successful in the UK Supreme Court. Was there a difference in treatment between Judge Gilham and others in relation to how their Article 10 rights were secured by the legislative regime? The ERA route that was not available to Judge Gilham provides protection from detriment, as well as from disciplinary action, and is more generous in its remedial elements, for example, by including damages for injury to feelings.[139] Thus, her exclusion from eligibility for this cause of action left her Article 10 rights *less* protected than those of other workers.

The next stage in the court's reasoning was to assert that '[a]n occupational classification is clearly capable of being a "status" within the meaning of article 14'.[140] This statement is not supported by any direct authority from the ECtHR, although the Strasbourg Court has adopted a fairly wide interpretation of this phrase.[141] Having found a distinction based on a relevant status in relation to the enjoyment of a Convention right, the court turned to the justification stage where proportionality to a legitimate aim should be examined. After some discussion of the appropriate standard of review, the Supreme Court noted that no legitimate aim had in fact been provided by the Ministry of Justice.[142] The justification process therefore never got underway. Judge Gilham was successful in her Articles 10 and 14 argument.

The Supreme Court finally turned to 'the most difficult question' of providing a remedy.[143] Applying the section 3 HRA duty of compatible interpretation, the court reconsidered the scope of the ERA definition of 'worker'. In particular, the key question was whether the requirement of a contract under that definition was one of its fundamental features. The inclusion of judges within the scope of 'worker' had already been achieved in litigation based upon EU law in *Ministry of Justice v O'Brien*.[144] This decision aided the court in finding that the extension of the definition to the judiciary was indeed possible without undermining a fundamental feature of the ERA 1996. The court was clear that the reinterpretation of the ERA's provision would only apply where its effects are incompatible with a Convention right. No precise phrasing was offered, instead the court stated that 'the Employment Rights Act 1996 should be read and given effect to extend its whistleblowing protection to the holders of judicial office'.[145]

139 ibid [30].
140 ibid [32].
141 See for example *Sidabras And Dziautas v Lithuania* (2006) 42 EHRR 6 where the treatment of ex-KGB agents was examined under Article 14.
142 *Gilham v Ministry of Justice* (n 4) [36].
143 ibid [38].
144 *Ministry of Justice v O'Brien* [2013] UKSC 6, [2013] 1 WLR 522.
145 *Gilham v Ministry of Justice* (n 4) [44].

C. An Unpredictable Artform: The Limits of Human Rights Argumentation

Gilham and *Vining* were very welcome decisions, after decades of the application of restrictive rules on the entitlement to employment rights and little judicial interest in developing the common law in a more inclusive direction. EU law and discrimination law have also proved to be powerful tools in altering boundaries of certain labour laws. In recent months, for example, the domestic legislation that implements EU health and safety directives has been successfully challenged where the scope of protection is limited to 'employees' rather than 'workers' in *R. (on the application of The Independent Workers' Union of Great Britain) v The Secretary of State for Work and Pensions.*[146] In *Puthenveettil v Alexander,*[147] the exemption from the national minimum wage that applies to 'family workers' was disapplied on the grounds that it constitutes unjustified indirect discrimination against women. Most recently, a union formed to represent foster carers won a major victory when the Court of Appeal, relying on Article 11, overturned a decision that they could not be listed as a trade union.[148]

It must be observed, however, that these decisions are only one side of the story. Elsewhere, groups struggle to secure the entitlement to claim employment rights that are intimately connected to their fundamental rights. We return to Article 11, the right to freedom of association and the rights that have been recognized as aspects of the right to form and join a trade union. Within the TULR(C)A 1992 framework, being 'recognized' by the employer as a trade union for the purpose of collective bargaining is a crucial step. Unions can seek to force an employer to recognize them through the statutory recognition procedure, which is administered by the Central Arbitration Committee (CAC).[149] The procedure is only available to unions that are on a list held by the Certification Officer and a union's membership must consist wholly or mainly of 'workers'.[150] At various points in the statutory process, unions have been prevented from representing members of the workforce on grounds related to their employment status. The progress shown elsewhere is far from uniform.

In *R. (on the application of Independent Workers' Union of Great Britain) v Central Arbitration Committee & University of London*, a union sought recognition via the statutory process. The union wished to represent outsourced workers

[146] *R. (on the application of the Independent Workers' Union of Great Britain) v The Secretary of State for Work and Pensions & The Secretary of State for Business, Energy and Industrial Strategy* [2020] EWHC 3050 (Admin).

[147] *Puthenveettil v Alexander, George & The Secretary of State for Business, Energy and Industrial Strategy* [2020] ET 2361118/2013.

[148] *National Union of Professional Foster Carers v Certification Officer* [2021] EWCA Civ 548.

[149] TULR(C)A 1992, schedule A1.

[150] TULR(C)A 1992, section 1.

who were hired by an agency, Cordant, to provide services to the University. Any potential recognition by Cordant was scuppered by the existence of a prior recognition agreement and collective bargain which included some of the relevant workers within its scope. In these circumstances, the incoming union cannot use the TULR(C)A procedure to oust the incumbent union, a situation that was upheld on appeal.[151]

In respect of seeking recognition by the University of London, the union was prevented from progressing further on the grounds of their members' employment status. As they were agency workers, there was no contract between the workers and the University.[152] As a consequence, the members of the union fell outside the definition of 'worker', which requires a contract between the parties, and the union was unable to apply to represent their interests in bargaining with the University of London. This decision is manifestly inconsistent with the ECtHR's decision outlined earlier in *Sindicatul Păstorul cel Bun*, where the Court made no mention of the need for a contract in order to be entitled to join and be represented by a trade union under Article 11. The workers were left without any opportunity to seek recognition for their chosen union and their reliance upon Article 11 was not sufficient to alter the courts' conclusions.

In the *Deliveroo* case, the Independent Workers Union applied for recognition on behalf of a group of riders. The CAC found that the riders were not 'workers' within the statutory definition because they did not have an obligation of personal service—they had a genuine right to substitute another rider to complete a particular job. The High Court upheld the CAC's decision that their union was not entitled to utilize the recognition procedure. The court considered that the ECtHR's jurisprudence, particularly *Sindicatul Păstorul cel Bun*, that the relevant aspects of Article 11 were restricted to those in an 'employment relationship', which was not present here.[153] The Court did not attempt to conduct an assessment of the overall characteristics of the relationship between the parties and whether the lack of personal service was sufficiently destructive of a relationship of employment that the riders should be disentitled from their rights under Article 11. The High Court's reasoning goes against the grain of the inclusive approach evidenced in Strasbourg and it is currently under appeal to the Court of Appeal. As it stands currently, the riders' capacity to claim statutory rights that are necessary to exercise their full freedom of association is obstructed by the requirement of personal service.

[151] See *R. (on the application of the Independent Workers' Union of Great Britain) v Secretary of State for Business, Energy and Industrial Strategy and others* [2021] EWCA Civ 260, [2021] IRLR 363.

[152] *R. (on the application of the Independent Workers' Union of Great Britain) v Central Arbitration Committee & University of London* [2019] EWHC 728 (Admin), [2019] IRLR 530, [75]. The union did not appeal this aspect of the decision.

[153] *R. (on the application of the Independent Workers Union of Great Britain) v Central Arbitration Committee & Roofoods Limited t/a Deliveroo* [2018] EWHC 3342 (Admin), [2019] IRLR 249, [39].

These cases demonstrate one drawback of a litigation-driven approach to tackling the personal scope problem. The results are inconsistent, depending to a great extent on the judge's viewpoint and their interpretation of the Convention and its case law. For example, the High Court in *Deliveroo* could be thought to have taken a restrictive or ungenerous reading of Article 11 whereas the Supreme Court in *Gilham* was willing to accept the occupational status of a judge as a relevant status under Article 14 without any prior ECtHR case law on the issue. Victory and defeat appear arbitrarily distributed, even turning on unusual events such as the fact that both defendants in *Vining* and *Gilham* declined to put forward any justification for the exclusionary legislative provisions. The absence of any justification left the courts with no choice but to find in the claimants' favour.[154] If the exclusionary rule in each case had been defended and supported by evidence of a legitimate aim, as occurred in the *Deliveroo* case for example,[155] the claimants may have found themselves without a remedy for the infringement upon their human rights.

I have also noted elsewhere a concern that these decisions create a tiering amongst the workforce.[156] Many claimants, when facing unfavourable treatment, may not be able to attach their argument to a Convention right and therefore the successes that hinged so heavily on Articles 10 and 11 ECHR are of no relevance to them. The structures noted in the early parts of this chapter, for the most part, persist in their exclusionary operation and generate a disadvantaged group who lack any avenue to challenge their treatment. This concern speaks directly to an anxiety regarding the effects of relying heavily upon human rights in the employment sphere raised in Chapter 2.[157] Any issues that cannot be phrased in language of human rights are neglected and many claimants have limited opportunity to defend themselves against abuse of managerial prerogative.

Conclusion

This chapter commenced by noting that the UK is under an obligation to offer universal protection of human rights in its jurisdiction, including against infringements by private actors such as employers. Any failure to provide the opportunity to all individuals to enforce their rights must be justified through the provision of a legitimate aim and be necessary and proportionate to achieve that aim. When the Strasbourg Court is required to assess whether an individual is party to an employment relationship for the purposes of Article 11's trade union rights, its starting

[154] Similarly, in *Puthenveettil v Alexander*, the Secretary of State declined to participate in the hearing and did not offer any justification or evidence to defend the existence of the 'family worker' exception: see *Puthenveettil v Alexander* (n 147) [42].

[155] *R. (IWUGB) v CAC & Deliveroo* (n 153) [55].

[156] Collins and Fradley (n 6) 239.

[157] See Chapter 2, section II.

assumption is that the individual *is* entitled to call upon Article 11 and it asks whether the relationship had enough features of 'traditional' employment to maintain that conclusion.

Even the most cursory examination of the legal framework that determines the personal scope of domestic employment rights reveals serious limitations upon employment law's capacity to meet those expectations. Although this area is rapidly evolving through a persistent stream of litigation based upon the Convention, EU law, and discrimination law, the restrictive structures still dominate the question of the personal scope of employment rights. Many groups within the workforce, such as contractors, agency workers, office holders, and new recruits, fall into gaps within the scope of protection and are therefore unable to vindicate their fundamental rights through employment law. For these workers, the narrow relational scope of employment rights remains—their fundamental rights are not protected against infringement by the entity for whom they work.

With relation to those important victories in cases such as *Vining* and *Gilham*, I would also argue that the creation of exceptions from the general rules may distract from the urgent need for a systematic review of the operation of this area of law.[158] As the application of section 3 HRA satisfies individual litigants, we are diverted from the wider fact that the contours of employment law's relational scope are consistently narrow and leave significant gaps between domestic law and the requirements of the Convention's positive obligations. Individual litigation has limited capacity to achieve wider structural change in respect of personal scope. Even a high-profile finding against the UK in this area in *Redfearn v UK* failed to prompt any substantial review. The verdict led to a very minor amendment to the qualifying period, the minimum capable of achieving compliance with the ECtHR's criticisms and inadequate to meet the full challenge posed by the Court's reasoning. I argue that a more concerted approach, deliberately conscious of the obligations entailed by the Convention, is necessary to reshape the rules of personal scope. Small adjustments are simply inadequate and *ad hoc* solutions to the points thrown up by litigation is not a satisfactory method of legal evolution. Careful and considered reform, taking into account human rights principles, is necessary and urgent. One possible approach to this process is outlined in Chapter 9.

[158] See Philippa Collins, 'Square Peg vs a Round Hole? The Necessity of a Bill of Rights for Workers' (2020) 11 European Labour Law Journal 199.

6

Human Rights and the Law of Unfair Dismissal

A concern for the employee's dignity and autonomy has been argued to underpin the right not to be dismissed unfairly.[1] Unfair dismissal law therefore seems well-placed, at least from a conceptual viewpoint, to step into the role of protecting the human rights of the employee, central as those two values are within human rights discourse. The Employment Rights Act 1996 (ERA 1996) aims to ensure that an appropriate reason is provided for a termination of the employee's contract and that employers follow proper procedures, including providing sufficient evidence to support the reason put forward and allowing the employee to challenge the evidence or give their account of the issue. Some structural elements of the law of unfair dismissal have also been considered to map onto human rights concerns.[2] Where discrepancies might exist, the statutory basis of the right provides scope for reinterpretation of its provisions via section 3 of the Human Rights Act 1998 (HRA 1998). The framework of unfair dismissal law will be discussed in section I.

The aim of this chapter is to assess whether the law of unfair dismissal can fulfil the most relevant positive obligations placed upon the UK by the European Convention on Human Rights (ECHR or the Convention).[3] If a dismissal amounts to an infringement upon an individual's human right, there is an obligation on the member state to ensure that the infringement is necessary and proportionate to achieve a legitimate aim. Domestic courts should take into account those factors that the European Court of Human Rights (ECtHR or the Court) considers relevant to cases of dismissal, such as the severity of the sanction and whether other, less severe measures might have been appropriate. Finally, there is an obligation to ensure that the employee receives an effective remedy that recognizes the infringement that they have suffered. In addition, Article 8 ECHR may be invoked more frequently in unfair dismissal disputes as a result of the recent articulation by the ECtHR of the 'consequence-based approach' to the right to respect for private life.[4]

[1] Hugh Collins, *Justice in Dismissal: The Law of Termination of Employment* (Oxford University Press 1992) 272.

[2] Hugh Collins and Virginia Mantouvalou, '*Redfearn v UK*: Political Association and Dismissal' (2013) 76 MLR 909, 915–16.

[3] See Chapter 3 for further detail on the content of these obligations.

[4] See generally Hugh Collins, 'An Emerging Human Right to Protection against Unjustified Dismissal' (2021) 50 ILJ 36.

Putting Human Rights to Work. Philippa Collins, Oxford University Press. © Philippa Collins 2022.
DOI: 10.1093/oso/9780192894595.003.0007

The individual's right to respect for their private life will be engaged by a dismissal if its consequences are sufficiently serious in terms of the individual's reputation or the impact upon their inner circle.[5] In these circumstances, a legitimate aim, the proportionality assessment, and a remedy for any unjustified infringement upon Article 8 will be required.[6] One can see that these positive obligations upon the UK may be invoked in a wide range of unfair dismissal cases but I will argue that claimants seeking to vindicate their human rights through this route are very likely to be disappointed.

Viewed through the lens of the UK's obligations under the Convention, a raft of difficulties will be exposed within the current approach to unfair dismissal cases.[7] As discussed in section II, the courts very swiftly accepted that human rights considerations, and in particular the proportionality test, should form part of the unfair dismissal enquiry.[8] Nevertheless, the practical impact of this recognition has been minimal. In fact, human rights arguments are yet to alter the reasoning or conclusion of a tribunal in any case on record.[9] Sections III and IV will argue that this is a result of two problems: the failure to recognize human rights dimensions within a case at all and, in the rare cases that the individual's rights are considered, the lacklustre engagement with the questions of proportionality and necessity. In the similarly unlikely event that a claimant is successful in arguing that their dismissal was unfair, there are serious gaps and deficiencies in the remedies that are available to them. Remedies will be discussed in section V.

I. The Framework of the Law of Unfair Dismissal

The right not to be dismissed unfairly could be considered the centrepiece of employment law. Introduced in 1971, it is only available to employees who must have satisfied a qualifying period of continuous employment in most cases.[10] The right itself is contained in section 94 of the ERA 1996. Once the individual has proved their entitlement to the right, there are four broad stages to the dispute: (1) a dismissal must have occurred, (2) the employer must demonstrate the reason for that dismissal, (3) an assessment of the fairness of the dismissal should be carried out, and (4) remedies awarded if the dismissal is considered to be unfair. A dismissal may occur either at the employer's or the employee's initiative.[11] A 'constructive

[5] *Denisov v Ukraine* Application no 76639/11 (ECtHR, 25 September 2018) [107]–[109].

[6] See *Pişkin v Turkey* Application no 33399/18 (ECtHR, 15 December 2020).

[7] See also Philippa Collins, 'The Inadequate Protection of Human Rights in Unfair Dismissal Law' (2018) 47 ILJ 504.

[8] *X v Y* [2004] EWCA Civ 662, [2004] ICR 1634.

[9] See Philippa Collins, 'Square Peg vs a Round Hole? The Necessity of a Bill of Rights for Workers' (2020) 11 European Labour Law Journal 199, 215.

[10] ERA 1996, section 108.

[11] ERA 1996, section 95.

dismissal' occurs where an employee resigns in response to their employer's behaviour and it must be shown that the employer committed a repudiatory breach of contract for the employee to be entitled to treat themselves as dismissed.[12]

At the second stage, the burden is on the employer to demonstrate the principal reason for the dismissal.[13] Under the statute, reasons are divided into two categories: potentially fair reasons for dismissal and automatically unfair reasons for dismissal. Potentially fair reasons are listed and the particular circumstances in which they have been relied upon will be assessed according to the standard of fairness at the third stage. Contained in section 98(1) and (2), these reasons for dismissal are: the employee's conduct, their capabilities or qualifications, a statutory requirement, redundancy, or some other substantial reason that may justify a dismissal. In cases where the reason that prompted the dismissal invokes a human right, for example, the employee's behaviour outside of work or their expression on social media, the reason relied upon will often be the employee's conduct. There is a low threshold for reliance on a person's conduct, as the employer is not required to prove that the conduct breached the terms of the contract.[14] If the circumstances of the dismissal do not easily match a listed reason, the 'some other substantial reason' category operates as a wide, catch-all category of permitted reasons for dismissal.[15]

Where human rights have been taken to come into play at this stage is the group of automatically unfair reasons for dismissal. If found to be proved upon the evidence available to a tribunal,[16] a dismissal for an automatically unfair reason leads directly to a conclusion of unfairness. The employer has no opportunity to explain their decisions and the standard of fairness is never applied. Whilst the list of automatically unfair reasons for dismissal have developed in a piecemeal way, Hugh Collins and Virginia Mantouvalou have observed that they fit within three categories.[17] Individuals who assert their statutory rights and employees who have faced retaliation for their role as a workplace representative are two broad categories. The third, loosely defined category relates to the enforcement of the fundamental rights of the employee. Some reasons relate to the exercise of trade union functions or activities as a member, which fall within the scope of Article 11 ECHR. Article 8, the right to respect for one's private life, could be considered to underlie the safeguards for employees who exercised their right to take leave in support of their family life, such as maternity and parental leave.[18] Article 10 is undoubtedly reflected in the protection of whistleblowers through a finding of

[12] *Western Excavating (ECC) Ltd v Sharp* [1978] QB 761, 769 (Lord Denning MR).
[13] ERA 1996, section 98(1).
[14] *Reilly v Sandwell Metropolitan Borough Council* [2018] UKSC 16, [2018] IRLR 558, [24].
[15] See John Bowers and Andrew Clarke, 'Unfair Dismissal and Managerial Prerogative: A Study of Other Substantial Reason' (1981) 10 ILJ 34.
[16] See *Kuzel v Roche* [2008] IRLR 530.
[17] Collins and Mantouvalou (n 2) 915.
[18] ibid, 916.

automatic unfairness in relation to their dismissal.[19] There is a perceptible connection between the fundamental rights of employees and some automatically unfair reasons for dismissal.

Nevertheless, the listed automatically unfair reasons are tightly confined and leave significant gaps in the protection of Convention rights. Would it be beneficial to strengthen the correlation between fundamental rights and automatically unfair reasons? It might be thought that an amendment to list any reason for dismissal linked to the exercise of a Convention right as automatically unfair would be desirable. This proposal faces the difficulty that the Convention rights most invoked in the employment relationship are qualified rights, which provide an opportunity for the employer to justify their decision. Within unfair dismissal law, this role is played by the fairness enquiry which is entirely absent from cases of automatically unfair dismissal. Secondly, we must consider situations where the infringement upon the Convention right is due to the consequences of or procedure leading up to the dismissal. These cases do not fit squarely within the reason-based approach which the automatically unfair route represents. We can see that, despite its initial appeal, this route to guaranteeing the protection of employees' fundamental rights is not appropriate.

If an employer satisfies the Employment Judge that they have dismissed for a legitimate reason under the statute, the main examination of the circumstances of the dismissal takes place through an assessment of the fairness of the dismissal. Section 98(4) ERA 1996 states that the question of fairness should be decided by asking whether:

> in the circumstances ... the employer acted *reasonably or unreasonably* in treating it as a sufficient reason for dismissing the employee, and shall be determined in accordance with equity and the substantial merits of the case.[20]

Although this phrase indicates a bare reasonableness standard, it has been interpreted by the courts to require the consideration of a 'range' or 'band' of reasonable employer responses.[21] Under the application of the range of reasonable responses (RORR) test, if the decision to dismiss was within a range of reasonable responses that a reasonable employer could have selected in those circumstances, then the dismissal must be considered fair. Dismissal is thus deemed to be a legitimate response in a much wider range of circumstances than would be the case under a reasonableness standard, particularly when combined with the instruction that the tribunal must not take account of how they, themselves, would have responded to the particular situation.[22]

[19] ERA 1996, section 103A.
[20] ERA 1996, section 98(4) emphasis added.
[21] See *British Leyland UK Ltd v Swift* [1981] IRLR 91, 93 (Lord Denning MR); *Iceland Frozen Foods Ltd v Jones* [1983] ICR 17, 24–25 (Judge Browne-Wilkinson).
[22] See *Beedell v West Ferry Printers* [2000] IRLR 650, 656.

For the tiny minority of claimants who are successful in their case,[23] the final stage is awarding remedies. Re-engagement orders were intended to be the primary remedy for an unfair dismissal.[24] Such orders are designed to ensure that the claimant gets either their old job back or a suitable alternative role with the same employer.[25] Currently, re-engagement orders are rare.[26] Two factors contribute to this situation: re-engagement orders depend on the claimant's desire to return to a company that they have litigated against[27] and employers tend to avoid such an order being issued or enforced if possible. Although commentators have proposed adjustments that would bolster the prominence of re-engagement orders within unfair dismissal law,[28] employers are likely to resist any attempts to introduce these suggestions as recognized by Joanne Howe in her comparative study of the remedy.[29]

In practice, the usual remedy for an unfair dismissal is a monetary award, comprising of two parts. The 'basic award' is calculated according to a statutory formula that takes into account age and years of service.[30] This unusual component may be an attempt to recognize less tangible losses, such as loss of seniority, rights accrued by working continuously with the employer and other lost expectations that are difficult to measure, such as time investment in firm-specific training that will no longer be useful or loss of job satisfaction.[31] A more substantial amount is available under the 'compensatory award'. The tribunal awards an amount it considers 'just and equitable in all the circumstances having regard to the loss sustained by the complainant in consequence of the dismissal'.[32] A significant component of this sum compensates the claimant for lost wages during the anticipated period of unemployment following the dismissal or, if the claimant has already found a new job, the estimated time it will take them to attain their prior salary. Both monetary elements are limited by an upper cap, meaning that in most cases the absolute limit that a successful claimant would receive in 2021 is £105,813.[33]

[23] In 2019–2020, 7 per cent of unfair dismissal claimants were successful at hearing: see Ministry of Justice, *Tribunal Statistics Quarterly: January to March 2020* (11 June 2020) Table ET_3.

[24] *O'Laoire v Jackel International Ltd* [1990] ICR 197, 200 (Lord Donaldson MR).

[25] ERA 1996, section 113–15.

[26] See Joanne Howe, 'Why Do So Few Employees Return to their Jobs? In Pursuit of a Right to Work Following Unfair Dismissal' in Virginia Mantouvalou (ed), *The Right to Work: Legal and Philosophical Perspectives* (Hart Publishing 2014) 258.

[27] ERA 1996, section 116(1)(a) and (3)(a).

[28] See, for example, David Lewis, 'Re-Employment as a Remedy for Unfair Dismissal: How can the Culture be Changed?' (1999) 28 ILJ 183.

[29] See Howe (n 26) 273.

[30] ERA 1996, section 119.

[31] Hugh Collins, Keith Ewing, and Aileen McColgan, *Labour Law* (2nd edn, Cambridge University Press 2019) 900.

[32] ERA 1996, section 123.

[33] This figure has been calculated using the amounts set out in the Employment Rights (Increase of Limits) Order 2021.

II. The Standard of Review

Having introduced the law of unfair dismissal, we can narrow in on a key area of discussion and litigation at the intersection between dismissal and human rights: the standard of review. David Cabrelli defines 'standards of review' as norms which are 'addressed to adjudicators and set the level at which the law expects independent adjudicators to scrutinise managerial action and decision making'.[34] The aim of this section is to expose the significant differences between the 'default approaches' adopted by the ECtHR and an Employment Tribunal (ET) in an unfair dismissal case. Where the Strasbourg Court is searching, the ET is limited by the parameters of the RORR test. This divergence prompted an attempt to reconcile the standard of fairness with the ECHR in *X v Y*, which will be discussed later.

A. Divergent Standards: Proportionality and the Range of Reasonable Responses

In the case of *Vogt v Germany*,[35] the ECtHR demonstrated the depth of the scrutiny that an infringement upon the qualified rights should entail. Ms Vogt was dismissed from her post as a teacher for a failure to adhere to her duty of loyalty to the constitution, evidenced by her attempt to be elected as a candidate for the Communist party. Before the ECtHR, the government had to demonstrate that the dismissal, as a serious infringement upon the applicant's Article 10 right, was justified. The Court accepted that the dismissal was prescribed by law and in accordance with several legitimate aims: protecting national security, preventing disorder, and protecting the rights of others. In assessing whether the dismissal was 'necessary in a democratic society', the Court noted that Ms Vogt's dismissal was a 'very severe measure': she was deprived of her livelihood, suffered reputation damage, and faced the prospect of being excluded from her vocation.[36] Despite extensive investigations, Ms Vogt had never been accused of attempting to indoctrinate her students.[37] Given the severity of the sanction and the impact upon the applicant and her lawful political activities, the Court concluded that the reasons produced to justify the interference were 'not sufficient to establish convincingly that it was necessary in a democratic society to dismiss her'.[38]

Fuentes Bobo v Spain[39] is an interesting case as it is the nearest analogy to dismissal for spontaneous expression via social media, a recurring theme in the

[34] David Cabrelli, 'The Hierarchy of Differing Behavioural Standards of Review in Labour Law' (2011) 40 ILJ 146, 148.
[35] (1996) 21 EHRR 205.
[36] ibid [60].
[37] ibid [60].
[38] ibid [61].
[39] (2001) 31 EHRR 50.

domestic tribunals. Mr Fuentes Bobo was a presenter who was engaged in a dispute with his employer, a public broadcasting service. During a live interview on radio, he was impolite and used vulgar language when raising criticisms of the broadcasting company and the way it was being managed. He was dismissed shortly afterwards. The dismissal infringed upon his right to freedom of expression under Article 10 and the Court accepted that the employer was acting to protect the reputations of the company and the people within it.[40] In examining the necessity of the infringement, it was important that less severe sanctions could have been envisaged by the Court in the light of the serious consequences for the complainant of a dismissal.[41] Ultimately, the ECtHR found that there was 'no reasonable relationship of proportionality' between the penalty and the legitimate aim pursued.

In terms of the expression itself, the Court noted that Mr Fuentes Bobo was adopting phrasing put to him by the radio hosts, rather than formulating his own descriptions.[42] The spontaneity of the comments, occurring during a live radio broadcast 'which eliminated the applicant's possibility of reformulating, perfecting or retracting them before they were made public',[43] was also taken account of in assessing the dismissal as a disciplinary response. In this sense, there is an echo of many 'social media dismissals'.[44] Often, on Facebook or Twitter, the expression is impulsive, ill-thought-through and in response to a particular event in the heat of the moment. From the discussion in *Fuentes Bobo*, it appears that the Court would expect employers to be understanding of such outbursts, particularly in the absence of proven damage to their reputation and in circumstances where the posts can be retracted and deleted. We will return to the theme of social media dismissals below.

In contrast to the stringent examination at the Convention level, the domestic tribunals apply the RORR test. In short, 'if a reasonable employer might reasonably have dismissed him, then the dismissal was fair'.[45] There are clear differences between the RORR test and the structured approach taken under the qualified Convention rights. Cabrelli observes that the RORR test:

> is generally one-dimensional in nature since it concentrates on the actions of the employer only, whereas [the proportionality test] is two-dimensional, focussing on the actions and needs of the employer and the harm caused to the employee, duly balancing them off against each other.[46]

[40] ibid [39].
[41] ibid [49].
[42] ibid [48].
[43] ibid [46].
[44] For a detailed discussion, see Virginia Mantouvalou, '"I Lost My Job over a Facebook Post: Was that Fair?" Discipline and Dismissal for Social Media Activity' (2019) 35 International Journal of Comparative Labour Law and Industrial Relations 101.
[45] *British Leyland v Swift* (n 21) 93 (Lord Denning MR).
[46] Cabrelli (n 34) 170.

The employer's decision does not have to correspond to a legitimate aim: they need only produce a potentially fair reason, which as we have seen is an open-ended category. The tribunal's assessment is centred on the perspective of the 'reasonable employer' and what range of options could be considered open to them. This perspective pushes aside the claimant, their interest in their job, the consequences for their life and, in some cases, their fundamental rights.

Even further, in applying the RORR test, the tribunal's own expertise in industrial relations must not be used in a manner that demonstrated the prohibited 'substitution mindset'. Judge Browne-Wilkinson, on behalf of the Employment Appeal Tribunal, described the prohibition as follows in *Iceland Frozen Foods v Jones*:

> in applying the section an industrial tribunal must consider the reasonableness of the employer's conduct, not simply whether they (the members of the industrial tribunal) consider the dismissal to be fair; ... in judging the reasonableness of the employer's conduct an industrial tribunal must not substitute its decision as to what was the right course to adopt for that of the employer.[47]

The deprivation of a tribunal's capacity to offer an objective adjudication on the reasonableness of a dismissal has been a consistent point of criticism of the RORR test.[48] If we were seeking to reflect the proportionality standard within the RORR framework, the impossibility of tribunals setting clear standards for employers and asserting what *an appropriate response would have been* is particularly problematic.

The problems with this approach can be demonstrated by reference to a classic example of a disciplinary dismissal, *Haddon v Van Der Bergh Foods Ltd.*[49] In *Haddon*, the events centred on an awards evening recognizing the achievements of the workforce. Mr Haddon was to be presented with a good service award, following fifteen years with the company. The presentation event occurred midway through one of Mr Haddon's scheduled shifts. His manager told Mr Haddon that he must return to that shift after the event, an instruction that Mr Haddon decided not to follow because he had consumed alcohol at the event and therefore could not work safely. He was dismissed because of his failure to return to work. The tribunal noted that in the event Mr Haddon's absence made no difference to the operation of the shift or the production levels that evening. Thus, for the company, there was no actual damage incurred by his failure to complete the shift.

47 *Iceland Frozen Foods v Jones* (n 21) 24.

48 David Cabrelli, 'Rules and Standards in the Workplace: A Perspective from the Field of Labour Law' (2011) 31 Legal Studies 21, 29; ACL Davies, 'Judicial Self-restraint in Labour Law' (2009) 38 ILJ 278, 291–93.

49 [1999] ICR 1150. The case has gained notoriety for Morison P's strong dissent in the EAT against the application of the RORR test, although his approach was swiftly overruled by the Court of Appeal in *Foley v Post Office, HSBC Bank plc v Madden* [2000] ICR 1283, [2000] IRLR 827.

In considering the fairness of his dismissal for this reason, the tribunal recalled the RORR test and warned itself of falling into the substitution mindset. Ultimately, the tribunal reluctantly found that it could not escape the conclusion that the dismissal was fair. Many factors mitigated against this conclusion: the irrelevance of Mr Haddon's absence to the operation of the business, his long and good service record, the apparent unreasonableness of the manager's instruction, and the impact of a dismissal upon Mr Haddon himself. The tribunal went as far as saying that 'most people would regard that [his dismissal] as harsh in the extreme'.[50] Further, '[i]t was a decision that many reasonable employers would not have taken'.[51] Despite expressing their strong disagreement with the choice that the employer made in this case, the high standard for demonstrating that a dismissal is unfair under the RORR approach left the tribunal with little choice but to find in favour of the employer.

Haddon is an apt example of a range of deficiencies of the operation of the RORR test when contrasted with a proportionality approach. I would argue that much of the harshness perceived by the tribunal derived from the lack of any proportionality between the misconduct and the penalty. The most severe sanction had been applied without any discernible benefit for the company or rationale beyond penalizing an employee for a minor misjudgment. A less severe sanction would clearly have been adequate to discipline Mr Haddon and assert the need to follow instructions from one's manager in the workplace, but the RORR test and the injunction against the 'substitution mindset' deprived the tribunal of the opportunity to reflect that in their decision regarding fairness. This factor would be crucial to a proportionality exercise. The gap between unfair dismissal law and the demands of a proportionality analysis could not have been clearer in Mr Haddon's case.

B. An Attempt at Reconciliation: The *X v Y* Framework for Fairness

The disparities between the two standards of review were confronted by the Court of Appeal in *X v Y*.[52] In section 3 of the HRA 1998,[53] employees had an interpretive technique that they could rely on to argue that the RORR test should give effect to their Convention rights. The claimant worked for a charity providing support to young offenders. He received a caution from the police for a sex offence which occurred with another man in a public toilet. He decided not to disclose it to his employer. His employer dismissed him after discovering the caution when running

[50] *Haddon v Van Der Bergh Foods* (n 49) [3].
[51] ibid [19].
[52] *X v Y* (n 8).
[53] For a discussion of the interpretive obligation in HRA 1998, section 3, see Chapter 4, section II.

standard checks six months later. The ET found that the dismissal was for gross misconduct: that he had committed a criminal offence and failed to tell his employer, which undermined the employer's trust and confidence in him. The tribunal found it was within the range of reasonable responses to consider dismissal to be the appropriate sanction. The Employment Appeal Tribunal (EAT) agreed and dismissed the claimant's appeal.

Mummery LJ gave the leading judgment for the Court of Appeal. His Lordship commenced by acknowledging that there are positive obligations upon states to protect Article 8 rights, which includes one's sexual orientation and sexual life.[54] He confined his comments to the specific issue of the applicability of ECHR rights such as Articles 8, 9, and 10 on private law cases and giving guidance to tribunals on how to deal with such cases. Lord Justice Mummery's 'short answer' was that Article 8 was not engaged upon the facts,[55] although his Lordship's reasoning on this point has been questioned.[56] In his longer answer, Lord Justice Mummery stated that if the dismissal was for reasons relating to 'private' conduct, Article 8 will be relevant to section 98. He directed as follows: 'it might be necessary for the employment tribunal then to consider whether there was a justification under article 8(2) for the particular interference'.[57]

Mummery LJ went on to express doubts as to whether Article 8 could have any real effect on section 98's application: it was 'not immediately obvious ... as to how [section 98(4)] could be incompatible with, or be applied so as to violate, article 8 and article 14'.[58] Section 98(4)'s core concepts (fairness, the RORR test, and equity and the substantial merits of the case) should be 'sufficiently flexible' to give effect to ECHR rights without relying on section 3 HRA's interpretative obligation.[59] However, in circumstances where the application of the RORR test could reach a 'fair' outcome but under Article 8 it would be an unjustified interference, Mummery LJ made it clear that section 3 HRA should be used to ensure the ERA's effects are compatible with Article 8.[60]

Lord Justice Mummery's recommended approach appears to retain the RORR as the primary standard of review. In a more recent Court of Appeal decision, *Turner v East Midlands Trains*, the court returned to the idea that the RORR test did not require adjustments to achieve compliance with the expectations of the ECtHR. Although the case focused on procedural aspects of the employer's decision to dismiss Ms Turner, Elias LJ stated that the RORR test provides for 'a sufficiently robust, flexible and objective analysis of all aspects of the decision to dismiss to

[54] *X v Y* (n 8) [38].
[55] ibid [51].
[56] Virginia Mantouvalou, 'Human Rights and Unfair Dismissal: Private Acts in Public Spaces' (2008) 71 MLR 912.
[57] *X v Y* (n 8) [56].
[58] ibid [59].
[59] ibid.
[60] ibid.

ensure compliance with article 8'.[61] This perception of the relationship between the ECHR and the standard of review in unfair dismissal law runs contrary to the observations that have been put forward in this chapter but, unfortunately, it has been taken up by the ETs. In *Austin v A1M Retro Classics*, a case regarding Mr Austin's dismissal following a series of comments on his Facebook page, it was stated by the ET that:

> In a case such as this it could also be added that Article 10 may be engaged. That protects the right to freedom of expression and the right to receive information. *In all such cases s98 remains adequate and does not need a different approach.*'[62]

One might hypothesize that this understanding of the RORR test lies behind some inadequacies discussed later, particularly regarding the reluctance to engage in a full analysis of the proportionality of a dismissal *after* the RORR test has been satisfied.

III. The Tribunals' Blindspot: An Absence of Human Rights Considerations

How has the framework set out in *X v Y* been integrated into the practice of the ETs? In this section, I observe how frequently tribunals make decisions in relation to unfair dismissals without any reference to the employee's human rights, amounting to a clear failure to comply with the positive obligations under the Convention. *GM Packaging Ltd v Haslem* concerned a small packaging company for whom the claimant had worked for fourteen years before the events took place.[63] Mr Haslem was seen engaging in sexual conduct with a colleague, LO, by his manager on company premises but outside of working time. LO was dismissed. During the period of investigation into Mr Haslem's conduct, an accidental recording of Mr Haslem and LO speaking in derogatory terms about the owner–manager of the company emerged. Mr Haslem was dismissed after an investigatory meeting. The ET considered that the principal reason for the dismissal was the sexual activity that took place on the company premises. Further, it found that this reason could not be categorized as gross misconduct and that the dismissal fell outside the RORR. The employer appealed to the EAT.

The EAT criticized the tribunal's finding that the sexual conduct between the two employees was the principal reason for dismissal. The reason for dismissal was the sexual activity between Mr Haslem and LO *and* the recorded conversation.

[61] *Turner v East Midlands Trains Ltd* [2012] EWCA Civ 1470, [2013] ICR 525, [56].
[62] *Austin v A1M Retro Classics Limited* [2020] ET 2500934/2020, [9].
[63] *GM Packaging (UK) Ltd v Haslem* (2014) UKEAT/0259/13/LA.

Based on this reasoning and relying on evidence of the sound procedure used by the employer to support their opinion, the EAT concluded that 'this is a plain example of the ET impermissibly substituting their views for that of the employer'.[64] The dismissal fell within the range of reasonable responses open to the employer and was therefore fair.[65]

Haslem shows how the RORR can be applied without any regard to the infringement on the individual's human rights. Under Article 8 ECHR, Mr Haslem's private and sexual life was invoked expressly by the EAT as one part of the reason for his dismissal. From the ECtHR case law, we know that Article 8 rights persist within professional and workspaces.[66] Secondly, reliance upon the recorded conversation could also be seen to breach Mr Haslem's right to respect for his private life as a form of workplace surveillance. Finally, the recorded conversation itself should have invoked a concern regarding Mr Haslem's freedom of expression under Article 10. We saw in *Fuentes Bobo* that Article 10 also applies to offensive or crude expression, as well as criticism of one's employer.[67] The EAT made no reference to these three serious infringements upon Mr Haslem's rights that were incurred through the reason and procedure leading to his dismissal.

If the EAT had acknowledged the applicability of Articles 8 or 10, following the guidance of Mummery LJ in *X v Y*, they would have been compelled to conduct a proportionality analysis.[68] Applying the ECtHR's proportionality standard would have highlighted a variety of factors that the EAT disregarded in its decision. For example, the EAT failed to weigh in the balance that Mr Haslem had spent a significant part of his career at the company—fourteen years—and had gained some seniority within the company. These factors made the dismissal a very severe sanction. The RORR test has been consistently criticized for failing to adequately consider a worker's interest in continued employment or their job security.[69] Further, the EAT did not examine whether a lesser sanction, such as being issued with a written warning, could have achieved the aim of ensuring the smooth running of the business. All these factors would have been relevant under Articles 8 and 10, with the consequence that Mr Haslem's dismissal was arguably a disproportionate interference with his human rights and should have been held to be unfair.

Haslem is not an isolated example of the neglect of the human rights dimensions of unfair dismissal cases. For example, 'social media dismissals' touch upon the employee's right to privacy and their freedom of expression.[70] Both are

[64] ibid [30].
[65] ibid [33].
[66] *Niemietz v Germany* (1993) 16 EHRR 97, [29]; *Pay v United Kingdom* (2009) 48 EHRR SE2, 24.
[67] See also *Sánchez v Spain* (2012) 54 EHRR 24, [72]–[76].
[68] See *X v Y* (n 8) discussed earlier.
[69] Collins and Mantouvalou (n 2) 921.
[70] Mantouvalou, '"I Lost My Job over a Facebook Post: Was that Fair?" Discipline and Dismissal for Social Media Activity' (n 44) 103.

commonly disregarded.[71] In *Plant v API*, the employee made irreverent comments on Facebook, not explicitly referencing (although related to) managerial decisions made by her employer.[72] Her dismissal was found to be fair. The ET made no reference to her right to freedom of expression. A starker instance of the disregard of human rights occurred in *Gibbins v British Council*.[73] Ms Gibbins expressed her republican views of a thread of comments that happened to be attached to an image of Prince George, with an offensive caption attached. Her employer dismissed her. The tribunal failed to consider the dismissal in terms of either its interference with her freedom of expression or her freedom to hold her own beliefs. The tribunal's reasoning strongly indicated that dismissal was not a proportionate response:

> [a more measured approach] was certainly an option, and the tribunal considered that some reasonable employers would have considered lesser discipline, such as a final warning, as a way of appeasing critics, and *being proportionate to the claimant's lack of intention to do harm*.[74]

If the tribunal had engaged with the Convention and the *X v Y* framework, the lack of proportionality between the aim and the dismissal should have been central to a finding of unfairness. The RORR test deprived the tribunal of the opportunity to criticize the employer on this ground.

Finally, during the argument in *Reilly v Sandwell MDC*,[75] Lady Hale queried why counsel for the claimant had not raised a human rights argument. A headteacher failed to disclose her friendship, outside of work, with an individual who had been convicted of sex offences. She was dismissed as a result. The case progressed all the way to the Supreme Court before anyone raised a human rights point, despite the obvious connection to the claimant's rights under Article 8. As counsel had not prepared the point, the case was decided without consideration of the human rights issues. This example shows how the narrow focus of the courts' decisions is often a result of the argument that is put before the court—one major problem with a model of dispute resolution that is entirely led by the parties.

IV. The Cursory Consideration of Human Rights Issues

The second criticism that is levelled at the tribunals in cases that invoke human rights is that the proportionality standard, as set out by the ECtHR, is never

[71] See also, for example, *Greenwood v William Hill Organisation Ltd* (2017) ET 2404408/2016; *Gibson v Dundee City Council* (2017) ET 4100314/2017.

[72] *Plant v API Microelectronics Ltd* (2017) ET 3401454/2016.

[73] (2017) ET 2200088/2017.

[74] ibid [139] emphasis added.

[75] *Reilly v Sandwell MBC* (n 14).

properly applied. Inadequate weight is given to the claimant's fundamental rights and those rights are quickly 'trumped' by the employer's arguments. I argue that the deference with which the tribunals have long approached the RORR test has diluted the approach to human rights interferences. This problem can be seen in cases where the reason for the dismissal related to the exercise of a human right[76] and those where the manner of the dismissal, such as the investigation or the disclosure of evidence, breached the employee's rights.[77] The tribunals lack sensitivity to the employee's exercise of their fundamental rights and the proportionality exercise is brief, unstructured, or missing entirely. Here, I will focus on examples drawn from the social media context—an area where the tribunals consistently fail to strike a balance between the employee's rights and the employer's desire to protect their reputation.

In *Game Retail Limited v Laws*,[78] the claimant was a risk investigator for the defendant retailer. As part of his duties, he created a Twitter account and formed online connections with accounts run by local Game Retail stores to monitor their activities. Using the same account, he also formed connections with his own friends and acquaintances and communicated with them via Twitter outside of working hours. A year later, the employer received notification from another employee that the claimant had posted some offensive material on his Twitter account. During the investigation, the claimant voluntarily deleted the Twitter account. He was charged with gross misconduct on the grounds that his tweets were offensive, threatening, and obscene and could be viewed by anyone, including the defendant's employees and customers. The company dismissed him without notice.

The ET found that the decision fell outside the RORR. It considered that the primary purpose of the Twitter account was for Mr Laws to communicate outside of work on matters that did not relate to his work. He only used it in his own time, and he had explained some of the offensive tweets further and their more innocuous meaning became clear. The tribunal also questioned the employer's assumptions that the public had accessed his Twitter account and had linked the claimant to the company as he did not mention his work or the company in his comments. The EAT took a different view. The EAT acknowledged that some balance must be achieved between an employer's desire to reduce reputational risk stemming from social media and the employee's right to freedom of expression.[79] The EAT criticized the ET for focusing on what *they* considered to be relevant, rather than the view that a reasonable employer could take.[80] The same conclusion was reached

[76] See, amongst others, *Pay v Lancashire Probation Service* [2004] ICR 187; *Lawrence v Secretary of State for Justice* (2017) ET 3401016/2016, [42]–[43]; *Q v Secretary of State for Justice* (2020) UKEAT/0120/19/JOJ, [2020] All ER (D) 83.

[77] See, amongst others, *McGowan v Scottish Water* [2005] IRLR 167; *Atkinson v Community Gateway Association* [2015] ICR 1; *O'Toole v DHL Services Limited* (2017) ET 1300625/2017.

[78] (2014) UKEAT/0188/14/DA.

[79] ibid [46].

[80] ibid [47].

on whether there was any offence actually caused—the judge had impermissibly substituted his own view of whether anyone had been offended.[81] The case was remitted for another hearing.

Laws can be criticized on several grounds. The EAT readily accepted that Mr Laws' online activity posed an actual threat to the employer's reputation. As Paul Wragg comments, 'the harm of the expression to the employer's interests is often either assumed or otherwise ignored, as if it were an apparently unimportant consideration'.[82] Yet it is only this harm (or a risk of it occurring) that could justify the infringement upon his freedom of expression. Instead of making a genuine attempt to assess the likelihood of harm being caused to the reputation or interests of Game Retail,[83] the EAT accepted the employer's assertion that Mr Laws' actions were sufficiently harmful to justify the deprivation of his livelihood. The judicial deference to the view of the employer at the centre of the RORR test remains, even where Convention rights are invoked by the employee.

The EAT's approach in *Laws* also confirms the 'dismissive treatment' of ECHR rights in dismissal cases.[84] In contrast to *Haslem*, the EAT mentioned Mr Laws' right to freedom of expression but there was no attempt to assess the proportionality of the dismissal in light of the ECHR. The facts of Mr Laws' case disclose a variety of considerations which could lead to the conclusion that the dismissal was a disproportionate interference with the claimant's Article 10 rights. There was very little evidence that the company had sustained damage to their reputation and Mr Laws closed his Twitter account immediately, removing any continuing risk to the company as the content could not be viewed or recovered from that point. The court could equally have considered the likely chilling effect upon the freedom of expression of others in the workplace in the light of such a severe sanction being meted out to a colleague. Once again, it is arguable that a less severe sanction may have been appropriate, but the EAT did not consider these factors.

In *Preece v J D Wetherspoons*,[85] the claimant removed two customers from the pub that she managed. They later called the pub on the telephone and began abusing the claimant. The claimant posted some comments on her personal Facebook page, expressing anger towards the customers and making some offensive comments about them. It was reported to the employer, and she was dismissed. The tribunal considered the dismissal to be within the RORR and went on to consider the dismissal in light of the HRA.[86] The tribunal held that Article 8 was

[81] ibid [49].

[82] Paul Wragg, 'Free Speech Rights at Work: Resolving the Differences between Practice and Liberal Principle' (2015) 44 ILJ 1, 2.

[83] We can see that the ET did attempt to assess the likelihood of actual harm to the employer's interests but received criticism for doing so as it strayed into the 'substitution mindset': *Game Retail v Laws* (n 78) [47].

[84] Wragg (n 82) 7.

[85] [2011] ET 2104806/10.

[86] ibid [40].

not engaged because the claimant's comments were in the public domain. Article 10 was engaged but the tribunal found the infringement to be justified. This conclusion was reached despite a revealing comment that indicated that the dismissal *should have* failed the proportionality test, had it been properly considered. The tribunal indicated that a lesser sanction could have been applied:

> it is irrelevant for the consideration of whether or not the decision to dismiss fell within the band of reasonable responses, that this is a case where the Tribunal may have been more inclined to award a final written warning.[87]

Preece clearly shows how the proportionality test, when it is applied, has been affected by the deference to the employer's decision-making that pervades the RORR test. The tribunals restrain themselves from setting standards of behaviour for employers. They fail to ensure that each dismissal was necessary to achieve the goal pursued. Given the significant differences between the RORR test and a Convention-compliant justification process, the application of the *X v Y* framework should occasionally lead to a finding of unfairness. Yet, as has already been pointed out, there are no reported cases where consideration of the human rights dimension of the case has changed the outcome of the case. This situation is very troubling and shows that unfair dismissal law is simply failing to protect the human rights of employees.

V. The Remedies for an Unfair Dismissal

It is questionable whether the remedies available upon a successful unfair dismissal claim are satisfactory when compared to their counterparts in human rights law.[88] There are several possible disparities between the remedies granted by the ECtHR and those available under the ERA 1996. This section focuses on three in particular: the refusal to recognize injury to feelings in the compensatory award, the cap on the total amount available, and the rules regarding adjustments to the amounts awarded.

Although there are several potential sources of guidance from the ECtHR on the issue of the appropriate remedy for an infringement, there has been limited engagement with this dimension of the state's obligations towards complainants in employment cases. The remedial element of the qualified rights themselves are only likely to be breached in cases where the national system offered no remedy at

[87] ibid [40].

[88] See Collins and Mantouvalou (n 2) 921–22; Hazel Oliver, 'Employment Law' in David Hoffman (ed), *The Impact of the UK Human Rights Act on Private Law* (Cambridge University Press 2011) 358–59.

all.[89] Article 13, which requires an effective remedy before a national authority for a breach of a Convention right, is often not examined by the Court if an infringement of a different Article has been found.[90] Under Article 41 which sets out the Court's own jurisdiction to offer 'just satisfaction' to complainants who have suffered a violation of a Convention right, the ECtHR relies upon a broad, 'equitable assessment' rather than any system of precedent or principled determination. This equitable approach is flexible but, as observed by Luzius Wildhaber who led the ECtHR between 1998 and 2007, the Court's remedial approach 'has made it even more difficult to extract clear criteria from the case-law'.[91] The lack of strong guidance from the ECtHR on the requirements for an effective remedy makes some of the conclusions herein tentative, but it is clear that some aspects of unfair dismissal law would be inconsistent with the expectations of the Court if they were expressly formulated.

A. Non-pecuniary Loss and Injury to Feelings

The monetary award in an unfair dismissal case is made up of a basic award, calculated according to a statutory formula, and a compensatory award. The latter is awarded in line with an open-textured measure: such amount as is considered 'just and equitable in all the circumstances having regard to the loss sustained by the complainant'.[92] There is no mention of non-pecuniary loss or injury to feelings in the statute. It has been argued that the justice and equity of redressing a dismissal could easily encompass injury to the ex-employee's feelings, particularly where there was bullying or other conduct intended to upset or humiliate the individual.[93] This approach would comply with the requirements of the Convention, where the ECtHR have been most clear and consistent on the issue of awards for non-pecuniary loss.

Despite the feasibility of the contrary interpretation, the most senior UK courts continue to reject any remedial claim for 'pure' non-pecuniary losses.[94] As some level of distress and anxiety is likely to follow from any dismissal, it has been argued that compensating for this is one function of the basic award discussed earlier. Where stigma is attached to the dismissed employee or they suffer psychiatric harm which leads to a longer period of unemployment, this may be covered in

[89] See *Taliadorou and Stylianou v Cyprus* Application nos 39627/05 and 39631/05 (ECtHR, 16 October 2008) [49] onwards.

[90] See, for example, *Redfearn v United Kingdom* (2013) 57 EHRR 2, [61]–[63].

[91] Luzius Wildhaber, 'Article 41 of the European Convention on Human Rights: Just Satisfaction under the European Convention on Human Rights' (2003) 3 Baltic Yearbook of International Law 1 6.

[92] ERA 1996, section 123.

[93] Hugh Collins, 'Compensation for the Manner of Dismissal' (2004) 33 ILJ 152, 155, 158.

[94] See *Norton Tool Co Ltd v Tewson* [1973] 1 WLR 45; *Dunnachie v Kingston upon Hull City Council* [2004] UKHL 36, [2005] 1 AC 226.

the compensatory award as a form of pecuniary damage.[95] But where exceptional injury to feelings have been caused by the employer's behaviour, there is no recompense unless it can be converted into a purely financial loss. This position has been maintained since the 1972 case of *Norton Tool v Tewson*.[96]

In contrast, awards for non-pecuniary harm are commonplace in employment law cases before the ECtHR. The awards range from €2,000 for Ms Eweida's anxiety, frustration, and distress[97] to £19,000 each to Ms Smith and Mr Grady in light of the 'profoundly destabilising events' of having one's private life investigated as well as the continuing emotional and psychological impact of those events.[98] In some cases, the Court even declines to separate the pecuniary and non-pecuniary damages due to evidential difficulties: in *Fuentes Bobo*, the complainant received a million pesetas for all aspects of the harm he sustained.[99] All of the aforementioned cases, and many others relating to different forms of infringement, demonstrate that non-pecuniary damages are a crucial part of the ECtHR's remedial package. Further, it has been stated that the same is true under Article 13's right to an effective remedy.[100] Thus, it appears that the approach of the judiciary towards non-pecuniary damages in unfair dismissal law is incompatible with the ECHR's requirements.

B. The Upper Limit on a Claimant's Award

In most unfair dismissal cases, there is an absolute limit upon the total that a claimant can receive. In 2021, the upper limit on the compensatory award—the more substantial component—is the lower of fifty-two weeks' pay or £89,493.[101] Collins and Mantouvalou have questioned whether the cap is compatible with effective protection of Convention rights.[102] Two points can be observed. Firstly, the just satisfaction award from the Strasbourg Court has been over the upper limit in unfair dismissal at the time.[103] This discrepancy indicates that an effective remedy may demand awards more significant that an Employment Judge is able to make. Although the cap on compensation does not affect most claimants,[104] for those that

95 These possibilities have been mentioned in *Norton Tool v Tewson* (n 94) 50 and *Vaughan v Weighpack Ltd* [1974] ICR 261, 265–66.

96 *Norton Tool v Tewson* (n 94).

97 *Eweida and others v United Kingdom* (2013) 57 EHRR 8, [114].

98 *Smith and Grady v United Kingdom (Just Satisfaction)* (2001) 31 EHRR 24, [13].

99 *Fuentes Bobo v Spain* (n 39) [57].

100 *Edwards v United Kingdom* (2002) 35 EHRR 19, [99].

101 See Employment Rights (Increase of Limits) Order 2021.

102 Collins and Mantouvalou (n 2) 921.

103 In *Smith and Grady v UK (Just Satisfaction)* (n 98), one complainant received £78,000 in just satisfaction whereas the statutory limit upon compensation that year was £50,000.

104 The median award in an unfair dismissal case was £6,000 in a 2013 survey: see Department of Business, Innovation and Skills, *Findings from the Survey of Employment Tribunal Applications 2013* (Research Series No. 117, 2014) Table 5.9.

it does, the upper limit operates as an arbitrary limit on their compensation which is arguably not compatible with the right to an effective remedy.

Secondly, it is noticeable that the narrow existing exceptions from the upper limit are associated with human rights concerns: whistleblowing and health and safety cases.[105] No general exception from the upper limit has been created for cases where an unjustified infringement of the employee's human rights has been found. In the future, the ECHR's prohibition on discrimination in Article 14 may prove useful to claimants who wish to challenge the differences in the upper limit in some categories of case. This has been demonstrated recently in *Steer v Stormsure*.[106] The challenge regarded the availability of interim relief, which ensures the claimant's continued employment pending trial, in different types of employment cases. Mrs Steer's claim was for discrimination under the EA, where interim relief is not available, whereas in some types of unfair dismissal claims it is.[107] Her argument under Article 6's right to a fair trial, combined with Article 14, was successful. The remedial framework across the various employment rights discriminated between different groups of claimants without justification.[108] Article 14 could thus be a potential avenue for litigants wishing to argue that the upper limit on compensation is in breach of the Convention, as it distinguishes between groups of claimants without justification.

C. An Unbalanced Approach to the Adjustment of Awards

The final concern that can be raised is the approach of the UK tribunals to adjusting the awards to take account of the specific circumstances of the case. Here, we can see a clear difference between how the tribunals respond to attempts to *decrease* the amount awarded to the claimant (positively) and attempts to *increase* the amount (negatively). Whilst claimants face a raft of potential deductions from their award, the only possibility for receiving a higher amount of compensation—a claim of punitive damages—has been rejected. The ECtHR has not stated clear principles on granular issues such as these, however, we can see that some of these positions would be problematic from a Convention perspective.

What would the Court's position be regarding the raft of reductions and deductions faced by successful claimants? In awarding just satisfaction in a case, the ECtHR will occasionally make no award, finding that the judgment itself is sufficient. Such a decision expresses the Court's disapproval of the complainant's

[105] The exceptions are listed in ERA 1996, section 124(1A).
[106] *Steer v Stormsure Ltd* [2021] IRLR 172.
[107] See ERA 1996, section 128; Trade Union and Labour Relations (Consolidation) Act 1992, section 161.
[108] *Steer v Stormsure Ltd* (n 106) [192].

behaviour in relation to the case.[109] Thus, the Convention may not be infringed by reductions of compensation on the grounds that the claimant's conduct contributed to their dismissal[110] or where gross misconduct was discovered after the dismissal took place.[111]

More troubling from a Convention viewpoint would be the '*Polkey* deduction'. If a dismissal is considered unfair on procedural grounds, the compensatory award may be reduced to reflect the possibility that a fair dismissal would have occurred shortly after.[112] In particularly serious cases, the award can be reduced to zero.[113] Hugh Collins has expressed concern about the *Polkey* deduction as it is 'no more than an unreliable estimation of risk' on the evidence, which operates to undermine the importance of the employer following a fair procedure.[114] The *Polkey* deduction has also been applied where the tribunal foresees that the claimant would have been dismissed for a different reason, for example, because they are a difficult or antagonistic colleague so would have generated problems for the employer in the future.[115] Given that the *Polkey* deduction can put the entire monetary award in jeopardy, this principle would be likely to be a concern for the ECtHR. The deprivation of any financial remedy based upon the tribunal's assessment of hypothetical futures runs contrary to the principle that a victim of a human rights violation should receive an effective remedy.

One last point of disparity concerns the tribunals' inability to award aggravated or exemplary damages against an employer whose behaviour was particularly capricious or unpleasant. In 2004, Lord Steyn went so far as to say that 'nobody could seriously suggest that Parliament intended to allow such awards'.[116] In contrast, the ECtHR is willing to grant more generous awards to reflect the fact that the complainant has suffered a serious infringement. For example, in *Smith and Grady v UK*, the complainants suffered intrusive investigations into their private lives and discriminatory dismissals from the armed forces on the grounds of their sexual orientation. The ECtHR noted 'profoundly destabilising events' which continued to have 'a significant emotional and psychological impact' on each complainant.[117] They were awarded £19,000 for non-pecuniary damage, plus £59,000 and £40,000 respectively for pecuniary losses. These were substantial amounts when they were made in 2000, indicating a punitive element to the amount awarded by the ECtHR. This is another point on which the UK tribunals and the ECtHR are out of step.

[109] Wildhaber (n 91) 6, 12, 17.
[110] ERA 1996, section 123(6).
[111] *W Devis & Sons Ltd v Atkins* [1977] 3 WLR 214, [1977] AC 931.
[112] *Polkey v AE Dayton Services Ltd* [1987] 3 WLR 1153, [1988] AC 344; *Thornett v Scope* [2006] EWCA Civ 1600, [2007] IRLR 155, [34]–[36].
[113] *Fisher v California Cake & Cookie Ltd* [1997] IRLR 212.
[114] Hugh Collins, 'Compensation for Dismissal: In Search of Principle' (2012) 41 ILJ 208, 224.
[115] See, for example, *O'Donoghue v Redcar and Cleveland Borough Council* [2001] EWCA Civ 701, [2001] IRLR 615.
[116] *Dunnachie v Kingston upon Hull City Council* (n 94) [19] per Lord Steyn.
[117] *Smith and Grady v UK (Just Satisfaction)* (n 98) [13].

Conclusion

When Hugh Collins studied the law of unfair dismissal in the early 1990s, he observed that 'a failure to respect civil liberties constitutes one of the principal sources of injustice in the law of unfair dismissal'.[118] Unfortunately, we can see that Collins' criticism remains true today. To achieve compliance with the Convention's obligations and make unfair dismissal law an effective vehicle for the enforcement of an employee's fundamental rights, a range of changes would be necessary. As discussed in Chapter 5, the qualifying period continues to exclude many individuals from launching an unfair dismissal claim, in addition to those excluded by the requirement of a contract of employment. The rules for awarding compensation would also require adjustments, particularly ensuring that all victims of a human rights infringement can recover their full losses, including non-pecuniary losses, regardless of hypothetical alternative scenarios.

At the heart of unfair dismissal law is the question of fairness and the RORR test. Despite the Court of Appeal's clear explanation of how tribunals should take the Convention into account in unfair dismissal cases, an understanding has developed within the tribunals that the RORR test is sufficient to offer protection for an employee's fundamental rights. Given that this chapter noted extensive differences between the ETs' and the ECtHR's approach to deciding cases and examining the employer's decision, this understanding is open to question. In the cases decided since *X v Y*, we see the complete neglect or only very cursory consideration of the potential infringement upon an individual's rights. The tribunals' approach to the question of fairness fails to protect employees' human rights. It appears that the RORR test, avoidance of a 'substitution mindset' and a strong sense of deference to the employer's judgment have become entrenched within the law of unfair dismissal. All these aspects of the fairness standard are problematic from a human rights perspective. It is reasonable to suggest, therefore, that even a second direction from a senior court to encourage the application of a Convention-compliant proportionality analysis may not be successful in bringing the tribunals fully into line with the Convention. Without a clean break from this deep-rooted approach, I argue that the statutory regulation of dismissal is unlikely to offer an acceptable route to the vindication of an employee's Convention rights.

[118] Collins, *Justice in Dismissal: The Law of Termination of Employment* (n 1) 185.

PART III

THE FUTURE OF HUMAN RIGHTS AT WORK

7
Human Rights and the Common Law of the Contract of Employment

The 2012 decision in *Smith v Trafford Housing Trust*[1] demonstrated the potential of the common law of the contract of employment to uphold the human rights of an individual worker. Mr Smith was disciplined after an online exchange regarding a news article about gay marriages taking place in churches. Mr Smith was even-tempered in expressing his views that were linked to his own Christian faith, however, some of his colleagues were offended and the Housing Trust became involved. Mr Smith challenged the disciplinary action taken against him, alleging that it was in breach of the terms of his contract of employment. When his freedom of religion and freedom of expression were raised in argument, Briggs J's response was that 'those rights of Mr Smith are undoubtedly relevant in the context of the interpretation of his employment contract with the Trust'.[2]

The judge carefully interpreted Mr Smith's terms and duties under his contract of employment, finding that none of the terms relied upon by the Trust were breached by Mr Smith's conduct. For example, on the point that he had been disciplined for mistreating his colleagues, the court observed that the upset caused was a 'necessary price to be paid for freedom of expression'.[3] Applying the employer's Code of Practice to every interaction with a colleague, including those outside of work, 'would be to impose a fetter on the employee's freedom of speech in circumstances beyond those to which a reasonable reader of the Code and Policy would think they applied'.[4] The court's approach in *Smith v Trafford Housing Trust* sought to ensure that Mr Smith's fundamental rights were not unnecessarily restricted through the employer's disciplinary code.

The method of contractual interpretation employed in *Smith* proved to be a viable way to give effect to Mr Smith's fundamental rights. It also complies with the UK's positive obligations under the European Convention on Human Rights (ECHR or the Convention), including the European Court of Human Rights' (ECtHR or the Court) expectation that private law instruments should be interpreted in a manner that corresponds to domestic law *and* to the Convention as it

[1] [2012] EWHC 3221 (Ch), [2013] IRLR 86.
[2] ibid [8].
[3] ibid [82].
[4] ibid [82].

Putting Human Rights to Work. Philippa Collins, Oxford University Press. © Philippa Collins 2022.
DOI: 10.1093/oso/9780192894595.003.0008

has been interpreted in the Court's case law.[5] Although not explicitly mentioned in Briggs J's judgment, the interpretation given to the contract aligns with the aims of the Human Rights Act 1998 (HRA 1998), particularly giving further effect to the ECHR rights,[6] as well as demonstrating compliance with the court's own obligation to act compatibly with those rights under section 6. Section I investigates whether the interpretation of contracts in a manner infused with respect for the employee's Convention rights is an approach which has taken hold more broadly.

Finding that there is strong evidence that *Smith v Trafford Housing Trust* is an exception rather than the general rule, sections II and III consider whether a duty to respect the Convention rights of one's employees could be implied into contracts of employment. Terms implied in law provide default rules that regulate the behaviour of any parties to a particular category of contract and could be used to protect the fundamental rights of employees through contractual means. In section II, I will discuss the possibility that an established implied term—the implied obligation of mutual trust and confidence—could evolve to encompass human rights concerns. Alternatively, the judiciary may be asked to imply a new term, in addition to the existing range of obligations, that requires employers to respect the human rights of their workers. This possibility will be discussed in section III. Although there are strong arguments in favour of the development or creation of implied terms along human rights lines,[7] I argue that both options are unlikely due to the cautious attitude of the judiciary towards the evolution of the common law in areas where Parliament is seen as the most appropriate regulatory actor. Chapter 8 goes on to assess the desirability and potential challenges of protecting workers' human rights via contractual means.

I. Contractual Interpretation and Human Rights

The contract between a worker and their employer is an important source of rights and obligations. The contract of employment contains a range of express terms and implied obligations, as well as being modified in some instances by statute.[8] The common law regarding the breach of a contract of employment combines the ordinary rules of contract law with unique principles that apply only to the context of work. In deciding whether an employer has breached the terms of the contract

[5] *Pla v Andorra* (2006) 42 EHRR 25, [62]. See further, Chapter 3, section III(B).

[6] HRA 1998, Introductory Text.

[7] See most recently Joe Atkinson, 'Implied Terms and Human Rights in the Contract of Employment' (2019) 48 ILJ 515; Hugh Collins and Virginia Mantouvalou, 'Human Rights and the Contract of Employment' in Mark Freedland (ed), *The Contract of Employment* (Oxford University Press 2016) 205–07.

[8] Prominent examples include the sex equality clause under section 66 of the EA 2010 and the contractual entitlement to additional remuneration where a worker has been paid below the minimum wage in a pay reference period under section 18 of the National Minimum Wage Act 1998.

of employment, the central allegation in a common law case, there are several ways in which the worker's human rights could be relevant. This section focuses on the interpretation of the terms of the contract of employment and whether the courts routinely take human rights into consideration in that process.

The common law counterpart of an unfair dismissal, a dismissal in breach of the terms of the contract of employment, is termed a 'wrongful dismissal'. The classic wrongful dismissal is the termination of the contract of employment without the benefit of a notice period, where the employee can demonstrate that they were so entitled. For example, an employee who has been dismissed summarily may argue that they did not commit conduct sufficiently serious to justify an immediate termination of their contract.[9] If successful, they would receive damages reflecting their wage for the period of notice to which they were entitled, applying the expectation measure of damages. Variants on the paradigm wrongful dismissal case include a claim that the employer has failed to carry out the required contractual disciplinary procedure. There, a successful claimant would receive award of damages reflecting their wages for the period during which the procedure should have been carried out[10] or possibly an injunction to prevent ongoing procedures in breach of the disciplinary terms.[11] The employee might also make an argument based on terms implied into the contract of employment, which will be discussed further below.

Smith v Trafford Housing Trust showed how straightforward interpretation could bring the employee's fundamental rights into the heart of a contractual dispute. As has already been mentioned, Mr Smith was disciplined after an incident on Facebook. On his personal Facebook page and outside of working time, Mr Smith posted an article regarding the possibility of gay marriages taking place in churches for the first time. A colleague asked him to elaborate upon his views. He said: 'I don't understand why people who have no faith and don't believe in Christ would want to get hitched in church … if the state wants to offer civil marriage to same sex then that is up to the state; but the state shouldn't impose [its] rules on places of faith and conscience.' As a result, three charges of misconduct were laid against Mr Smith by his employer: bringing the Trust into disrepute, impermissibly promoting his religious or political views, and mistreating his fellow employees. Mr Smith was demoted from his managerial position and suffered a 40 per cent reduction in his salary.

Mr Smith argued before the High Court that his demotion had been in breach of contract. He claimed that the demotion had no basis as he was not guilty of misconduct under the terms of his employment. Briggs J found in his favour. Upon their correct interpretation, the terms relied on by the Trust had not been breached

[9] See *Laws v London Chronicle Ltd* [1959] 1 WLR 698.
[10] See *Gunton v Richmond upon Thames LBC* [1981] Ch 448.
[11] See *Irani v Southampton and South West Hampshire HA* [1985] ICR 590.

by Mr Smith's actions. The true interpretation of the contract's terms is determined from the perspective of the 'reasonable reader' of the contract, an objective approach. Throughout the decision, the High Court showed concern that an employee is entitled to understand, from reading their employer's codes and policies, the extent to which their obligations to their employer extend beyond the workplace and into their personal and social life.[12] This factor informed the perspective of the 'reasonable reader' of Mr Smith's contract of employment and worked to curb attempts by the employer to regulate their employees' behaviour outside of work.

On the first issue of disrepute, the court was not persuaded that a reasonable reader would believe him to be representing the views of the Trust. Further, Briggs J found that the posts were not such that they 'did, or even could, bring the Trust into disrepute'.[13] Regarding the allegation of impermissible proselytization, Briggs J held that the employer's prohibition of promotion of one's religious or political beliefs only applied to activities that had a sufficiently work-related context. As Mr Smith's Facebook page was 'inherently non-work related', he was free to express his views if he did so lawfully.[14] Finally, as mentioned earlier, the charge that Mr Smith had mistreated and upset his colleagues was similarly dismissed. Upon the reasonable reader's view, the Code of Practice could not be considered to apply to all interactions between colleagues.[15] As the employer failed to establish any misconduct on Mr Smith's behalf, his demotion amounted to a breach of contract[16] and a wrongful dismissal.[17] He was entitled to recover the damages for his dismissal.[18]

In *Smith v Trafford*, the court was sensitive to how the interpretation of the terms of employment would affect Mr Smith's expression outside of working time. Briggs J was keen to preserve space free from the influence of the employer's Code of Conduct, implicitly giving regard to Mr Smith's freedom of expression and freedom of belief. For the protection of human rights to be uniform, however, this method of interpreting contracts of employment must be shown to be adopted consistently. Do we see this approach reflected elsewhere?

A case that shows what I argue is a more typical approach to a similar pattern of facts is *Gibbins v British Council*.[19] Ms Gibbins worked for the British Council. She was a dedicated socialist, atheist, and republican. On Facebook, she became involved in discussions about the place of the Royal family in modern society. The claimant stated her wish that Britain should be a democracy with no monarchy.

[12] *Smith v Trafford Housing Trust* (n 1) [53].
[13] ibid [64].
[14] ibid [75]–[79].
[15] ibid [82].
[16] ibid [86].
[17] ibid [94].
[18] In Chapter 8, section I, we will return to the issue of damages for a breach of the contract of employment and the negligible amount that Mr Smith in fact received after the court found in his favour.
[19] (2017) ET 2200088/2017.

The thread of conversation focused upon Prince George and his position of privilege and wealth. The original author had described a photograph of the Prince in colourful and offensive language. Although Ms Gibbins kept her own Facebook page very private, adding her comments to this existing thread had the consequence that they were open to a wider audience. Reports of Ms Gibbins' Facebook comments were reported by *The Sun* newspaper, and the British Council became a focus of public outrage.

After a very brief investigation, the employer decided that Ms Gibbins should be summarily dismissed. It considered that the claimant had been reckless in posting on Facebook in the manner that she had and that her actions had done serious damage to the reputation of the Council. Particularly problematic was that the claimant had associated herself with abusive comments about a child. Ms Gibbins challenged her dismissal in the Employment Tribunal (ET) on several grounds, including discrimination and unfair dismissal. On the latter argument, the dismissal was held to be fair.[20] This finding was despite the tribunal's comment that other reasonable employers may have decided upon a lesser sanction, a clear indication that the dismissal was a disproportionate interference with her rights to freedom of expression and to the manifestation of her beliefs.

Finally, the tribunal considered her common law claim. Ms Gibbins argued that her actions did not amount to gross misconduct and therefore the employer's failure to provide her with a period of notice was in breach of contract. The tribunal agreed with the employer, concluding that an instance of reckless lack of judgment that had damaged the employer's reputation constituted gross misconduct.[21] She was not entitled to a period of notice. Ultimately, all of Ms Gibbins' claims failed.

How does the judgment in *Gibbins* compare with that of Briggs J in *Smith*? The tribunal agreed with the employer's interpretation of the contract's terms and with how they had been applied to the incidents in question. Although reference was made to the fact that Ms Gibbins was expressing her personal beliefs on what she had thought was a private forum, the tribunal did not take into account how the employer's interpretation and actions based upon the terms of the contract affected Ms Gibbins' exercise of her fundamental rights. Her freedom of expression and her freedom of thought and belief were clearly infringed upon, as well as the employer reading her private, out-of-work communications in breach of her rights under Article 8. The tribunal did not attempt to read the Code of Conduct in a manner that would minimize the infringement upon Ms Gibbins' freedom of expression. The analysis of her wrongful dismissal was untouched by human rights concerns. *Gibbins* demonstrates that the courts do not consistently apply contracts

[20] ibid [141].
[21] ibid [147].

of employment in a manner sensitive to human rights considerations in common law cases.[22] *Smith v Trafford Housing* is an exception, rather than the rule.

Does the *Gibbins* approach meet the ECtHR's expectations of a national court adjudicating an employment dispute in which fundamental rights are invoked? As explained in Chapter 3,[23] there is an obligation upon member state adjudicators to interpret contracts in a manner that avoids unjustified interferences with an individual's Convention rights. National courts have been criticized for deciding upon the lawfulness of dismissals purely on the basis of contractual terms.[24] We can see that the decision in *Gibbins* would be liable to criticism on this basis.

Even further, in *Bărbulescu v Romania*, the ECtHR held that an unambiguous workplace rule should not be permitted to eliminate an employee's right to privacy in the workplace.[25] The right to exercise a Convention right should outweigh contractual considerations, where necessary. On an approach in line with *Bărbulescu*, even if the British Council had a clear rule that Ms Gibbins' behaviour amounted to gross misconduct, she could still succeed in her claim. The judge would have to find a way to protect her fundamental rights in their reading and application of the contract's terms to the facts. This proactive approach is well outside the routine methods of interpretation applied by the courts.[26] I would doubt whether the court in *Smith* would have disapplied an express contractual term if that was what was required in order to give effect to the Convention rights in the dispute.

II. A New Function for the Mutual Trust and Confidence Term?

Whilst *Smith v Trafford Housing Trust* showed us the *potential* of straightforward contractual interpretation to achieve a rights-respecting result, *Gibbins* demonstrates that this approach is far from systematic. No express terms contained in the contract of employment require employers to act in accordance with the employee's human rights. One alternative is to imply a term into the contract of employment that requires the employer to respect the human rights of the employee. Whilst Chapter 8 will consider whether contractual means are the most appropriate method for guaranteeing the human rights of workers, the focus of these sections is the likelihood in practice of the implied terms developing in a rights-centred direction. Here we will investigate the probability of an existing implied obligation evolving to offer protection for the employee's fundamental rights

[22] See also *Williams v Leeds United Football Club* [2015] EWHC 376 (QB), [2015] IRLR 383; *Wells and another v Cathay Investments 2 Ltd* [2019] EWHC 2996 (QB), [2020] IRLR 281, [149]–[154].
[23] See Chapter 3, section III(B).
[24] See *Herbai v Hungary* (2020) 70 EHRR 35, [50].
[25] *Bărbulescu v Romania* Application no 61496/08 (ECtHR, 5 September 2017) [80].
[26] See H G Beale (ed), *Chitty on Contracts* (33rd edn, Sweet & Maxwell 2018) [1-094].

before turning to the possibility of a new term being implied into the contract of employment for this particular purpose below.

Bob Hepple speculated that the introduction of the HRA 1998 would result in the implied obligation of mutual trust and confidence (IOMTAC) developing into a duty to respect the Convention rights of employees.[27] In *Malik v Bank of Credit and Commerce International S.A.*,[28] the House of Lords confirmed the existence of an obligation, implied into all contracts of employment, as follows:

> the employer will not, without reasonable and proper cause, conduct itself in a manner calculated (or) likely to destroy or seriously damage the relationship of confidence and trust between employer and employee.[29]

Others have been optimistic regarding the overlap between human rights infringements and a breach of the IOMTAC.[30] Indeed the term's two-part structure seems apt to protect the qualified rights contained in the Convention where one examines the infringement and then assesses the necessity of that infringement. Under the implied obligation, one party suffers a detriment (conduct calculated or likely etc.) and the other party is permitted an opportunity to justify that conduct (was there any reasonable or proper cause?). In addition, as observed by Lord Steyn in *Malik*, the term has been applied to a diverse range of workplace situations.[31] The open-ended nature of the term admits the possibility that it could be extended to encompass instances where an employee's human rights have been infringed upon. Could a guarantee of non-interference with human rights be offered through the evolution of the implied term of mutual trust and confidence?

The question of whether the term may be stretched to cover circumstances in which the individual's human rights have been infringed upon must be answered by reference to the current focus and foreseeable direction of the term. The case law applying the obligation can be grouped into three broad themes, each tackling a particular type of behaviour: procedural impropriety, employers acting without reasonable and proper cause, and situations where employers failed to treat their

[27] Bob Hepple, 'Human Rights and Employment Law' [1998] Amicus Curiae 19; Bob Hepple, *Rights at Work: Global, European and British Perspectives* (Sweet & Maxwell 2005) 56.

[28] [1998] AC 20.

[29] ibid 45 (Lord Steyn) with the correction added that has been accepted in later cases: *Amnesty International v Ahmed* [2009] ICR 1450 at note 12.

[30] See, for example, Mark Freedland, *The Personal Employment Contract* (Oxford University Press 2003) 162; Douglas Brodie, 'Mutual Trust and Confidence: Catalysts, Constraints and Commonality' (2008) 37 ILJ 329, 335; Hazel Oliver, 'Employment Law' in David Hoffman (ed), *The Impact of the UK Human Rights Act on Private Law* (Cambridge University Press 2011) 350–51, 356; Simon Deakin and Gillian S Morris, *Labour Law* (6th edn, Hart Publishing 2012) 364; Gillian Morris, 'Protection of Employees' Personal Information and Privacy in English Law' in Hiroya Nakakubo and Takashi Araki (eds), *Protection of Employees' Personal Information and Privacy* (The Japan Institute for Labour Policy and Training 2014) 79.

[31] *Malik v BCCI* (n 28) 46.

employees with respect and concern. Examining each theme allows the observer to assess how close the implied obligation is to offering substantive human rights protection and how it might evolve in order to do so. Although this section offers a more detailed assessment of the implied obligation than has been offered in previous works, I share the reservations regarding the future of the implied obligation in relation to the human rights of employees that have been expressed elsewhere.[32]

Whilst the first theme of procedural justice has a clear link to Article 6 of the Convention, the connections between the themes that will be outlined here and the substance of the qualified Convention rights are tenuous. There are clear routes of evolution that the courts could follow in order to offer general protection to the fundamental rights of employees but there seems to be no immediate interest in pursuing them. Even further, there are points of clear divergence between the application of the implied term and Convention rights in both scope and manner of application, a source for significant concern. Litigants could seek to hasten the development of the implied term through an argument based on the indirect horizontal effect of Convention rights. The HRA 1998 gives this argument impetus, but it is difficult to predict how the courts would respond. A factor that we might expect to be important is the extent to which the judiciary feel that the domestic system of employment law already protects an individual's Convention rights sufficiently.

A. Procedural Justice and the Implied Obligation

Paul Davies and Mark Freedland have noted that the jurisprudence of the implied obligation is partially concerned with 'procedural propriety'.[33] Potential wrongs falling within this line of cases include disregarding the requirements of natural justice, failing to give an employee a fair hearing, or conducting inadequate investigations. For example, in *Gogay v Hertfordshire County Council*,[34] Ms Gogay received a letter from her employer, a care home for children, suspending her with immediate effect and referring to an allegation of child abuse made against her. This action clearly had the capacity to destroy the relationship between employer and employee. An important part of the employer's breach of the implied obligation was that it had not taken adequate investigatory steps before making the decision to suspend Ms Gogay. The Court of Appeal considered that the employer wrote the letter without 'reasonable and proper cause' to do so.[35] The courts indicated that

[32] Collins and Mantouvalou (n 7) 205–06; Atkinson (n 7) 531–35; Alan Bogg, 'Good Faith in the Contract of Employment: A Case of the English Reserve?' (2010) 32 Comparative Labour Law and Policy Journal 729, 733.

[33] Paul Davies and Mark Freedland, 'The Impact of Public Law on Labour Law, 1972–1997' (1997) 26 ILJ 311, 325.

[34] [2000] IRLR 703.

[35] ibid [56].

the employer should have considered alternatives such as reallocating responsibilities whilst the investigation was ongoing.[36]

In *TSB v Harris*, the bank included information in a reference to a prospective employer about complaints against Miss Harris. She was not aware of the complaints, nor was she given an opportunity to respond to their content. The tribunal found this conduct to be in breach of the IOMTAC.[37] In contrast, in *Stevens v University of Birmingham*,[38] the dispute arose because of the employer's refusal to permit Mr Stevens to bring his chosen companion to an investigatory meeting. Although Mr Stevens' choice of companion was not strictly in accordance with the University's rules, the court was anxious that 'equality of arms' was achieved as far as possible, and that Professor Stevens was given an opportunity to explain the situation with the benefit of appropriate assistance. The High Court held that forcing Mr Stevens to go to a meeting without any support would be a breach of the IOMTAC.[39]

These cases demonstrate that one role of the implied obligation is to provide some procedural guarantees for employees, particularly where the employer's actions entail serious consequences for their future. Cases like *Harris* and *Stevens* thus reflect the values and elements of the right to a fair hearing which is protected by Article 6 ECHR, as well as the elements of the qualified Convention rights that relate to the procedure by which any disciplinary decisions are made. Article 6 requires, for example, a fair balance between the parties in proceedings, ensuring that both are afforded a reasonable opportunity to present their case and any evidence under conditions where neither party is placed at a substantial disadvantage in relation to the other.[40] By strengthening the processes by which decisions are made, this aspect of the IOMTAC may indirectly improve the substantive treatment of employees but the potential of cases of this kind to develop into substantive human rights protection is limited.

B. Acting 'Without Reasonable and Proper Cause'

This theme can be divided into two strands: instances where an employer drew a distinction between workers without justification and cases where there was no lawful cause for the employer's treatment of the employee. An example of the first type of case is *Transco Plc v O'brien*.[41] Mr O'brien did not receive a bonus made

[36] ibid [57].
[37] *TSB Bank Plc v Harris* [2000] IRLR 157, 166.
[38] [2015] EWHC 2300 (QB), [2015] IRLR 899.
[39] ibid 910.
[40] *Regner v Czech Republic* (2018) 66 EHRR 9, [146]. For a consideration of the role of Article 6 in workplace proceedings, see Astrid Sanders, 'Does Article 6 of the European Convention on Human Rights Apply to Disciplinary Procedures in the Workplace?' (2013) 33 OJLS 791.
[41] [2002] EWCA Civ 379, [2002] ICR 721 .

available to other members of staff due to the employer's misunderstanding regarding his employment status. The Court of Appeal held that '[t]o single out an employee on capricious grounds and refuse to offer him the same terms as were offered to the rest of the workforce is ... a breach of the implied term of trust and confidence'.[42] This case could be seen to link to the prohibition of non-discrimination under Article 14 of the ECHR, as it relates to discriminatory treatment without justification, but there is no connection to the other qualified Convention rights.

Elsewhere, however, we can see how the 'reasonable and proper cause' element can—upon occasion—give effect to the human rights of employees. As explained in Chapter 4, several labour statutes reflect a partial duty not to interfere with an individual's human rights through, for example, not subjecting them to detriment on the grounds of their trade union activities or membership.[43] If this unlawful reason appeared to the court to motivate the employer's behaviour, then they may be found to lack a reasonable and proper cause and the implied obligation will be breached. The implied contractual duty bolsters the existing statutory provisions by preventing the employer from relying on unlawful motivations in justifying their actions.

In *Avsar v Wilson James Ltd*,[44] Mr Avsar was an active trade union member who campaigned against the outsourcing of labour. Wilson James was an outsourcing company who hired Mr Avsar as a security officer and subsequently suspended him pending a probation hearing to discuss the future of the employment relationship. The employer cited the 'conflict of interest' between Mr Avsar's continued employment and his views on outsourcings and trade union activities as its grounds for questioning his suitability for employment. Mr Avsar sought an interim injunction to prevent the probation meeting and to end his suspension on the grounds that the employer had breached the IOMTAC. The courts were required to answer whether there was a serious issue to be tried that would justify an interim injunction. The High Court found that there was,[45] although the court found against the claimant on a different point.[46] The suspension and invitation to a hearing could breach the implied obligation and, as those actions appeared to be for reasons connected to Mr Avsar's trade union activities, the employer could be shown to lack 'reasonable and proper cause'. The court's acceptance that the facts disclosed a serious issue to be tried shows how the implied obligation can reinforce statutory prohibitions that protect the individual's human rights from infringement by their employer.

42 ibid [17].
43 Trade Union and Labour Relations (Consolidation) Act 1992, section 146.
44 [2020] EWHC 3412 (QB).
45 ibid [56].
46 ibid [59].

Currently, cases such as *Avsar* show how the common law implied term can offer a secondary form of protection for the employee's fundamental rights. The primary protection is contained in the statute, such as the Trade Union and Labour Relations (Consolidation) Act 1992 (TULR(C)A 1992) or discrimination law.[47] The breach of contract claim will not be permitted to subvert the effect of those provisions. The implied term could evolve to offer direct protection to the employee's human rights by progressing further along this line. For example, we might think that any decision taken by an employer for reasons connected to the employee's exercise of their fundamental rights should not be considered to have a 'reasonable and proper cause'. The decision or behaviour would therefore lack justification and the implied obligation would be breached. Combined with the procedural elements outlined above, this route could provide protection from human rights infringements that originate in the reason for *or* the procedure leading to the employer's decision. Despite the existence of such a direct avenue to the protection of Convention rights, there is no evidence that the courts intend to pursue it.

C. A Lack of Respect and Concern for the Employee

The final group of cases relate to employers' conduct that breaches the IOMTAC by failing to treat the employee with respect and concern. Such conduct can take a variety of forms. For example, in *Buckland v Bournemouth University Higher Education Corporation*,[48] the claimant was a professor of Archaeology who had been responsible for marking a number of exam scripts. His marks were checked and confirmed by the board of examiners. Without permission from the board of examiners or Professor Buckland, another member of the faculty re-marked the papers which ultimately led to several marks being increased. Despite a university inquiry finding in favour of Professor Buckland, he resigned from his post and claimed that he had been constructively dismissed by reason of the university's breach of the IOMTAC and that the dismissal was unfair under the statute. The ET, the Employment Appeal Tribunal (EAT), and the Court of Appeal agreed that the IOMTAC had been breached by the university's acceptance of the re-mark which amounted to 'an unequivocal affront to his integrity'.[49] Professor Buckland was entitled to resign in response to this fundamental breach of the contract. By failing to respect Professor Buckland's expertise and undermining his position within the university, the university had breached the implied obligation.

[47] See, for example, *Greenhof v Barnsley Metropolitan Borough Council* [2006] IRLR 98, [10]; *Shaw v CCL Ltd* [2008] IRLR 284, [18].
[48] [2010] EWCA Civ 121, [2010] 4 All ER 186.
[49] ibid [12].

Other ways in which the employer may fail to treat their employees with respect include campaigns of hostile behaviour. In *Horkulak v Cantor Fitzgerald International*,[50] the chief executive of a financial brokerage company engaged in a sustained campaign of unpleasant behaviour against Mr Horkulak, including outbursts in which he used 'foul and abusive language' in criticizing Mr Horkulak. As Mr Horkulak was a managing director, the chief executive's consistent and aggressive criticism undermined his authority to manage other employees and made his position intolerable. The High Court judge found that this conduct amounted to a breach of the IOMTAC.[51]

Reed v Stedman regarded the employer's failure to investigate sexual harassment and bullying.[52] The wrongdoer was Ms Stedman's manager and she made it clear that his behaviour was unwelcome. Ms Stedman complained informally to her colleagues about his behaviour and suffered from deteriorating health, which she considered to be caused by the harassment. Her ill-health resulted in Ms Stedman leaving her job. The repudiatory breach of the IOMTAC had two elements: first, the manager's course of behaviour and, second, the company's failure to investigate the situation in light of the complaints made by Ms Stedman and her deterioration in health.[53] *Reed* is not the only instance where an employer's failure to take seriously an allegation of sex discrimination has amounted to a breach of the IOMTAC.[54]

Alan Bogg has argued that dignity is a key value underlying the IOMTAC, using *Stedman* as a specific example.[55] A grounding in dignity would be a substantial step forward in developing the potential of the implied obligation to embrace a concern for human rights, however, I would put forward an alternative interpretation of these cases. The crux of the issue appears to me to be that the employer failed to treat an employee with due respect and concern. A violation of the employee's dignity was not the obvious tipping point into a breach of contract in the cases that have been outlined. In *Buckland*, the university's actions amounted to an affront to his academic integrity. In *Horkulak*, the chief executive undermined Mr Horkulak's authority as a manager. In *Stedman*, her manager's conduct certainly injured her dignity, but the *employer's* wrong lay in failing to demonstrate concern for her situation by embarking upon an investigation. Although the sample of cases here is limited, it demonstrates that conduct that breaches the IOMTAC does not always involve a substantial injury to the dignity of the employee. Nevertheless, by concentrating on the impact of the employer's conduct upon the claimant, this

50 [2003] EWHC 1918 (QB), [2004] ICR 697.

51 ibid [78]–[79].

52 *Reed and Bull Information Systems v Stedman* [1999] IRLR 299.

53 ibid [19].

54 See also *Bracebridge Engineering v Darby* [1990] IRLR 3.

55 Alan Bogg, 'Bournemouth University Higher Education Corporation v Buckland: Re-establishing Orthodoxy at the Expense of Coherence?' (2010) 39 ILJ 408, 414–15.

line of cases moves closer to a human rights focus. This potential to protect fundamental rights, however, remains unrealized.

D. The Divergence between the Implied Obligation and Human Rights Protection

There are several points of connection between the implied obligation and human rights concerns. Although the courts have not embraced the connection thus far, guaranteeing procedural propriety, providing secondary support for existing statutory prohibitions, and tackling hostile behaviour align well with the rights-focused direction. Any optimism must be dampened, however, when one looks elsewhere in the IOMTAC case law. Not only the content of the implied term but also how it is applied to particular cases can be troubling from a rights-based perspective. We turn first to the EAT's decision in *Amnesty International v Ahmed*.[56]

Ms Ahmed worked for Amnesty International and applied for a new role which related to the country of her own ethnic origin, Sudan. Amnesty International refused to offer her the role in accordance with its policy, on the grounds that her employment may lead others to question the impartiality of the organization and that her ethnicity may place her at an increased security risk in the field. Ms Ahmed left her position at Amnesty International. She was successful in her claim for direct discrimination on the grounds of ethnic origin.[57] Her unfair dismissal claim, however, was rejected.

The first stage in her unfair dismissal claim was to demonstrate that a 'constructive dismissal' had occurred—that she was entitled to treat herself as dismissed because of her employer's behaviour.[58] In accordance with the established test,[59] Ms Ahmed had to demonstrate that she left her employment in response to a serious breach of the IOMTAC. The EAT concluded that the employer's conduct was not sufficient to breach the implied obligation.[60] Unlawful discrimination does not 'inevitably' breach the term nor did the discriminatory conduct violate the claimant's dignity, as Amnesty International's reasoning was not prejudiced and 'could not reasonably be regarded as offensive to the claimant as an individual'.[61] Ms Ahmed may have felt hurt but, examined objectively, the court was of the view that the relationship with Amnesty International was not destroyed or seriously damaged as required by the phrasing of the implied obligation.

56 *Amnesty International v Ahmed* (n 29).
57 ibid [57].
58 See Employment Rights Act 1996, section 95(1)(c).
59 See *Western Excavating (ECC) Ltd v Sharp* [1978] QB 761.
60 *Amnesty International v Ahmed* (n 29) [72].
61 ibid [72].

Other cases illustrate the disconnect between the IOMTAC and a concern for the employee's fundamental rights. In *Grant v South-West Trains Ltd*, the company refused to extend a work-related benefit to Ms Grant's same-sex partner as their policy granted the entitlement only to a spouse or common law spouse of the opposite sex. The High Court rejected the claimant's argument that the employer's discriminatory conduct amounted to a breach of the implied obligation.[62] Such actions and policies would now be contrary to the Equality Act 2010 (EA 2010) and an infringement of Ms Grant's Article 8 and Article 14 ECHR rights, but were not considered to reach the threshold at which they could be 'fairly be said to destroy or seriously damage the relationship between employer and employee'.[63]

These cases bring to the fore a number of issues. First, in some situations, there is a divergence between when a breach of the implied term occurs and what would constitute an infringement upon the individual's human right. This deviation is demonstrated by the difference between the IOMTAC and discrimination law. Second, although the term does focus on the impact of the employer's behaviour on the claimant rather than the employer's intention, that effect is judged objectively.[64] In contrast, in human rights cases, the Court's focus is on the impact of the other party's actions on the particular claimant, the consequences for them, and whether the infringement can be justified in the specific circumstances that arose. No mention is made of whether the reasonable person would have felt their rights were infringed. A further chasm between the operation of the IOMTAC and the correct approach to Convention rights is thus revealed.

Finally, the threshold which must be surpassed before the implied obligation will be breached is set at high point. The Court of Appeal has noted that the test for a breach of the IOMTAC is a 'severe one'.[65] Underhill P, whilst he was President of the EAT, emphasized in two cases that 'the phrases "without reasonable and proper cause" and "destroy or seriously damage" must be given their full weight'.[66] Simultaneously, the 'reasonable and proper cause' element could permit justification of an employer's behaviour in circumstances far broader than would be permitted by the qualified rights.[67] These components of the implied term have no role to play in substantive human rights protection, further distancing the implied obligation from this potential role.

62 [1998] IRLR 188, [18].
63 ibid.
64 See *Malik v BCCI* (n 28) 47.
65 *Gogay v Hertfordshire CC* (n 34) [55].
66 *Ministry of Justice v Sarfraz* [2011] IRLR 562, [34]; *Amnesty International v Ahmed* (n 29) [72].
67 Atkinson (n 7) 533.

E. Human Rights as a Mandatory Influence on the Implied Obligation?

Even in face of the divergence between the IOMTAC and substantive human rights protection, the provisions of the HRA 1998 might be considered to compel the judges to develop the IOMTAC in this direction. Hepple argued that:

> since the court must act compatibly with convention rights, the duty of trust and confidence also embodies a duty to respect the Convention rights of an employee. This may be regarded as horizontal enforcement of the Convention by the back-door, but it seems to me altogether legitimate and strongly arguable.[68]

Under section 6 of the HRA 1998, all public authorities, including courts and tribunals, must act in a way that is compatible with Convention rights.[69] We can see an argument that, if the UK would otherwise fail to protect the Convention right invoked by the claimant, the court *must* develop the implied obligation in order to protect that right. Joe Atkinson suggests that effective protection for fundamental rights through this route would 'require the courts to automatically deem violations of Convention rights as "conduct likely to destroy trust and confidence", and to apply a strict interpretation of "reasonable and proper cause" when employees' human rights are at stake'.[70]

In practice, however, I anticipate that the chance of this modification occurring is slim. There are two main reasons for this. The first factor that may hold the judiciary back is the argument that the development outlined earlier is not necessary to fulfil the positive obligations of the UK. The ECtHR grants member states a margin of appreciation in determining precisely how Convention rights should be protected and balanced against other rights and the community interests. The law of unfair dismissal, particularly after the *X v Y* decision that added a human rights component, could be thought to place the UK well within its margin of appreciation. Such reasoning has been relied upon in cases where the Convention has been invoked to challenge statutory regulation in the area of trade union rights.[71] From this perspective, overlapping common law protection would be extraneous. In tort law, we see that the judiciary are extremely reluctant to extend existing causes of action if there are other private law rights that offer equivalent protection

[68] Hepple, 'Human Rights and Employment Law' (n 27) 22–23.

[69] HRA 1998, section 6.

[70] Atkinson (n 7) 535.

[71] *Pharmacists' Defence Association Union v Boots Management Services Ltd and another* [2017] EWCA Civ 66, [2017] IRLR 355, [68] (Underhill LJ), although the interpretation of the ECHR's requirements in *Boots* has been criticized: see Alan Bogg and Ruth Dukes, 'Article 11 ECHR and the Right to Collective Bargaining: Pharmacists' Defence Association Union v Boots Management Services Ltd' (2017) 46 ILJ 543, 559–61.

to Convention rights.[72] In employment law, this reasoning would result in a refusal to restyle the IOMTAC to include an obligation to respect the human rights of workers.

To counter this line of thought, one might reference the kinds of arguments made in Chapter 6 that demonstrate the inadequacies of unfair dismissal as a method of vindicating an individual's human rights. Some judges might be convinced by this counterargument. A second reason might instead trouble them: developing a duty to respect the human rights of workers under the auspices of the IOMTAC goes beyond an incremental step in the progress of the common law. This reasoning has been found to be persuasive elsewhere in the development of the implied term of mutual trust and confidence. In *Johnson v Unisys Ltd*, Lord Hoffman for the majority of the House of Lords refused to apply the implied obligation to the manner of an employee's dismissal on these grounds.[73] In light of this judicial caution, in addition to the margin of appreciation argument that has already been outlined, I would agree with Douglas Brodie that 'it is by no means inevitable' that the domestic courts will follow the path set out by Hepple and develop the implied term into a wide-ranging obligation to respect the human rights of one's employees.[74]

III. A New Implied Obligation to Respect an Employee's Human Rights

There are two routes to the implication of a term into a contract: an implied term in fact, which is particular to the contract in question, and an implied term in law, which is considered 'a necessary incident of a definable category of contractual relationship'.[75] Although it is possible that an implied term in fact might be used in particular instances to protect an employee's human rights,[76] here I focus on whether a term might be implied in law for this purpose. An implied term in law has the benefit that it is implied into an entire category of contracts. The individual does not have to demonstrate in each case that they benefit from the implied obligation provided that they are party to a contract of that kind. In this section I will argue that, although there are strong arguments in favour of the implication of a term for this purpose, the judicial response is likely to be very cautious. A new implied term is unlikely to emerge in the near future.

There are several ways in which the term could be phrased. Hugh Collins and Virginia Mantouvalou mention that a possible mechanism for protecting the

[72] See *Michael v Chief Constable of South Wales Police* [2015] UKSC 2, [2015] AC 1732, [125] (Lord Toulson).
[73] [2001] UKHL 13, [2003] 1 AC 518, 541 (Lord Hoffman).
[74] Brodie (n 30) 335.
[75] *Scally v Southern Health and Social Services Board* [1992] 1 AC 294, [1991] 3 WLR 778, 307.
[76] See Atkinson (n 7) 537–39.

human rights of employees is an implied term requiring that employers respect their autonomy and dignity.[77] The generality of the IOMTAC itself demonstrates that this is a possibility and many of the considerations that will be discussed here would be relevant if the courts were called upon to imply a term based upon the autonomy and dignity of their staff. Although such an implied term would encompass human rights obligations, I would argue that a more concrete and narrowly defined implied obligation would be more likely to be judicially accepted after a consideration of the policy factors that will be outlined below.[78] An obligation upon the employer to respect the human rights of their employees, as defined and protected by the ECHR and the HRA, might be suitable for implication.[79]

In general, it must be noted that the courts tend to take a restrictive approach to the implication of a new term in law, possibly due to the judges' 'preference for rules rather than policy'.[80] The process of acceptance of a new implied term in law is somewhat ill-defined. The first stage is to identify the 'definable category of contractual relationship' into which the term would be implied. The court will then consider whether the term is a necessary element of that type of contract.[81] There may be a third stage, or a part of the second stage, in which 'the court will naturally ask itself whether in the general run of such cases the term in question would be one which it would be reasonable to insert'.[82] What conclusions might the courts reach if presented with a claimant arguing for the development of a new term to protect their human rights in the workplace? Guidance will be taken in this section from a useful article by Elizabeth Peden on the process of implication in law[83] and the *dicta* of the House of Lords in *Malik v BCCI* as the leading English authority on the implication of terms into the contract of employment.[84]

The first stage is easily satisfied. A new obligation could be implied into all contracts of employment, alongside the existing obligations of mutual trust and confidence, obedience and loyalty, and so forth. Once the implication of a human rights term has been accepted, an extension into other contracts for work—'limb (b) worker' contracts or the EA contracts personally to do work—might be considered. In the light of the arguments made in Chapter 3 regarding the inclusive scope of the Convention's protection, this would certainly be justified. However, this chapter will focus on the possibility of implication into all contracts of employment as a starting point.

[77] Collins and Mantouvalou (n 7) 205.

[78] For a contrasting view, see Roger Rideout, 'Implied Terms in the Employment Relationship' in Roger Halson (ed), *Exploring the Boundaries of Contract* (Dartmouth Publishing 1996) 125.

[79] Atkinson (n 7) takes a similar approach.

[80] Elizabeth Peden, 'Policy Concerns behind Implication of Terms in Law' (2001) 117 LQR 459, 466.

[81] *Scally v SHSSB* (n 75) 307.

[82] *Liverpool City Council v Irwin and Another* [1976] 2 WLR 562, [1977] AC 239, 258.

[83] Peden (n 80).

[84] *Malik v BCCI* (n 28).

A. A 'Necessary Incident' of a Contract of Employment?

The commonly cited test for determining whether a new obligation should be implied into a particular category of contract is necessity. In practice, however, 'the courts do not confine themselves to a narrow test of necessity but instead can draw upon a broader range of factors, such as the reasonableness of the term, its fairness and a range of competing policy considerations'.[85] We might observe that contracts of employment have existed and functioned for many decades without the implication of a term that protects employee's human rights. This observation, along with the existing statutory protection for human rights at work, could place the *necessity* of an additional implied obligation in doubt. This perspective on the question is put forward in *Chitty on Contracts*: 'under the established test for the implication of such terms that they are necessary as well as reasonable, and where neither party to the contract is a public authority it is difficult to see the genuine necessity of the implication of such a term'.[86]

Several counterarguments can be made to undermine this stance.[87] Firstly, we would not expect a worker to continue to work for an employer who has committed an unjustified breach of their human rights. Without some contractual recognition of an obligation to respect the human rights of a worker, they have no grounds on which to repudiate the contract and resign their position. The worker would be in breach of their own obligation to provide notice and perform work for the employer if they resigned without cause. Second, workers who are secure in the knowledge that their employer must respect their human rights may be more likely to invest in their employment relationship and in the business as a whole. As observed by Atkinson, '[r]elationships of trust are important for efficient production, and employees who know their human rights are subject to the whims of their employer will lack the sense of co-operation that is central to productive enterprise'.[88] He argues that this social benefit of the term is one element of the justification for its implication.

Finally, it could be argued that an implied term of this kind is a necessary incident of contracts of employment by reason of the UK's obligations under the ECHR. *Redfearn v UK* requires that a claimant be able to access a court capable of balancing their rights against an employer's in each particular case.[89] *Pla v Andorra* placed an obligation upon the domestic courts to read contracts in a manner that closely corresponds to the Convention.[90] There are difficulties with the contractual mechanism itself and the narrow boundaries of the 'contract of employment'

[85] Beale, *Chitty on Contracts* (n 26) [14-005]. See, for example, *Scally v SHSSB* (n 75) 307.
[86] Beale, *Chitty on Contracts* (n 26) [1-095].
[87] See further Atkinson (n 7) 539–48.
[88] ibid 544.
[89] (2013) 57 EHRR 2, discussed in Chapter 3.
[90] *Pla v Andorra* (n 5).

which will be discussed in Chapter 8. Nevertheless, a new implied obligation could offer a forum to some individuals, like Mr Redfearn, who would otherwise fall through the cracks of the existing legislative framework.

B. A 'Sound Development' of the Common Law?

The judges would also consider whether a new implied obligation is a sound development,[91] in line with the common law and its surrounding legal context, or a development that is akin to the creation of a new cause of action and therefore beyond the powers of the judiciary. Despite strong arguments in favour of the implication, my argument here is that the case law on the implication of new terms is distinctly cautious. The impact of contextual factors such as the surrounding legislative frameworks is difficult to predict, although the presence of so much statutory material in this area might persuade the judges that Parliament should retain the leading role in determining how human rights should be protected at work.

Looking at the legal context in which it would arise, the implication of a new implied term in the human rights area sits on a very fine balance. On one hand, the term would cohere well with the statutory and common law themes which protect human rights at work elsewhere. Members of the judiciary have been keen to emphasize the role of the common law in the protection of human rights[92] and in some of the cases discussed already, the IOMTAC can be viewed in this light. Key statutes that regulate contracts of employment are reflective of human rights concerns.[93] As observed by Lord Hoffman, the common law of the contract of employment has 'adapted itself to the new attitudes, proceeding sometimes by analogy with statutory rights.'[94] The development of an implied term would seem, on this evidence, to be a sound development of the common law which aligns well with its surrounding context.

On the other hand, the existence of statutory regulation could lead the judges to two conclusions to the contrary. First, the courts might think that the implied obligation would add little to the law regulating contracts of employment. The judges might examine legislation such as TULR(C)A 1992 and the EA 2010, combined with the more general right not to be unfairly dismissed and its newer human rights components, and conclude that this range of actions is sufficient to protect employees' Convention rights. On this point, I would argue that the outcome would depend heavily upon the particular facts of the case. If the claimant

[91] *Malik v BCCI* (n 28) 46.

[92] See, for example, Lord Toulson, 'Fundamental Rights and the Common Law' (The Fundamental Rights Conference, London, 10 October 2015); Lord Reed, 'The Common Law and the ECHR' (Inner Temple Lecture Series, London, 11 November 2013).

[93] See Chapter 4.

[94] *Johnson v Unisys* (n 73) [35].

had already made a successful claim under one of the statutory rights, the courts would be very unlikely to permit a 'second bite of the cherry'[95] via the common law. If the individual had no alternative avenue through which to claim, then the courts may be more sympathetic. Nevertheless, I would see the development of an entirely new implied term as a fairly extreme reaction to such an individual, where the IOMTAC might be deployed instead.

Secondly, the judges might take the view that the implied obligation would stray onto territory that is or should be occupied by Parliament. ACL Davies has observed that the courts currently view 'statute as the primary source of regulation of employment', with the common law playing a supplementary role.[96] This view has been shown most prominently in cases regarding the relationship between unfair dismissal and the IOMTAC. In *Johnson v Unisys*, Lord Hoffman's judgment shows clear deference to Parliament's regulation of dismissals, which is justified particularly by reference to the clear compromises and decisions grounded upon policy that were made in drafting the legislation.[97] Only dissenting voices advocate for the common law's evolution in tandem with the statutory provisions.[98] Although this line of reasoning has been criticized,[99] the fairly extensive list of statutes that attempt to prevent infringements upon the human rights of employees could be taken as strong evidence that the most appropriate regulator here is Parliament. On this view, the development of a new implied term would constitute an undesirable advance onto Parliamentary territory, even if the choices made by the legislator are open to criticism.

The likelihood of an unreceptive judicial attitude is reinforced when we examine the evolution of the existing terms implied into the contract of employment. The courts appear to resist taking large steps by implying strong and generalized duties into wide subsets of the contract of employment.[100] In *Crossley v Faithful & Gould Holdings Ltd*,[101] the court refused to imply a term that the employer should take reasonable care of the financial well-being of their employees. It was considered to impose an unfair burden on the employer and to lead to a variety of practical problems. Where the implication has been accepted in principle, the courts keep the obligation tightly defined and narrowly applicable to a small subgroup of contracts of employment.[102] Even the recognition of the IOMTAC, a significant milestone, can

95 A metaphor borrowed from Catherine Barnard, 'Cherries: One Bite or Two?' (2006) 65 CLJ 27.

96 ACL Davies, 'The Relationship between the Contract of Employment and Statute' in Mark Freedland (ed), *The Contract of Employment* (Oxford University Press 2016) 74.

97 *Johnson v Unisys* (n 73) [54]–[58] (Lord Hoffman).

98 ibid [22]–[23] (Lord Steyn); later *Edwards v Chesterfield Royal Hospital NHS Foundation Trust, Botham v Ministry of Defence* [2011] UKSC 58, [2012] 2 AC 22, [121] (Baroness Hale).

99 Hugh Collins, 'Claim for Unfair Dismissal: Johnson v Unisys Ltd' (2001) 30 ILJ 305, 306–07; Lizzie Barmes, 'The Continuing Conceptual Crisis in the Common Law of the Contract of Employment' (2004) 67 MLR 435, 464.

100 One way to avoid this difficulty would be to imply a term *in fact* in a particular case as a precursor to an implied term in law: see Atkinson (n 7).

101 [2004] EWCA Civ 293, [2004] ICR 1615.

102 See *Scally v SHSSB* (n 75) 781 and *Spring v Guardian Assurance plc* [1994] ICR 596, 647.

be regarded as following on from an existing implied obligation of cooperation.[103] The term was also in use for many years in the lower courts prior to coming before the House of Lords in *Malik*.[104] Their Lordships had plenty of evidence as to the term's impact and operation before confirming its implication in all contracts of employment. Without such evidence, there may be reluctance to develop the common law through a new implied term in law.

Overall, I see little cause for optimism regarding the possibility of the courts implying a new term in law that requires respect for an employee's human rights. The dominance of statutory regulation in this area, combined with a cautious approach to the implication of new obligations, indicates that there would be limited judicial enthusiasm for such a step. The judges may form a reasonable belief that choosing the means to safeguard the employee's human rights at work would most appropriately be done by Parliament, particularly in the absence of evidence as to the consequences of such an implied term. This view was articulated by Lady Hale when answering the question 'where should judges fear to tread?':

> Never say never, but I think that the judges are unlikely to create an entirely new cause of action ... This they would now regard themselves as institutionally incompetent to do, even if they might on occasions have done so in the past, when Parliament was less active and there were no Law Commissions to show how it should be done.[105]

Conclusion

Although the capacity of the courts to read contracts in a manner respectful of the individual's human rights has been proved, it is not exercised consistently. Whilst implied terms offer an alternative solution to the problem of how to protect human rights at work, the likelihood of this form of protection being developed is difficult to predict. Regarding the implied term of mutual trust and confidence, the current content of the term offers tangential protection to the Convention rights of employees and at some points clearly runs counter to those rights. In addition, despite the potential for a claimant to put forward a strong argument under the HRA 1998 and the state's positive obligations under the Convention, it is likely that the courts would consider the existing range of protection for human rights at work sufficient to keep the UK within its margin of appreciation. Galvanizing the courts into action under the existing obligation of mutual trust and confidence would thus be

[103] Douglas Brodie, 'The Heart of the Matter: Mutual Trust and Confidence' (1996) 25 ILJ 121, 129–30.

[104] See, for example, *Courtaulds Northern Textiles v Andrew* [1979] IRLR 84, [10].

[105] Baroness Hale, 'Legislation or Judicial Law Reform: Where Should Judges Fear to Tread?' (Annual Society of Legal Scholars Conference, Oxford, 7 September 2016) 17–18.

difficult. An argument for the second route, implying a new term in law requiring that employers should not unjustifiably infringe the human rights of their workers, would likely be met with similar reasoning. The development would be considered neither sufficiently necessary nor sufficiently incremental to be accepted by the courts.

These conclusions are subject to a significant caveat. If Parliament remains inactive in this area and individuals who have suffered an infringement of their human rights have no other opportunity to gain a remedy, then the courts have an obligation to develop the law. In these instances, as argued by Alan Bogg, 'the judicial responsibility to protect the claimant's fundamental human rights might override the judicial responsibility to respect the unfair dismissal legislation as a ceiling'.[106] If an interpretive exercise such as the one found in *Smith* is not possible, I would argue that the most likely judicial response is the application of the existing IOMTAC, flexible and open-ended as it is, rather than the more drastic step of the implication of a new obligation. This limit on the judiciary's deference was recognized by Lord Hoffman in a cryptic comment in his judgment in *Johnson*:

> Employment law requires a balancing of the interests of employers and employees ... *Subject to observance of fundamental human rights,* the point at which this balance should be struck is a matter for democratic decision.[107]

[106] Alan Bogg and Hugh Collins, 'Lord Hoffman and the Law of Employment: The Notorious Episode of Johnson v Unisys Ltd' in Paul S Davies and Justine Pila (eds), *The Jurisprudence of Lord Hoffman* (Hart Publishing 2015) 205.

[107] *Johnson v Unisys* (n 73) [37].

8
The Merits of Contractual Human Rights Protection

Even if contractual methods could be used to protect the human rights of workers, the question remains whether they would be a desirable means to protect those rights. There are several benefits of using contractual means to protect human rights. One of the advantages of this route to protection is that scope of the common law extends beyond a dismissal to other forms of detriment such as Mr Smith's demotion or the rejection of Ms Ahmed's application for an internal transfer.[1] To receive the unfair dismissal protection discussed in Chapter 6, employees who suffer detriment other than dismissal must follow the risky path of resigning in protest and making a claim of constructive unfair dismissal. Another benefit of the common law of the contract of employment is its remedial range. Although damages are most often sought, the courts can issue an injunction to prevent a breach of contract if it is ongoing.[2] An injunction is not available in unfair dismissal law, and it may be useful for claimants who wish to preserve their employment relationship despite a breach of contract by their employer. These benefits are significant and should not be dismissed. Nevertheless, problems remain.

Mark Freedland and Alan Bogg have argued that 'a narrowly contractual version of the idea of wrongful dismissal' has been embraced, underpinned by a 'normative position ... which is strongly defensive of employers' managerial prerogative and very weakly protective of employees' security of employment'.[3] This view of the common law provides crucial context to this chapter, as it also leads to a low standard of protection for workers' human rights. The common law of the contract of employment has been central in shaping the employer–employee relationship as one of subordination to direction and control. The employer benefits from implied obligations of loyalty and obedience that have been placed upon their employees and enjoys residual powers to direct, manage, and determine the rules and policies of the workplace. Whilst the case law of the European Court of Human Rights

[1] *Smith v Trafford Housing Trust* [2012] EWHC 3221 (Ch), [2013] IRLR 86; *Amnesty International v Ahmed* [2009] ICR 1450.

[2] *Irani v Southampton and South West Hampshire HA* [1985] ICR 590; *West London Mental Health NHS Trust v Chhabra* [2013] UKSC 80, [2014] 1 All ER 943.

[3] Alan Bogg and Mark Freedland, 'The Wrongful Termination of the Contract of Employment' in Mark Freedland (ed), *The Contract of Employment* (Oxford University Press 2016) 538, 540.

Putting Human Rights to Work. Philippa Collins, Oxford University Press. © Philippa Collins 2022.
DOI: 10.1093/oso/9780192894595.003.0009

(ECtHR) demonstrates that an employee's human rights *should* make inroads into this swathe of prerogatives and lead to the examination of the proportionality of particular decisions or practices, there is no evidence in the decisions at common law that the human rights of individuals will circumscribe the employer's managerial authority. This chapter seeks to demonstrate that the common law of the contract of employment, as it currently operates, is not an appropriate mechanism for safeguarding the human rights of workers.

In section I, I focus on the likely difficulties of using the existing implied obligation of mutual trust and confidence (IOMTAC) to protect the human rights of employees. Beyond structural issues regarding the scope of protection, we can see how the view described earlier has manifested in relation to the remedies for a breach of the IOMTAC. The measure of damages, the heads of damage that can be claimed, and the exclusion of common law damages for any breach related to the manner of dismissal are significant problems. If these principles are applicable to cases in which human rights have been invoked, they would severely hinder the capacity of the law to provide an effective remedy.

The second and third section examine in more detail the relationship between the contractual context of the common law and principles of the European Convention on Human Rights (ECHR or the Convention). There is a prospect that employers would use their bargaining power to attempt to contract out of their human rights duties under an implied term. This could be through the insertion of a contradictory express term or by avoiding the implication altogether by designing the arrangement so that it is not one of 'employment'. I predict that such efforts could be met with success in the domestic courts, but any contracting out is unlikely to meet the high level of scrutiny currently used in Strasbourg regarding waivers of Convention rights.

Finally, we turn to the relationship between the common law of the contract of employment, the employer's managerial powers, and the individual's human rights. The ECtHR's decisions emphasize that employees continue to enjoy human rights throughout an employment relationship and those rights may only be 'restricted in so far as necessary' in the pursuit of a legitimate aim.[4] In contrast, the domestic courts and tribunals adopt a view of the relationship of employment that is one of control and subordination, in which the employer retains the power to manage and supervise its staff in any manner it considers appropriate. The courts have stated that employees cannot expect to enjoy some fundamental rights during working time because of the existence of an employment relationship and the employer's right to control and direct their workforce. Decisions made in the name of protecting the employing business, such as dismissals for reasons that infringe upon an individual's freedom of expression or investigative actions that violate

[4] *Bărbulescu v Romania* Application no 61496/08 (ECtHR, 5 September 2017), [80].

their privacy, are accepted uncritically, with no recognition that the employer's prerogative must be circumscribed by reference to the employee's human rights.

I. The Limitations of the Mutual Trust and Confidence Term

Adapting a pre-existing mechanism for a new purpose brings challenges. The question addressed in Chapter 7 was whether the terms implied into *a contract of employment* could be pushed to cover situations where human rights have been infringed. As explained in Chapter 5, the contract of employment is narrowly defined and is the most difficult employment status to satisfy. If an individual sought human rights protection through, for example, the IOMTAC, they would need to first be classified as an employee under a contract of employment. Whilst it is possible that parties to other types of contracts for work could benefit from a wider range of implied obligations in the future, until that point, the scope of protection offered by either implied obligation would be narrow.

In terms of remedies, the common law is not generous. Contractual damages entitle the claimant to the sum they would have had if the contract had been lawfully performed—the expectation measure. This measure is then combined with the assumption of minimal lawful performance by the employer. The effect of these two principles, and the right of the employer to terminate the contract of employment by giving a reasonable period of notice,[5] is that claimants may only be entitled to damages representing lost wages for a period of weeks. For example, Mr Smith was wrongfully dismissed from his managerial position and demoted in breach of contract and in arguable violation of his human rights. He received only £98 in damages.[6] This figure represented the difference between his managerial salary and his reduced salary for a period of twelve weeks, after which the employer could have dismissed him lawfully and reappointed him in the more junior position.[7] Even claimants who have suffered infringements upon their human rights may be left with an extremely limited remedy.

Beyond pecuniary damages, *Addis v Gramophone Company Ltd* remains authority for the principle that damages for anxiety, frustration, or disappointment as a result of the fact or manner of dismissal are not recoverable at common law.[8] Recognized psychiatric injury is now recoverable,[9] mitigating the most serious effects of this rule. Nevertheless, the *Addis* principle is firmly out of line with ECHR principles. The ECtHR may award damages covering anxiety, humiliation, or

[5] See Employment Rights Act 1996, section 86 for the minimum periods of notice guaranteed by statute.

[6] *Smith v Trafford Housing Trust* [2012] EWHC 3320 (Ch), [2012] All ER (D) 273, [4].

[7] *Smith v Trafford Housing Trust* (n 1) [104]–[105].

[8] [1909] AC 488, 491.

[9] See *Gogay v Hertfordshire County Council* [2000] IRLR 703.

distress,[10] which is well outside the common law's remedial capacity. Questions might also be raised regarding the lack of non-pecuniary 'stigma damages' at common law, which would reflect 'damage to employability resulting from the manner of the dismissal or breach of contract that had the effect of wrongfully impugning the conduct or competence of the employee'.[11] This gap in the common law's damages is questionable under Article 8 ECHR. Several recent cases, notably *Denisov v Ukraine* and *Pişkin v Turkey*, have made it clear that Article 8 can be engaged where an employer's actions impugn the reputation of an individual.[12] This line of cases suggests that an effective remedy for such infringements would not be restricted to pecuniary losses only.[13]

More serious remedial limitations could be placed on the common law's capacity to vindicate an individual's human rights by the decision in *Johnson v Unisys Ltd* and its successors.[14] The principles expressed in these cases determine if an employee can recover damages at common law where the breach of their contract of employment is linked to their dismissal. The principles are very restrictive and have been termed the '*Johnson* exclusion zone'. Damages will not be recoverable for any breaches of the IOMTAC that relate to the manner of the dismissal or any breaches of a contractual disciplinary procedure that are not separable from the process of dismissal.[15] These types of claims must be litigated through unfair dismissal, in accordance with the majority of the House of Lords' understanding of Parliament's intention upon introducing the statutory framework.[16] Breaches of contractual terms, express or implied, that were independent of and separable from the dismissal remain actionable.[17] In order to receive common law damages for a breach of the implied term, an individual has two options: affirm the contract and make a claim whilst still employed or prove that the employer's actions were independent of the dismissal. Only in these two narrow situations would the common law offer any kind of effective remedy.

These remedial limitations seriously hinder the common law's ability to offer any effective remedy to claimants. However, if we see *Johnson* as a 'constitutional law case that happens to be played out against the backdrop of an employment dismissal dispute',[18] the constitutional context could be thought to change

[10] See Chapter 3, section IV.

[11] Hugh Collins, 'Compensation for Dismissal: In Search of Principle' (2012) 41 ILJ 208, 216.

[12] See, for example, *Denisov v Ukraine* Application no 76639/11 (ECtHR, 25 September 2018); *Pişkin v Turkey* Application no 33399/18 (ECtHR, 15 December 2020).

[13] See, for example, the award of £4,000 in non-pecuniary losses in *Pişkin v Turkey* (n 12) [239].

[14] [2001] UKHL 13, [2003] 1 AC 518; *Eastwood v Magnox Electric Plc* [2004] UKHL 35, [2005] 1 AC 503; *Edwards v Chesterfield Royal Hospital NHS Foundation Trust, Botham v Ministry of Defence* [2011] UKSC 58, [2012] 2 AC 22.

[15] *Johnson v Unisys* (n 14) and *Edwards v Chesterfield* (n 14).

[16] *Johnson v Unisys* (n 14) [54]–[55] and [58].

[17] See *Eastwood v Magnox Electric Plc* (n 14).

[18] Alan Bogg and Hugh Collins, 'Lord Hoffman and the Law of Employment: The Notorious Episode of Johnson v Unisys Ltd' in Paul S Davies and Justine Pila (eds), *The Jurisprudence of Lord Hoffman* (Hart Publishing 2015) 200.

dramatically upon the introduction of human rights arguments. If the IOMTAC is extended to protect the human rights of an employee, the claimant might argue that an exception from the '*Johnson* exclusion zone' should be created to permit them to receive damages where the manner of their dismissal infringed upon the individual's rights. The need to ensure that individuals receive an effective remedy if they have suffered a violation of their human rights could be an influential factor in deciding this issue.[19]

Drawing on the reasoning in *Johnson* and *Edwards*, the outcome would turn upon the courts' perception of the role of the common law in this scenario. It is plausible to think that the courts would perceive the law of unfair dismissal with its in-built limitations and subsequent adaptations through section 3 of the Human Rights Act 1998 (HRA 1998), as well as the HRA itself, as providing the appropriate vehicles for human rights claims.[20] This line of reasoning could persist *even if* the claimant has no other avenue to a remedy in their particular circumstances. Despite the injustice of such a situation and the potential breach of the UK's obligations under the ECHR that would result, the judiciary may accept this outcome as a consequence of their understanding of Parliament's intentions and the legislative compromises that have been struck. Although there would undoubtedly be resistance to this approach,[21] the extension of the '*Johnson* exclusion zone' to human rights cases would stunt the capacity of the common law to act as a vehicle for the full and effective vindication of the fundamental rights of the individual.

II. Contractual Waivers of Convention Rights and the Implied Terms

Human rights are inalienable and non-negotiable norms. These characteristics are reflected in the strict scrutiny applied by the ECtHR to any argument that an individual has contracted out of or waived their Convention rights. A government seeking to rely on such a waiver must demonstrate the following:[22]

1) The waiver must be established in an unequivocal manner.
2) It must be given in full knowledge of the facts.
3) It must be based upon informed consent and offered without constraint.
4) The waiver cannot be accepted if such acceptance would run counter to an important public interest.

[19] See the comment of Lord Hoffman in *Johnson v Unisys* (n 14) at [37].

[20] Hugh Collins and Virginia Mantouvalou, 'Human Rights and the Contract of Employment' in Mark Freedland (ed), *The Contract of Employment* (Oxford University Press 2016) 207.

[21] ibid; Bogg and Collins (n 18) 207.

[22] See *DH and others v Czech Republic* (2008) 47 EHRR 3, [202]; *Markin v Russia* (2013) 56 EHRR 8, [150].

These stringent standards have not yet been met in any ECtHR cases regarding a relationship between an employer and a working individual. Instead, contractual restrictions will be weighed in the balance during the assessment of whether an infringement upon a qualified right was necessary and proportionate.[23]

An argument before the Court that an employee or applicant for employment had waived a Convention right would face numerous obstacles.[24] If, as a result of a refusal to waive a particular right, one's job is at risk, this consideration would weigh heavily under the third criteria.[25] The ECtHR has long recognized the difficult position that employees or candidates may be placed in when responding to a request from an employer. In *Sørensen and Rasmussen v Denmark*, the Court took into account that 'individuals applying for employment often find themselves in a vulnerable situation and are only too eager to comply with the terms of employment offered'.[26] A threat of dismissal and loss of one's livelihood has also been described as 'a most serious form of compulsion'.[27] In addition, it could be considered seriously detrimental to the public interest to permit rights to be waived in the context of work,[28] which is so crucial to our daily lives and personal development.

Turning to the possibility that implied terms could be relied upon to guarantee the human rights of employees, would the mandatory nature of those rights be reproduced? Roger Rideout observed that an 'obvious weakness' of any attempt to regulate a relationship through contractual mechanisms is 'the existence of the veto which either party must be able to exercise over that external control'.[29] In practice, the employer is the only party to an employment relationship who possesses an effective veto in most cases, due to their superior bargaining power. This 'veto' might be exercised by inserting express terms that are either inconsistent with or directly exclude the operation of a particular implied term. In this section, I will discuss the likelihood of employers successfully ousting human rights protection in the form of, first, an extended IOMTAC, and second, a new implied obligation. Whilst I argue that the current conception of the obligation of mutual trust and confidence would permit it to be excluded, there is more cause for optimism in relation to a dedicated, rights-protective implied term.

[23] See, for example, *Martínez v Spain* (2015) 60 EHRR 3, [131] and [135].

[24] See also Olivier de Schutter, 'Human Rights in Employment Relationships: Contracts as Power' in Filip Dorssemont, Klaus Lörcher, and Isabelle Schömann (eds), *The European Convention on Human Rights and the Employment Relation* (Hart Publishing 2013) 152–55.

[25] Gillian Morris, 'Fundamental Rights: Exclusion by Agreement?' (2001) 30 ILJ 49, 54; Hazel Oliver, 'Email and Internet Monitoring in the Workplace: Information Privacy and Contracting-out' (2002) 31 ILJ 321, 333.

[26] (2008) 46 EHRR 29, [59].

[27] *Young, James and Webster v United Kingdom* (1981) 3 EHRR 20, [55].

[28] Morris (n 25) 55; Oliver (n 25) 333.

[29] Roger Rideout, 'Implied Terms in the Employment Relationship' in Roger Halson (ed), *Exploring the Boundaries of Contract* (Dartmouth Publishing 1996) 125.

A. Displacing the Implied Obligation of Mutual Trust and Confidence

The observation of Bogg and Freedland regarding the dominance of a strictly contractual view of wrongful dismissal law foreshadows the answer to the question of whether employers would be permitted to exclude the operation of the IOMTAC. From their work, and Freedland's earlier scholarship,[30] we can draw two different ways of thinking about the implied obligation: the traditional, contractual approach and the 'core component' or tortious perspective. These two models entail very different consequences in terms of the possibility of avoiding the operation of implied obligation by contrary express terms.

On the 'core component' view, the IOMTAC is seen as 'so inherent to the core concept of the contract of employment as to be incapable of exclusion from that contract'.[31] Whilst the *content* of the implied obligation draws on public law, its *form* is closer to a tortious duty: 'a non-voluntary obligation, based upon fault-based liability ... with the particular normative content of the general duty elaborated by the courts incrementally in a range of specific factual contexts'.[32] The obligation would be viewed as imposed by the common law and therefore its direction and application firmly within the sole control of the courts. The external and non-derogable nature of the IOMTAC on the 'core component' view would be in keeping with a new role of safeguarding the fundamental rights of the employee. Despite scholarly support for the 'core component' account of the implied term,[33] it does not appear to represent the courts' current understanding of the term.

The traditional, contractual approach holds that the source of the implied obligation is the parties' assumed intentions which can be displaced by an express contrary intention. On this view, the only question for the courts would be whether the parties had demonstrated a contrary intention through their express terms. There would be no assessment of the *quality* of the employee's consent to contract out of this core obligation or whether the agreement was achieved without constraint, pursues the public interest, and so forth. The contractual view therefore poses significant difficulties if the implied obligation evolves to provide human rights protection.

Hugh Collins observes with regret that the 'traditional' approach to the exclusion of the implied obligation remains the orthodoxy.[34] Whilst there are some examples of implied terms shaping the exercise of express contractual powers,[35] the

[30] Mark Freedland, *The Personal Employment Contract* (Oxford University Press 2003) 164.
[31] ibid 166.
[32] Bogg and Freedland (n 3) 548.
[33] Freedland (n 30) 164, 166; Rideout (n 29) 128; Douglas Brodie, 'Beyond Exchange: The New Contract of Employment' (1998) 27 ILJ 79, 85–86; Bob Hepple, *Rights at Work: Global, European and British Perspectives* (Sweet & Maxwell 2005) 62.
[34] Hugh Collins, 'Implied Terms in the Contract of Employment' in Mark Freedland (ed), *The Contract of Employment* (Oxford University Press 2016) 487 onwards.
[35] See, for example, *Gogay v Hertfordshire CC* (n 9); *United Bank Ltd v Akhtar* [1989] IRLR 507.

general thrust of the case law is that the implied obligation will not be defended against express terms that may whittle it down. In *Johnson v Unisys* itself, the majority erred on the side of preserving the absolute right to give reasonable notice to terminate a contract rather than requiring that the right be exercised in accordance with the IOMTAC.[36] Not long after, the orthodox view was affirmed by the Privy Council in *Reda v Flag Ltd.*[37] Lord Millett stated that the IOMTAC 'must yield to the express provisions of the contract'.[38] The possibility that the implied obligation may somehow persist despite contrary express terms has not be pressed in litigation since.

It appears from the evidence available that the IOMTAC is at least vulnerable to exclusion or limitation via express terms. The insertion of any term inconsistent with the implied obligation could displace its operation, such as an entire agreement clause or express powers that are incompatible with its operation. An alternative method would be to avoid the implication of the term altogether by ensuring that the relationship between the parties will not be classified as a 'contract of employment'.[39] The employer could use their bargaining and bureaucratic power to ensure that the relationship is conducted in a manner inconsistent with such a classification, thereby avoiding the term's operation completely. If the IOMTAC was extended to protect the Convention rights of employees, any displacement or exclusion of the term would operate as a waiver of the employee's right to protection of their human rights. The continued influence of the contractual conception of the implied obligation would, in these circumstances, render it an unsuitable vehicle for human rights protection.

B. Would a New Human Rights Term be Derogable?

If an independent term is implied by law to offer protection for the human rights of workers, a bold employer may attempt to insert a clause that excludes its operation. The question of whether the employer could do so successfully would be crucial to the standard of protection guaranteed by the novel term. As has been observed, it is unlikely that any provision that contracts out of Convention guarantees in the employment context would pass ECtHR scrutiny in light of the unique relational dynamics between an employee and employer. Could the new term be entrenched to a sufficient degree that it would comply with the Convention's principles on contracting out of rights?

36 *Johnson v Unisys* (n 14) [42] and [47] (Lord Hoffman).
37 *Reda v Flag Ltd* [2002] UKPC 38, [2002] IRLR 747, [44] onwards.
38 ibid [45].
39 See Hepple (n 33) 62; Brodie (n 33) 102. Douglas Brodie observes that such manoeuvres 'constitute the most radical form of contracting-out of fundamental obligations'.

Here, one might permit a degree of optimism, although it must be tempered by the untested nature of the arguments that follow. To prevent the waiver of an implied term to respect human rights, one could make an argument founded upon public policy: it would be contrary to public policy to permit employers to avoid an obligation to respect the human rights of their employees. There is no general principle of contract law that terms contrary to public policy will not be enforced by the courts. We can see pockets of case law, however, that are motivated by public policy and a concern to protect the fundamental rights of the individual.

A particular high point is Lord Denning's judgment in *Lee v Showmen's Guild*, tackling a membership contract between Mr Lee and his former union. 'Although the jurisdiction of a domestic tribunal is founded on contract, express or implied, nevertheless the parties are not free to make any contract they like. There are important limitations imposed by public policy.'[40] In several areas, we can see that rights-based concerns are a key aspect of these public policy limitations. For example, public policy has been considered to motivate doctrines of restraint of trade.[41] If one considers the right to work in a chosen occupation as a fundamental right,[42] the courts' refusal to enforce excessive restraints of trade can be seen as a refusal to enforce a waiver of a fundamental right.[43] Elsewhere, the operation of the illegality defence balances public policies on either side. Maintaining consistency across the legal system and preventing individuals from profiting from their wrongdoing are set against other policies such as the UK's international human rights obligations and importance of protecting the fundamental rights of the claimant.[44]

If a new implied term was introduced, I would argue that there are exceptionally strong reasons of public policy that dictate that the employer should not be allowed to exclude a term requiring that they respect the human rights of their employees. We might cite the UK's positive obligations under the European Convention which include an obligation to protect individuals from infringements on their rights by other private parties, as well as the common law's role in the protection of fundamental rights.[45] In addition, any court that enforced a deliberate evasion of a duty

[40] *Lee v Showmen's Guild of Great Britain* [1952] 2 QB 329.

[41] Edwin Peel, *Treitel on the Law of Contract* (14th edn, Sweet & Maxwell 2015) [11-032].

[42] See The Charter of Fundamental Rights of the European Union [2016] OJ C202/389, Article 15; European Social Charter, Article 1; Hugh Collins, 'Is There a Human Right to Work?' in Virginia Mantouvalou (ed), *The Right to Work: Legal and Philosophical Perspectives* (Hart Publishing 2015).

[43] See the framing of restraint of trade in Chantal Mak, *Fundamental Rights in European Contract Law: A Comparison of the Impact of Fundamental Rights on Contractual Relationships in Germany, the Netherlands, Italy and England* (Kluwer Law International 2008).

[44] See *Hounga v Allen and another* [2014] UKSC 47, [2014] 1 WLR 2889, discussed further in Chapter 5, section II(B).

[45] See Lord Reed, 'The Common Law and the ECHR' (Inner Temple Lecture Series, London, 11 November 2013); Philip Sales, 'Rights and Fundamental Rights in English Law' (2016) 75 CLJ 86, particularly 104.

to respect an employee's human rights would appear to in breach of its own obligation under section 6 HRA to act compatibly with the Convention.

A specific method by which the courts could give effect to this public policy argument is by severing the exclusion term from the remainder of the contract. The exclusion term could be rendered unenforceable. The courts will not use the severance of terms to rewrite the parties' bargain and the remaining terms must not require modification, as well as being supported by adequate consideration.[46] If applied to a term that attempts to exclude the implied obligation, these criteria would not pose any difficulty. In addition, severance will not be used to rewrite the parties' contract or alter its essential nature.[47] Here, it would be difficult to argue that removing a term that denies respect for the employee's human rights would change the fundamental nature of a contract of employment. Finally, the courts will not sever the unenforceable parts of the contract unless such a step is in accordance with public policy.[48] Severance of a term that ousts the protection of the human rights of the individual would cohere with and contribute to the overarching direction of public policy, as expressed by common law doctrines and in legislation such as the HRA 1998. There is at least a chance that the non-derogable nature of a new implied term could be protected through the mechanism of severance.

III. The Common Law's Relationship to the Employer's Managerial Prerogative

The common law of the contract of employment has played a key role in shaping the relationship between employer and employee. Significant developments within the common law operate to protect the employee, notably the implied obligation of trust and confidence and the implied duty of care. Nevertheless, the employer's right to manage their employees is firmly entrenched within common law thinking about the nature of the employment relationship. Hugh Collins describes the relationship as:

> a power relationship constructed by the contract of employment and supported by the law. The employer is the dominant power—the boss—and in accordance with the contract of employment the employee must serve as an instrument of the employer's commands.[49]

[46] H G Beale (ed), *Chitty on Contracts* (33rd edn, Sweet & Maxwell 2018) [16-239]–[16-240].
[47] ibid [16-240A].
[48] ibid [16-244].
[49] Hugh Collins, 'Is the Contract of Employment Illiberal?' in Hugh Collins, Gillian Lester, and Virginia Mantouvalou (eds), *Philosophical Foundations of Labour Law* (Oxford University Press 2018) 52.

The common law perspective, I argue, has not made any significant concessions to the need to respect and protect the human rights of workers from infringement by their employer since the introduction of the HRA. It remains centred upon the preservation of the employer's prerogative to manage and control the workforce.

Common law duties and developments have been important in maintaining and reinforcing the subordination of employees to the demands of their employer. Implied duties of obedience and loyalty on behalf of employees are longstanding. The common law places employees under wide-ranging duties including to obey all lawful and reasonable instructions issued by their employer[50] and to serve the employer faithfully and in a manner that does not obstruct the efficient running of the business.[51] The employer also possesses residual powers of management, including hiring and firing employees and setting and enforcing standards of behaviour within the workplace. The common law offers an effective buttress for the managerial powers of employers and reinforces the subordination of workers to the demands and decisions of their employer. As observed by Simon Deakin:

> A work relationship that did not give the employer a certain residual discretion of this kind would lack the element of personal subordination (or 'control' in an extended sense) which separates the contract of employment (or service) from the contract for services.[52]

Deakin describes the current incarnation of managerial prerogative, protected by the common law, as a 'relic of the old master–servant regime'.[53]

A concern to protect the human rights of workers poses a challenge to the view of the contract of employment preserved by the common law. For example, it may require courts to question how employers interpret their rulebook or respond to an allegation that an employee has committed misconduct if either decision results in an infringement of the individual's human rights. In *Herbai v Hungary*,[54] the ECtHR was asked to decide whether Mr Herbai's right to freedom of expression had been infringed by his dismissal. Mr Herbai was a human resources professional. He established a blog to share information amongst the human resources community and wrote a piece about national tax changes, which was published online. He was dismissed for breaching the employer's confidentiality standards and code of conduct. As he was found to have breached the employer's rules, the national courts held that his dismissal was lawful. In contrast, the ECtHR found

50 See *Pepper v Webb* [1969] 1 WLR 514, 518.

51 See *Secretary of State for Employment v Associated Society of Locomotive Engineers and Firemen and Others (No. 2)* [1972] 2 QB 455.

52 Simon Deakin, 'Formation of the Contract of Employment' in Mark Freedland (ed), *The Contract of Employment* (Oxford University Press 2016) 389.

53 ibid 388.

54 (2020) 70 EHRR 35.

that Mr Herbai's Article 10 right had been infringed upon and asked whether the national courts had taken his rights into consideration. The ECtHR stated that it could not find 'any meaningful balancing of the interests at issue by the domestic courts'.[55] Further, '[t]he substantive outcome of the labour dispute was dictated purely by contractual considerations ... and voided the applicant's reliance on freedom of expression of any effect'.[56] In upholding the employer's decision to dismiss, the national authorities had failed to fulfil their positive obligations under Article 10.

The decision in *Herbai v Hungary* demonstrates that the human rights of an individual may curtail the employer's prerogative to determine the rules of the organization and apply them through disciplinary action. The inapplicability of these kinds of restraints upon employers under the common law was clear in *Gibbins v British Council*,[57] discussed in Chapter 7. Ms Gibbins was associated with a contentious and offensive thread of conversation on Facebook about the Royal Family. After a media furore, she was dismissed for recklessly causing damage to the employer's reputation. Amongst other claims before the tribunal, Ms Gibbins argued that her behaviour was not gross misconduct and that she was entitled to pay during her notice period as a result. Similarly to the domestic courts' consideration of Mr Herbai's dismissal, the Employment Tribunal (ET) only assessed the wrongfulness of Ms Gibbins' dismissal from the perspective of the terms of the contract of employment and accepted how the employer had interpreted them. There was no consideration of whether the disciplinary powers of the employer should be circumscribed by a need to respect Ms Gibbins' right to freedom of expression and to belief.

The lack of appreciation for the constraints that human rights may place upon the employer's power to manage their employees is perhaps strongest in relation to steps taken to investigate misconduct alleged against an individual. The ECtHR case law shows clearly that employees continue to enjoy the right to respect for private life within the workplace itself, as well as a right to be free of employer interference outside of working time. In *Antović and Mirković v Montenegro*,[58] for example, employees invoked their Article 8 rights to challenge the use of video recordings in lecture halls. The ECtHR held that Article 8 was applicable because the lecture hall was the workplace of teachers, where they interact with students and build relationships with them.[59] Thus, employees retain privacy rights under Article 8 within the workplace and during working time. In *Bărbulescu v Romania*, the Court stated clearly that employees may retain a reasonable expectation of privacy in relation to their correspondence and online activities even in the face of

[55] ibid [50].
[56] ibid [50].
[57] (2017) ET 2200088/2017.
[58] Application no 70838/13 (ECtHR, 28 November 2017).
[59] ibid [45].

contrary workplace rules or instructions.[60] There, the employer relied upon a notice that prohibited the use of working time and equipment for personal matters. This express direction was not sufficient to oust the employee's rights under Article 8 ECHR. Any interference with these rights, through monitoring or accessing personal information about the employee, must be shown to correspond to a legitimate aim and be necessary and proportionate to achieve that aim.[61]

In contrast, the national courts struggle to appreciate the consequences of the fact that individuals possess the right to respect for their private life within and despite the existence of an employment relationship. The managerial powers of employers have been reinforced for so many years through the common law cases that any suggestion that they should be limited or circumscribed by a right to privacy is hastily dismissed. The perspective of the courts was exhibited in *City and County of Swansea v Gayle*.[62] The employer had a suspicion that the employee was engaging in leisure activities during working time. Mr Gayle was subject to covert surveillance by a private investigator, arranged by the employer, over the course of five weeks. He was dismissed without notice on grounds of misconduct and challenged his dismissal through unfair dismissal law. On the issue of the surveillance, which constituted the employer's investigation before dismissal, the Employment Appeal Tribunal (EAT) ruled against Mr Gayle. The EAT stated 'we do not accept that here there was any breach of art 8(1) so as to require the tribunal to consider the requirements of 8(2) at all'.[63]

Langstaff P, then President of the EAT, put forward a justification for this conclusion on Article 8, invoking as he did so a very clear perception of the relationship between employee and employer:

> It is a feature of an employment contract that an employee is subject to the reasonable direction of his employer. An employer is thus entitled to know where someone is and what they are doing in the employer's time. *An employee can have no reasonable expectation that he can keep those matters private and secret from his employer at such a time. To do so would be to run contrary to the contract he had entered with his employer.*[64]

The passage clearly expresses the idea that the employment contract entails a right to manage and direct an employee which displaces any expectation of privacy whilst the employee is 'on the clock'. This reasoning runs contrary to the ECtHR's case law on the subject. As seen in cases such as *Antović and Mirković*,[65] surveillance

[60] *Bărbulescu v Romania* (n 4) [80].
[61] ibid [121].
[62] [2013] IRLR 768.
[63] ibid [23].
[64] ibid [15] emphasis added.
[65] See *Antović and Mirković v Montenegro* (n 58) [44].

during working time, even in a notionally public space such as the workplace, engages Article 8. The court should then consider whether the employer's policy or decision was necessary to pursue a legitimate aim. In contrast, the EAT in *Gayle* approached the question of Article 8 from the opposite direction. Rather than asking whether the employer's right to supervise their workers was justified in its exercise here, given the infringement upon Mr Gayle's private life, the court's starting point was that right to supervise. There was no thought that the employee's fundamental rights should be the primary concern in the case or that they might override or constrain the employer's managerial prerogative.

The failure to recognize how employees' privacy rights may require the re-examination of the employer's right to manage a workplace is most noticeable in cases involving online behaviour. Employers are able to delve ever further into the private lives of their employees by investigating their online activities on social media sites such as Facebook and Twitter. Personal correspondence is also easily accessible, particularly where the employee uses equipment owned by their employer to open their messages or correspond with others. In recent cases, employers have even relied on messages exchanged on mobile phone applications such as WhatsApp (a messaging service known for its privacy protections) in their investigations of employee conduct.[66] Employers regularly use these new avenues of information about their employees to investigate allegations of misconduct with no regard to the consequences for their employees' privacy rights. In turn, the courts accept this probing by employers as a legitimate extension of the managerial prerogative to discipline their staff. Individuals thereby lose any protection of their reasonable expectations of privacy, which must be considered to persist in correspondence and social activities even if they occur online or electronically.[67]

In *Williams v Leeds United Football Club*,[68] Mr Williams held a senior position within Leeds United Football Club. In 2013, the management of the Club decided to make him redundant. They simultaneously resolved to find a way not to pay Mr Williams' wages for the lengthy notice period to which he was contractually entitled. To this end, the Club hired forensic investigators. The investigators were asked to find evidence that would justify Mr Williams' dismissal on grounds of gross misconduct, which would disentitle Mr Williams from any remuneration during his notice period. The investigators were successful. Mr Williams had forwarded an email containing pornographic photographs from his Club account

66 See, for example, *Wells and another v Cathay Investments 2 Ltd* [2019] EWHC 2996 (QB), [2020] IRLR 281, [149]; under the unfair dismissal jurisdiction, see *Sharp and Lewis v Xylem Water Solutions UK Limited* [2020] ET 1400459/2019; 1400652/2019, *Case v Tai Tarian* [2019] ET 1601297/2018; *Faraz v Core Education Trust* [2018] ET 1303060/15.

67 See *Pay v United Kingdom* (2009) 48 EHRR SE2, 25, although in that case Mr Pay's online activities were anonymised which was relevant to the Court's assumption that Article 8 was engaged and *Bărbulescu v Romania* (n 4) [74].

68 [2015] EWHC 376 (QB), [2015] IRLR 383.

to colleagues at other clubs and one internal member of staff. Mr Williams at the time had found these emails amusing and believed that his colleagues would do so too. The email at issue was sent five years and four months before the redundancy announcement. No complaints or offence had been caused by the email at the time nor had it been raised as an issue in the intervening period. The day after Mr Williams was informed of his redundancy, he was called into a disciplinary hearing and dismissed without notice on grounds of gross misconduct.

Mr Williams brought a wrongful dismissal claim. The main issue for the High Court was whether forwarding the email amounted to gross misconduct: was his conduct a fundamental breach of the IOMTAC that entitled the Club to dismiss him summarily? The court found that the breach of the implied term was sufficiently serious to warrant summarily dismissal.[69] This finding was made even though the Club's Code of Conduct indicated that such behaviour would be a serious disciplinary matter, rather than gross misconduct. The court disregarded Mr Williams' argument that the employment relationship, having continued for more than five years after the incident, was sufficiently robust to survive the discovery.[70] The employer's motives—the Club's prior decision to breach its own contractual obligation and search out a reason for dismissal in its own financial interests—were irrelevant in the court's consideration of whether they could rely on the repudiatory breach.[71] The unfairness and injustice of the situation did not affect the court's findings.[72]

The serious breach of Mr Williams' Article 8 rights also failed to enter the court's deliberations. It was established as early as 1993 in *Niemietz v Germany* that professional activities and correspondence are covered by the right to privacy.[73] In *Bărbulescu v Romania*, the ECtHR also emphasized that member states, whilst exercising their discretion within the margin of appreciation, must ensure that monitoring measures by employers are accompanied by 'adequate and sufficient safeguards against abuse'.[74] Investigations and monitoring undertaken for the express purpose of depriving an individual of their contractual rights may well constitute an employer abusing their disciplinary powers. The court's approach to the issue reflected clearly the perspective described earlier where the employer's right to manage and direct their workers is placed at the centre of the reasoning, and the employer is assumed to possess any powers required to investigate and discipline their staff. No consideration was given to the employer's abuse of those powers for a profiteering motive or the infringement upon Mr Williams' Article 8 rights in the exercise of their managerial authority.

69 ibid [55].
70 ibid [67] and [68].
71 ibid [84].
72 ibid [84].
73 (1993) 16 EHRR 97.
74 *Bărbulescu v Romania* (n 4) [120].

This disregard for Article 8 ECHR has been reflected in other cases regarding investigations into private correspondence or out-of-work communications where the employee is suspected of misconduct.[75] In *Ministry of Justice v Sarfraz*,[76] the claimant's Facebook page was accessed during a disciplinary investigation. Mr Sarfraz sought to argue that this action amounted to a breach of the employer's legal obligations for the purposes of a whistleblowing claim under section 103A of the ERA 1996. Mr Justice Underhill, then President of the EAT, was dismissive of the claimant's Article 8 argument: 'I do not think it likely that the tribunal will find that any belief on the part of the claimant that this amounted to a breach of his Article 8 rights was reasonable.'[77] Similarly in *Wells v Cathay Investments*, the employer investigated the contents of a private conversation between the claimants and other colleagues on the mobile application WhatsApp.[78] Whilst considering whether the claimants' conduct amounted to gross misconduct that warranted summary dismissal, the High Court did not take into account that the employer's investigation had breached the right to respect for privacy and correspondence of the individuals involved. There was no debate regarding the legitimacy of this investigatory process from a human rights perspective. The lack of engagement with the possibility that Article 8 may place limits upon the scope of an employer's misconduct investigation is disappointing.

These cases demonstrate that the courts readily accept that the employer's managerial powers extend to intrusive investigations that infringe upon the privacy rights of their staff. The common law's conception of the relationship between employer and employee which reinforces the individual's daily subordination to their manager has been extended beyond the workplace and well into the private life and correspondence of the employee. The way that cases are decided under the common law runs contrary to the clear statements by the ECtHR that human rights persist in the context of employment relationship and cannot be ousted easily by an employer's rulebook or instructions. Equally the courts do not examine the employer's classification of behaviour as gross misconduct or serious misconduct where the employee's conduct amounts to an exercise of their human rights. Rather than questioning the necessity and proportionality of dismissing an employee in such circumstances, as is required under the ECHR, the courts decide the cases purely on the basis of contractual interpretation and the contract's application to the facts. These cases cast serious doubts over the capacity of the common law to vindicate the human rights of an individual and to become an effective source of protection for the human rights of workers in the future.

[75] See, for example, *Farnan v Sunderland Association Football Club Ltd* [2015] EWHC 3759 (QB), [2016] IRLR 185, [48]; *Mason v Huddersfield Giants Ltd* [2013] EWHC 2869 (QB), [35].

[76] [2011] IRLR 562.

[77] ibid [41].

[78] *Wells and another v Cathay Investments 2 Ltd* (n 66) [149]–[154].

Conclusion

Whilst there are ways in which the implied obligations of the contract of employment could be configured in a fashion that would make them passable vehicles for an employee's human rights, these developments are deeply speculative. Not only would the content of the implied obligations have to develop rapidly, and in a new direction, but the common law's remedial principles and the relationship between implied and express terms would have to be redefined in a radical way. Finally, an extension beyond the narrow 'contract of employment' would be essential to reflect the universal entitlement to exercise and receive protection of one's Convention rights. There is therefore a series of significant structural adjustments that would be required before the contractual route to human rights protection could provide an adequate solution for working people.

Beyond these essential mechanical changes, there is a clash between the common law's conception of the relationship of employment and the pursuit of effective protection of the individual's human rights. The relationship between employer and employee is viewed as one of subordination, direction, and control, a perspective that is braced by implied duties on behalf of employees and residual powers of management that are vested in employers. The courts in recent years have accepted that these powers of management extend well into the private lives of their employees through monitoring or investigations of electronic and online communications, without reflection upon the human rights consequences of such an expansion of the employer's influence. The lack of engagement with the human rights dimensions of disciplinary decisions made by employers is also present in cases where the reason for the disciplinary action touches upon the rights of the employee. Even *Smith v Trafford Housing Association*, the best example thus far of an approach that is sensitive to human rights, failed to reference any of the case law of the ECtHR that discusses disciplinary actions that interfered with Convention rights. For the common law of the contract of employment to offer effective protection for the human rights of individuals, an appreciation for the need to guarantee those rights despite the power that an employer otherwise holds over their workforce would be necessary.

9
A Bill of Rights for Workers

The preceding chapters conducted a comprehensive review of employment law's protection of the human rights of working people. The initial chapters argued that safeguarding those rights is an important aim of labour law and set out the clear expectations imposed through the European Court of Human Rights' (ECtHR or the Court) doctrine of positive obligations. Although piecemeal protection of the rights contained in the European Convention on Human Rights (ECHR or the Convention) is in place, Chapters 5 and 6 exposed the substantial barriers that prevent individuals vindicating their fundamental rights. Large groups within the workforce do not enjoy the protection of some, or all, employment rights. Unfair dismissal law remains the predominant route through which litigants seek to enforce their fundamental rights. There, we found that an ECHR-compliant framework has been introduced in theory, but in practice, it is either omitted completely or applied half-heartedly. Although human rights arguments are yet to influence the outcome of an unfair dismissal dispute, if they were to do so, the remedies are arbitrarily limited by the statutory cap and do not include recompense for non-pecuniary loss, an important aspect of the harm of a human rights infringement.

Chapters 7 and 8 examined the common law alternative to a statutory claim. Finding that the implied term of mutual trust and confidence is a long distance away from providing human rights safeguards, I observed that the likelihood of the implication of a new term alongside it is small. The courts could either see the new term as an unnecessary addition to the suite of existing rights or view it as tantamount to the judicial creation of a new cause of action. In addition, I argued that this contractual, common law route to protection has several other possible drawbacks. The subordination of any implied term to the express terms of the contract places this form of guarantee at risk of express or implied exclusion. Further, the tribunals are ready to defer to the contractual obligations and duties that place restrictions on the exercise of fundamental rights. Both features of the current case law would severely curtail the effectiveness of protection via the common law.

In the absence of adequate existing protection for the human rights of individuals in their working relationships, this chapter presents one possible solution to the issue.[1] The chapter suggests the introduction of a Parliamentary bill, a Bill of Rights, that would require employers to act compatibly with the human rights of

[1] An outline of this proposal was put forward in Philippa Collins, 'Square Peg vs a Round Hole? The Necessity of a Bill of Rights for Workers' (2020) 11 European Labour Law Journal 199.

Putting Human Rights to Work. Philippa Collins, Oxford University Press. © Philippa Collins 2022.
DOI: 10.1093/oso/9780192894595.003.0010

the people that they employ. The suggestions here take inspiration from discrimination law, labour law statutes, and the Human Rights Act 1998 (HRA 1998). In making these proposals, this chapter draws together many of the themes that have been present throughout this work and proposes a novel solution to the issues and inadequacies that have been explored earlier.

The chapter will first defend the choice of suggesting a new framework which would be set out in legislation. Section II outlines the central duty placed on employers not to infringe upon the human rights of their workers and discusses important issues such as how to confine the range of legitimate aims that employers can rely upon and how the courts should assess the proportionality of an employer's action or measure. In section III, another major challenge will be confronted: the definition of the relational and personal scope of the Bill. The theme of ensuring effective protection for the human rights of workers in a variety of situations continues in section IV, in a discussion of complementary mechanisms that would aid the Bill's operation such as a pre-emptive capacity to challenge rights-restrictive practices and prevent avoidance via contract. Section V turns to the question of how to fashion an appropriate link between the Bill's interpretation and the case law of the Strasbourg Court, before considering in section VI the role that fundamental social rights could have in the operation of the Bill.

I. The Need for Legislative Action

Before turning to the detail of the Bill itself, the recommended mechanism must briefly be justified. Whereas some might hope that we could rely on the common law to evolve to protect the human rights of workers, I argue that legislative action is the preferable option. From the perspective of the appropriate division of responsibilities between the judicial and Parliamentary branches of government, as well as from a pragmatic viewpoint, Parliamentary enactment is the most desirable choice.

To offer a comprehensive and democratically legitimate solution to the issues raised in the preceding chapters, remedial measures must be taken by Parliament rather than the courts. Courts and tribunals, ruling on narrow facts between two parties, are not well-equipped to enunciate a comprehensive set of rights in a novel context and establish new mechanisms by which those rights should be enforced.[2] There are many different routes, methods, and compromises that could be adopted in order to protect the fundamental rights of workers.[3] Each may have different

[2] For further discussion of why judicial law reform can be problematic, see Baroness Hale, 'Legislation or Judicial Law Reform: Where Should Judges Fear to Tread?' (Annual Society of Legal Scholars Conference, Oxford, 7 September 2016) 8–13.

[3] See Maris Köpcke, 'Why It Takes Law to Realise Human Rights' in Grégoire Webber and others (eds), *Legislated Rights: Securing Human Rights through Legislation* (Cambridge University Press 2018) on the role of the legislature in specifying the duties required to realize rights.

benefits, drawbacks, and consequences that must be reviewed and carefully taken into consideration. In most instances, judges are not presented with the evidence necessary to make such choices and would be justified in their likely reluctance to reform the law from the bench. In contrast, legislatures have a central role to play in setting out the detailed duties, rules, and standards that are required to implement human rights effectively.[4] Parliamentary enactments enjoy democratic legitimacy, and one would hope that the process of building consensus in favour of a Bill of this kind could be inclusive of a wide cross-section of civil society groups.

Enactment by primary legislation also has several other benefits. There would be symbolic and expressive importance to the introduction of a piece of primary legislation with the singular aim of providing protection for the fundamental rights of workers. We might consider the possibility of increasing this expressive value by incorporating a long title or a purpose clause to articulate the values that motivate the Bill and should guide its interpretation in the future. Even the brief statement the precedes the HRA 1998—that it is '[a]n Act to give further effect to rights and freedoms guaranteed under the European Convention on Human Rights'—has been important to its subsequent implementation and encouraged the courts to take a purposive approach to its application.[5] In this instance, the proposed Bill might commence:

> A Bill to ensure that all workers enjoy human rights in their working lives and to protect those rights from infringement by any employer, in order to ensure broad-minded, tolerant and diverse workplaces in which all people are respected.

We might also consider the benefit of *de facto* entrenchment through enactment by primary legislation, when contrasted with the common law's vulnerability to subsequent judicial decisions. Complete repeal or significant amendments could be difficult to achieve if the Bill attained enough support to be enacted initially, particularly in light of the moral urgency of the safeguards that the Bill contains. As observed by Patrick Elias recently in relation to the HRA itself, 'it would be politically difficult for any government to pass legislation which would be perceived as precluding judges from protecting human rights, whatever the merits of such legislation may be'.[6] We can see this demonstrated in the fact that the HRA has survived

[4] For a recent perspective on the role of legislation in realizing human rights, see Grégoire Webber and others (eds), *Legislated Rights: Securing Human Rights through Legislation* (Cambridge University Press 2018).

[5] Baroness Hale, '*Argentoratum Locutum*: Is Strasbourg or the Supreme Court Supreme?' (2012) 12 Human Rights Law Review 65, 69.

[6] Patrick Elias, 'Reflections on Judicial Power and Human Rights' in Alan Bogg, Jacob Rowbottom, and Alison L Young (eds), *The Constitution of Social Democracy: Essays in Honour of Keith Ewing* (Bloomsbury Publishing 2020) 19.

untouched, despite years of political criticism and several Conservative Party commitments to repeal the Act and replace it with a British bill of rights.[7]

Nevertheless, one might wonder why this chapter embarks upon the elaboration of a new statutory framework rather than suggesting a simple amendment to the HRA. Sections 6 and 7 of the HRA 1998 could be amended in order to render employers liable for human rights infringements in the same way as public authorities. Such an amendment might appear to be a neat solution to the problems that we have exposed. It would pose several serious difficulties. Many of the obligations and duties that the ECHR entails, including the positive obligations discussed in Chapter 3, are only placed upon state authorities. Employers should not be subject to them, and it would not be appropriate to impose the same kind of general duty to comply with Convention rights upon employers as is placed upon public authorities. Employers owe duties to those individuals with whom they come into contact *as an employer*, rather than as a business partner or consumer, for example.[8] The duties proposed here are narrower in application than those that would be created through an amendment to the HRA, thereby avoiding imposing an excessive burden upon employers in their other business dealings and tackling the specific risks that arise in the employment relationship.

II. A Duty to Respect the Human Rights of Workers

There are different ways in which one might approach the regulation of human rights infringements by employers. On one approach, a long but comprehensive list of actions by employers would be targeted by the provisions. Unfurling the key contents of each qualified right would be challenging, but this approach has benefits such as a greater degree of certainty for employers. On the other hand, one might consider an open-ended duty to respect the qualified rights of workers. This option would be more adaptable, adjusting more straightforwardly to new directions in the ECtHR case law, but also places a great deal of responsibility with the courts in defining the scope of the obligation. As either approach would offer an effective standard of rights protection, no preference will be expressed between them.

One could take a similar route as that taken by the Trade Union and Labour Relations (Consolidation) Act 1992 (TULR(C)A 1992) in relation to the protection of the right to freedom of association. Specific types of behaviour are prohibited,

[7] David Cameron, 'Balancing Freedom and Security—A Modern British Bill of Rights' *The Guardian* (London, 26 June 2006) <https://www.theguardian.com/politics/2006/jun/26/conservatives.constitution> 24 September 2021; The Conservative Party, *Invitation to Join the Government of Britain: The Conservative Manifesto 2010* (2010) 79; The Conservative Party, *Strong Leadership. A Clear Economic Plan. A Brighter, More Secure Future: The Conservative Party Manifesto 2015* (2015) 60.

[8] The point made here draws upon Tarunabh Khaitan, *A Theory of Discrimination Law* (Oxford University Press 2015) 196–200.

such as subjecting a worker to detriment or dismissing an employee for a reason relating to their trade union activities, or refusing to employ an individual because they are or are not a union member. One could envisage statutory provisions that prevent employers from subjecting a worker to any detriment because they exercised their freedom of expression and opinion or because of activities in their private life. Detriments connected to the expression of deeply held beliefs, the individual's adherence to or manifestation of their religious beliefs, or their association with political, religious, or other groups would have to be regulated. Under each of the qualified rights, protection from detriment—up to and including dismissal—for any reason linked to the exercise of the right by the worker would have to be spelled out. Employers should also be prevented from infringing upon their workers' privacy of correspondence in the form of monitoring their social media presence, workplace correspondence, or messages on other forums such as WhatsApp or online chatrooms. The provisions could be extended to cover employers' decisions in relation to hiring candidates, as in both TULR(C)A 1992 and the Equality Act 2010 (EA 2010).

This method of regulation would have advantages. A detailed regulatory framework would give less room for cautious or regressive judicial decisions on human rights issues. From the perspective of the employer, it would be easier to establish from the legislation precisely what types of acts are prohibited. It could be tailored to fit alongside existing legislation to avoid overlap and confusion. Such a proposition is not without its own difficulties, however. As noted in Chapter 5, most labour legislation has a narrow personal scope so the proposed Bill may have to overlap with existing regulation where its protections are not available sufficiently widely. There are other complexities with this option. Even preparing a comprehensive list of the categories of unlawful actions would be a difficult task. The extent of TULR(C)A's provisions indicates that the result would be substantial in length, particularly if each fundamental right had a collection of dedicated proscriptions. Similarly, with each prohibition, a drafter would have to consider whether the infringement could ever be justified by the employer, and if so, when. As the ECtHR's jurisprudence develops, it would be necessary for the shape and scope of protections to evolve with the case law of the courts and be duly amended. An exhaustive list of prohibitions is less flexible and less responsive to changing circumstances and new challenges or threats to fundamental rights at work. This more detailed approach to regulating human rights infringements in the workplace may nevertheless be considered desirable for its value of certainty and comprehensibility.

Alternatively, the Bill might impose an open-ended, general duty upon employers. It could read:

> An employer must not interfere with the human rights of its workers, as defined by the European Convention on Human Rights, and in particular an employer must respect each worker's right to respect for their private and family life, his/

> her/their freedom of thought, conscience and religion, his/her/their freedom of expression and his/her/their freedom of assembly and association.
>
> In accordance with the principles set out in the Convention, where a qualified right has been breached, an interference will only be justified if it satisfies the requirements set out in this Bill.

In section V, I will tackle the question of crafting an appropriate link between the Bill's interpretation and the case law of the ECtHR. This connection would be particularly important in determining the precise scope of each fundamental right under an open-ended duty. This alternative approach has the capacity to adapt to evolving interpretations of the scope of each Article of the Convention without amendments. It would also sit alongside existing legislation, allowing potential litigants to assess whether they fit within the protection of existing labour rights or need to rely upon the more flexible protection of the Bill.

The discussion of dismissal law in its common law and statutory forms demonstrated how the courts' examination of the employer's justification is crucial to the level of protection given to the claimant's human rights. The justification process in the Bill must balance several functions. It should be implemented in a manner that ensures that the individual's human rights are not outweighed too readily and that those rights remain central in the dispute. However, the justification process is also the mechanism by which employer's rights are weighed in the balance[9] and the size of the burden imposed upon employers by the Bill is managed.[10] The detail, interpretation, and application of the process of justification must be fine-tuned to adequately take into account legitimate employer concerns, but not to excuse employers on grounds that are insufficiently weighty. Unlike in unfair dismissal law, the standard for justification should be objectively determined by the court and applied rigorously to ensure that workers' human rights are properly secured.

A. The Requirement of Legality in the Context of Work

To maximize the clarity of the provision and the consistency of its application, all the components of the justification exercise should be set out clearly in the legislative text. In the ECHR framework for qualified rights, the first requirement is that an infringement must be 'in accordance with law'. In the employment context, it would be essential that infringement was lawful, that is, not in breach of any other regulation or rule of the domestic legal system. In addition, there could

[9] Hugh Collins, 'Justice for Foxes: Fundamental Rights and Justification of Indirect Discrimination' in Hugh Collins and Tarunabh Khaitan (eds), *Foundations of Indirect Discrimination Law* (Hart Publishing 2018) 269–70.

[10] Khaitan (n 8) 197–98.

be a requirement that the employer follows their own policies and procedures. In some instances where established disciplinary procedures are fairly basic, this requirement would not pose any substantial issue for the employer. Some organizations have more elaborate rules regarding discipline so this element would provide certainty when an individual is assessing the options open to them. For example, if an employer's rule book does not permit them to demote, suspend, or dock pay for misconduct of particular types, the individual can be sure that they should not be punished in that way and, if they are, they will be entitled to a remedy under the Bill's provisions. The requirement that an infringement must be lawful and in accordance with the employer's internal 'laws' would incentivize employers to follow their own processes and lend some predictability from the claimant's perspective.[11]

B. The Definition of an Employer's Legitimate Aims

The next demand within a justification analysis is that the infringement must be in pursuit of an aim that is legitimate within the Convention system. The stated aims contained in the Convention are tailored to state action, so the Bill would have to take a different approach. Stephen Gardbaum highlights this question of which 'private reasons' can justify infringing the rights of an individual as one of the most challenging issues in the move from vertical to horizontal rights enforcement.[12] As observed in Chapter 2, we must be careful to avoid a situation where the economic interests of business are permitted to 'trump' the fundamental rights of workers.

The EA 2010's formulation—'a proportionate means of achieving a legitimate aim'—relies on the courts to decide whether the employer's declared aim is legitimate.[13] On the whole, the courts have proceeded carefully in accepting legitimate aims in anti-discrimination law and have rightfully refused to accept commercial competitiveness[14] or cost savings, without other valid reasons,[15] as legitimate aims capable of justifying discrimination. But how could this reluctance to accept comparatively unimportant commercial aims be maintained under the Bill, whilst

[11] This function is comparable to protecting employees' legitimate expectations regarding their employer's response: see Hugh Collins, 'Market Power, Bureaucratic Power and the Contract of Employment' (1986) 15 ILJ 1, 5–6; Muayad Kamal Hattab, 'The Doctrine of Legitimate Expectation & Proportionality: A Public Law Principle Adopted into the Private Law of Employment' (2018) 39 Liverpool Law Review 239.

[12] Stephen Gardbaum, 'Positive and Horizontal Rights: Proportionality's Next Frontier or a Bridge Too Far?' in Vicki Jackson and Mark Tushnet (eds), *Proportionality: New Frontiers, New Challenges* (Cambridge University Press 2017) 246.

[13] See EA 2010, section 19(2)(d) and Schedule 9, paragraph 1(1)(b).

[14] In *Ratcliffe v North Yorkshire CC* [1995] All ER 587, [1995] ICR 883, female catering assistants were paid less than their male comparators and the House of Lords held that this was not justified by the competitive pressure of a tendering process.

[15] See the Court of Appeal's recent analysis of this area of justification in *Heskett v Secretary of State for Justice* [2020] EWCA Civ 1487, [2020] All ER (D) 72, [78]–[90].

incorporating the flexibility that is needed to respond to a wide range of factual circumstances?

The Bill could adopt the approach of unfair dismissal law, which sets out four 'potentially fair' reasons that the employer can point to (capacity/qualification needed to do the work, conduct, redundancy, statutory prohibition) and adds 'some other substantial reason of a kind such as to justify the dismissal of an employee'.[16] Each enumerated reason is identified by the legislator as being a legitimate aim that is sufficiently serious to justify a dismissal. The inclusion of 'some other substantial reason' can be interpreted as a 'safety valve, allowing a potentially fair dismissal in situation closely analogous to those listed'.[17] On Simon Deakin and Gillian Morris' reading of the legislation, implicit in the provision's phrasing is that the reason cited by the employer reaches the same level of seriousness or substance as the listed reasons, although the courts have not adopted this interpretation.[18]

The style of drafting seen in section 98 of the Employment Rights Act 1996 (ERA 1996) could be adopted by the Bill along the following lines:

> A 'legitimate aim' for the purpose of the Bill is limited to:
> (a) the protection of the employer's fundamental rights as defined by the ECHR, or
> (b) the protection of the fundamental rights of others as defined by the ECHR, or
> (c) a similarly pressing and substantial aim.

Subsection (b) would cover decisions by employers implemented in order to protect the rights of their other workers, customers, or service users. Policies that require equal treatment amongst service users or disciplinary action taken against an employee for derogatory comments about particular groups or individuals could fall within subsection (b)'s scope. Subsection (a) would include conduct intended to protect an employer from a serious and immediate risk to its reputation or its property through theft or defamation by an employee, for example. Policies or decisions that give effect to the rights of those that the employer represents, such as union members or adherents to a particular faith, could be captured under (a) or (b).[19]

Regarding subsection (a), the courts must pay particular attention where the employer is alleging that the employee's conduct put their business at risk. Too

[16] Employment Rights Act 1996 (ERA 1996), section 98(1) and (2).

[17] Simon Deakin and Gillian S Morris, *Labour Law* (6th edn, Hart Publishing 2012) 526.

[18] See *RS Components v Irwin* [1973] ICR 535, 56; *Cobley v Forward Technology Industries Plc* [2003] EWCA Civ 646, [2003] ICR 1050, [22].

[19] For example, the employer may be an institution, such as a church group or political party, which is a collective through which others exercise their rights: see Anat Scolnicov, 'Lifelike and Lifeless in Law: Do Corporations Have Human Rights?' (2013) University of Cambridge Legal Studies Research Paper Series, Paper No 13/2013 <http://ssrn.com/abstract=2268537> accessed 16 November 2020.

deferential an attitude to this question risks seriously damaging the standard of protection given to the claimant. The employer must be required to prove that they were responding to a real risk to their business at the time of the decision. Reliance upon a threat that has long since passed should not be permitted. This rule would mean that Leeds United Football Club, for example, was not justified in dismissing Mr Williams in response to an incident that had occurred five years previously and had not produced any damage to the Club's reputation.[20] The ECtHR has emphasized that a 'mere allegation' of a threat to an employer's rights is insufficient: the risk to the employer must be 'real and substantial' and the interference must not serve any other purpose that is unrelated to the exercise of their fundamental rights.[21] These safeguards should be reflected in the Bill's operation.

C. The Proportionality of an Employer's Policy or Decision

The remaining aspects of the proportionality analysis have been stated clearly by the UK Supreme Court in *Bank Mellat (No 2)*. The court summarized the relevant questions as follows:

> (1) whether the objective of the measure is sufficiently important to justify the limitation of a protected right,
> (2) whether the measure is rationally connected to the objective,
> (3) whether a less intrusive measure could have been used without unacceptably compromising the achievement of the objective, and
> (4) whether the impact of the rights infringement is disproportionate to the likely benefit of the impugned measure.[22]

The final limb of the *Bank Mellat (No. 2)* framework provides an opportunity for the tribunal to check the overall balance between the seriousness of the infringement and the strength of the legitimate aim and benefits that flow from the decision or policy. Here, the courts should consider the wider impact within the employing organization of the decision at issue, considering, for example, if a policy would also affect candidates applying for a role with the company or have a 'chilling effect' upon other workers. Practices that would lead to the exclusion of particular groups from that workplace or create a situation where a fundamental right cannot be exercised effectively must be supported by particularly weighty and urgent justifications.

[20] *Williams v Leeds United Football Club* [2015] EWHC 376 (QB), [2015] IRLR 383.
[21] *Sindicatul Păstorul cel Bun v Romania* (2014) 58 EHRR 10, [159].
[22] *Bank Mellat v HM Treasury* [2013] UKSC 38, [2014] AC 700, 790 (Lord Reed).

Concerns have been expressed about the applicability of proportionality to horizontal disputes.[23] In this situation, the proportionality analysis would be performing its established role of prohibiting certain types of actions by a powerful actor, here the employer, and a comparable assessment is undertaken regularly by the Employment Tribunals (ETs) in examining indirect discrimination claims. When considered fully, these elements strike a good balance between giving respect to the claimant's fundamental rights and permitting the defendant some scope to pursue other, equally important aims.

III. The Parties: Defining the Duty Bearer and the Rights Holder

The focus of this section is upon who can bring a claim and against whom. Contrary to the current dominant approach taken to drafting employment statutes, I suggest that the Bill should define the scope of its application by reference to the duty bearer: the employer. In so doing, I follow Brian Langille's recommendation regarding how to determine the appropriate scope of a piece of regulation: 'we rationally seek out those who are in a position to advance our purposes—those who can prevent the harms, remedy them when they occur, and who can and will respond to incentives and liability'.[24] This section adds detail to this proposal and also examines the issue of granting standing to challenge an employer in the absence of an identified claimant.

A. Who Is 'an Employer'?

Defining the protective scope of the Bill appropriately is crucial. It is one of the most significant areas of difficulty in relation to current employment law mechanisms, as highlighted in Chapter 5. The approach must reflect the universality of human rights, as well as the myriad of ways that an employer-like entity can impose disadvantage upon a working individual or deter them from exercising their fundamental rights. The guarantees set out here should be extended as broadly as possible to encompass any individual (A) who provides work for another (B) and that 'other' holds the capacity to impose detriment upon A for exercising their fundamental rights or to otherwise prevent or deter A from doing so. How this functional or risk-centred approach could be structured will be the focus of this section.

[23] See Gardbaum (n 12) 244.

[24] Brian Langille, 'If Labour Law is a Subset of Employment Law, What is Employment Law a Subset of?' (2020) 43 Dalhousie Law Journal 581, 602.

There are several problems that the Bill's provisions must tackle to provide an adequate solution. First, the modern world of work is complex. Individuals earn a living through a 'portfolio' of jobs of different kinds, leading to a diverse set of potential employers and making it difficult to identify one employer as *the* employer upon which the individual depends. A person may work under a multilateral arrangement, where several entities and individuals devise mechanisms for the provision of work but the management role may be split across them or even performed by an algorithm.[25] Any proposal must tackle carefully 'the *complication* of the employing organisation'.[26]

In addition, the approach that has been adopted under existing employment statutes has permitted large scale avoidance of obligations by putative employers. We saw in Chapter 5 that the current approach is to categorize and attach rights to the individual, and the definition of 'the employer' follows from that process. This method presents an opportunity for the organization providing work to manipulate the terms of the relationship so that the individual does not resemble the subordinated or dependent employee that the courts seek. Any drafter must be alive to this problem in crafting a solution to the problem of the Bill's relational applicability.

I would advocate a reversal of the current analysis. Attention should be focused on which individual(s) or organization(s) possess the powers of an employer or perform the employing functions.[27] This approach undoubtedly creates a reach far broader than any existing labour or employment rights. It would represent a fusion between the principles of human rights law and the lessons that we have learnt about the dynamics of working relationships through many years of labour law scholarship. The duty would be triggered by the presence of a sufficient degree of risk to human rights, which in turn arises from the relationship of authority, subordination, and dependence that arises between employer (broadly defined) and worker (broadly defined). Any entity that exercises these powers over an individual in the context of work would be considered a potential duty bearer under the Bill.

A key advantage of adopting such a different approach is that the Bill would benefit from a clean break from the 'accumulation of case law [that] has added weight rather than wisdom'[28] on the issue of who is entitled to employment law's protection. The unhelpful and restrictive concepts associated with the 'contract of employment' explored in Chapter 5 would necessarily be left behind if a

[25] See Jeremias Prassl, *Humans as a Service: The Promise and Perils of Work in the Gig Economy* (Oxford University Press 2018) chapter 3.

[26] Paul Davies and Mark Freedland, 'The Complexities of the Employing Enterprise' in Guy Davidov and Brian Langille (eds), *Boundaries and Frontiers of Labour Law: Goals and Means in the Regulation of Work* (Hart Publishing 2006) 287.

[27] Prassl sets out a developed account of what a functional approach to the identification of the employer means in Jeremias Prassl, *The Concept of the Employer* (Oxford University Press 2015), particularly chapter 5.

[28] Mark Freedland, *The Personal Employment Contract* (Oxford University Press 2003) 20.

very different strategy regarding the identification of relevant relationships was adopted. An analogy might be drawn to the boundaries drawn under health and safety instruments which deliberately straddle the divide seen elsewhere between employees and the self-employed. The European definition of 'worker' in the health and safety context is very broad.[29] In the domestic Health and Safety at Work etc. Act 1974, the employer's duties extend not only to their own employees but anyone who may be placed at risk by the conduct of its undertaking,[30] and a broad definition of 'work' specifically includes self-employed persons.[31] The health and safety provisions show that it is eminently possible to attach duties to the actor that creates the risk and benefits from the rewards, regardless of existing technical boundaries drawn within the workforce.

The next question, therefore, is how to give effect to the inclusive protective scope suggested. The first step in building a robust approach to identifying an employer in this scheme would be a rebuttable presumption that the defendant is an employer of the individual, until they produce evidence to the contrary. A presumption of this kind has been suggested by scholars.[32] The Workers (Definition and Rights) Bill, introduced by Chris Stephens MP in 2018, included a presumption of inclusion as one aspect of the proposed single statutory definition for both employees and workers.[33] As Hugh Collins noted many years before, such a presumption would impose 'a high hurdle before the duties of an employer can be evaded'.[34] A presumption of this sort aligns well with the approach of the Strasbourg Court in borderline cases where the applicant wishes to benefit from specific protections associated with the employment relationship: 'the question to be determined is rather whether such *special features are sufficient to remove* the relationship between members of the clergy and their church from the ambit of Article 11'.[35] This statement indicates that the ECtHR's assumption is that all individuals are entitled to the Convention's protection.

Once the presumption has been applied, the employer must be given the opportunity to prove they are *not* an entity with responsibilities under the legislation.

[29] See Klaus Lörcher, 'Article 31—Fair and Just Working Conditions' in Filip Dorssemont and others (eds), *The Charter of Fundamental Rights of the European Union and the Employment Relation* (Hart Publishing 2019) 549; Mark Freedland and Nicola Kountouris, *The Legal Construction of Personal Work Relations* (Oxford University Press 2011) 395. This was crucial in recent domestic litigation: see *R. (on the application of the Independent Workers' Union of Great Britain) v The Secretary of State for Work and Pensions & The Secretary of State for Business, Energy and Industrial Strategy* [2020] EWHC 3050 (Admin).

[30] Health and Safety at Work etc. Act 1974, section 3.

[31] Health and Safety at Work etc. Act 1974, section 52.

[32] Alan Bogg, 'Sham Self-employment in the Supreme Court' (2012) 41 ILJ 328, 343; Hugh Collins, 'Independent Contractors and the Challenge of Vertical Disintegration to Employment Protection Laws' (1990) 10 OJLS 353, 379; Freedland (n 28) 54–55.

[33] Workers (Definition and Rights) HC Bill (2017–19).

[34] Collins, 'Independent Contractors and the Challenge of Vertical Disintegration to Employment Protection Laws' (n 32).

[35] *Sindicatul Păstorul cel Bun v Romania* (n 21) [145].

Here, I propose the adoption of a functional approach to targeting the actors that should be constrained by a duty to respect the human rights of their workers. If the putative employer can demonstrate that both parties were able to negotiate at arm's length, seek such guarantees for their rights as they desired, and walk away from the bargaining table if they did not receive an offer of satisfactory terms, they would avoid the imposition of a duty under the Bill. Truly independent and entrepreneurial enterprises must turn to the norms of contract law for their safeguards. In order to enact an approach that tackles all relevant risks to the human rights of workers, we must identify the capacities and powers that one entity holds over a worker which could be deployed in a manner that breaches their human rights.

From the cases and examples contained in the proceeding chapters, key capacities emerge that can be used in a manner that interferes with the rights of an individual. The authority to appoint and dismiss a working person is a crucial power within the work setting, which in turn reinforces all other disciplinary measures available to an employer. Lesser disciplinary measures, as well as the capacity to withdraw payment or suspend the supply of work, can be used very effectively to disincentivize behaviour that the employer considers undesirable. Where an entity hires from amongst a group of candidates, it is possible to differentiate between individuals who have chosen to exercise their rights in particular ways and those who have not. As work is such a valuable opportunity, socially and economically, this power is important even for very short periods of work. Finally, managing the workforce, organizing and regulating the workplace, deploying individuals to particular tasks, and determining the terms and conditions of the relationship all have a determinative influence on the working environment and whether individuals are able to exercise their rights during working time and beyond it.

I argue that an entity that holds authority to do any one of these functions presents a risk to the exercise and enjoyment of the fundamental rights of the individuals subject to their authority. It is worth noting that the powers that have been listed do not necessarily have to be *actually exercised* in order to generate a risk to an individual's exercise of their human rights. Simply the fact that an entity holds these powers, even without exercising them, can affect the behaviour of a workforce or individual. This 'vulnerability to interference' was highlighted by Alan Bogg and Cynthia Estlund.[36] The threat to human rights simply by one entity's potential to generate detriment for another person must be reflected in any attempt to define the employer within the Bill.

Drawing the two elements together in a statutory provision, I suggest the following:

[36] Alan Bogg and Cynthia Estlund, 'Freedom of Association and the Right to Contest' in Alan Bogg and Tonia Novitz (eds), *Voices at Work: Continuity and Change in the Common Law World* (Oxford University Press 2014) 151.

(1) For the purposes of this Act, an 'employer' means any person who performs or could perform any of the following functions or exercises or could exercise any of the following powers:
  (a) to initiate or terminate the worker's employment, contract, or engagement,
  (b) to determine or affect the terms and conditions of work, including but not limited to location, job description, pay, and policies or practices of the workplace,
  (c) to manage the worker or the process of work,
  (d) to remunerate the worker or provide them with other benefits associated with the provision of work, or
  (e) to discipline the worker, including by suspension of pay or allocation of work.

(2) It shall be for the respondent to show in any legal proceedings that the respondent is not an employer.

This definition would undoubtedly include a far broader range of entities and offer safeguards to people currently outside the scope of employment law. It does not attach accountability based on the terms of a contract which are dictated unilaterally by the more powerful party. Rather, a duty to respect human rights is imposed because an entity has the capacity to disadvantage another and thereby affect that person's willingness to exercise their fundamental rights. At this point, the proposed regime treads a new path that is deliberately separate from the established approach of employment law, which has been shown to run counter to the inclusive protection offered by the Convention.

B. Who Can Bring a Claim?

To correspond with the earlier definition of 'employer', a worker entitled to make a claim would be defined as:

> A 'worker' for the purposes of this Bill is an individual who provides work or services to an employer or a number of employers.

Unlike the entitlement to make an unfair dismissal claim, the protection of the Bill must not be subject to a qualifying period of continuing employment. The requirement to work under a contract, common to all current employment statuses and exclusionary in its operation, is also absent. The definition also makes clear that a worker may work for several employers who hold the above-listed powers, and that does not deprive them of their status as a worker. In the knowledge that the Bill would not anticipate every working arrangement that will come before the tribunals, this provision might be supplemented by a direction to tribunals to interpret and apply the definition of 'worker' as broadly as possible and in line with the statutory purpose set out in the preamble.

For clarity, the Bill or related statutory instrumentation might enumerate specific groups that are entitled to the Bill's protection. Examples might be job applicants and workers in the post-employment phase, groups that are both protected by the EA 2010,[37] and individuals who provide their work through personal service companies. The drafters might also consider clearly stating that migration or visa status are irrelevant to a person's right to make a complaint, as these members of two groups are particularly vulnerable to maltreatment in the UK labour market. The earlier definition of 'worker' makes no mention of working in return for remuneration, which leaves the status of volunteers and interns open. In a 2010 survey, 37 per cent of adults had volunteered in the last year.[38] Internships are now an established stage of many career paths, but interns are not entitled to most forms of employment protection.[39] Debating the personal scope of the Bill's protection may provide an opportunity to reconsider the position of volunteers and interns within employment law.[40]

Another significant decision would be whether actors other than individuals, or groups of individuals, should be permitted to bring claims to the tribunals. A less controversial step would be allowing representative actions by unions or nongovernment organisations (NGOs) who bring a claim on behalf of an individual or group and litigate the issues in their place. This would reduce the burden on an individual bringing a claim.[41] The possibility of representative actions should be seriously considered as a way to improve access to justice and the enforcement of the Bill.

Alongside this option, it may be useful for the Equality and Human Rights Commission (EHRC) to possess more generalized enforcement and investigatory powers of the kind currently provided for by discrimination law. Under the EA 2006, the Commission can investigate any suspected wrongdoing, launch inquiries into any issue related to its remit, and apply to a court for an injunction where it suspects that an actor is likely to commit an unlawful act.[42] Although these powers are deployed subject to resource constraints,[43] it might aid the enforcement of the Bill in practice.

More controversially, the Bill could permit other bodies—such as unions, NGOs, public interest groups, or institutions like the EHRC—to make a complaint to a tribunal *without* identifying an individual who has been affected by an

[37] EA 2010, sections 39(1) and 108.

[38] Department for Communities and Local Government, *Citizenship Survey: April–June 2010, England* (Cohesion Research, Statistic Release Number 13, 2010) 8.

[39] See *X v Mid Sussex Citizens Advice Bureau* [2012] UKSC 59, [2013] 1 All ER 1038.

[40] For a powerful contestation of the current boundary between volunteers and employees, see Sabine Tsuruda, 'Volunteer Work, Inclusivity, and Social Equality' in Hugh Collins, Gillian Lester, and Virginia Mantouvalou (eds), *Philosophical Foundations of Labour Law* (Oxford University Press 2018).

[41] Sandra Fredman, *Discrimination Law* (2nd edn, Oxford University Press 2011) 228.

[42] EA 2006, sections 16, 20, 24, and 25.

[43] Joint Committee on Human Rights, *Enforcing Human Rights* (Tenth Report of Session 2017–19, HC 669, HL 171, 19 July 2018) [131]–[132].

infringement of their human rights. This issue is one that is currently prominent in discrimination law.[44] The Court of Justice of the European Union has held that member states may provide for associations with an interest in the issue to bring proceedings without acting on behalf of a specific claimant.[45] Closer to home, the Blacklisting Regulations are designed in such a way that unions themselves can challenge an employer or employment agency which they suspect of breaching regulation 3, which prohibits the compilation, use, sale, or supply of a blacklist, through a claim for breach of statutory duty under regulation 13.[46] Permitting complaints to be launched without an individual litigant at their heart would certainly challenge the narrow view that the judiciary's role is 'to do no more than protect individuals who can point to personal detriment as a result of an alleged breach of a human right'.[47]

Introducing non-representative litigation could be particularly useful in challenging policies that deter individuals from applying for a role in a particular company or target organizational activities at an early stage. However, this mechanism also carries a risk of encouraging strategic litigation in favour of interests that have strong financial backing. With regard to the HRA, for example, Sir Stephen Sedley observed that freedom of speech 'is constantly at the head of the queue for rights adjudication' due to its financial value to the mass media.[48] If the rights of some groups are litigated heavily in the early years of a provision's life, it could be perceived that these groups influence its application unduly. A compromise might be to retain a claimant-led model, but 'to enrich the process of deliberation by bringing to the notice of the judiciary expert information, perspectives, and arguments which a bipolar process could not bring to light' by allowing interventions and contributions by interest groups and experts in the litigation process.[49]

IV. Implementing Effective Protection for Human Rights at Work

Several additional forms of protection would be necessary to ensure the central prohibition operates effectively in practice. Protection from retaliatory behaviour,

[44] See C-54/07 *Centrum voor Gelijkheid van Kansen en voor Racismebestrijding v Firma Feryn* [2008] 3 CMLR 22; C-81/12 *Asociatia ACCEPT v Consiliul National pentru Combaterea Discriminarii* [2013] 3 CMLR 26.

[45] *Centrum voor Gelijkheid van Kansen en voor Racismebestrijding v Firma Feryn* (n 44).

[46] The Employment Relations Act 1999 (Blacklists) Regulations 2010.

[47] Sandra Fredman, 'Scepticism under Scrutiny: Labour Law and Human Rights' in Tom Campbell, K D Ewing, and Adam Tomkins (eds), *Sceptical Essays on Human Rights* (Oxford University Press 2001) 212.

[48] Stephen Sedley, 'Human Rights: A Twenty-first Century Agenda' [1995] Public Law 386, 396.

[49] As envisaged by Fredman, 'Scepticism under Scrutiny: Labour Law and Human Rights' (n 47) 206.

including dismissal or any other type of detriment, on the grounds that a worker has launched a claim against an employer would be important. Protection from this kind of victimization is common across employment law[50] and it should extend to protection from detriment imposed by Employer B where the claim has been launched against Employer A. The remaining possibilities can be divided into two groups: mainstreaming and pre-emptive duties, and issues connected to the contract for the provision of work. I will also consider the remedies that should follow a successful claim.

A. A Pre-emptive Duty to Consider Fundamental Rights

Whilst the core prohibition that has been outlined is retroactive and centred on a past wrong, the Bill could include measures that would accelerate the process of embedding a 'human rights culture'[51] across workplaces. In terms of moving beyond tackling retrospective wrongs, employers could be placed under a proactive duty to consider their impact on the exercise of human rights by their staff. This duty could be modelled on the public sector equality duty contained within section 149 of the EA 2010, which requires public sector actors to give due regard to discrimination issues *in advance* of introducing a policy or making a decision.

In addition, we could imagine introducing a cause of action with a purpose similar to indirect discrimination to hasten the achievement of the Bill's aims. These additional provisions would incorporate, but go beyond, Gillian Morris' suggestion of 'a mechanism for workers to challenge the propriety of contractual clauses which they consider violate a Convention right without having to await the imposition of a disciplinary sanction for breach of contract'.[52] An individual could be provided with the opportunity to come before a tribunal if they believe that the employer is maintaining a workplace hostile to or incompatible with the enjoyment and exercise of their human rights.

This possibility would tackle two types of rules or terms. Firstly, it would permit challenges to rules that themselves constitute an interference with an individual's rights. Secondly, it would call into question rules that have the effect of preventing individuals from exercising their rights, either in the workplace or elsewhere. This second function is similar to that of indirect discrimination: although there is no overt infringement upon the human right, the impact of the rule or policy in practice can be such that the exercise of that right is negatively affected. In order to be

[50] See in particular the group of automatically unfair dismissal reasons in the ERA 1996, section 43M onwards.

[51] ACL Davies, 'Workers' Human Rights in English Law' in Tonia Novitz and Colin Fenwick (eds), *Human Rights at Work: Perspectives on Law and Regulation* (Hart Publishing 2010) 183.

[52] Gillian Morris, 'Fundamental Rights: Exclusion by Agreement?' (2001) 30 ILJ 49, 70.

lawful, any such negative impact must be justified in accordance with the process set out earlier.

What conduct would be prohibited by this suggested provision? We might imagine a wide range of practices that have an adverse effect upon the claimant's ability to enjoy their Article 8 right to respect for their private and family life but are not tackled by existing legislation. The EA 2010, for example, offers protection where unwanted workplace conduct or indirect discrimination is linked to a protected characteristic such as sex, sexual orientation, or gender reassignment. Whilst such behaviour would likely violate Articles 8 or 14 ECHR, the EA's provisions are only applicable where a listed protected characteristic is invoked. The suggested provision would tackle a much wider variety of issues connected to Article 8 such as employment practices that demand extensive or unpredictable hours of work and thereby make it very difficult for workers to reconcile their personal or family life with their professional life.[53] Similarly a workplace that is managed in a way that prevents workers from developing relationships with their colleagues during working time[54] or an employer that enforces computer and internet use policies that severely delimit their workforces' online privacy could be considered hostile to the exercise of Article 8. All these practices would have to be justified under the proposal here.

Elsewhere, this provision could offer safeguards to claimants who hold opinions on political or social issues but feel unable to express them, either during or outside working time. As observed in Chapter 4,[55] the EA 2010 may not come to the aid of claimants in these circumstances. A gamut of workplace policies and practices can operate to chill employees' freedom of speech and association. Employers may have strict policies regarding the public speech or associations of their employees, including monitoring employees' social media profiles. For example, in late 2020, there was media coverage regarding new guidance issued by the BBC to its staff on impartiality and avoiding public perceptions of bias.[56] The reports indicate that

[53] Deirdre McCann, 'Decent Working Hours as a Human Right: Intersections in the Regulation of Working Time' in Tonia Novitz and Colin Fenwick (eds), *Human Rights at Work: Perspectives on Law and Regulation* (Hart Publishing 2010) 519–20.

[54] See an Amazon worker's account of working life in one of their warehouses, highlighting particularly the impact of work processes on collective organizing and creating connections with fellow workers: John Holland, 'Amazon Inquiry' (2020) 13 *Notes from Below* 7.

[55] See the discussion in Chapter 4, section III(B).

[56] See 'BBC issues staff with new social media guidance' (*BBC News*, 29 October 2020) <https://www.bbc.co.uk/news/entertainment-arts-54723282> accessed 7 November 2020; Jim Waterson, 'BBC "No Bias" Rules Prevent Staff Joining LGBT Pride Marches' *The Guardian* (London, 29 October 2020) <https://www.theguardian.com/media/2020/oct/29/bbc-no-bias-rules-prevent-staff-joining-lgbt-pride-protests> accessed 7 November 2020; Nick Duffy, 'Media Unions Demand BBC Meeting Over New Bias Rules as Legal Challenge Threatened Over Pride Row' *iNews* (London, 30 October 2020) <https://inews.co.uk/news/uk/media-unions-bbc-meeting-bias-rules-legal-challenge-743939> accessed 7 November 2020.

the guidance applies to all use of social media by employees, whether using the platforms privately or publicly, and to attendance at public events, even in a private capacity. Such policies are very likely to have a detrimental impact on the exercise of the employees' right to freedom of expression. The additional cause of action recommended here would demand that an employer show that their policies or practices are justified by a legitimate aim and a proportionate infringement on the rights of their staff.

B. Tackling Avoidance by Contract

It would be essential to the Bill's operation to ensure that attempts to evade, contract-out of, or contradict its provisions are tackled. One of the main difficulties exposed in Chapter 8 with relation to using implied terms as a method of human rights protection was that any safeguards could be ousted by express terms to the contrary. A requirement that contracts for the provision of work that fall within the scope of the Bill must be interpreted compatibly with the Bill could be expressed alongside the provisions regarding the development of the common law, discussed in section V. Several additional preventative mechanisms could also be considered.

Any term directly contrary to the provisions of the Bill must be rendered unenforceable. This rule should apply to an attempt to exclude the operation of the Bill altogether, as well as contractual requirements that would run contrary to it. Here the model adopted by the EA 2010 could be incorporated. It contains the following components:

1) Any term of a contract that 'constitutes, promotes or provides for' prohibited treatment against that person *or another person* is unenforceable.[57]
2) Any term of a contract is unenforceable by a person in whose favour a term of a contract would operate in so far as it 'purports to exclude or limit a provision of or made under this Act.'[58]

This approach could be applied to any rule of the employer or non-contractual aspects of the employer's policies, such as disciplinary procedures. The Bill might go further and state that any affected term is unenforceable by the employer at any time, including during the existence of the employment relationship. This provision would ensure that employees can insist on exercising their rights where a dispute arises, knowing that the employer cannot enforce the incompatible term. Finally, there should be specific protection for workers who refuse to waive their

[57] EA 2010, section 142(1).
[58] EA 2010, section 144.

Convention rights or sign a contract containing terms inconsistent with those rights.[59]

C. An Effective Remedy for an Interference

There are a variety of other matters that would influence the effectiveness of the Bill substantially. Here, I will not discuss procedural matters such as the limitation period or the appropriate choice of forum in detail. One might perceive ETs as the obvious choice for claims relating to the workplace but equally the daily work of the Administrative Courts involves hearing human rights cases and considering Strasbourg jurisprudence. Guaranteeing straightforward access to justice, in terms of ensuring the support of legal advisers and minimizing the financial risks associated with bringing a claim, would be essential. Similarly, we might consider a reversal to the burden of proof, as applied in discrimination law,[60] given that there is often an informational disbalance between the worker and employer regarding the events and practices of the workplace. All these matters would have significant consequences for the effectiveness of the Bill but are beyond the scope of this chapter.

In order to ensure that the protection offered by the Bill is practical and effective, the relevant court should possess a range of remedial powers to redress an infringement. These powers should include the ability to modify or remove terms in a contract or other provisions that regulate the working relationship that are inconsistent with the Bill,[61] ordering an employer to cease a particular form of conduct if it is ongoing and giving broader, enforceable recommendations regarding the employer's practices.[62] If the claimant wishes to return to their job, the tribunal should be able to make an order to that effect or ensure that the worker is offered an alternative role within the employing entity if a return to the same job is not possible or appropriate.[63] Although these powers are valuable, individual workers are likely to consider financial compensation to be the primary remedial option.

The 'employment law torts' provide a reasonable starting point for the financial awards available to a successful litigant. Following the model set out by discrimination law and the law of unfair dismissal,[64] the measure of compensation should

[59] Morris (n 52) 70.

[60] See Council Directive 97/80/EC of 15 December 1997 on the burden of proof in cases of discrimination based on sex [1998] OJ L14/6, Article 4(1) and EA 2010, section 136(2).

[61] Drawing upon the comparable power in EA 2010, section 143.

[62] In the manner of the EA, section 124(3) as it was originally enacted: a recommendation that 'the respondent takes specified steps for the purpose of obviating or reducing the adverse effect of any matter to which the proceedings relate (a) on the complainant; (b) on any other person'.

[63] Drawing upon the re-instatement and re-engagement remedies in the ERA 1996, sections 114 and 115.

[64] EA 2010, section 119(2)(a) and ERA 1996, section 123.

be tortious and permit recovery for all losses that flowed from the wrong. The aim should be to put the claimant in the position that they would have occupied had the infringement not occurred. The award would include, for a dismissed worker, wages for periods spent out of work and potentially future loss of earnings. 'Stigma damages' should represent the increased difficulty in finding a new job as a result of being dismissed, bringing a claim or other reputational harm, as well as non-pecuniary damages for any reputational impact. In order to offer an effective remedy in the Convention sense, damages for non-pecuniary loss must be available including for distress, anxiety, and injury to feelings. Exemplary damages could also be available where the employer has acted in an oppressive or malicious manner towards the claimant.[65] There must be no upper limit on the damages that can be awarded to a worker after a successful claim.

V. A Tailored Connection to the ECHR

This section turns to the relationship between the proposed Bill and the case law of the ECtHR. The suggestion here must balance the need to 'keep pace' with Strasbourg's decisions in order to ensure that the UK fulfils its obligations under the Convention with the recognition that ECtHR case law should not be slotted into the common lawyer's system of precedent.[66] A more sophisticated approach is necessary, based upon extracting general principles from the reasoning in ECtHR cases, so that the Court's case law that is decided in an applicant-state context can be presented in a way that is applicable and appropriate to the enforcement of rights between worker and employer. After setting out this mode of addressing the jurisprudence of the ECHR, this section will also set out ways in which the Bill could go beyond provisions for its own interpretation. I will suggest a provision that the principles taken from the Convention and its case law should influence the interpretation and evolution of other labour law instruments, as well as the common law. Where alignment between statutes and the Convention's principles cannot be achieved, the Bill could provide the capacity for a declaration of incompatibility as under section 4 of the HRA.

A. A Distinctive and Dynamic Approach to the Court's Case Law

The aim of the Bill is to ensure that workers receive full and effective protection for their human rights in their relationship with an employer. Akin to the HRA's

[65] Exemplary damages are available in discrimination cases, see *London Borough of Hackney v Sivanandan* (2011) UKEAT/0075/10/CEA, [32] and *Armitage v Johnson* [1997] IRLR 162, [40].

[66] See Roger Masterman, 'Deconstructing the Mirror Principle' in Roger Masterman and Ian Leigh (eds), *The United Kingdom's Statutory Bill of Rights* (Oxford University Press 2013) 125.

requirement that domestic courts 'take into account' any relevant Strasbourg decisions,[67] the interpretation of the Bill's provisions should be connected to the ECHR and the case law of the ECtHR. Courts and tribunals would thereby have the benefit of a rich and evolving body of jurisprudence to guide their decisions in particular matters. From this starting point, there are several potential difficulties that we should address. Are Strasbourg's decisions the 'floor' or the 'ceiling' of the protection under the Bill? How should judges approach case law that is cited before them in a private employment dispute, but was decided in the Convention's vertical context? I propose an approach based upon the *principles* extracted from the Court's caselaw, which is also *dynamic*, meaning that the domestic standards are encouraged to go beyond the levels of protection offered by the ECtHR where appropriate.

There are several likely challenges of drawing upon Strasbourg decisions in the consideration of a domestic employment dispute regarding Convention rights. The first is what tribunals should do when Strasbourg decisions do not give guidance that is sufficiently concrete or useful in the case before a domestic court. The ECtHR has not ruled conclusively on every issue, and each case is decided on its own unique facts. In addition, the Court's decisions are 'declaratory' in nature, finding only whether a particular state action has violated the Convention and imposing an obligation upon that member state to end the breach and make reparations for its consequences.[68] In work-related complaints, this issue is exacerbated by the deployment of the doctrine of positive obligations and margin of appreciation. These principles of decision-making can obscure the clarity of the Court's declarations regarding what is required in order to adequately protect Convention rights in a particular situation. These doctrines have led to most uncharitable interpretations of the Convention's input in domestic employment litigation.[69]

To tackle these potential difficulties, I advocate for an approach based on the principles which can be derived from the ECtHR jurisprudence on a particular point, such as the proper scope of a particular right or the factors that must be considered in assessing the proportionality of an infringement.[70] This approach echoes the suggestions made by Roger Masterman in relation to section 2 HRA.[71] Strasbourg's decisions should be regarded 'as a source of guidance as to the philosophy, values or

[67] HRA 1998, section 2(1).

[68] *Papamichalopoulos v Greece* Application no 14556/89 (ECtHR, 31 October 1995) [34].

[69] See, for example, the Court of Appeal decision in *Pharmacists' Defence Association Union v Boots Management Services Ltd and another* [2017] EWCA Civ 66, [2017] IRLR 355. See the critique of the court's reasoning in Alan Bogg and Ruth Dukes, 'Article 11 ECHR and the Right to Collective Bargaining: *Pharmacists' Defence Association Union v Boots Management Services Ltd*' (2017) 46 ILJ 543.

[70] For an example of how this approach might be conducted in the employment context, see Chapter 3 which draws out the common principles in relation to the doctrine of positive obligations by reading many cases together.

[71] See Roger Masterman, 'Section 2(1) of the Human Rights Act 1998: Binding Domestic Courts to Strasbourg?' [2004] Public Law 725, 735–37; Roger Masterman, 'Taking the Strasbourg Jurisprudence into Account: Developing a 'Municipal Law of Human Rights' under the Human Rights Act' (2008) 54 International and Comparative Law Quarterly 907.

considerations to be weighed in the balance by national courts when applying their own domestic law'.[72] By reading the ECtHR's body of cases as indicating a broad set of principles, and carefully translating these principles into a form that is suitable for the employment context, the Bill could provide a high standard of protection whilst conforming to the UK's obligations under the ECHR. This method of handling the Court's case law coheres with its own statements regarding the purpose of its judgments: 'judgments in fact serve not only to decide those cases brought before the Court but, more generally, to elucidate, safeguard and develop the rules instituted by the Convention, thereby contributing to the observance by the States of the engagements undertaken by them as Contracting States'.[73]

A frame of reference orientated towards the principles enunciated through the Court's case law also assists us in addressing a second conceivable problem: how to tackle issues where a domestic tribunal may wish to go beyond the standards set out by Strasbourg. There may be points where the ECtHR has been cautious and incremental in taking decisions or areas where there is a wide diversity of regulation across the member states, so the Court relies upon the margin of appreciation. Here, the domestic approach should be dynamic[74]—going beyond the standard of protection set out in ECtHR decisions. As observed by Baroness Hale:

> There is no reason why either Strasbourg or the other member states should object if we go forging ahead in interpreting the scope of the Convention rights in UK law. Indeed, there is good reason to think that they do not.[75]

A dynamic approach which is respectful of the principles that can be drawn from ECtHR cases, whilst going beyond it in situations where the Court is bound by the margin of appreciation, would ensure a high standard of rights protection for people at work.

B. The Interpretation and Incompatibility of Labour Law and the Common Law

A discussion of how the Bill's own provisions would be applied in the light of the ECtHR's principles are half the story. We must also look to the legal landscape into which the Bill would be inserted. Chapter 4 demonstrated that a significant proportion of labour law touches on human rights questions. Partial duties and specific protections of some aspects of an individual's Convention rights are included

[72] Paul Mahoney, 'Effect, Non-Compliance and Enforcement of Judgments of International/Supranational Courts: The European Court of Human Rights as a Case-Study' in Carl Baudenbacher (ed), *Dispute resolution*, vol III (German Law Publishers 2009) 111.

[73] *Rantsev v Cyprus and Russia* (2010) 51 EHRR 1, [197].

[74] Francesca Klug and Helen Wildbore, 'Follow or Lead? The Human Rights Act and the European Court of Human Rights' (2010) 6 EHRLR 621, 626.

[75] Hale, '*Argentoratum Locutum:* Is Strasbourg or the Supreme Court Supreme?' (n 5) 71.

in legislation such as TULR(C)A 1992, EA 2010, and the Public Interest Disclosure Act 1998. In some areas, legislative provisions or the common law create significant barriers to the exercise or vindication of one's Convention rights. The interaction between the novel safeguards set out here and the existing mass of regulation via statutes and the common law is thus essential to the practical protection of fundamental rights. This section will focus on two mechanisms that mirror the provisions of the HRA: an interpretive obligation and the capacity to issue a declaration of incompatibility.

One might consider whether something comparable to the duty contained in section 3 HRA could be useful. The duty therein reads as follows: 'So far as it is possible to do so, primary legislation and subordinate legislation must be read and given effect in a way which is compatible with the Convention rights.'[76] A duplication of section 3 would be extraneous. Instead, the Bill might usefully include an interpretive obligation which states that statutes regulating work must be read in a way that respects the principles and requirements drawn from ECHR jurisprudence in the manner that has been described here. This more ambitious interpretive obligation would extend the approach I have set out to other legislative provisions, in addition to those contained in the Bill itself. It would prevent lapses into minimalist readings of our obligations under the Convention and ensure a high standard of human rights protection across the entire suite of rights and duties that have already been put in place.

Statutory rights often interact with, or are layered onto, a common law foundation, such as a contract of employment or a contract for the personal provision of work. Common law developments in areas such as the economic torts, which interact with strikes and industrial action, and the contract of employment could substantially hinder the achievement of the Bill's goals. Thus, rather than leaving open the question of the impact of Convention rights upon the common law as it was in the drafting of the HRA 1998, any debate should be settled by an express requirement to develop the common law in line with the Convention rights and principles assembled from the case law.

There must, however, be limits on the judiciary's ability to reshape the effects of a statute on human rights grounds. Simply in practical terms, it is most difficult to mitigate the cumulative effect of a piece of legislation by granular reinterpretation. For example, looking at legislation such as TULR(C)A 1992, it is this cumulative effect that could be argued to prevent the effective exercise of one's right to associate with others through a trade union, to strive for better terms and conditions through bargaining and ultimately to strike if necessary.[77] In these circumstances, a claimant may wish to challenge the legislation itself as incompatible with the rights and principles set out by the Convention and developed by the ECtHR.

[76] HRA 1998, section 3.

[77] The European Committee on Social Rights (ECSR) has long criticized the legal regime on the grounds that the right to take collective action is 'excessively circumscribed' by the totality of measures that regulate the right to strike: see ECSR, *Conclusions XXI-3— United Kingdom— Article 6-4* (2019).

The domestic courts are not able to rewrite legislation on the scale necessary to achieve compliance and are not institutionally competent to select from a range of detailed ways in which the freedom to associate could be given substance.[78] Instead, it would be desirable for the legislative scheme for the Bill of Rights to include an ability for the court to issue a declaration that the piece of legislation is incompatible with the Convention, its rights and its principles. Whilst this remedy does not offer respite for the litigant before the court, which Tom Hickman rightly notes may limit the enthusiasm of potential claimants,[79] this feature is a necessary compromise between the need to guarantee Convention rights and respect for Parliamentary sovereignty and its democratic mandate.[80]

VI. What Role for Fundamental Social Rights?

For reasons of space, the primary focus of this book has been the rights contained in the European Convention. Nevertheless, the potentially important role of fundamental social rights in a legal instrument that relates to the world of work cannot be neglected. To do so would ignore the indivisibility of all human rights that has been recognized expressly by the Court and distinguish between groups of human rights, all of which are essential to human dignity and flourishing. It would also risk the establishment of what Keith Ewing termed the 'unbalanced constitution' within the workplace, wherein civil and political rights are awarded priority and fundamental social rights are side-lined.[81] There remains significant debate on the nature of guarantees that fundamental social rights should receive within constitutions and human rights documents and particularly the extent to which they should be justiciable.[82] This section is confined to the ways in which social rights could be integrated into the proposed framework.

There are several potential sources that one may look to for social and economic rights and their details, including conventions and recommendations of the International Labour Organization (ILO), the UN International Covenant on Economic, Social and Cultural Rights, and the Charter of Fundamental Rights

[78] See further Alan Bogg and Ruth Dukes, 'Statutory Interpretation and the Limits of a Human Rights Approach: Royal Mail Group Ltd v Communication Workers Union' (2020) 49 ILJ 477, 490.

[79] Tom Hickman, 'Bill of Rights Reform and the Case for Going Beyond the Declaration of Incompatibility Model' (2015) New Zealand Law Review 35.

[80] Secretary of State for the Home Department, *Rights Bought Home: The Human Rights Bill* (CM 3782, 1997) [2.13].

[81] Keith Ewing, 'The Unbalanced Constitution' in Tom Campbell, Keith Ewing, and Adam Tomkins (eds), *Sceptical Essays on Human Rights* (Oxford University Press 2001).

[82] See, for example, Jeff King, *Judging Social Rights* (Cambridge University Press 2012) chapter 3; Sandra Fredman, *Human Rights Transformed: Positive Rights and Positive Duties* (Oxford University Press 2008) chapter 4; Conor Gearty and Virginia Mantouvalou, *Debating Social Rights* (Hart Publishing 2010).

of the European Union. In the context of this work, the European Social Charter (ESC) assumes natural prominence, due to its status as the companion treaty of the ECHR. The Charter contains numerous fundamental social rights of relevance to workers, including the right to safe and healthy working conditions, the right to fair remuneration, and rights to organize and bargain collectively.[83] The ESC's implementation in by its signatory member states is monitored by the European Committee of Social Rights (ECSR) through national reports and a collective complaints procedure.

The UK has ratified the ESC, although it is not subject to the complaints procedure and its implementation of the Charter has consistently been found by the ECSR to be defective.[84] The neglect of the Charter by successive UK governments may lead to a pessimistic outlook for any attempt to render Charter rights more strongly applicable in the domestic setting. Nonetheless, to present a full picture of how a Bill might be framed, it is useful to consider some options for how social rights might be incorporated into the statutory design. The Bill might integrate respect for fundamental social rights as a guiding principle, either in the purpose clause or elsewhere in the text. Such a choice would give these rights greater prominence within the Bill.[85]

As a first step to giving fundamental social rights greater prominence within the domestic legal regime, one could argue that fundamental social rights should be given *indirect* horizontal effect through the Bill. Respect for fundamental social rights could shape how existing measures that give effect to key labour rights are implemented by the courts and other authorities. One can take inspiration from the ECtHR's own approach to the interpretation of the Convention rights. The Court has been willing to consider fundamental social rights documents, particularly the ESC and conventions of the ILO, in shaping their reading of ECHR rights. Virginia Mantouvalou has termed this interpretive mode an 'integrated approach', as it integrates the two groups of rights—civil/political and social/economic—that were previously regarded as separate.[86] The integrated approach has been instrumental in the development of key human rights within the labour sphere, notably the right to freedom of association and the prohibition on forced labour.[87] Guiding

[83] ESC, Articles 3–6.

[84] Colm O'Cinneide, 'The European Social Charter and the UK: Why it Matters' (2018) 29 Kings Law Journal 275, 275. See, for example, ECSR, *UK Article 6-4* (n 77); ECSR, *Conclusions XXI-3—United Kingdom—Article 6-2* (2019).

[85] As Jeff King points out, the lack of full justiciability may be viewed as a sign that social rights have an inferior status and that must be a consideration in any debate about the appropriate guarantees for these rights: King (n 82) 53.

[86] Virginia Mantouvalou, 'The Human Rights Act and Labour Law at 20' in Alan Bogg, Jacob Rowbottom, and Alison L Young (eds), *The Constitution of Social Democracy: Essays in Honour of Keith Ewing* (Bloomsbury Publishing 2020) 56–59.

[87] See Virginia Mantouvalou, 'Labour Rights in the European Convention on Human Rights: An Intellectual Justification for an Integrated Approach to Interpretation' (2013) 13 Human Rights Law Review 529.

the interpretation of the Bill's provisions in a similar manner could avoid the sense of disbalance highlighted by Ewing[88] and give some legal effect to the fundamental social rights of workers.[89]

Conclusion

This chapter has given detail to the proposal that an Act of Parliament should enact specific, enforceable, and horizontally effective human rights protection for workers against their employers. The design put forward here tackles the many pitfalls and inadequacies of the existing mechanisms of domestic employment law that have been exposed over the course of this work. The suggestions are ambitious and aspirational. Although placing duties upon businesses to prevent human rights abuses has been recommended before,[90] the provisions that have been outlined surpass any previous proposals in the level of detail and tailored nature of the guarantees that have been explored.

Unfortunately, it would be unrealistic to end on this high note. As Sir Stephen Sedley observed, human rights campaigners in the UK engage in debate and activism from a 'low and defensive base'.[91] The Conservative government has recently announced an independent review of the HRA itself, with a particular focus on the relationship between the UK courts and the ECtHR case law as reflected in section 2.[92] In the media, human rights are 'frequently portrayed as undermining traditional freedoms and legal protections, rather than empowering and enhancing citizenship'.[93] Public opinion is deeply mixed, with groups that both strongly support and strongly oppose human rights present as well as a majority that are conflicted or disinterested in them.[94] Commentators observe that more must be done to educate and persuade the public of the value of human rights and their relevance to our daily lives.[95] One might hope that demonstrating the usefulness of Convention rights to all workers in Britain might lead to an increase in support for

88 Ewing (n 81).

89 Niklas Bruun and others, 'Conclusions: The Potentials for the Charter to be Used' in Niklas Bruun and others (eds), *The European Social Charter and the Employment Relation* (Hart Publishing 2016).

90 Joint Committee on Human Rights, *Human Rights and Business 2017: Promoting Responsibility and Ensuring Accountability* (Sixth Report of Session 2016–17, HL 153, HC 443, 5 April 2017) [193]. The proposal is elaborated upon in Irene Pietropaoli and others, *A UK Failure to Prevent Mechanism for Corporate Human Rights Harms* (British Institute of International and Comparative Law 2020).

91 Stephen Sedley, 'Bringing Rights Home: Time to Start a Family?' (2008) 28 Legal Studies 327, 332.

92 Ministry of Justice, 'Government launches independent review of the Human Rights Act' (7 December 2020) <https://www.gov.uk/government/news/government-launches-independent-review-of-the-human-rights-act> accessed 11 January 2021.

93 JCHR, *Enforcing Human Rights* (n 43) [141].

94 Equally Ours, *Telling the Story of Everyone's Rights, Every Day* (November 2013) 7.

95 JCHR, *Enforcing Human Rights* (n 43) [139].

human rights more broadly, as well as highlighting to the British public one benefit amongst many that membership of the Council of Europe provides.

The sensible conclusion to draw, in the current political climate, is that the enactment of legislation of the kind proposed here is unlikely in the extreme. A consensus regarding its necessity and desirability would have to be built in a time where the UK's relationship with Europe is fraught. The EU has been the source of a floor of mandatorily maintained rights for three decades. As Britain leaves the EU, we might ask what impact that constitutional shift will have on the position of workers in the UK. The forecast is not optimistic. Without the minimum standards provided through membership of the EU, a concern that workers' rights will be gradually eroded, and workers exposed to managerial prerogative to a greater degree, is justified.[96] In that context, a widespread desire to ensure that an individual's most basic rights—which include but certainly go beyond those considered in this work—are visibly embedded within the legal system may well arise. The nonchalance towards the rights of workers which is prevalent in the public consciousness today may be disrupted sufficiently to gain popular and political momentum for campaigns in favour of fundamental rights at work.

[96] See, for example, the ministerial response to questioning about worker's rights by the JCHR at [76]–[77] and the Committee's concern that fundamental rights should not be repealed without full debate for reasons of 'expediency' at [92]: Joint Committee on Human Rights, *The Human Rights Implications of Brexit* (Fifth Report of Session 2016–17, HL 88, HC 695, 19 December 2016).

Bibliography

Alston P, 'Conjuring up New Human Rights: A Proposal for Quality Control' (1984) 78 American Journal of International Law 614

Anderson E, *Private Government: How Employers Rules our Lives (and Why We Don't Talk about It)* (Princeton University Press 2017)

Atkinson J, 'Human Rights as Foundations for Labour Law' in Collins H, Lester G, and Mantouvalou V (eds), *Philosophical Foundations of Labour Law* (Oxford University Press 2018)

Atkinson J, 'Implied Terms and Human Rights in the Contract of Employment' (2019) 48 ILJ 515

Atkinson J and Dhorajiwala H, '*IWGB v RooFoods*: Status, Rights and Substitution' (2019) 48 ILJ 278

Barmes L, 'The Continuing Conceptual Crisis in the Common Law of the Contract of Employment' (2004) 67 MLR 435

Barnard C, 'Cherries: One Bite or Two?' (2006) 65 CLJ 27

Barnard C, 'So Long, Farewell, Auf Wiedersehen, Adieu: Brexit and the Charter of Fundamental Rights' (2019) 82 MLR 319

Barnard C and Blackham A, 'Discrimination and the Self-Employed: The Scope of Protection in an Interconnected Age' in Collins H (ed), *European Contract Law and the Charter of Fundamental Rights* (Intersentia 2017)

Barnard C and Ludlow A, 'Enforcement of Employment Rights by EU-8 Migrant Workers in Employment Tribunals' (2016) 45 ILJ 1

Beale HG (ed), *Chitty on Contracts* (33rd edn, Sweet & Maxwell 2018)

Beijer M, *The Limits of Fundamental Rights Protection by the EU* (Intersentia 2017)

Bellace JR and ter Haar B, 'Perspectives on Labour and Human Rights' in Bellace JR and ter Haar B (eds), *Research Handbook on Labour, Business and Human Rights Law* (Edward Elgar Publishing 2019)

BeVier L and Harrison J, 'The State Action Principle and its Critics' (2010) 96 Virginia Law Review 1767

Bogg A, '*Bournemouth University Higher Education Corporation v Buckland*: Re-establishing Orthodoxy at the Expense of Coherence?' (2010) 39 ILJ 408

Bogg A, 'Good Faith in the Contract of Employment: A Case of the English Reserve?' (2010) 32 Comparative Labor Law and Policy Journal 729

Bogg A, 'Sham Self-employment in the Supreme Court' (2012) 41 ILJ 328

Bogg A, 'Illegality, Public Policy and the Contract of Employment' in Freedland M (ed), *The Contract of Employment* (Oxford University Press 2016)

Bogg A, '"Individualism" and "Collectivism" in Collective Labour Law' (2017) 46 ILJ 72

Bogg A, 'Freedom of Association: Courts and Legislatures' (2020) 36 International Journal of Comparative Labour Law and Industrial Relations 409

Bogg A and Collins H, 'Lord Hoffman and the Law of Employment: The Notorious Episode of *Johnson v Unisys Ltd*' in Davies PS and Pila J (eds), *The Jurisprudence of Lord Hoffman* (Hart Publishing 2015)

Bogg A and Dukes R, 'Article 11 ECHR and the Right to Collective Bargaining: *Pharmacists' Defence Association Union v Boots Management Services Ltd*' (2017) 46 ILJ 543
Bogg A and Dukes R, 'Statutory Interpretation and the Limits of a Human Rights Approach: *Royal Mail Group Ltd v Communication Workers Union*' (2020) 49 ILJ 477
Bogg A and Estlund C, 'Freedom of Association and the Right to Contest' in Bogg A and Novitz T (eds), *Voices at Work: Continuity and Change in the Common Law World* (Oxford University Press 2014)
Bogg A and Ewing K, 'The Implications of the *RMT* Case' (2014) 43 ILJ 221
Bogg A and Ford M, 'Between Statute and Contract: Who is a Worker?' (2019) 135 LQR 347
Bogg A and Freedland M, 'The Wrongful Termination of the Contract of Employment' in Freedland M (ed), *The Contract of Employment* (Oxford University Press 2016)
Bogg A and Green S, 'Rights Are Not Just for the Virtuous: What *Hounga* Means for the Illegality Defence in the Discrimination Torts' (2015) 44 ILJ 101
Bogg A and others (eds), *Criminality at Work* (Oxford University Press 2020)
Bowers J and Clarke A, 'Unfair Dismissal and Managerial Prerogative: A Study of Other Substantial Reason' (1981) 10 ILJ 34
Brems E and Lavrysen L, '"Don't Use a Sledgehammer to Crack a Nut": Less Restrictive Means in the Case Law of the European Court of Human Rights' (2015) 15 HRLR 139
Brodie D, 'The Heart of the Matter: Mutual Trust and Confidence' (1996) 25 ILJ 121
Brodie D, 'Beyond Exchange: The New Contract of Employment' (1998) 27 ILJ 79
Brodie D, 'Mutual Trust and Confidence: Catalysts, Constraints and Commonality' (2008) 37 ILJ 329
Bruun N and others, 'Conclusions: The Potentials for the Charter to be Used' in Bruun N and others (eds), *The European Social Charter and the Employment Relation* (Hart Publishing 2016)
Busby N and McDermont M, 'Fighting with the Wind: Claimants' Experiences and Perceptions of the Employment Tribunal' (2020) 49 ILJ 159
Cabrelli D, 'Rules and Standards in the Workplace: A Perspective from the Field of Labour Law' (2011) 31 Legal Studies 21
Cabrelli D, 'The Hierarchy of Differing Behavioural Standards of Review in Labour Law' (2011) 40 ILJ 146
Cherednychenko O, 'Towards the Control of Private Acts by the European Court of Human Rights?' (2006) 13 Maastricht Journal of European & Comparative Law 195
Cherednychenko O, 'Subordinating Contract Law to Fundamental Rights: Towards a Major Breakthrough or towards Walking in Circles?' in Grundmann S (ed), *Constitutional Values and European Contract Law* (Kluwer Law International 2008)
Christodoulidis E and Dukes R, 'Dialogue & Debate: Labour, Constitution and A Sense of Measure: A Debate with Alain Supiot' (2010) 19 Social & Legal Studies 217
Clapham A, *Human Rights Obligations of Non-State Actors* (Oxford University Press 2006)
Clément D, 'Human Rights or Social Justice? The Problem of Rights Inflation' (2018) 22 International Journal of Human Rights 155
Collins H, 'Market Power, Bureaucratic Power and the Contract of Employment' (1986) 15 ILJ 1
Collins H, 'Independent Contractors and the Challenge of Vertical Disintegration to Employment Protection Laws' (1990) 10 OJLS 353
Collins H, *Justice in Dismissal: The Law of Termination of Employment* (Oxford University Press 1992)
Collins H, 'The Productive Disintegration of Labour Law' (1997) 26 ILJ 295
Collins H, 'Claim for Unfair Dismissal: *Johnson v Unisys Ltd*' (2001) 30 ILJ 305

Collins H, 'Compensation for the Manner of Dismissal' (2004) 33 ILJ 152
Collins H, 'Utility and Rights in Common Law Reasoning: Rebalancing Private Law Through Constitutionalization' (2007) 30 Dalhousie Law Journal 1
Collins H, 'Theories of Rights as Justifications for Labour Law' in Langille B and Davidov G (eds), *The Idea of Labour Law* (Oxford University Press 2011)
Collins H, 'Compensation for Dismissal: In Search of Principle' (2012) 41 ILJ 208
Collins H, 'On the Incompatibility of Human Rights Discourse and Private Law' in Micklitz HW (ed), *Constitutionalization of European Private Law* (Oxford University Press 2014)
Collins H, 'Is There a Human Right to Work?' in Mantouvalou V (ed), *The Right to Work: Legal and Philosophical Perspectives* (Hart Publishing 2015)
Collins H, 'Implied Terms in the Contract of Employment' in Freedland M (ed), *The Contract of Employment* (Oxford University Press 2016)
Collins H, 'The Challenges Presented by Fundamental Rights to Private Law' in Barker K, Fairweather K, and Grantham R (eds), *Private Law in the 21st Century* (Hart Publishing 2017)
Collins H, 'Is the Contract of Employment Illiberal?' in Collins H, Lester G, and Mantouvalou V (eds), *Philosophical Foundations of Labour Law* (Oxford University Press 2018)
Collins H, 'Justice for Foxes: Fundamental Rights and Justification of Indirect Discrimination' in Collins H and Khaitan T (eds), *Foundations of Indirect Discrimination Law* (Hart Publishing 2018)
Collins H, 'Justice at Work' (2020) 1 Revista Forumul Judecatorilor 59
Collins H, 'An Emerging Human Right to Protection against Unjustified Dismissal' (2021) 50 ILJ 36
Collins H, Ewing K, and McColgan A, *Labour Law* (2nd edn, Cambridge University Press 2019)
Collins H, Lester G, and (eds) Mantouvalou V, *Philosophical Foundations of Labour Law* (Oxford University Press 2018)
Collins H and Mantouvalou V, '*Redfearn v UK*: Political Association and Dismissal' (2013) 76 MLR 909
Collins H and Mantouvalou V, 'Human Rights and the Contract of Employment' in Freedland M (ed), *The Contract of Employment* (Oxford University Press 2016)
Collins P, 'The Inadequate Protection of Human Rights in Unfair Dismissal Law' (2018) 47 ILJ 504
Collins P, 'Square Peg vs a Round Hole? The Necessity of a Bill of Rights for Workers' (2020) 11 European Labour Law Journal 199
Collins P and Fradley P, 'Policing the Boundaries of Articles 8 and 11 ECHR' (2019) 48 ILJ 225
Costello C, 'Migrants and Forced Labour: A Labour Law Response' in Bogg A and others (eds), *The Autonomy of Labour Law* (Hart Publishing 2015)
Cruft R, Liao SM, and Renzo M (eds), *Philosophical Foundations of Human Rights* (Oxford University Press 2015)
Davidov G, 'Joint Employer Status in Triangular Employment Relationships' (2004) 42 British Journal of Industrial Relations 727
Davidov G, *A Purposive Approach to Labour Law* (Oxford University Press 2016)
Davidov G and Langille B (eds), *Boundaries and Frontiers of Labour Law: Goals and Means in the Regulation of Work* (Hart Publishing 2006)
Davidov G and Langille B (eds), *The Idea of Labour Law* (Oxford University Press 2011)
Davies ACL, 'Judicial Self-restraint in Labour Law' (2009) 38 ILJ 278

Davies ACL, 'Workers' Human Rights in English Law' in Novitz T and Fenwick C (eds), *Human Rights at Work: Perspectives on Law and Regulation* (Hart Publishing 2010)

Davies ACL, 'Labour Law as Public Law' in Bogg A and others (eds), *The Autonomy of Labour Law* (Hart Publishing 2015)

Davies ACL, 'The Relationship between the Contract of Employment and Statute' in Freedland M (ed), *The Contract of Employment* (Oxford University Press 2016)

Davies P and Freedland M, 'The Impact of Public Law on Labour Law, 1972–1997' (1997) 26 ILJ 311

Davies P and Freedland M, 'The Complexities of the Employing Enterprise' in Davidov G and Langille B (eds), *Boundaries and Frontiers of Labour Law: Goals and Means in the Regulation of Work* (Hart Publishing 2006)

Deakin S, 'The Changing Concept of "Employer" in Labour Law' (2001) 30 ILJ 72

Deakin S, 'Formation of the Contract of Employment' in Freedland M (ed), *The Contract of Employment* (Oxford University Press 2016)

Deakin S and Morris GS, *Labour Law* (6th edn, Hart Publishing 2012)

Dorssemont F, 'The European Convention on Human Rights as a Fountain of Labour Rights' in Bellace JR and ter Haar B (eds), *Research Handbook on Labour, Business and Human Rights Law* (Edward Elgar Publishing 2019)

Drooghenbroek SV, 'Labour Law Litigation and Fair Trial under Article 6' in Dorssemont F, Lörcher K, and Schömann I (eds), *The European Convention on Human Rights and The Employment Relation* (Hart Publishing 2013)

Dukes R, 'Constitutionalizing Employment Relations: Sinzheimer, Kahn-Freund, and the Role of Labor Law' (2008) 35 Journal of Law and Society 341

Dukes R, 'The Right to Strike under UK Law: Something More Than a Slogan?' (2011) 40 ILJ 302

Dworkin R, *Taking Rights Seriously* (Harvard University Press 1977)

Elgar J and Simpson B, 'The Impact of the Law on Industrial Disputes Revisited: a Perspective on Developments over the last Two Decades' (2017) 46 ILJ 6

Elias P, 'Reflections on Judicial Power and Human Rights' in Bogg A, Rowbottom J, and Young AL (eds), *The Constitution of Social Democracy: Essays in Honour of Keith Ewing* (Bloomsbury Publishing 2020)

Estreicher S and Hirsch JM, 'Comparative Wrongful Dismissal Law: Reassessing American Exceptionalism' (2014) 92 North Carolina Law Review 343

Ewing K, 'The Right to Strike' (1986) 15 ILJ 143

Ewing K, 'Rights at the Workplace: An Agenda for Labour Law' in McColgan A (ed), *The Future of Labour Law* (Cassell 1996)

Ewing K, 'The Human Rights Act and Labour Law' (1998) 27 ILJ 275

Ewing K, 'The Unbalanced Constitution' in Campbell T, Ewing K, and Tomkins A (eds), *Sceptical Essays on Human Rights* (Oxford University Press 2001)

Ewing K, 'The Implications of *Wilson and Palmer*' (2003) 32 ILJ 1

Ewing K, 'The Implications of the *ASLEF* Case' (2007) 36 ILJ 425

Ewing K, *Ruined Lives: Blacklisting in the UK Construction Industry* (Institute of Employment Rights 2009)

Ewing K and Hendy J, 'The Trade Union Act 2016 and the Failure of Human Rights' (2016) 45 ILJ 391

Ford M, 'The Fissured Worker: Personal Service Companies and Employment Rights' (2020) 49 ILJ 35

Frantziou E, *The Horizontal Effect of Fundamental Rights in the European Union: A Constitutional Analysis* (Oxford University Press 2019)

Fredman S, 'Scepticism under Scrutiny: Labour Law and Human Rights' in Campbell T, Ewing KD, and Tomkins A (eds), *Sceptical Essays on Human Rights* (Oxford University Press 2001)
Fredman S, *Human Rights Transformed: Positive Rights and Positive Duties* (Oxford University Press 2008)
Fredman S, *Discrimination Law* (2nd edn, Oxford University Press 2011)
Fredman S, 'Equality Law: Labour Law or an Autonomous Field?' in Bogg A and others (eds), *The Autonomy of Labour Law* (Hart Publishing 2015)
Fredman S, *Comparative Human Rights Law* (Oxford University Press 2018)
Freedland M, *The Personal Employment Contract* (Oxford University Press 2003)
Freedland M, 'Employment Law' in Bell J, Boyron S, and Whittaker S (eds), *Principles of French Law* (2nd edn, Oxford University Press 2008)
Freedland M and Davies P, *Kahn-Freund's Labour and the Law* (3rd edn, Stevens 1983)
Freedland M and Kountouris N, *The Legal Construction of Personal Work Relations* (Oxford University Press 2011)
Freedland M and Kountouris N, 'Some Reflections on the 'Personal Scope' of Collective Labour Law' (2017) 46 ILJ 52
Fudge J, 'The New Discourse of Labor Rights: From Social to Fundamental Rights' (2007) 29 Comparative Labor Law and Policy Journal 29
Fudge J, *Constitutionalizing Labour Rights in Europe* (Oxford University Press 2011)
Fudge J, 'Labour As a 'Fictive Commodity': Radically Reconceptualizing Labour Law' in Davidov G and Langille B (eds), *The Idea of Labour Law* (Oxford University Press 2011)
Gardbaum S, 'Positive and Horizontal Rights: Proportionality's Next Frontier or a Bridge Too Far?' in Jackson V and Tushnet M (eds), *Proportionality: New Frontiers, New Challenges* (Cambridge University Press 2017)
Gardner J, 'Liberals and Unlawful Discrimination' (1989) 9 OJLS 1
Gearty C and Mantouvalou V, *Debating Social Rights* (Hart Publishing 2010)
Gerards J, 'Procedural Review by the ECtHR: A Typology' in Gerards J and Brems E (eds), *Procedural Review in European Fundamental Rights Cases* (Cambridge University Press 2017)
Gerards J, *General Principles of the European Convention on Human Rights* (Cambridge University Press 2019)
Gerstenberg O, 'Private Law and the New European Constitutional Settlement' (2004) 10 European Law Journal 766
Gilabert P, 'Labor Human Rights and Human Dignity' (2015) 42 Philosophy & Social Criticism 171
Gilabert P, 'Dignity at Work' in Collins H, Lester G, and Mantouvalou V (eds), *Philosophical Foundations of Labour Law* (Oxford University Press 2018)
Griffin J, *On Human Rights* (Oxford University Press 2008)
Gross JA, *A Shameful Business: The Case for Human Rights in the American Workplace* (Cornell University Press 2010)
Hale B, '*Argentoratum Locutum*: Is Strasbourg or the Supreme Court Supreme?' (2012) 12 Human Rights Law Review 65
Hart HLA, 'Rawls on Liberty and Its Priority' (1973) 40 University of Chicago Law Review 534
Hattab MK, 'The Doctrine of Legitimate Expectation & Proportionality: A Public Law Principle Adopted into the Private Law of Employment' (2018) 39 Liverpool Law Review 239
Hepple B, 'European Rules on Dismissal Law?' (1997) 18 Comparative Labour Law Journal 204

Hepple B, 'Human Rights and Employment Law' [1998] Amicus Curiae 19
Hepple B, *Rights at Work: Global, European and British Perspectives* (Sweet & Maxwell, 2005)
Hickman T, 'Bill of Rights Reform and the Case for Going Beyond the Declaration of Incompatibility Model' [2015] New Zealand Law Review 35
Holland J, 'Amazon Inquiry' (2020) 13 Notes from Below 7
Howe J, 'Why Do So Few Employees Return to their Jobs? In Pursuit of a Right to Work Following Unfair Dismissal' in Mantouvalou V (ed), *The Right to Work: Legal and Philosophical Perspectives* (Hart Publishing 2014)
Hunt M, 'The "Horizontal Effect" of the Human Rights Act' [1998] Public Law 423
Kay RS, 'The European Convention on Human Rights and the Control of Private Law' (2005) 5 EHRLR 466
Kennedy D, 'International Human Rights Movement: Part of the Problem?' (2002) 15 Harvard Human Rights Journal 101
Khaitan T, *A Theory of Discrimination Law* (Oxford University Press 2015)
King J, *Judging Social Rights* (Cambridge University Press 2012)
Klare K, 'The Public/Private Distinction in Labour Law' (1981) 130 University of Pennsylvania Law Review 1358
Klug F and Wildbore H, 'Follow or Lead? The Human Rights Act and the European Court of Human Rights' (2010) 6 EHRLR 621
Köpcke M, 'Why It Takes Law to Realise Human Rights' in Webber G and others (eds), *Legislated Rights: Securing Human Rights through Legislation* (Cambridge University Press 2018)
Kumm M, 'Who is Afraid of the Total Constitution? Constitutional Rights as Principles and the Constitutionalization of Private Law' (2006) 7 German Law Journal 341
Langille B, 'Labour Law is a Subset of Employment Law' (1981) 31 University of Toronto Law Journal 200
Langille B, 'Labour Law's Theory of Justice' in Davidov G and Langille B (eds), *The Idea of Labour Law* (Oxford University Press 2011)
Langille B, 'If Labour Law is a Subset of Employment Law, What is Employment Law a Subset of?' (2020) 43 Dalhousie Law Journal 581
Lavrysen L, *Human Rights in a Positive State: Rethinking the Relationship between Positive and Negative Obligations under the European Convention on Human Rights* (Intersentia 2017)
Laws J, 'Public Law and Employment Law: Abuse of Power' (1997) Public Law 455
Leigh I, 'Horizontal Rights, the Human Rights Act and Privacy: Lessons from the Commonwealth?' (1999) 48 International & Comparative Law Quarterly 57
Leigh I and Masterman R, *Making Rights Real: The Human Rights Act in its First Decade* (Hart Publishing 2008)
Letsas G, 'Two Concepts of the Margin of Appreciation' (2006) 26 OJLS 705
Lewis D, 'Re-Employment as a Remedy for Unfair Dismissal: How can the Culture be Changed?' (1999) 28 ILJ 183
Lörcher K, 'Article 31—Fair and Just Working Conditions' in Dorssemont F and others (eds), *The Charter of Fundamental Rights of the European Union and the Employment Relation* (Hart Publishing 2019)
Mahoney P, 'Effect, Non-Compliance and Enforcement of Judgments of International/Supranational Courts: The European Court of Human Rights as a Case-Study' in Baudenbacher C (ed), *Dispute resolution*, vol III (German Law Publishers 2009)
Mak C, *Fundamental Rights in European Contract Law: A Comparison of the Impact of Fundamental Rights on Contractual Relationships in Germany, the Netherlands, Italy and England* (Kluwer Law International 2008)

Mangan D, 'Social Media in the Workplace' in Mangan D and Gillies LE (eds), *The Legal Challenges of Social Media* (Elgar Publishing 2017)

Mantouvalou V, 'Human Rights and Unfair Dismissal: Private Acts in Public Spaces' (2008) 71 MLR 912

Mantouvalou V, 'Are Labour Rights Human Rights?' (2012) 2 European Labour Law Journal 151

Mantouvalou V, 'Labour Rights in the European Convention on Human Rights: An Intellectual Justification for an Integrated Approach to Interpretation' (2013) 13 Human Rights Law Review 529

Mantouvalou V, 'The Prohibition of Slavery, Servitude and Forced and Compulsory Labour under Article 4 ECHR' in Dorssemont F, Lörcher K, and Schömann I (eds), *The European Convention on Human Rights and The Employment Relation* (Hart Publishing 2013)

Mantouvalou V, '"I Lost My Job over a Facebook Post: Was that Fair?" Discipline and Dismissal for Social Media Activity' (2019) 35 International Journal of Comparative Labour Law and Industrial Relations 101

Mantouvalou V, 'Structural Injustice and the Human Rights of Workers' (2020) 73 Current Legal Problems 1

Mantouvalou V, 'The Human Rights Act and Labour Law at 20' in Bogg A, Rowbottom J and Young AL (eds), *The Constitution of Social Democracy: Essays in Honour of Keith Ewing* (Bloomsbury Publishing 2020)

Masterman R, 'Section 2(1) of the Human Rights Act 1998: Binding Domestic Courts to Strasbourg?' [2004] Public Law 725

Masterman R, 'Taking the Strasbourg Jurisprudence into Account: Developing a 'Municipal Law of Human Rights' under the Human Rights Act' (2008) 54 International and Comparative Law Quarterly 907

Masterman R, 'Deconstructing the Mirror Principle' in Masterman R and Leigh I (eds), *The United Kingdom's Statutory Bill of Rights* (Oxford University Press 2013)

McCann D, 'Decent Working Hours as a Human Right: Intersections in the Regulation of Working Time' in Novitz T and Fenwick C (eds), *Human Rights at Work: Perspectives on Law and Regulation* (Hart Publishing 2010)

McCrea R, 'Religion in the Workplace' (2014) 77 MLR 277

Morgan J, 'Questioning the True Effect of the Human Rights Act' (2002) 22 Legal Studies 259

Morgan J, 'Privacy, Confidence and Horizontal Effect: "Hello" Trouble' (2003) 62 CLJ 444

Morris G, 'Fundamental Rights: Exclusion by Agreement?' (2001) 30 ILJ 49

Morris G, 'Protection of Employees' Personal Information and Privacy in English Law' in Nakakubo H and Araki T (eds), *Protection of Employees' Personal Information and Privacy* (The Japan Institute for Labour Policy and Training 2014)

Mowbray A, *The Development of Positive Obligations under the European Convention on Human Rights by the European Court of Human Rights* (Hart Publishing 2004)

Moyn S, *Not Enough: Human Rights in an Unequal World* (Harvard University Press 2018)

Mundlak G, 'Human Rights and the Employment Relationship: A Look Through the Prism of Juridification' in Friedmann D and Barak-Erez D (eds), *Human Rights in Private Law* (Hart Publishing 2002)

Murray J, 'Taking Social Rights Seriously: Is There a Case for Institutional Reform of the ILO?' in Novitz T and Fenwick C (eds), *Human Rights at Work: Perspectives on Law and Regulation* (Hart Publishing 2010)

Novitz T and Fenwick C, 'The Application of Human Rights Discourse to Labour Relations: Translation of Theory into Practice' in Novitz T and Fenwick C (eds), *Human Rights at Work: Perspectives on Law and Regulation* (Hart Publishing 2010)

O'Cinneide C, 'The European Social Charter and the UK: Why It Matters' (2018) 29 Kings Law Journal 275

Oliver D, *Common Values and the Public–Private Divide* (Cambridge University Press 2010)

Oliver D and Fedtke J (eds), *Human Rights and the Private Sphere: A Comparative Study* (Routledge-Cavendish 2007)

Oliver H, 'Email and Internet Monitoring in the Workplace: Information Privacy and Contracting-out' (2002) 31 ILJ 321

Oliver H, 'Employment Law' in Hoffman D (ed), *The Impact of the UK Human Rights Act on Private Law* (Cambridge University Press 2011)

Pannick D, 'Principles of Interpretation of Convention Rights under the Human Rights Act and the Discretionary Area of Judgment' [1998] Public Law 545

Peden E, 'Policy Concerns behind Implication of Terms in Law' (2001) 117 LQR 459

Peel E, *Treitel on the Law of Contract* (14th edn, Sweet & Maxwell 2015)

Phillipson G, 'The Human Rights Act, 'Horizontal Effect' and the Common Law: A Bang or a Whimper?' (1999) 62 MLR 824

Phillipson G, 'Privacy: The Development of Breach of Confidence—The Clearest Case of Horizontal Effect?' in Hoffman D (ed), *The Impact of the UK Human Rights Act on Private Law* (Cambridge University Press 2011)

Pietropaoli I and others, *A UK Failure to Prevent Mechanism for Corporate Human Rights Harms* (British Institute of International and Comparative Law 2020)

Prassl J, *The Concept of the Employer* (Oxford University Press 2015)

Prassl J, *Humans as a Service: The Promise and Perils of Work in the Gig Economy* (Oxford University Press 2018)

Prassl J and Albin E, 'Employees, Employers, and Beyond: Identifying the Parties to the Contract of Employment' in Freedland M (ed), *The Contract of Employment* (Oxford University Press 2016)

Priel D, 'The Political Origins of English Private Law' (2013) 40 Journal of Law and Society 481

Raday F, 'Constitutionalization of Labour Law' in Blanpain R and Weiss M (eds), *The Changing Face of Labour Law and Industrial Relations* (Nomos 1993)

Rakoff TD, 'Enforcement of Employment Contracts and the Anti-Slavery Norm' in Friedmann D and Barak-Erez D (eds), *Human Rights in Private Law* (Hart Publishing 2003)

Rideout R, 'Implied Terms in the Employment Relationship' in Halson R (ed), *Exploring the Boundaries of Contract* (Dartmouth Publishing 1996)

Sales P, 'Rights and Fundamental Rights in English Law' (2016) 75 CLJ 86

Sanders A, 'Does Article 6 of the European Convention on Human Rights Apply to Disciplinary Procedures in the Workplace?' (2013) 33 OJLS 791

Sanders A, 'The Law of Unfair Dismissal and Behaviour Outside Work' (2014) 34 Legal Studies 328

de Schutter O, 'Human Rights in Employment Relationships: Contracts as Power' in Dorssemont F, Lörcher K, and Schömann I (eds), *The European Convention on Human Rights and the Employment Relation* (Hart Publishing 2013)

Scolnicov A, 'Lifelike and Lifeless in Law: Do Corporations Have Human Rights?' (2013) University of Cambridge Legal Studies Research Paper Series, Paper No 13/2013 <http://ssrn.com/abstract=2268537> accessed 16 November 2020

Sedley S, 'Human Rights: a Twenty-first Century Agenda' [1995] Public Law 386

Sedley S, 'Bringing Rights Home: Time to Start a Family?' (2008) 28 Legal Studies 327Shue H, *Basic Rights: Subsistence, Affluence, and U.S. Foreign Policy* (40th Anniversary edn, Princeton University Press 2020)

Smits J, 'Private Law and Fundamental Rights: A Sceptical View' in Barkhuysen T and Lindenberg S (eds), *Constitutionalisation of Private Law* (Martinus Nijhoff Publishers 2006)
Spector H, 'Philosophical Foundations of Labor Law' (2006) 33 Florida State University Law Review 1119
Spieler EA, 'Risks and Rights: The Case for Occupational Safety and Health as a Core Worker Right' in Gross JA (ed), *Workers' Rights as Human Rights* (Cornell University Press 2003)
Spielmann D, 'The European Convention on Human Rights: The European Court of Human Rights' in Oliver D and Fedtke J (eds), *Human Rights and the Private Sphere: A Comparative Study* (Routledge-Cavendish 2007)
Starmer K, *European Human Rights Law: the Human Rights Act 1998 and the European Convention on Human Rights* (Legal Action Group 1999)
Stewart P, 'Tortious Remedies for Deliberate Wrongdoing to Victims of Human Trafficking and Slavery in Australia' (2011) 34 University of New South Wales Law Journal 898
Stoyanova V, *Human Trafficking and Slavery Reconsidered: Conceptual Limits and States' Positive Obligations in European Law* (Cambridge University Press 2017)
Summers CW, 'The Privatization of Personal Freedoms and Enrichment of Democracy: Some Lessons from Labor Law' (1986) 1986 University of Illinois Law Review 689
Thomas J, *Public Rights, Private Relations* (Oxford University Press 2015)
Toulson R, 'Fundamental Rights and the Common Law' (The Fundamental Rights Conference, London, 10 October 2015)
Tsuruda S, 'Volunteer Work, Inclusivity, and Social Equality' in Collins H, Lester G, and Mantouvalou V (eds), *Philosophical Foundations of Labour Law* (Oxford University Press 2018)
Varuhas JNE, 'Damages: Private Law and the HRA—Never the Twain Shall Meet?' in Hoffman D (ed), *The Impact of the UK Human Rights Act on Private Law* (Cambridge University Press 2011)
Vickers L, *Freedom of Speech and Employment* (Oxford University Press 2002)
Vickers L, *Religious Freedom, Religious Discrimination and the Workplace* (Hart Publishing 2016)
Wade SW, 'Horizons of Horizontality' (2000) 116 LQR 217
Weatherill S, 'Use and Abuse of the EU's Charter of Fundamental Rights: On the Improper Veneration of "Freedom of Contract"' (2014) 10 European Review of Contract Law 167
Webber G and Yowell P, 'Securing Human Rights through Legislation' in Webber G and others (eds), *Legislated Rights: Securing Human Rights through Legislation* (Cambridge University Press 2018)
Webber G and others (eds), *Legislated Rights: Securing Human Rights through Legislation* (Cambridge University Press 2018)
Wedderburn B, 'Freedom of Association or Right to Organise?' (1987) 18 Industrial Relations Journal 244
Wedderburn B, *Labour Law and Freedom: Further Essays in Labour Law* (Lawrence & Wishart 1995)
Weil D, *The Fissured Workplace: Why Work Became So Bad for So Many and What Can Be Done to Improve It* (Harvard University Press 2014)
Weiss M, 'Re-Inventing Labour Law?' in Langille B and Davidov G (eds), *The Idea of Labour Law* (Oxford University Press 2011)
Wildhaber L, 'Article 41 of the European Convention on Human Rights: Just Satisfaction under the European Convention on Human Rights' (2003) 3 Baltic Yearbook of International Law 1

Wintemute R, 'Belief vs. Action in *Ladele, Ngole* and *Forstater*' (2021) 50 ILJ 104

Wragg P, 'Free Speech Rights at Work: Resolving the Differences between Practice and Liberal Principle' (2015) 44 ILJ 1

Yamada DC, 'Human Dignity and American Employment Law' (2009) 43 University of Richmond Law Review 523

Young A, 'Mapping Horizontal Effect' in Hoffman D (ed), *The Impact of the UK Human Rights Act on Private Law* (Cambridge University Press 2011)

Youngdahl J, 'Solidarity First: Labor Rights are Not the Same as Human Rights' (2009) 18 New Labour Forum 31

Index

For the benefit of digital users, indexed terms that span two pages (e.g., 52–53) may, on occasion, appear on only one of those pages.

agency workers 85, 105–6, 107–8, 124–25
Anderson, Elizabeth 39–40
applicants for work 21–22, 27, 85, 87
association and assembly, right to freedom of
  blacklisting *see under* trade union members
  industrial action *see* strike, right to
  political associations *see* political activities/expression
  Trade Union and Labour Relations (Consolidation) Act 1992, and 85–88
  trade union members *see* trade union members
  trade unions *see* trade unions
Atkinson, Joe 35, 165, 168

Bellace, Janice 47–48
Bogg, Alan 29–30, 44, 162–63, 172, 173–74, 179, 202
Brodie, Douglas 166

Cabrelli, David 133, 134
Collins, Hugh 11–12, 17, 27, 31, 36, 49, 54, 110–11, 118, 130–31, 145–46, 147, 148, 166–67, 179–80, 182, 201
common law, doctrines of the
  development in accordance with human rights *see under* horizontal effect, indirect horizontal effect
  existing protection of human rights 6, 48–49, 180–82
  illegality 108–10
  implication of a contract 105–6
contract of employment
  constructive unfair dismissal, and 129–30, 168, 176
  implied terms, and *see* implied terms
  inequality of power between parties 3–4, 26, 49, 174, 178
  interpretation of terms in accordance with ECHR 151–56, 183–84
  means of human rights protection, as a 6, 152–56, 173, 182–88, 189
  personal scope of labour rights, role in *see* personal scope of labour rights
  remedies for breach of 3, 153, 173
    expectation measure 153, 175
    limitations 3, 174, 175–76
  restrictions upon exercise of human rights 27, 55, 174–75, 182–88, 189
  subordination of employees, and 23–24, 49, 173–75, 182–83, 189
  waiver of human rights, and *see* waiver
  wrongful dismissal *see* wrongful dismissal

Davidov, Guy 25–26
Davies, ACL 43–44, 50–51, 170
Davies, Paul 107–8, 158–59
Deakin, Simon 183, 197
de Schutter, Olivier 69
discrimination, the prohibition of
  Article 14 and 9–10, 60, 84–85
  direct discrimination 84
  Equality Act 2010 and 83–85
  equal pay 82–83
  EU law and 83–84
  grounds 83–84
    contentious beliefs 97–100
    philosophical beliefs 97–99
    political beliefs 97, 98
  implied term of mutual trust and confidence and 162, 163–64
  indirect discrimination 84–85, 94–97
    group disadvantage requirement 94–97
Dorssemont, Filip 14, 77–78
Dworkin, Ronald 35

ECHR, the
  common law, and the development of 72, 88, 174–75, 184–85, *see under* horizontal effect, indirect horizontal effect
  contractual/professional obligations, and 72, 88, 174, 184
  duty of compatible interpretation of legislation and *see under* horizontal effect, statutory horizontal effect
  integrated approach to interpretation of 8–9, 43–44, 103–4, 215–16
  legitimate aims *see* legitimate aims
  margin of appreciation 52, 211–12
  necessity *see* necessity standard, the
  positive obligations 9–11, 58, 62–69, *see* positive obligations, ECHR doctrine of
  qualified rights, the 9, 58, 62
  scope of entitlement 58, 60–62, 101, 103–4

Elias, Sir Patrick 192–93
employers
duty bearers of workers' human rights, as 22–23, 24–31, 32, 81, 82, 85, 88, 89
Bill of Rights for workers, and 193, 199–203
gatekeepers of work opportunities, as 24–25
institutional status of employers, the 24–25
implied obligations of *see* implied terms
multiple employing entities 13, 107–8, 200, 204
powers/functions of *see* employers' powers
protective motives 30–31, 197
employers' powers
as distinct from states' powers 17, 54–55, 193
Bill of Rights for workers, relevance to 201–3
bureaucratic power over workplace 26–27, 173–74
discipline 1–2, 12, 27, 151–52, 153–55, 173, 188
dismissal 11–12, 27, 28–29, 128–48, 154–56, 184, 188
financial incentives, offer of 12, 87
influence beyond work 2, 28–29, 136–37, 154–56, 184, 186–88
investigation of misconduct 12, 67–68, 138–43, 153–56, 158–59, 174–75, 184–88
management of work 26–27, 173–74
monitoring/surveillance 28, 200–1
need for proportionate use of 2, 133–34, 188
selection between applicants 22, 26, 27
terms and conditions, determination of 12, 26, 27–28, 70–71, 173–75
employment relations
dependence of workers 4–5, 25–26
inequality of power between parties 4–5, 26
subordination, and 4–5, 26–27, 31–32
tailored understanding of human rights 17, 50–57
tension between free exercise of human rights, and 4–5, 24, 25–29
vulnerability of workers 21–22
enforcement 102, 203–5, 209
equality *see* discrimination, prohibition of
Estlund, Cynthia 29–30, 202
Ewing, Keith 40–41, 43, 93–94, 214, 215–16
expression, right to freedom of
chilling effect of employer's sanctions 2, 88
contentious views 2, 97–100, 154–56, 184
Equality Act 2010, and 97–99
interpretation of the right 63–64, 97, 183–84
necessity of an interference, examination of 133–34, 183–84
political expression *see* political activities/expression
professional obligations, treatment of 72, 88
religious beliefs, and *see* religion and belief, right to freedom of
social media 1, 2, 28–29, 130, 134, 139–43, 153–56, 184
unfair dismissal law, and 134, 137–38, 139
whistleblowers, and *see* whistleblowing

fair trial, right to a 10–11, 158, 159
Fenwick, Colin 38
forced labour, prohibition of 10, 41, 48–49, 81, 82–83
Ford, Michael 106–7
Frantziou, Eleni 23–24
Freedland, Mark 107–8, 110–11, 114–15, 158–59, 173–74, 179
Fudge, Judy 45
fundamental social rights 7–9, 44–46
Brexit and 7
lack of judicial enforcement 8
necessity within foundations of labour law 8–9, 40–42
role in Bill of Rights for workers 214–16

Gardbaum, Stephen 196
Gardner, John 24
Gilabert, Pablo 46–47

ter Haar, Beryl 47–48
Hale, Baroness 171, 212
health and safety 41, 48, 82–83, 124, 200–1
duty of care, common law 81
Hepple, Bob 4, 157, 165, 166
Hickman, Tom 214
horizontal effect of human rights 15–18, 89–93
direct horizontal effect 90
Bill of Rights for workers, and 190–91
duties of labour law as *de facto* direct horizontal effect 5, 90
forms of horizontal effect 16–17, 90–91
indirect horizontal effect 90–93, 151–67, 168–69, 171–72, 176–77, 213–14
positive obligations, ECHR and 58–59, 74–75
statutory horizontal effect 5, 81, 91–93, 95–97, 102–3, 120–26, 128, 136–43, 212–13
Howe, Joanne 132
human rights
basic minimum, as a 38–40
centrality of the state 23–24
ECHR *see* ECHR, the
foundations of labour law, as 34, 37–46
horizontal effect and *see* horizontal effect of human rights
inalienability 35–36, 177
public/private divide, and 15, 23–24
universal entitlement to human rights 4, 13–14, 35–36, 58, 60–62, 101

human rights at work
Bills of Rights for workers
comparison between specific and general duties 193–99
legislative action, desirability of 191–93
pre-emptive duty to consider fundamental rights 206–8
relationship to ECHR and ECtHR 210–14
collective power, and 42–44
contextual understanding of rights 17–18, 34, 50–57, 69–75, 184–85
employers' powers 54–55
employers' rights 55
objective of labour law, as an 17–18, 34, 35–49
beneficial consequences 35–37
limitations 38–46
tension between employment relations and 32–33

implied terms 152, 156–71
divergence from human rights protection 163–64
duty of loyalty and obedience 173–74, 183
duty to respect employees' human rights, implication of 166–71, 180–82
necessity of implication 168–69
relationship to surrounding context 169–71
evolution to protect human rights 6, 152, 156–71, 189
exclusion of implied terms 179–82, 189
mutual trust and confidence 156–66, 175–77, 179–80, 186–87
actions without lawful cause 160–61
arbitrary treatment of employees 159–60
failure to show respect and concern 161–63
HRA 1998 and 165–66
procedural justice 158–59
relationship to Parliamentary interventions 165–66, 169–70, 172, 176–77
remedies for breach 153, 173–74, 175–76
workers' contracts, and 167, 189
wrongful dismissal, and *see* wrongful dismissal

Kahn-Freund, Otto 23–24, 26
Kay, Richard 74
Kennedy, David 42
Kountouris, Nicola 114–15

labour law
human rights, and
common law, development of *see under* horizontal effect, indirect horizontal effect
external standard for examination, as an 36–37, 93
historic protection of human rights 31–32, 47–49
statutory interpretation *see under* horizontal effect, statutory horizontal effect
personal scope *see* personal scope of labour rights
public/private divide, and 16, 23–24, 49, 100
social rights, and *see* fundamental social rights
values/objectives of labour law 26, 42, 46–49
human rights as a foundation for labour law 37–46
Langille, Brian 199
Lavrysen, Laurens 53, 58–59
legitimate aims
Bill of Rights for workers, and 196–98
profit/costs savings 56–57, 68–69, 196–97
protection of employer's reputation 1–2, 68, 141–42
protection of others 1–2, 30–31, 68, 197
protection of property 56
protection of worker 30–31
public interest, and 17
scope under the ECHR 56–57, 65, 68
substantial threat to employing organization, need for 56, 68–69, 197–98

Mantouvalou, Virginia 36, 46–47, 49, 118, 130–31, 145–46, 166–67, 215–16
Masterman, Roger 211–12
McCann, Deirdre 40–41
McCrea, Ronan 95–96
Morris, Gillian 71, 197, 206
Moyn, Samuel 38–39
Murray, Jill 39–40, 44–45

necessity standard, the
application by the ECtHR 65–69, 133–34
Bill of Rights for workers, and 194–95, 198–99
dismissal, seriousness of 66–67, 128–29, 133–34
'less restrictive means' test, the 67, 128–29, 133–34
proportionality 66–67, 133–34
relevance of employer's disciplinary procedure 67–68, 195–96
standard of scrutiny 66
unfair dismissal law and *see under* unfair dismissal
whistleblowing and 88
work-related restrictions on exercise of rights 72, 174–75, 184–85

Novitz, Tonia 38

O'Cinneide, Colm 45
office holders 60–61, 105, 106, 122–23

pay 27
equal pay *see* discrimination, prohibition of
Peden, Elizabeth 167
personal scope of labour rights
agency workers *see* agency workers
Bill of Rights for workers, and 199–205
continuous employment, qualifying period of 61–62, 103–4, 116–18, 127, 129–30
contract, requirement of a 105–8, 122–23, 124–25
contract of employment, the 113–16
common law tests 110–11, 113
dismissal law and 110–11, 113, 115–16, 129–30, 175
discrimination law 85, 111, 112–13
ECtHR approach 103–4, 107–8, 110, 126–27
embassy staff 119
gig/platform economy 111–12, 125
human rights, contrast with entitlement to 13–14, 60–61, 101, 107–8
illegality 60–61, 108–10
interpretation compatible with the ECHR
examples 120–23, 124
limitations 102–3, 124–26, 127
migration/visa status 60–61, 108–10, 204
personal service companies 106–7, 204
police service, members of 119–22
subcontractors 106–7
terms inconsistent with employment status, treatment of 112, 120
union membership/activities, rights associated with 103–4, 105, 107, 111–12, 114–15, 120–22, 124–26
worker status 105, 111–13, 122–23, 124–26
political activities/expression 2–3, 29, 154–56, 184
affiliation with a political party 98, 117
disciplinary sanctions and 2–3, 154–56, 184
positive obligations, ECHR doctrine of
contractual obligations, treatment of 69–75, 151–52, 173–75, 183–84
effective remedy, right to an 58, 75–77, 128–29
expectation of alignment with ECHR principles/case-law 62–65, 66, 73–75, 151–52, 155–56
fair balance, striking a 53–54, 59, 183–84
inclusive scope of protection, need for 58, 60–62, 101, 117–18, 168–69
interference, examination of 63–65, 70
exit, possibility of employee's 70, 71
justification, examination of 58, 62–63, 65–69, 128–29, 133–34, 184–85
legislation/legislatures and 52–53, 59, 62–63, 78
national courts' decisions, and 35–36, 63–65, 66, 73–75, 78, 151–52, 155–56, 173–74, 183–84
necessity of an interference *see* necessity standard, the
role in domestic cases 52–53, 211–12
standard of scrutiny 53–54, 66
private and family life, right to respect for
activities outside work 28–29, 41, 130, 136–37, 153–56, 184–85, 188
consequence-based approach to dismissals 41, 121, 128–29
correspondence 28, 184–85
email 2–3, 186–87
instant messages 186, 188
social media 28–29, 130, 139–43, 153–56, 186, 188
data privacy 22, 82–83
discrimination, prohibition of, and 94
interpretation of the right 64, 137, 184–85
reasonable expectation of privacy 72–73, 184–85, 186
relevance of employer's policies 73, 156, 184–85
investigations of employee conduct and 2–3, 12, 63, 138–43, 154–56, 184–88
monitoring/surveillance of workers 2–3, 27, 28, 29, 184–86
reason for dismissal, as a 12, 29, 63, 130, 136–40, 186–88
safeguards for workers' privacy 67–68
proportionality *see under* necessity standard, the

Raday, Frances 24–25
Rawls, John 56–57
religion and belief, right to freedom of
Equality Act 2010, and 94–97
expression of non-religious beliefs 97, 98–99, 139–40, 184
expression of religious beliefs 1–2, 28–29, 94, 98–99, 153–55
manifestation of religious beliefs 2–3
dress codes 28, 95
working hours 28, 96
remedies
Bill of Rights for workers, and 209–10
breach of contract 3, 153, 173, 174, 175–76
ECHR, and *see* remedy, right to an effective

unfair dismissal, and 132, 143–47, *see also* unfair dismissal
wrongful dismissal, and 153, 174, 175–77, *see also* wrongful dismissal
remedy, right to an effective 75–76, 143–44
non-pecuniary losses 76–77, 144, 145, 175–76
qualified rights, states' obligations under the 75, 77, 143
positive obligation upon states 58, 75–77, 128–29
reputation, damage to
employer's reputation *see* legitimate aims
worker's reputation 3, 22, 76–77, 175–76
Rideout, Roger 178

Sedley, Sir Stephen 205, 216–17
Shue, Henry 22–23
slavery and servitude, prohibition of *see* forced labour, prohibition of
Stoyanova, Vladislava 10
strike, right to
derivative of freedom of association, as a 42
protection of strikers 87
recognition under Article 11 43–44, 85–86, 92
union immunity from tortious liability 86, 91–94
wage deductions 27
Summers, Clyde 24

thought, right to freedom of *see* religion and belief, right to freedom of
trade union members
blacklisting 21–23, 107
dismissal/detriment 87, 160–61
personal scope of rights *see* personal scope of labour rights
rights of 86–88, 93–94, 103–4
use of disciplinary power, and 2–3, 87
trade unions
autonomy 43–44, 86, 93–94
definition of a union/union member *see* personal scope of labour rights
formation/registration of unions 85–86, 124
recognition by employer 86, 124–26
right to bargain collectively 42, 43–44, 85–86
right to strike *see* strike, right to
treatment by ECtHR 43–44, 85–86

unfair dismissal
basis in human rights concepts 41–42
continuous employment, qualifying period of *see* personal scope of labour rights
fairness standard 131, 133, 134–35, 148
application of fairness standard 135–36, 138–43
interpretation of fairness standard 131, 134–35
substitution mindset, prohibition of 135
interpretation compatible with the ECHR 128–29, 136–38
application in cases 137–40
personal scope of right *see* personal scope of labour rights
procedural fairness 128, 137–38
reason for dismissal 128, 130
automatically unfair reasons 130–31
fair reasons 130
remedies 132, 143–47
basic award 132
compensatory award 132
deductions from award 146–47
injury to feelings 144–45
re-engagement orders 132
upper limit on monetary awards 132, 145–46
values underpinning right 128

Van Drooghenbroeck, Sébastian 10–11
Vickers, Lucy 97–98

waiver
and the contract of employment 55, 178
application to employment relations 71, 178
Bill of Rights for worker, and 208–9
ECtHR's approach, the 70–71, 174–75, 177–78
Wedderburn, Lord 43
Weiss, Manfred 56–57
whistleblowing 29, 81
detriment/dismissal, and 2–3, 88, 89, 130–31
employees' duties to employer, and 88
last resort, as a 88–89
personal scope of protection 106, 111–12, 122–23
Public Interest Disclosure Act 1998, and 88–89
remedies 89
Wildhaber, Luzius 143–44
work
dependence upon work 4–5, 25–27, 200
inequality of power between workers and employers 4–5, 21–22, 26
right to work 22
social importance of work 4–5, 25
value of work 4–5, 25

workers
contract, requirement of a *see* personal scope of labour rights
genuine independent contractors, contrast to 14, 201–2
subordination, position of 4–5, 26–27, 31–32, 200
terms inconsistent with status *see* personal scope of labour rights
vulnerability to interference with rights 29–30, 202
working time 28, 31–32, 82–83
Wragg, Paul 142
wrongful dismissal 153, 154–56, 173–74, 184, 186–87
Johnson exclusion zone 176–77
personal scope of right *see* personal scope of labour rights
remedies 153, 174, 175–77

Youngdahl, Jay 42